FEMALE MONASTIC NETWORKS IN LATE BYZANTIUM

SPIRITUALITY AND MONASTICISM, EAST AND WEST

Further Information and Publications

www.arc-humanities.org/series/book-series/

FEMALE MONASTIC NETWORKS IN LATE BYZANTIUM

TEXTUAL, SPATIAL, AND CULTURAL ENTANGLEMENTS

by

EKATERINI MITSIOU

ARC HUMANITIES PRESS

British Library Cataloguing in Publication Data
A catalogue record for this book is available from the British Library.

ISBN (Hardback): 9781641890656
ISBN (Paperback): 9781802703870
e-ISBN (PDF): 9781802702194
e-ISBN (ePUB): 9781802703863

www.arc-humanities.org

Printed and bound in the UK (by CPIGroup [UK] Ltd), USA (by Bookmasters), and elsewhere using print-on-demand technology.

Publisher (manufacturer) details: Arc Humanities Press, 14 Clifton Moor Business Village, James Nicolson Link, York YO30 4XG, United Kingdom.

EU Authorized Representative details (for GPSR purposes): Amsterdam University Press, Nieuwe Prinsengracht 89, 1018 VR Amsterdam, The Netherlands. www.aup.nl

CONTENTS

LIST OF ILLUSTRATIONS

Figures

All figures were created with ORA, © author.

Maps

All maps were created with Quantum GIS, © author.

Tables

ABBREVIATIONS

ACHCByz	Association des Amis du Centre d'histoire et civilisation de Byzance.
BHG	Halkin, François. *Bibliotheca hagiographica graeca*. 3 vols. Société des Bollandistes, 1957.
Diktyon	*Réseau numérique pour les manuscrits grecs*. Accessed March 11, 2025, https://diktyon.irht.cnrs.fr/en/.
ODB	*Oxford Dictionary of Byzantium*. Edited by Alexander Kazhdan, 3 vols. Oxford University Press, 1991.
PBW	*Prosopography of the Byzantine World*. Accessed March 11, 2025, https://pbw2016.kdl.kcl.ac.uk/.
PLP	*Prosopographisches Lexikon der Palaiologenzeit*. Edited by Erich Trapp et al. Österreichische Akademie der Wissenschaften, 1977–1994.
PmbZ	*Prosopographie der mittelbyzantinischen Zeit/Prosopography of the Middle Byzantine Period*. Edited by Ralph-Johannes Lilie et al. De Gruyter, 2013. Accessed March 11, 2025, https://www.degruyter.com/view/db/pmbz.
TLG	*Thesaurus Linguae Graecae*. Accessed March 11, 2025, https://stephanus.tlg.uci.edu/.

ACKNOWLEDGEMENTS

THIS BOOK IS the result of the postdoctoral project, "Female Monasticism in the Late Byzantine Period (1204–1453)," conducted in Athens from 2012 to 2015 at the National Hellenic Research Foundation, with financial support from the European Social Fund and the Hellenic State. After expanding the content and adding further material, it was finalized during the ENCHANT Project: Entangled Charters of Anatolia, 1200–1300 (PI: J. Preiser-Kapeller; funded by the Austrian Science Fund FWF P 36403-G).

I would like to express my gratitude to those who supported this endeavour. I am especially thankful to Eleonora Kountoura-Galake for her guidance and support as well as the fruitful discussions we had in Athens during the project. The exchange of ideas with colleagues at the Institute for Medieval Research (Austrian Academy of Sciences) and the Institute of Byzantine and Modern Greek Studies (University of Vienna) was also immensely helpful. The Faculty of Historical and Cultural Studies of the University of Vienna generously supported the publication of this book.

Throughout the long process of producing this volume, I had the constant support of the publishing house, for which I am deeply grateful.

Finally, I would like to extend my heartfelt thanks to my husband, Johannes, to all my friends, and to my mother Vassiliki and my sister Helen for their unconditional love and support.

GUIDE FOR THE READER

Some clarifications are necessary regarding references, transliteration, and useful links.

For the spelling of Byzantine words in transliteration and the abbreviations of journal and series titles, we follow the *ODB* (1991). In the interest of standardization, I have transliterated most Greek technical terms and names of people and places according to the forms used in the *ODB*. Technical terms, such as *modioi* and *hyperpyra*, are italicized.

References and links to online prosopography databases like *PmbZ* and the *PBW* are provided in the footnotes or in the indices. All *Diktyon* and *BHG* numbers for manuscripts can be found in the relevant text or footnotes, while the *PLP* numbers are listed in the indices and the list of nuns. Modern names of cities and places will be provided in the index if not in the text.

INTRODUCTION

BLACK ROSE, a Modern Greek television series that aired from autumn 2022 to 2023, centres on the story of Elisabeth, a nun who briefly leaves her monastery and, while in the secular world, falls in love with a young man. The series captivated audiences eager for a romantic narrative and a "happily-ever-after" ending. However, such an outcome would be deeply troubling from the perspective of the monastic community, as it challenges the moral integrity of the group and threatens its internal cohesion. The departure of one nun could encourage others to follow, thereby destabilizing the entire institution. To mitigate such risks, both civil and canon law—along with the foundation charters of monastic communities—sought to regulate nearly every aspect of monastic life. Yet, despite this regulatory rigour, such measures were not always effective. The story of a "fallen" monk or nun has recurred throughout history, reflecting the persistent tension between individual desire and communal discipline.

The ideal of monastic life envisioned virtuous monks and nuns striving to draw closer to God through fasting, prayer, and spiritual devotion. This ideal also embraced those who emulated the martyrs by steadfastly professing their faith as well as those who resisted temptation and renounced worldly pleasures. Alongside the early Christian martyrs, medieval monastics revered the founders of monasticism and a distinguished lineage of male and female saints. The *vitae*—narratives of their lives—were widely read, copied, and disseminated across medieval contexts. In Eastern Christianity, their examples were also memorialized visually through monumental paintings and icons, which served as constant reminders of the "right path" and the proper mode of monastic living. This path was gradually shaped from the third century onward by influential ecclesiastics, monastics, and theologians.

Each successive generation drew upon the authority of established monastic tradition while simultaneously adapting it to meet contemporary needs and challenges. This dynamic of continuity and transformation remained evident well into the late Byzantine period—the focus of this study—when Byzantium, or the Eastern Roman Empire, had ceased to be a dominant global power and had instead become a more peripheral actor within increasingly interconnected world systems.[1]

Finally, the presence of Western Orders in the Eastern Mediterranean after the Crusades—particularly after 1204—influenced Byzantine monasticism, especially in matters of debate and theological discourse.[2] Initially marked by suspicion and animosity, the coexistence of Catholic and Orthodox monastics eventually became common, particularly in Latin-dominated areas such as Crete and Cyprus. Many Orthodox monuments, manuscripts, texts, and wall paintings depicting nuns originate from these regions, attesting to the presence and influence of Orthodox female monastics within a non-Byzantine cultural environment.

Before delving into the central focus of this study, however, it is important to review the current state of research and outline the methodological framework that guides this analysis.

State of Research

Christian asceticism, along with the origins and development of monasticism, has been extensively studied.[3] Significant emphasis has been placed on the life and works of Antony the Great and the Desert Fathers, the emergence and spread of coenobitic life, and the role of the monastic rules established by Pachomios and Basil the Great.[4] Influenced by anthropological and philosophical theories, recent scholarship has shifted its focus to more specific thematic areas, such as the body, diet, sexuality, and the performative aspects in the lives of saints. In this regard, the contributions of Peter Brown and Stavroula Constantinou have been particularly important.[5]

On the other hand, since the introduction of feminist theories and gender studies into historical research in the 1980s, Byzantine women have become

1 On world systems, see Abu-Lughod, *Before European Hegemony*, 34 (map) and 137–45.

2 Mitsiou, "Die Netzwerke einer kulturellen Begegnung," 359–74; Mitsiou, "Die Dominikaner als Experten in der Romania," 43–53.

3 Cf. Harpham, *The Ascetic Imperative in Culture and Criticism*.

4 Veilleux, *Pachomian Koinonia*; Basil of Caesarea, *Regulae fusius tractatae*, ed. Migne, cols. 901–1052; Basil of Caesarea, *Regulae brevius tractatae*, ed. Migne, cols. 1052–1305.

5 Brown, *The Body and Society*; Constantinou, *Female Corporeal Performances*; cf. Hatzaki, *Beauty and the Male Body in Byzantium*; Ringrose, "The Byzantine Body," 362–78.

a vibrant field of study.[6] Their social and economic circumstances have been analyzed by scholars such as Angeliki Laiou, Judith Herrin, Liz James, and Joëlle Beaucamp. Laiou focused on their socio-economic conditions,[7] while Herrin and James explored issues of power,[8] and Beaucamp examined women's legal status.[9]

There has also been extensive research on the role of women in the monastic movement. Susan Elm's book *Virgins of God* has been a milestone in this regard.[10] Additionally, studies like Theresa Shaw's *The Burden of the Flesh*, which focuses on the sexuality and asceticism of nuns, have analyzed the perception of the female body and the practice of fasting in ascetical texts.[11] However, there is a distinct lack of focused studies on female coenobitical monasticism in Byzantium from Late Antiquity up to the twelfth century, with the topic typically receiving only indirect mentions or brief treatments within broader studies. Examples of this approach can be seen in the otherwise excellent works by Peter Hatlie and Rosemary Morris, where no dedicated sub-chapter on nuns is included.[12] This contrasts with the scholarly research on female monasticism in the West, which has seen an increase in publications in recent years.[13] A more recent study by Daniel Oltean on the stages before becoming a monk or nun is extremely helpful and insightful, though it is not gender-focused.[14]

Morris's statement that "we know next to nothing about female monasticism in the period up to *c.* 1100" reflects more the lack of information about the economic and administrative aspects of female monasticism in the Middle Byzantine period than a lack of sources. In fact, a significant corpus of hagiographical works highlights other areas of interest, such as social and spatial entanglements, while archaeology continues to bring new evidence to light.

---

6 On the role of women and especially of nuns in the Western Middle Ages, see Shahar, *The Fourth Estate*, 22–64; Erler and Kowaleski, *Gendering the Master Narrative*.

7 Laiou, *Gender, Society and Economic Life in Byzantium*; Laiou, *Mariage, amour et parenté à Byzance*; Laiou, "Sex, Consent and Coercion in Byzantium," 109–221.

8 Herrin, "'Femina Byzantina,'" 115–32; Herrin, *Women in Purple*; Herrin, *Unrivalled Influence*; James, *Empresses and Power in Early Byzantium*.

9 Beaucamp, "La situation juridique de la femme à Byzance," 145–76; Beaucamp, *Le statut de la femme à Byzance*.

10 Elm, *"Virgins of God."*

11 Shaw, *The Burden of the Flesh*; cf. Bynum, *Holy Feast and Holy Fast.*

12 Hatlie, *The Monks and Monasteries of Constantinople*; Morris, *Monks and Laymen.*

13 See, for example, Lähnemann and Schlotheuber, *Unerhörte Frauen.*

14 Oltean, *Devenir moine à Byzance.*

Although Morris notes that "from the beginning of the twelfth century, the figure of the Byzantine nun appears much more frequently in the sources," a dedicated monograph on this topic in the late Byzantine period is still missing.[15]

Nevertheless, some important articles have been published on certain aspects of female monasticism during the Palaiologan period. Alice-Mary Talbot has done significant preliminary work on the subject, contributing numerous dictionary entries on women and monasticism as well as several pathbreaking articles. A key focus of her research is the age at which nuns entered the convent as well as their initial motivations for doing so.[16] Additionally, Talbot has explored the concept of gendered space within a nunnery. She has also addressed topics such as female piety, the founding of monasteries, and the lives of saints—areas that have been examined by many other scholars as well.[17]

At this point, we must mention the congresses and collective volumes.[18] One of the few congresses exclusively focused on female monasticism was held in Athens in 1988 ("Les femmes et le monachisme byzantine"), with many contributions dedicated to female monasticism in the late Byzantine period. Monasticism has been systematically included in round tables at international congresses and symposia, with the proceedings typically published soon after, such as *Monastères, images, pouvoirs et société à Byzance*. In the proceedings of the International Symposium "Τάσεις του Ορθόδοξου Μοναχισμού (Trends in Orthodox Monasticism)," only Elisabeth Malamut's contribution, "La moniale à Byzance aux 8e–12e siècles," specifically addressed female monasticism, focusing on the nuns of the Middle Byzantine period.

Additionally, the important papers from the section entitled "Women and Monasticism," presented at the Seventh Annual Byzantine Studies Conference at Boston University, were published in volume nine of the journal *Byzantinische Forschungen*. Finally, it is worth mentioning the workshop "Women and Monasticism in the Medieval Eastern Mediterranean: Decoding a Cultural Map," which sought to explore the role of women not only within the Byzantine Empire but also in comparison with Western and Eastern traditions.[19]

---

15 Morris, *Monks and Laymen in Byzantium*, 52.

16 On these topics, see Chapter 3.

17 See Talbot's publications and especially her latest books, *Varieties of Monastic Experience* and *Studies in Byzantine Monasticism.*

18 The full titles of the cited volumes in this section can be found in the bibliography.

19 Kountoura-Galake and Mitsiou, *Women and Monasticism in the Medieval Eastern Mediterranean.*

In conclusion, I would like to draw attention to the often-overlooked contributions of modern nunneries. Their publications primarily address the development of Orthodox female monasticism and offer spiritual resources valuable to their communities, although their scope is not limited to these subjects.[20]

The Present Study: Framework, Sources, and Methods

This book examines female monasticism in Late Byzantium (1204–1453), with a particular emphasis on the coenobitic tradition rather than semi-monastic brotherhoods. This focus provides a lens through which to explore how monasticism—a long-standing social institution—was shaped by an era marked by political collapse and widespread social transformation. It is important to recognize that after 1204, not only did the political landscape undergo significant change, but the ecclesiastical framework was also profoundly altered. In regions under Latin rule, a new ecclesiastical structure was imposed, and Orthodox monasteries were frequently converted into Latin ones.

Given the fluidity of political borders during this period, this study focuses on regions that remained under the jurisdiction of the Patriarchate of Constantinople. These include substantial parts of Asia Minor, the Balkan Peninsula (excluding Serbia and Bulgaria), and the Aegean and Ionian islands. For practical reasons, areas such as Russia, Wallachia, and Moldavia fall outside the scope of this research.

The research question is closely tied to the availability and nature of the written evidence. The primary sources include *typika*—monastic foundation documents—that offer detailed regulations concerning the governance and daily life of nunneries. Additional insight is provided by the rulings of ecclesiastical courts, notably those issued by Archbishop Demetrios Chomatenos of Ohrid in the thirteenth century.[21] Equally important are the synodic and patriarchal decisions from the Patriarchate of Constantinople during the fourteenth century.[22] These documents illuminate broader ecclesiastical policies and the Church's responses to various monastic issues, offering a

20 Cf., for example, Theotekne (Hagiostephanitissa), *Ἡ θέση τῆς μοναχῆς στὴν Ὀρθόδοξη Ἐκκλησία*.

21 Demetrios Chomatenos, *Ponemata*, ed. Prinzing.

22 *Patriarchal Register*, vols. 1–3; Miklosich and Müller, *Acta et Diplomata graeca Medii Aevi sacra et profana*, vols. 1–2; Darrouzès, *Le registre synodal*.

comprehensive view of the administrative and spiritual governance of Byzantine nunneries in the late Byzantine period.

The *typika* represent some of the most thoroughly analyzed and frequently cited sources in Byzantine studies. Several of these documents are available through the *Thesaurus Linguae Graecae* (*TLG*), and many have been translated and compiled in the volumes of *Byzantine Monastic Foundation Documents*, edited by Dumbarton Oaks. For the period under consideration, the most pertinent texts include the Constantinopolitan *typika* of Lips (1294–1301), Anargyroi (1294–1301), Bebaia Elpis (1327–1335), and Philanthropos Soter (after 1307) as well as the Cretan *typikon* of Baionaia (1400). The twelfth-century *typikon* of Kecharitomene will also be referenced for comparative purposes.[23]

Additional sources include original documents and cartularies, such as the one from Lembos in the region of Smyrna.[24] Contemporary historians and chroniclers—most notably George Pachymeres—also offer valuable testimonies, as do the letter collections of key figures, such as Gregory of Cyprus, Athanasios I, Theoleptos of Philadelphia, and Irene Choumnaina, the foundress and abbess of the Philanthropos Soter monastery.[25] A 1455 Ottoman survey of Constantinople, now available in English translation, provides unique insight into the urban context of nunneries in the Byzantine capital.[26] Furthermore, archaeological evidence—including monuments (churches, monasteries, and dwellings) as well as religious and liturgical objects such as icons, vessels, and manuscripts—constitutes an indispensable part of the research. Less frequently encountered are lead seals from female monasteries and nuns, as the number of such seals declined after the thirteenth

23 *Typicon monasterii Lips*, ed. Delehaye, 106–36; *Typicon monasterii Theotoci Bebaias Elpidos*, ed. Delehaye, 18–105; Meyer, "Bruchstücke zweier τυπικά κτητορικά," 45–58; Pétridès, "Le *typikon* de Nil Damilas," 95–109. Contrary to other documents, the official *typikon* of Baionaia was written in Latin by the notary George Delagronda and was later translated into Greek by Damilas for the nuns. Pétridès, "Le *typikon* de Nil Damilas," chaps. 18 and 20, p. 108; Talbot, "*Neilos Damilas*," 1477–78; Gautier, "Le *typikon* de la Théotokos Kécharitômènè," 5–165.

24 Miklosich and Müller, *Acta et Diplomata graeca Medii Aevi sacra et profana*, vol. 4, pp. 1–291.

25 Pachymeres, *History*, ed. Failler and Laurent, vols. 1–5; Gregory of Cyprus, *Letters*, ed. Kotzabassi; Gregory of Cyprus, *Letters*, ed. Eustratiades; Athanasios I, *Epistulae*, ed. Talbot; Irene Eulogia Choumnaina, *Correspondence*, ed. Constantinides Hero; Theoleptos of Philadelphia, *Letters*, ed. Constantinides Hero.

26 İnalcık, *The Survey of Istanbul*.

century in comparison to earlier periods.[27] Taken together, these sources offer a comprehensive perspective on the religious, social, and cultural life of Byzantine female monastic communities, enabling a multidimensional analysis that integrates both textual and material evidence.

This study is not structured according to generational categories (such as childhood, adulthood, or old age);[28] while such an approach may prove useful in broader surveys on the role of women in society, the complexity of female monasticism necessitates analysis within a continuous and integrated framework. The material is being structured according to the framework: chronology, geography, the organization of monastic life, and the economic and social dimensions of Byzantine nunneries. In addition, the methodological approach of Social Network Analysis (SNA) will sometimes be used in an attempt to further visualize specific aspects of Byzantine monasticism. This framework, which has been significantly refined in recent years, is increasingly employed by scholars working in the field of medieval history.[29]

SNA allows us to examine the research topic from the perspective of social entanglements. Female monasticism is understood as a network of actions, agents, and objects that form, constitute, and sustain complex systems. This approach enables us to perceive the foundation, administration, and economy of nunneries as well as the involvement of nuns in the ecclesiastical controversies of their time as complex networks of spatial, political, and economic relations. Based on evidence from *typika*, documents, and other sources, this study describes the networks of patronage, female monastic spaces, and cultural production and, in some cases suited for a digital approach, visualizes aspects of these networks.[30]

---

27 See now Cheynet, "Le bullaire monastique à Byzance," 271–73. The number of seals belonging to women dated after the thirteenth century is significantly smaller than the specimens from the eleventh and twelfth centuries. See the search results for women's seals in "Coins and Seals Collection, Dumbarton Oaks." https://www.doaks.org/resources/seals. Byzantine women preferred the image of Theotokos for their seals, Cotsonis, "Onomastics, Gender, Office and Images on Byzantine Lead Seals," 10–18. An example is the seal of the nun Zoe Senacheirina (first half of the twelfth century), which features the bust of Theotokos orans on the obverse. See Seibt, "The Sons of Senek'erim Yovhannēs," 126–27.

28 This tendency can be detected, for example, in Davies, "From Womb to the Tomb."

29 Mitsiou, "Networks of Nicaea," 91–104; Mitsiou and Preiser-Kapeller, "Moving Hands," 29–67; Mitsiou, "Byzantine Monastic Space," 365–81.

30 On women and Network Analysis, see Preiser-Kapeller, "Mapping Networks of Women in the Late Medieval Eastern Mediterranean," 349–63.

At this point, it is necessary to shortly explain the meaning of a social network within the framework of Social Network Analysis (SNA). According to Stanley Wasserman and Katherine Faust, "a social network consists of a finite set or sets of actors and the relation or relations between them. The presence of relational information is a critical and defining feature of a social network."[31] SNA maps relations (called "links" or "edges") between actors (called "nodes") in social networks.[32] In addition to individuals and groups, nodes can also represent corporate actors, such as organizations, nation-states, or economic firms. In SNA, actors and their actions are viewed as interdependent rather than independent, autonomous units. Furthermore, the relational ties (or "linkages") between actors (nodes) serve as channels for the transfer, or "flow," of resources, whether material or non-material. Memberships, relations, interactions, and flows are the most important forms of social ties.[33]

Network models that focus on individuals view the network's structural environment as providing either opportunities or constraints on individual actions. In general, network models conceptualize structure[34]—whether social, economic, political, and so forth—as enduring patterns of relations among actors.[35] The elementary forms of structure in networks are dyads (constellations of two nodes) and triads (three nodes), with the latter playing a significant role in maintaining structural balance.[36] Finally, in SNA terms, a society is seen as the superposition of various socioeconomic networks constructed at the local level, which can represent different types of relations and exchanges. Per Szell et al., "this superposition is typically referred to as a multiplex, multirelational, multimodal, or multivariate network."[37]

SNA focuses on nodes and their ties (links or edges) to other nodes. There are quantitative markers for nodes, such as their number and strength,[38] as

---

31 Wasserman and Faust, *Social Network Analysis*, 20; Kadushin, *Understanding Social Networks*, 14.

32 Rawlings et al., *Network Analysis*, 47–50.

33 Rawlings et al., *Network Analysis*, 49.

34 On the meaning of structure, see Rawlings et al., *Network Analysis*, 2–5.

35 Wasserman and Faust, *Social Network Analysis*, 4.

36 Kadushin, *Understanding Social Networks*, 22–26, 29; Crossley et al., *Social Network Analysis for Ego-Nets*, 15–16; Rawlings et al., *Network Analysis*, 148–59.

37 Szell et al., "Trade, Conflict and Sentiments," 1.

38 Rawlings et al., *Network Analysis*, 50.

well as qualitative markers for links, such as homophily,[39] and for nodes, such as types.[40] Additionally, there are concepts describing an entire network, such as structural holes,[41] distance,[42] and segmentation through clusters and cliques.[43] All of these elements can be analyzed using various measures and visualized with the help of graphs.[44] Where possible, some metrics are used in this book:[45]

Degree measures the number of links a node has in a network.[46]

Degree Centralization assesses whether some nodes are significantly more strongly connected than others, indicating the overall centralization of connections within the network.

Clustering Coefficient indicates the likelihood that two associates of a node are also associates themselves. A higher clustering coefficient reflects greater "cliquishness."[47]

Betweenness measures the extent to which a node lies between other nodes in the network. It reflects the connectivity of a node's neighbours

39 Kadushin, *Understanding Social Networks*, 18–21. Homophily means that "if two people have characteristics that match in a proportion greater than expected in the population from which they are drawn or the network of which they are a part, then they are more likely to be connected." At the same time, "if two people are connected, then they are more likely to have common characteristics or attributes," Kadushin, *Understanding Social Networks*, 18; Crossley et al., *Social Network Analysis for Ego-Nets*, 7, 14.

40 Rawlings et al., *Network Analysis*, 195–98.

41 Kadushin, *Understanding Social Networks*, 27: "a category concerned with the lack of connections"; see also 29–30.

42 Kadushin, *Understanding Social Networks*, 27: "the radius of distances from any given node"; Crossley et al., *Social Network Analysis for Ego-Nets*, 11–12.

43 Kadushin, *Understanding Social Networks*, 46–49; Crossley et al., *Social Network Analysis for Ego-Nets*, 13; Rawlings et al., *Network Analysis*, 176–78.

44 For more on the concepts of SNA, see Newman, Barabási, and Watts, *The Structure and Dynamics of Networks*; Kadushin, *Understanding Social Networks*, 13–55; Preiser-Kapeller, "Mapping Networks of Women in the Late Medieval Eastern Mediterranean," 349–52, with further references. The SNA tool used in all network graphs in this book is ORA. "ORA-LITE," https://www.cmu.edu/casos-center/research/tools/ora-lite.html.

45 Kadushin, *Understanding Social Networks*, 27: it "demonstrates that some nodes have more connections than others and those connections serve as links to other nodes." See also Crossley et al., *Social Network Analysis for Ego-Nets*, 14.

46 Crossley et al., *Social Network Analysis for Ego-Nets*, 14; Rawlings et al., *Network Analysis*, 50, 198.

47 Kadushin, *Understanding Social Networks*, 120–21.

and gives higher values to nodes that bridge clusters. A high betweenness indicates a node's potential importance in connecting otherwise disconnected clusters.

Betweenness Centralization measures the degree to which the potential for connecting nodes is concentrated among a small number of nodes in the network.[48]

Closeness measures the sum of all path distances from a node to all other nodes, providing a relative measure of its centrality. A node with high closeness is closer, on average, to all other nodes in the network.[49]

Density is the proportion of possible links that are actually present in the network. A network where every node is connected to every other node has a density of 1.[50]

Female monastics—especially those from aristocratic backgrounds—were members of various networks (such as kinship networks) before taking their monastic vows. Entering a nunnery did not sever their connections to the outside world; rather, they transferred the benefits of their social position and entanglements to their new environment. A recent example of the application of SNA in Gender Studies is the article "Mapping Networks of Women" by Johannes Preiser-Kapeller.[51] This study explores female aristocratic networks and highlights a specific, well-documented case in the sources: that of the nun and scholar Theodora Raoulaina. This paper is exemplary for various reasons, and it demonstrates the significant advantages of SNA in researching complex social phenomena in the Middle Ages.

In relation to women of the late Byzantine elite, Preiser-Kapeller demonstrated that:

> Even if fragmentary tradition does not allow the use of quantitative methods or only to a limited extent [as in the present volume, Ekaterini Mitsiou], it is worthwhile to take systematically in the focus the social connections between individuals and groups as the context of their actions. Every single actor was embedded in an abundance of relationships, which she or he had received by birth (e. g. kinship), or that she or he actively established and

48 Kadushin, *Understanding Social Networks*, 95–96; Rawlings et al., *Network Analysis*, 199–200.

49 Kadushin, *Understanding Social Networks*, 96.

50 Kadushin, *Understanding Social Networks*, 27: density indicates "the number of connections contained within the network."

51 Preiser-Kapeller, "Mapping Networks of Women in the Late Medieval Eastern Mediterranean," 349–63.

> maintained (e. g., the membership in a literary circle). These links could be connected with different positions in more or less formalized and institutionalized systems of order (as the patron of followers or as a follower of a higher-ranking patron, for instance) and could play an essential role for the identity and overall social position of an individual (e.g., the integration into networks of peers as a confirmation of the noble status). Such networks could serve as a resource (support from relatives, friends, allies, patrons), but also limit the room for manoeuvre, due to obligations as a follower of a patron, for instance.[52]

On various occasions, this study demonstrates some of the possibilities of SNA with specific examples and case studies. The second chapter explores life inside nunneries, analyzing their foundation as networks of patronage and the spatial consequences of these networks. The subsequent chapter focuses on another driving force of human activity: finances. Here, maps and, to a certain extent, Network Analysis enables the visualization of complex economic relations in specific geographic areas. Based on the *typikon* of individual institutions, we have mapped the landed properties of nunneries and, in one instance, we reconstructed the entanglements of individuals, landed properties, land prices, and locations. The fourth chapter examines networks of art and knowledge, including the donation and possession of movable objects by female monasteries and nuns. The final chapter addresses the involvement of female monastics in social and ecclesiastical upheavals, such as the Arsenite Schism and the Anti-Union movement following the Synod of Lyons (1274) and the Council of Ferrara-Florence. In addition, it detects the church efforts to protect and supervise the nunneries under its authority.

52 Preiser-Kapeller, "Mapping Networks of Women in the Late Medieval Eastern Mediterranean," 354.

Chapter 1

(FEMALE) MONASTICISM

AN OUTLINE

LATE BYZANTINE FEMALE monasticism can be better understood when placed in its historical perspective and context. The following provides a brief outline of the formation, establishment, and development of the Byzantine monastic experience, setting the foundation for this book's investigation.

From the Emergence of Monasticism up to the Twelfth Century[1]

The emergence of monasticism cannot be attributed to specific individuals or regions alone; rather, it appears as a near-simultaneous phenomenon in various locations, such as Egypt, Syria, and Palestine. On one hand, an anchoritic form of monasticism developed with major figures such as Antony the Great in Egypt and Ephraim in Syria. On the other hand, coenobitic (communal) monasticism emerged as an effort to bring order to unregulated anchoritic practices. A significant figure in coenobitic monasticism in Egypt was Pachomios, who founded a monastic community at Tabennisi, in Upper Egypt, around 321. This community was governed by rigid rules covering all aspects of communal life, including prayer, work, clothing, and food. The monks were accountable to an abbot and were prohibited from owning personal possessions. While there was no formal novitiate or vows, there was an obligation to obey all superiors within the community's hierarchy.[2]

The roots of what we now refer to as Byzantine monasticism can be traced back to the teachings and rules of Basil the Great in fourth-century Asia Minor. Recent studies highlight the significant influence of Basil's older sister, Makrina,[3] who established a monastery well before her brother and served as abbess over a mixed community of women and men. However, Basil, as a bishop, wielded greater authority and imposed order on monastic

---

1 Mitsiou and Preiser-Kapeller, "Church and Religion," 251–79.

2 Harmless, *Desert Christians*. On the Coptic monasteries in Egypt, such as the famous White Monastery of Shenoute, see Gabra and Vivian, *Coptic Monasteries*, 94–100.

3 Silvas, *Macrina the Younger*.

life through his leadership. His most notable works include the *Longer* and the *Shorter Rules*, which are collections of responses to questions posed by monks.[4] Basil advocated for a monastic life within a community under the supervision of the Church, expressing skepticism towards the often-extreme behaviours of anchorites. His approach was later emulated by other significant figures, such as Theodore of Stoudios and Athanasios the Athonite.[5]

In another significant monastic centre, Palestine, a blend of anchoritism and communal life was practiced through the formation of *lavrai*. A *lavra* was a community of hermits under the authority of an abbot. The monks lived in separate cells connected by paths (from the Greek *lavra*, meaning "alley" or "lane"). During the week, they lived and worked individually, but on Saturdays and Sundays they gathered to celebrate the liturgy and share a meal. The most renowned example was the Great Lavra (*Mar Saba*), founded by St. Sabas in 483.[6] Sabas' rule, known as the Jerusalem *typikon* (a liturgical book detailing Church rites), was widely circulated in Asia Minor after 800 and throughout the Byzantine territories during and after the eleventh century.

In contrast to the medieval West, monastic orders (in the strict sense) did not develop in Byzantium. However, rules such as those of Basil and the *typika* of certain monasteries—like the Theotokos Evergetis (Mother of God, the Benefactress) near Constantinople (eleventh/twelfth centuries)—served as models for other communities.[7] Authors would typically copy previous *typika*, keep some parts, modify others, and adapt them to the needs of the new community. By the tenth century, founders began to assert their independence from episcopal supervision, secure tax privileges, and ensure that their status was officially recognized by both lay and ecclesiastical authorities.[8] New monasteries continued to increase in number steadily, and many of them, such as those on Mount Athos,[9] also became significant economic institutions.

---

4 Silvas, *The Asketikon of St. Basil the Great.*

5 Dennis, "*Ath. Typikon*," 205–31.

6 Patrich, *Sabas, Leader of Palestinian Monasticism.*

7 Gautier, "Le *typikon* de la Théotokos Évergétis," 5–101; Jordan and Morris, *The Hypotyposis of the Monastery of the Theotokos Evergetis*. It should not be confused with Gül Mosque (Christ Evergetis) in Constantinople. See Ivanov, *In Search of Constantinople*, 289.

8 Morris, *Monks and Laymen in Byzantium.*

9 On the Athonite monasticism, see Papachryssanthou, *Ο αθωνικός μοναχισμός*.

Female Monasticism (Third–Twelfth Centuries)

In the first Christian centuries, the traditional form of asceticism for women often involved living as virgins, typically in their own homes. A document from Oxyrhynchus in Middle Egypt, dated June/July 400, indicates that ascetic women resided in towns, owned property, and engaged in business with locals, including members of the Jewish community.[10] The *Life of St. Antony* (*BHG* 140a–g) also attests to the existence of separate women's communities as early as the late third century. In the fourth century, Pachomios allowed his sister, Maria, and a group of women to join his community and established a special monastery for them.

The Egyptian monastic tradition records numerous exemplary lives of Desert Mothers, whose stories were collected—mostly by men—in compilations such as the *Sayings of the Desert Fathers* (and *Desert Mothers*), which have survived in various collections.[11] Among these figures, Mary of Egypt stands out as particularly notable; her story provides evidence of the presence of ascetic women along the Jordan River in the fourth and fifth centuries. Her narrative also sparked significant debate about gender, femininity, and masculinity due to her rejection of traditional femininity, which included total nudity, as depicted in various pictorial representations.[12] In contrast, late Byzantine nuns concealed their feminine features with long, dark cloaks. Another symbolic gesture of shedding femininity involved wearing male clothing, as demonstrated by around twelve saintly nuns between the fifth and eleventh centuries.[13] Notably, Matrona, a fifth-century foundress of a nunnery in Constantinople, clothed her entire community in male monastic habits.

There were also more extreme forms of asceticism, such as nuns who barricaded themselves in enclosed spaces without leaving for extended

---

10 Harmless, *Desert Christians*, 24.

11 The *Apopthegmata Patrum (Sayings of the Fathers)* (or *Gerontikon* or *Paterikon*; *BHG* 1442–1450) is a collection of stories attributed to the Desert Fathers. They have an original oral tradition in Coptic and a later written tradition in Greek. They have survived in many languages and in collections (e.g., *collectio alphabetica* and *collectio* systematica). See Harmless, *Desert Christians*; Guy, *Les Apophthegmes des Pères*; Ward, *The Sayings of the Desert Fathers*.

12 For an understanding of Mary's bodily appearance as transmasculinity, see Betancourt, *Byzantine Intersectionality*, 1–17.

13 On this category of nuns, see Patlagean, "L'histoire de la femme déguisée en moine," 597–623; Lubinsky, *Removing Masculine Layers to Reveal a Holy Womanhood*; Constantinou, "Holy Actors and Actresses," 343–62.

periods. Additionally, the phenomenon of holy fools, or *saloi* (from Greek, meaning "of disturbed mind"), emerged. These individuals sought sanctity through social ridicule, aiming to serve Christ and attain spiritual elevation by engaging in outrageous behaviour, seemingly irrational acts, and self-humiliation.[14]

After Late Antiquity, textual testimonies highlight the role of nuns in resisting Iconoclasm (726–787 and 814–843),[15] while the number of eremitic women diminished. Theodosia, a legendary urban nun, is said to have been martyred while protesting the removal of the Christ icon from the Chalke Gate at the Great Palace in Constantinople.[16] Her cult remained extremely popular in Constantinople, reaching its peak during the Palaiologan period, and the nunnery of St. Theodosia became a significant pilgrimage destination in the capital.[17]

From the fourth century onwards, nunneries—such as those of St. Melania and St. Paula in the Holy Land—became significant pilgrimage centres. In some cases, they rivaled the popularity of early Christian martyrs. For instance, the nunnery of St. Theodora of Thessaloniki attracted pilgrims to the extent that her cult rivaled that of St. Demetrios (patron saint of the city). This is evidenced by the distribution of lead flasks, known as *koutroubia*, which depicted both saints.[18]

After the ninth century, many female monastic communities continued the tradition of maintaining contact with spiritual fathers and prominent monastic figures. For example, Theodore of Stoudios regularly corresponded with convents and individual nuns in Asia Minor and received their support during his various exiles.[19]

---

14 Ivanov, *Holy Fools in Byzantium and Beyond*, 7, 55–58; Rydén, "The Holy Fool," 106–13.

15 Brubaker and Haldon, *Byzantium in the Iconoclast Era: The Sources*; Brubaker and Haldon, *Byzantium in the Iconoclast Era: A History*; Bryer and Herrin, *Iconoclasm*; Kazhdan and Talbot, "Women and Iconoclasm," 391–408.

16 Halkin, "Théodosie de Césarée," 63–68; Constas, "Life of Saint Theodosia," 1–8.

17 On the nunnery of St. Theodosia (Gül Camii and Ayakapı Mescidi), see Effenberger, "Theodosia von Konstantinopel," 121–34.

18 Mitsiou, "'Ευλογίες,'" 195–229. On travel and pilgrimage to the Holy Land, see now Luckhardt, *The Charisma of Distant Places*, 54–90.

19 "Theodoros Studites, no. 7574," in *PmbZ*; Pratsch, *Theodoros Studites*, 45–56 (especially on the female members of his family with whom he corresponded).

At the same time, nuns and nunneries are featured in sources concerning saintly abbesses, such as Irene of Chrysobalanton.[20] Her *Life* recounts a story of temptation similar to that faced by nun Elisabeth in *Black Rose*, where Irene is on the verge of leaving the nunnery for the love of a man. However, the intervention of St. Basil and St. Anastasia, along with the prayers of the entire community, led to a virtuous resolution. Irene also experienced visions (or possibly hallucinations) of demons and saints, yet she was not deemed insane or foolish by her contemporaries.

Irene of Chrysobalanton was an aristocratic nun, and her story highlights how nunneries often served as a refuge for women of high status—both fallen empresses and those destined to become empresses. Such nunneries were frequently motivated by political considerations and served as penitential sanctuaries or retirement homes for the wealthy and powerful.

A prime example is the Kecharitomene Monastery in Constantinople. Founded by Empress Irene Doukaina, wife of Emperor Alexios I (1081–1118), it served as a retreat for female members of her family, including her daughter, the historian Anna Komnena. The *typikon* of Kecharitomene had a significant influence on later Palaiologan female foundations (1258–1453).[21] Despite the political turmoil following the Crusaders' capture of Constantinople in 1204 and the subsequent fragmentation of power, the *typikon* was copied and continued to be a model for aristocratic women, including another empress in the late thirteenth century.

Byzantine Female Monasticism, Thirteenth–Fifteenth Centuries: An Outline

The Fourth Crusade and the subsequent capture of Constantinople in 1204 had a profound and lasting impact on Byzantine female monasticism. Contemporary accounts frequently highlight the violence inflicted by the Crusaders on women (including nuns), underscoring the traumatic consequences of the conquest.[22] The aftermath in Constantinople is well documented, revealing widespread disruption and hardship for monastic communities. Many churches and monasteries were seized by Latin clergy and

20 Rosenqvist, *The Life of Saint Irene*, 52–56.

21 Gautier, "Le *typikon* de la Théotokos Kécharitôménè," 5–165; Jordan, "*Kecharitomene*," 649–724; Mitsiou, "The Monastery of Kecharitomene and the Contribution of the Assumptionists," 327–44.

22 Darrouzès, "Le mémoire de Constantin Stilbès contre les Latins," 50–100.

repurposed for Catholic worship.[23] Others, such as the Monastery of St. Anargyroi, were abandoned and fell into disrepair, only to be restored following the Byzantine reconquest of the city in 1261.[24]

The Latin Crusaders were particularly intent on asserting control over the assets of Greek monasteries. A preliminary agreement dated March 17, 1206, placed all monasteries within and beyond Constantinople under the authority of the Latin ecclesiastical hierarchy. In the final agreement of 1219, Emperor Robert (r. 1219–1228) exempted all churches, clerics, and religious individuals—whether Greek or Latin—from lay jurisdiction. Although this arrangement likely extended to nuns, detailed evidence concerning the presence and activities of Orthodox nuns in former Byzantine territories under Latin control remains limited. A notable exception is the *praktikon* (tax record) of 1264 from the village of Avion on the island of Kephalenia, which documents a field owned by a nun.[25] Additional attestations of Orthodox nuns appear in Venetian Crete and Latin-ruled Cyprus, suggesting their continued—if constrained—presence in these Latin-dominated regions.

The scarcity of information extends to the territories of the Greek successor polities of Nicaea and Epiros. Records concerning nuns and female monastic communities during the Nicaean exile (1204–1261) and the immediate post-recovery period are particularly limited. A cartulary from the Smyrna region offers some insight, documenting individual donations by nuns to the Lembos Monastery and its dependent institutions (*metochia*). Similarly, in Philadelphia, there is a record of a single donation made by a nun to the Monastery of Boreine. Athanasia Mangaphaina is also mentioned in the sources, though without any clear affiliation to a specific monastic community.[26]

Documentation concerning the activities of female monastic communities during this period remains generally limited, especially when compared to the relatively abundant historical evidence concerning imperial policy toward monasticism.[27] Contemporary sources emphasize the support of

---

23 The numerical estimates of modern historians vary. On this, see Chapter 3.

24 *Typicon monasterii sanctorum Anargyrorum*, ed. Delehaye, chap. 56, p. 137; Talbot, "*Anargyroi*," 1291; Kidonopulos, *Bauten in Konstantinopel*, 1–4.

25 Tzannetatos, *Πρακτικόν τῆς Λατινικῆς Ἐπισκοπῆς Κεφαλληνίας*, p. 33, line 58.

26 *Diataxis et inventarium Maximi fundatoris monasterii Boreinae*, ed. Bompaire et al., p. 155, lines 81–83; Dennis, "*Skoteine* [Boreine]*," 1182; Ahrweiler, "La region de Philadelphie au XIVe siècle," 175–97.

27 On the power relations between Byzantine emperors and monasteries, see now Benoit-Meggenis, *L'empereur et le moine*.

Emperor John III Vatatzes (1221–1254) for monasteries under Latin control, including those on Mount Athos, in Thessaloniki, and in Attika.[28] They also record several Imperial foundations established by John III and his wife, Irene Laskarina, such as the monasteries of Sosandra and Kouzenas in Magnesia, St. Prodromos in Prousa, and St. Antony in Nicaea.[29] Of these, however, only the Nicaean foundation—likely identifiable as Church C in the Roman theatre—can be confirmed as a female convent.[30]

In contrast to other regions, Epiros offers more detailed evidence concerning female monasticism. A notable account is provided by John Apokaukos, the metropolitan of Naupaktos, who describes the Monastery of Blachernitissa in Arta.[31] According to Apokaukos, this monastery—originally inhabited by monks—was converted into a nunnery to provide refuge for nuns who had fled Constantinople following its fall in 1204.

Apokaukos's commentary is particularly noteworthy for its progressive perspective on gender and spiritual equality. He challenges the prevailing belief that salvation is secured exclusively through the prayers of monks, emphasizing instead the equal spiritual efficacy of nuns' prayers. Apokaukos also draws attention to the difficult circumstances faced by nuns who had fled Constantinople, lamenting the stark imbalance between the number of male monasteries and the scarcity of female convents. He vividly describes how these displaced nuns were forced to live in improvised and inadequate conditions—often residing in the forecourts of churches, with little more than broken beds for shelter.[32]

In the decades that followed, the capacities of the so-called Despotate of Epiros evolved, with an increasing number of nunneries becoming active. One such institution was the Monastery of St. George, later rededicated to St. Theodora of Arta. Theodora is notable as the only female saint canonized

28 Theodore Skoutariotes, *Additamenta*, ed. Heisenberg and Wirth, p. 287, fragment no. 33; Laurent, *Regestes*, nos. 1235, 1241, 1297, 1233, 1291, and 1303.

29 Mitsiou, "The Monastery of Sosandra," 665–83; Ahrweiler, "L'histoire et la géographie de la région de Smyrne," 96; Cheynet, "Le bullaire monastique à Byzance," 253, 273–77 (on Kouzenas); Belke, *Bithynien und Hellespont*, 816 (on St. Antony).

30 Foss, *Nicaea*, 108–9. Belke (*Bithynien und Hellespont*, 816, 822) does not specify which of the churches in the Roman theatre the convent was.

31 Acheimastou-Potamianou, "The Basilissa Anna Palaiologina of Arta and the Monastery of Vlacherna," 43–49; Parani, "'The Joy of the Most Holy Mother of God the Hodegetria,'" 113–45.

32 John Apokaukos, *Praxis on the Blachernitissa Monastery*, 17; Lampropoulos, *Ιωάννης Απόκαυκος*, 284–86; Talbot, "Affirmative Action in the 13th Century," 405–6.

from the thirteenth century, and her cult remains active to this day. Her *Vita*—likely composed by Job Iasites—bears resemblance to middle Byzantine hagiographies of married saints, such as that of Maria the Younger.[33] As the wife of Michael II Doukas, ruler of Epiros (1237–1266), Theodora experienced significant hardship, including five years of exile. Following her husband's death, she embraced monastic life and was ultimately buried in the convent she had entered.

The return to Constantinople in 1261 ushered in a dynamic period for Byzantine monasticism, distinguished by a revival in monastic activity and the establishment of numerous new foundations. This era, spanning the second half of the thirteenth century and extending into the 1320s, is noted for its prolific building activity, significant textual contributions to monastic organization, and vibrant cultural expressions.

During this period, Constantinople saw the foundation of several prominent nunneries. Among these were the Monastery of *kyra* Martha, St. Andrew *in Krisei* (modern-day Koca Mustafa Pasha Camii), the Mouchliotissa Monastery (now known as Kanlı Kilise), as well as the convents of *tes Glabaines* and Bebaia Elpis. Particularly significant is the double monastery of Philanthropos Soter (the Merciful Saviour), founded by Irene—later Eulogia—Choumnaina.[34] These foundations underscore the enduring importance of monasticism in Late Byzantium and reflect the central role of aristocratic and imperial patronage in shaping 'Constantinople's religious and cultural topography.

High-ranking officials also played a significant role in this monastic revival, with regional foundations often emulating models established in Constantinople.[35] A notable example from the Byzantine periphery is the Monastery of Lykousada in Thessaly, founded between 1282 and 1289 by the wife of the *sebastokrator* John Doukas.[36] This foundation exemplifies how local elites adopted and adapted the monastic ideals and institutional patterns promoted in the capital. However, after the mid-fourteenth century, the rate of monastic foundations by the aristocracy and imperial family declined considerably. Shifts in the economic landscape altered both

---

33 Talbot, "Saint Theodora of Arta," 323–33.

34 On the Constantinopolitan monasteries localised with certainty, see Kidonopulos, *Bauten in Konstantinopel*, 288–89. See also Mitsiou, "Historisch-Geographisches aus dem Patriarchatsregister," 141–65. See also Chapter 2 of this volume.

35 Cf. the case of Maroules nunnery, see Kidonopulos, *Bauten in Konstantinopel*, 66.

36 Koder and Hild, *Hellas und Thessalien*, 208–9; Pitouli, *A Vlach Nun and Her Thirteenth-Century Monastery*, 7–12.

the social profile of monastic founders and the underlying motivations for establishing such institutions.

During this period, the influence of the traditional landowning aristocracy—long the principal patrons of monastic institutions—began to wane. In their place, a new class of aristocrats emerged, distinguished by their engagement in trade and commerce. Having amassed considerable wealth and social standing, members of this mercantile elite began to allocate portions of their capital toward the support of monasteries and convents, thereby reshaping the landscape of monastic patronage in the late Byzantine era.

A notable illustration of this shift is the case of George Goudeles, a prominent figure of the late fourteenth century who embodies the emerging class of monastic patrons. Goudeles financed the establishment of the Nunnery of St. Nicholas in the Forum Tauri in Constantinople, demonstrating how mercantile wealth had begun to supplant traditional, land-based aristocratic patronage in sustaining and expanding monastic foundations during the late Byzantine period.[37]

The Nunnery of St. Nicholas not only exemplifies a shift in the profile of monastic patrons but also reflects the broader financial and social transformations of the late Byzantine period. This development underscores the ability of monastic institutions to adapt to an evolving economic and societal landscape.

The final centuries of Byzantium—particularly the period leading up to and including the Fall of Constantinople in 1453—offer valuable insight into the roles, resilience, and challenges of female monastics. Despite political instability, nuns remained active participants in ecclesiastical debates, contributed meaningfully to cultural and literary production, and sustained monastic life under increasingly difficult conditions.

Preliminary Conclusions

Women played a significant role in the ecclesiastical controversies that shaped the Byzantine Empire during this period. The active engagement of nuns and other female monastics in theological debates and church disputes—examined in detail in Chapter Five—underscores their influence and the esteem they held within the religious sphere. Their participation reflects

---

37 Ganchou, "L'ultime testament de Géôrgios Goudélès," pp. 346, line 1, p. 52, line 96; Harris, "The Goudelis Family in Italy After the Fall of Constantinople," 168–79; Oikonomidès, *Hommes d'affaires*, 68.

not only their intellectual and spiritual authority but also the broader visibility of women within Byzantine religious life.

The late Byzantine period also witnessed a marked increase in the visibility of nuns within literary and intellectual circles, particularly in Constantinople. This era offers substantial evidence of correspondence between nuns and prominent ecclesiastical figures, including George/Gennadios Scholarios (ca. 1400–1472). Both literate and non-literate nuns played an active role in the cultural and artistic life of the empire by commissioning or donating books, icons, and other devotional objects. Their contributions—often recorded through dedicatory inscriptions and donor portraits—not only reflect their engagement with the intellectual currents of their time but also ensured the preservation of their memory and spiritual legacy (see Chapter Four).[38]

The administration of nunneries was primarily overseen by the Patriarchate and local ecclesiastical authorities. Issues such as land disputes and internal conflicts were adjudicated in Church courts, with the Patriarchal Register offering detailed documentation of the Church's role in supporting convents and resolving such matters. This framework of institutional oversight reflects both the centralized and localized mechanisms of ecclesiastical governance and is examined in depth in Chapter Five.

Despite the political and social upheavals, including the Fall of Constantinople, nunneries remained active, particularly in major cities like Constantinople and Thessaloniki during the early fifteenth century. The Fall of Constantinople did not mark the end of Orthodox monasticism. Nunneries continued to operate and even saw new establishments under Ottoman rule. Notable examples include:

St. Theodora Nunnery in Thessaloniki: continued to function and by 1669 had 150 nuns.

Panagia Myrsiniotissa in Lesbos: founded in 1527.

St. Philothei in Athens: founded around 1572.

St. Anargyroi Kolokynthis in Athens: established in the mid-seventeenth century.[39]

---

38 Female donor portraits are attested also in areas not under the Byzantine rule. See Karamaouna et al., "Female Donors in Thirteenth Century," 231–42.

39 Charalampous, *Γυναικείος ορθόδοξος μοναχισμός κατά τα Πατερικά Κείμενα*, 237–39nn22–24.

Chapter 2

FEMALE MONASTERIES IN LATE BYZANTIUM

FOUNDATION, ORGANIZATION, AND NETWORKS

MODERN STUDIES REGARD medieval monastic foundations as a form of patronage, viewing them as expressions of power and unequal social relations.[1] However, the reasons behind their widespread prevalence in Byzantium—and particularly the role of women in this process—are still not fully understood.[2] Margaret Mullett has argued that while the Greek word *ktetor* can mean both "patron" and "founder," in English we can make the distinction that "founders are monks and patrons are secular, or at least secular becoming monastic."[3] Of course, this is only a general idea, and numerous exceptions can be traced. On the other hand, Michael Grünbart has correctly pointed out that while "foundation" can mean the construction of a building, it can also refer to the network of people associated with the foundation.[4]

As we will argue, foundations and patronage represent not only networks of individuals but also networks of material culture, including rules, texts, and spaces. This study approaches monastic foundations as complex systems composed of multilayered networks. Employing Network Analysis, we focus on specific components, such as textual and spatial networks. Our aim is to visualize and (if possible) to quantify these foundations as networks of unequal relations while also tracing the expressions of female power embedded within their intricate spatial and textual structures.

---

1 Hill, *Imperial Women in Byzantium*, 155–61.

2 Konidares, *Το δίκαιον της μοναστηριακής περιουσίας*, 16, 101; Konidares, *Νομικὴ θεώρηση τῶν μοναστηριακῶν τυπικῶν*, 26–43; Thomas, *Private Religious Foundations in the Byzantine Empire*; Herman, "Ricerche sulle istituzioni monastiche byzantine," 293–375; De Meester, "Les typiques de fondation," 489–508; Beck, *Kirche und theologische Literatur im byzantinischen Reich*, 130; Janin, "Le monachisme byzantine au Moyen Âge," 5–15; Geelhaar and Thomas, *Stiftung und Staat im Mittelalter*; Stathakopoulos, "I Seek Not My Own," 383–97; Kambourova, "Le don de l'Église—une affaire couple?," 213; Mullett, "Founders, Refounders, Second Founders, Patrons," 1–27; Alivisatos, *Die kirchliche Gesetzgebung des Kaisers Justinian I*, 98–112; Frazee, "Late Roman and Byzantine Legislation on the Monastic Life," 263–79; Troianos, *Οι πηγές*, 64, 151–56, 242–45, 270, 314–15, 276, 306–8; Janin, "Le monachisme byzantine au Moyen Âge," 5–44.

3 Mullett, "Founders, Refounders, Second Founders, Patrons," 1–27.

4 Grünbart, "Female Founders—Das Konzept," 21–28.

Founders and Patrons

> The aforementioned most-honourable nun, our celebrated foundress, lady Eugenia Kantakouzene Philanthropene, as a true [great] granddaughter and heir of her celebrated forebears, our founders, generously demonstrated the same zeal and enthusiasm and concern for this holy and venerable convent of ours until her dying breath. For she was tonsured at a youthful age, and spent all her fortune on this holy convent. It was her dying wish to bequeath 100 *hyperpyra* so that the garden of the holy great martyr George might be planted and restored as a vineyard, and joined with the large vineyard of our convent for the sake of her spiritual salvation. Thus our convent and the nuns who dwell in it from now on and in the future ought to celebrate a commemoration annually for the sake of her soul on the anniversary of her departure to God, which is February 11 of the year 6910 [=1402 A.D.]. For this is the day of her death, when we should customarily celebrate a commemoration, just as for our other celebrated founders, her forebears, since she displayed the same zeal and ardor and concern for her ancestral convent, in her longing to attain the heavenly bridal chamber and in her desire for the kingdom of Christ our God. May she be granted these [wishes] through the intercessions of our all-holy, immaculate, and exceedingly praised Lady, the Mother of God *Bebaia Elpis*, and all the saints, Amen.[5]

The passage above is a later and final addition to the *typikon* of the Bebaia Elpis nunnery in Constantinople. It identifies Eugenia Kantakouzene Philanthropene (d. 1402) as an additional *ktetor* of the nunnery. A member of the fourth generation of the Synadenoi family residing there, she continued the familial tradition of patronage.[6]

Sources such as this *typikon* (foundation charter) reveal a range of motives—political, economic, and cultural—underlying the act of founding a monastic institution. Primarily, it served as an expression of gratitude to God, a means of commemorating the founder, and a way to preserve the memory of the founder and their family. At the same time, it functioned as a demonstration of piety. In many ways, foundation and donation fulfilled a role similar to that of pilgrimage; they were a public offering to God—recorded and recognized by society—in hopes of receiving something in return, such as health, peace, or a "secure refuge for women who have chosen the ascetic way of life."[7]

---

5 *Typicon monasterii Theotoci Bebaias Elpidos*, ed. Delehaye, chap. 159, pp. 104–5; Talbot, "*Bebaia Elpis*," 1568.

6 Hannick and Schmalzbauer, "Die Synadenoi," 134–35, 140–41.

7 Gerstel and Kalopissi-Verti, "Female Church Founders," 204.

In practical terms, a foundation meant that a person of means (who often later became a nun) built or rebuilt a monastery (most cases deal with renovation, and only a few with completely new monasteries). In Byzantium, nunneries could be founded by men (emperors, members of the imperial family, monks, and bishops),[8] despite the decision of Patriarch Alexios the Stoudite in 1027 that there should be no male founders for female monasteries and vice versa (this decision was renewed in 1169 by Patriarch Loukas Chrysoberges).[9] Female founders were empresses, wives of local rulers, members of the aristocracy, and, finally, common nuns.

Existing textual and visual evidence links monastic foundations to the tradition of imperial philanthropy—a model that both male and female aristocrats, in the capital and the provinces, emulated to enhance their prestige and accumulate social capital. It is no coincidence that the most prominent female patrons belonged to powerful families, such as the Palaiologoi, Synadenoi, Raoul, Strategopouloi, and Tarchaneiotes. These elite lineages sought to reestablish landmarks within the Constantinopolitan landscape as enduring symbols of their familial significance and legacy.

Among female patrons, widows played a significant role.[10] Indeed, the connections between widowhood, monastic life, and foundation are extremely close, as Byzantine women very often took the monastic habit during widowhood. Sharon Gerstel and Sophia Kalopissi-Verti argue:

> The ability of widows to participate in church foundation...reflected the strong juridical rights of widows in Byzantium and their critical position within families where they served, on occasion, as heads of household.... The increased involvement of widows — even humble women of the Byzantine village — in the foundation of churches in the late Byzantine period, appears to benefit from changes in attitude toward the alienation of dowry properties in the last centuries of imperial rule.[11]

Dionysios Stathakopoulos proposed that female patronage is influenced by the so-called "bag-lady syndrome": women, who as a rule outlive men by several years, are concerned about a potential lowering of their financial

8 Loukaki, "Monastères de femmes à Byzance du XIIe siècle," 35.

9 Grumel, *Regestes*, nos. 833 and 1086.

10 Konidares, "Η θέση της χήρας στη βυζαντινή κοινωνία," 35–42. For information on widows in middle Byzantine hagiographical texts, see Nikolaou, *Η γυναίκα στη μέση βυζαντινή εποχή*, 172–82. For dowry and inheritance in traditional (modern) villages in Greece and Cyprus, see Piault, *Familles et biens en Grece et a Chypre*.

11 Gerstel and Kalopissi-Verti, "Female Church Founders," 195–96.

status and, as a result, only make their largest donations after their death.[12] On the other hand, we can assume that women—especially widows who did not choose to remarry—owned property that they could dispose of freely.

Widowhood offered economic freedom of action, and this freedom had a basis in the legislation of Justinian and in the *Ecloga* (726). The former enabled female ownership of property as a dowry or as *parapherna*.[13] Nevertheless, it was the *Ecloga* that stipulated a widow could become the head of the family, thus obtaining legal control of her dowry properties.[14] Along with a variety of legal freedoms, widowhood also provided wealthy women with further motivation to adopt the monastic life. The construction and re-foundation of a monastery allowed them to express their own wishes and enabled them to live a monastic life in line with their personal tastes. Women could take their lives into their own hands.

The Rules of Foundation

The foundation of monasteries in Byzantium is strongly connected to the *ktetorika typika* (founding statutes). The first known *typikon* for a Byzantine nunnery is that of Kecharitomene in Constantinople (first half of the twelfth century).[15] In the Palaiologan era, five more *typika* are dated: Lips, Anargyroi, Bebaia Elpis, Philanthropos Soter, and Baionaia. The *typika* constituted an essential part of a larger dossier that included the founder's testament and additional documents. By the thirteenth century, they had already acquired their main form, characteristics, and topics. They addressed all possible matters, such as the election of the abbot/abbess and the monastic *offikia* (offices) and their duties as well as constitutional, financial, and liturgical issues.

12 Stathakopoulos, "I Seek Not My Own," 385.

13 *Parapherna* (or *exoproika*) denoted usually the movable property of the wife, e. g. household items and clothing that she brought into the matrimonial home. It remained her personal property, but as these objects were used to cover the needs of the family, they were recorded in the marriage contract and were managed by the husband.

14 *Ecloga*, ed. Burgmann, title 2, chap. 5, §1; Freshfield, *A Revised Manual of Roman Law*, 28. For earlier legislation, see White, "Property Rights of Women," 539–48. See also Buckler, "Women in Byzantine Law About 1100 A.D.," 410. For inheritance disputes concerning the dowry, see Macrides, "Dowry and Inheritance in the Late Period," 89–98.

15 Mitsiou, "The Monastery of Kecharitomene and the Contribution of the Assumptionists," 327–44.

The very existence of the *typika* may seem paradoxical, as state and church legislation regulated the foundation proceedings and aspects of monastic life. Nevertheless, laws and canons provided only a general framework, whereas a *typikon* organized a specific community and addressed the wishes of a particular founder within the existing legislation. The canon and civil law related to monastic foundations are based principally on Justinian's *Novels* (*Novellae constitutiones*), the legislation of Leo VI, and the canons of the ecumenical and local synods. Justinian established a basic juridical framework by reinforcing and broadening the ecumenical synods, especially the Ecumenical Council of Chalcedon.[16]

Briefly, it should be mentioned that since Chalcedon, all monasteries were placed under episcopal authority. According to Canon 4, "no monastery should be built without the local bishop's permission, who will then exercise supervision in the monastery."[17] Justinian reinforced this canon, arguing that "he who wishes to build a monastery must first speak with the bishop of the region, so that the bishop will go there, say a prayer, and fix the cross; only then must the foundation commence."[18] Nevertheless, as we shall see, the bishop's rights were questioned, and many founders tried to replace them with imperial or patriarchal protection or even with total independence.

In addition, the canonical and legal framework regulated the maintenance of the original status of the foundation. Canon 24 of Chalcedon determined that "once a monastery, always a monastery, and its material goods must remain in its possession."[19] Chapter 7 of Justinian's Novel 120[20] forbade the alienation of monastic properties. Finally, both Justinian's Novel 131 and Novel 14 of Leo VI (886–912)[21] imposed the compulsory conclusion of all construction works undertaken by a monastery. Specifically, Justinian maintained that "he who has begun to build a new monastery or to restore an old one will be compelled to complete it."

16 This study does not address in detail the legal regulations but will refer to laws and canons whenever they are relevant to its argument.

17 *Council of Chalcedon*, ed. Alberigo et al., Canon 4, pp. 139–40.

18 Justinian, *Novellae*, ed. Schöll and Kroll, no. 5, chap. 1, pp. 28–29.

19 *Council of Chalcedon*, ed. Alberigo et al., Canon 24, pp. 148.

20 Justinian, *Novellae*, ed. Schöll and Kroll, no. 120, chap. 7, pp. 585–87; Justinian, *Novellae*, ed. Schöll and Kroll, no. 7, prefatio-chap. 2, pp. 48–54.

21 Justinian, *Novellae*, ed. Schöll and Kroll, no. 131, chap. 7, p. 657; Leo VI, *Novellae*, ed. Troianos, no. 14, pp. 76–79.

In a *typikon*, the status of a monastic foundation is normally declared in its first chapters. Since the so-called Evergetian reform,[22] there has been an increased desire among founders to establish independent and self-administered monasteries (both imperial and private). The first chapter of the Kecharitomene *typikon* declared that the nunnery:

> [S]hould be independent and under its own control, a stranger to all mastery and ownership, and that no one at all should have any right or privilege in respect of it but it should remain independent in every way, separate and in control of itself, and be administered in accordance with what will be expressly laid down here by me. It should neither be made subject to imperial or ecclesiastic or personal rights at any time nor assigned as a gift or *epidosis* or for reasons of *ephoreia*, stewardship or superintendence or for any other reason to any kind of person whatsoever or monastery or holy house or orphanage or other bureau or any hospital but remain for ever only under the authority of the Virgin Mother of God *Kecharitomene*.[23]

Theodora Palaiologina (d. 1303) also declared that the Lips foundation was to keep the right to govern itself (*autodespoton*).[24] The dowager empress rejected any efforts by the emperor or patriarch to attach it or subordinate it as a dependency to another convent. She made similar regulations for the Anargyroi nunnery, stipulating that it be "separate and independent," and she omitted the customary list of perceived threats to the independence of her foundation. This convent was to remain unattached to any other foundation and was not to be united by the emperor or patriarch with the Lips convent. The empress decided, rather innovatively, that although Lips and Anargyroi had to remain separate entities and could never become one monastery, they were allowed to cooperate to a certain extent.[25] Similar concerns and regulations regarding the independence and freedom of the institution are found in the *typikon* of Bebaia Elpis. Any involvement of individuals via *epidosis*,

22 Thomas, *Private Religious Foundations in the Byzantine Empire*, 214–43. On the *Evergetis typikon*, see Jordan and Morris, *The Hypotyposis of the Monastery of the Theotokos Evergetis*.

23 Gautier, "Le *typikon* de la Théotokos Kécharitôménè," chap. 1, pp. 29–31; Jordan, "*Kecharitomene*," 667–68.

24 *Typicon monasterii Lips*, ed. Delehaye, chaps. 1–2, pp. 106–7; Talbot, "*Lips*," 1265–66. On Theodora Palaiologina, see Melichar, *Empresses of Late Byzantium*, 71–103.

25 *Typicon monasterii sanctorum Anargyrorum*, ed. Delehaye, chap. 57, pp. 137–38; Talbot, "*Anargyroi*," 1291.

or union, with another institution should be avoided; moreover, it should be regarded as treason and, therefore, deserving of capital punishment.[26]

Related to the status of the nunneries is the issue of the "protectorate." Most *typika* of nunneries foresee the existence of a protector (*ephoros*) who mediates between them and the outside world and who has an overall controlling function. The Kecharitomene *typikon* made provision for a female protector. More specifically, the foundress Irene Doukaina referred to those individuals who would take over the supervision (*antilepsis*) of the nunnery after her death: her daughter Eudokia, followed by Anna Komnena (the well-known historian), her daughter Maria, and so on. However, it always had to be a member of her family.[27]

Contrary to the ideas of the Komnenian Empress, Theodora Palaiologina imposed a male protector upon the foundation. For the Lips Monastery, she nominated her son Andronikos II (1282–1328) and his successors as guardian and protector, arguing that women need strong protection "inasmuch as they are accustomed to staying at home and the silence which is most appropriate to [them]."[28] Such a gender-oriented statement merely disguises the effort to ensure the most powerful protector for the monastery. Similarly, the foundress of Bebaia Elpis authorized a male relative to be "protector and helper" after asserting that the nature of women is frail.[29] Her eldest son should be followed by her next eldest son and other suitably powerful and pious relatives.

John Philip Thomas has argued that "one of the most significant developments of the Palaiologan era was a drastic curtailment of the once very extensive and arbitrary rights of lay patrons of ecclesiastical institutions."[30] These lay patrons—primarily protectors (*ephoroi*)—were responsible for the maintenance (*systasis*) and improvement (*beltiosis*) of the monasteries, but they often failed to fulfill their duties. The difficulties faced by the nunnery *tes Panagiotisses* (also known as Mouchliotissa) due to its protector offer a good example. After the death of the foundress Maria Palaiologina (after 1307) and her daughter Theodora, her son-in-law, Isaakios Palaiologos Asanes, obtained the protection (*ephoreia*) of the monastery. Asanes

26 *Typicon monasterii Theotoci Bebaias Elpidos*, ed. Delehaye, chaps. 14–16, pp. 27–29; Talbot, "*Bebaia Elpis*," 1527–28.

27 Gautier, "Le *typikon* de la Théotokos Kécharitôménè," chap. 80, pp. 143–47; Jordan, "*Kecharitomene*," 709–10.

28 *Typicon monasterii Lips*, ed. Delehaye, chaps. 3–4, pp. 108–9; Talbot, "*Lips*," 1266.

29 *Typicon monasterii Theotoci Bebaias Elpidos*, ed. Delehaye, chaps. 18–20, pp. 29–31; Talbot, "*Bebaia Elpis*," 1528–29.

30 Thomas, *Private Religious Foundations in the Byzantine Empire*, 253.

contributed to its decay by putting a financial burden upon the monastic community for his own gain.[31]

The fear, attested in the *typika*, that powerful individuals might try to exploit even a *monydrion* (small monastery) is supported by various sources. The monk Theodosios' final wish was for the small nunnery *tes Kryoneritisses*, which he founded in Herakleia, to remain under the ownership of the nuns.[32] However, a certain George Kounales prevented this by producing a fake testament that favoured the deceased *mesazon* (chief minister), Nikephoros Choumnos. A *terminus ante quem* for the testament is 1327, the year Choumnos died as the monk Nathaniel and was buried in the Monastery of Philanthropos Soter in Constantinople.[33] The key point, however, is that after Choumnos' death and the fall of Andronikos II (1328), a certain nun, Agathonike, appeared before the synodic court, likely in the hope of securing a favourable ruling under the new regime.[34]

In some cases, the Patriarch and synod transferred the rights of the administration of a nunnery not to a male or a layperson but to a nun who could promise to improve the financial situation of the monastery. This occurred in the cases of Maroulina from the Varangiotissa convent[35] and Eleodora Tarchaneiotissa.[36] The nun Martha Syriana succeeded in securing not only the administration rights but also the *ktetorika dikaia* of Pausolype Monastery for the rest of her life after making improvements in the nunnery.

---

31 *Patriarchal Register*, vol. 3, Koder et al., pp. 62–77, no. 184 (October 1351); Darrouzès, *Les regestes des Actes du patriarcat de Constantinople*, no. 2330; Thomas, *Private Religious Foundations in the Byzantine Empire*, 261; Smyrlis, *La fortune des grands monastères byzantins*, 68–69.

32 Perhaps the monastery' name *tes Kryoneritisses* was the same as that of the monastery they left behind in Skamandros. In Thrace, there almost certainly existed a *proasteion* (a rural estate or suburban property) named Kryon Neron (meaning "Cold Water") near the village of Melandros, close to Rhaidestos; there was also a Kryoneron in the region of Bizye. See Külzer, *Ostthrakien*, 477.

33 Verpeaux, *Nicéphore Choumnos*, 45. Darrouzès (*Les regestes des Actes du patriarcat de Constantinople*, no. 2157) dates monastery's acquisition by Choumnos between 1316 and 1320.

34 *Patriarchal Register*, vol. 1, ed. Hunger and Kresten, pp. 586–88, no. 103 (April 1330); Darrouzès, *Les regestes des Actes du patriarcat de Constantinople*, no. 2157.

35 *Patriarchal Register*, vol. 3, ed. Koder et al., pp. 516, no. 258 (February 1361), lines 10–13; Darrouzès, *Les regestes des Actes du patriarcat de Constantinople*, no. 2433.

36 Miklosich and Müller, *Acta et Diplomata graeca Medii Aevi sacra et profana*, vol. 2, pp. 468–69, no. 628 (March-April 1401); Darrouzès, *Les regestes des Actes du patriarcat de Constantinople*, no. 3190.

The previous *ktetor*, nun Kallinike, agreed to give away her rights. Syriana was obliged, however, to undertake the restoration of the church and the improvement of the monastic properties.[37]

The nun Theodoule Tzouroulene rebuilt the Church *tes Gabraines*, which was in a sorry state. In her absence, a neighbour, Kontostephanos, used the area around the church to plant a vineyard. After expelling him, patriarch Matthew I in 1400 granted Theodoule ownership (*ktetoreia*) and protection (*ephoreia*) of the church.[38] According to John Philip Thomas, "the conversion of *ktetoreia*, the traditional Byzantine concept of private ownership of an ecclesiastical institution, to *ktetorikon dikaion* (founder's right) took place in the Palaeologan era, just as had occurred earlier in the medieval West."[39]

The obtainment and possession of the founder's right enabled changes to be made even to the original form and status of nunneries. By the will of the founder, male monasteries could be transformed into female monasteries and vice versa. The patriarchal Monastery of Theotokos Hodegetria in Didymoteichon was abandoned by its monks and later inhabited by nuns. However, this monastery soon fell into decay, and the nuns were relocated to other convents. To avoid further financial losses, the unknown *oikeios* of the emperor, who held the founder's rights (*ktetorikon dikaion*), in May 1340 requested the synod's permission to return the monastery to its former status.[40]

---

37 Miklosich and Müller, *Acta et Diplomata graeca Medii Aevi sacra et profana*, vol. 1, pp. 454–55, no. 200 (January 1365); Darrouzès, *Les regestes des Actes du patriarcat de Constantinople*, no. 2476. See Zhishman, *Das Stifterrecht (Τὸ κτητορικὸν δίκαιον) in der morgenländischen Kirche*, 65–66.

38 Miklosich and Müller, *Acta et Diplomata graeca Medii Aevi sacra et profana*, vol. 2, pp. 395–99, no. 579 (June 1400); Darrouzès, *Les regestes des Actes du patriarcat de Constantinople*, no. 3138. On the church *tes Gabraines*, see Janin, *La géographie ecclésiastique de l'Empire byzantine*, 172.

39 Thomas, *Private Religious Foundations in the Byzantine Empire*, 253. On the differences between *ktetorikon dikaion*, *despoteia*, and *ktetoreia*, see now Neyzi, "Monasticism in Late Byzantine Constantinople," 121–51, who distances from Thomas's view. Generally, the *ktetorikon dikaion* is based on the *jus patronatus*, which concerns the property rights of the monastery's founder. These ownership rights stem specifically from the act of establishing the monastery as well as the spiritual and administrative rights outlined in the ownership deed, known as the *typikon*, which can be inherited. The authority responsible for granting the founding rights is the relevant ecclesiastical body, which also holds the power to revoke these rights if the founder fails to meet their obligations regarding the monastery's maintenance and operation.

40 *Patriarchal Register*, vol. 2, ed. Hunger et al., p. 190, no. 127 (May 1340); Darrouzès, *Les regestes des Actes du patriarcat de Constantinople*, no. 2199; Soustal, *Thrakien*, 241; Bakirtzes, *Byzantine Thrace*, 70–73. For the title of *oikeios* and its meaning, see Verpeaux, "Les *oikeioi*," 89–99.

Church courts often found it difficult to decide upon the correctness of such transformations.[41] A case from the year 1341 serves as a good example. On the old ruins of a church, the military official Phokas Maroules built a new church dedicated to Theotokos.[42] The newly founded nunnery (sometime after 1305 but before 1320) was to become a residence for his wife and daughters; he also built cells and a circuit wall and endowed the monastery with adequate lands. Some years after Maroules' death, his son, John Synadenos, with his mother's assistance planned to transform it into a male monastery. The synod declared that the Holy Fathers forbade the conversion of a female monastery into a male monastery.[43] Nevertheless, these conversions were often tolerated. The Patriarchate generally did not react immediately but only after being requested to do so by individuals who had a personal interest in the matter.

According to a patriarchal document (*sigillion*) of Joseph I (1266–1275), the Nea Petra—founded circa 1271 by Anna Palaiologina near Velestinos in Thessaly—was also transformed into a male monastery. A *chrysobull* (imperial golden bull charter) of Michael VIII confirmed this transformation. The Patriarch offers no canonical justification for this decision, simply mentioning that it was the wish of its founders, Anna Palaiologina and John Maliasenos. There were probably political reasons for fulfilling the wishes of the Maliasenoi, ardent supporters of the Palaiologoi in Thessaly. The *chrysobull* ordered that the local bishop should refrain from annoying the existing and future nuns.[44]

---

41 Talbot, "The Conversion of Byzantine Monasteries from Male to Female," 360–64.

42 Darrouzès, *Les regestes des Actes du patriarcat de Constantinople*, no. 2207; Kidonopulos, *Bauten in Konstantinopel*, 65–67; Janin, *La géographie ecclésiastique de l'Empire byzantine*, 196, 336; Talbot, "A Comparison of the Monastic Experience," 7–8. On Maroules, see Efthymiadis and Mazarakis, "Questions de chronologie sur Ramon Muntaner," 313.

43 *Patriarchal Register*. vol. 2, ed. Hunger et al., pp. 280–82, no. 135 (May 1341); Darrouzès, *Les regestes des Actes du patriarcat de Constantinople*, no. 2207. Prior to the thirteenth century, the monasteries of Dalmatou, Zaoutzes, Theotokos Panachrantos, Areia, and Panagia in Thebai (known as Dekane) as well as the Monastery in Megalopolis had been turned into nunneries. See Magdalino, "Some Additions and Corrections to the List of Byzantine Churches," 278–79; Janin, *La géographie ecclésiastique de l'Empire byzantine*, 214–15; Talbot, "The Conversion of Byzantine Monasteries from Male to Female," 360–64. On the other hand, the nunnery of Myrelaion was converted into a monastery. Janin, *La géographie ecclésiastique de l'Empire byzantine*, 352.

44 Miklosich and Müller, *Acta et Diplomata graeca Medii Aevi sacra et profana*, vol. 4, pp. 361–62, no. 11 (December 1271); Dölger and Wirth, *Regesten der Kaiserurkunden*

Networks of Patrons and Texts

Foundation as a form of patronage is widely regarded as an expression of power and social hierarchy. Michael Grünbart has further highlighted that foundation entails not only material and institutional acts but also the creation of a network of individuals associated with the monastic establishment.[45] The Bebaia Elpis nunnery provides a compelling case for examining such networks. Its foundress, Theodora, married into the influential Synadenos family, becoming the wife of the *megas stratopedarches* John Angelos Doukas Synadenos. Theodora Synadene entered the convent alongside her daughter, Euphrosyne, who was still a child at the time. Her husband, John—later known by his monastic name Joachim—was likewise honoured as a founder. All three family members are represented as founders in the *typikon*, accompanied by some of the most striking examples of Byzantine illumination.[46]

The *typikon* preserves the Synadenos family's vision in two distinct versions. The original *typikon* was composed at the time of the foundation, while a later part was added by Euphrosyne Synadene as abbess of the convent. Euphrosyne adapted the original to reflect her own intentions and the evolving needs of the community. Notable modifications included increasing the allowable number of nuns, instituting commemorative practices for members of the monastic community, and prohibiting the education of lay children within the monastery. In addition, Euphrosyne crafted a kind of familial album, incorporating references to her grandparents, parents, siblings, and their descendants. In this way, the *typikon* offers a distinctive portrayal of both the monastic community and the founder's extended family. Remarkably, Euphrosyne and her parents are the only individuals depicted twice, highlighting different stages of their lives: her parents are shown

des Oströmischen Reiches, vol. 3, no. 2031a; Laurent, *Regestes*, no. 1411; Giannopoulos, "Αἱ παρὰ τὴν Δημητριάδα βυζαντιναὶ μοναί," 210–40.

45 Grünbart, "Female Founders—Das Konzept," 21–28.

46 Other *typika* contained also illuminations and portraits of the founders. For example, the lost manuscript Torino, Biblioteca Nazionale Universitaria, MS B. VI. 01 (Pasini 237) (1286) (*Diktyon*: 63769), which contained the cartulary of Makrinitissa and Nea Petra, featured portraits of Anna/Anthousa Maliasene and her husband holding a model of their foundation. Anna Maliasene was a cousin of Theodora Synadene. For a similar case, see Fugger and Stefec, "Das illuminierte *Typikon* des Eugenios-Klosters in Trapezunt," 41–66. On the illuminated manuscripts in Byzantium, see now the volume by Tsamakda, *A Companion to Byzantine Illustrated Manuscripts*. Nonetheless, illustrated *typika* have not been included in this Companion.

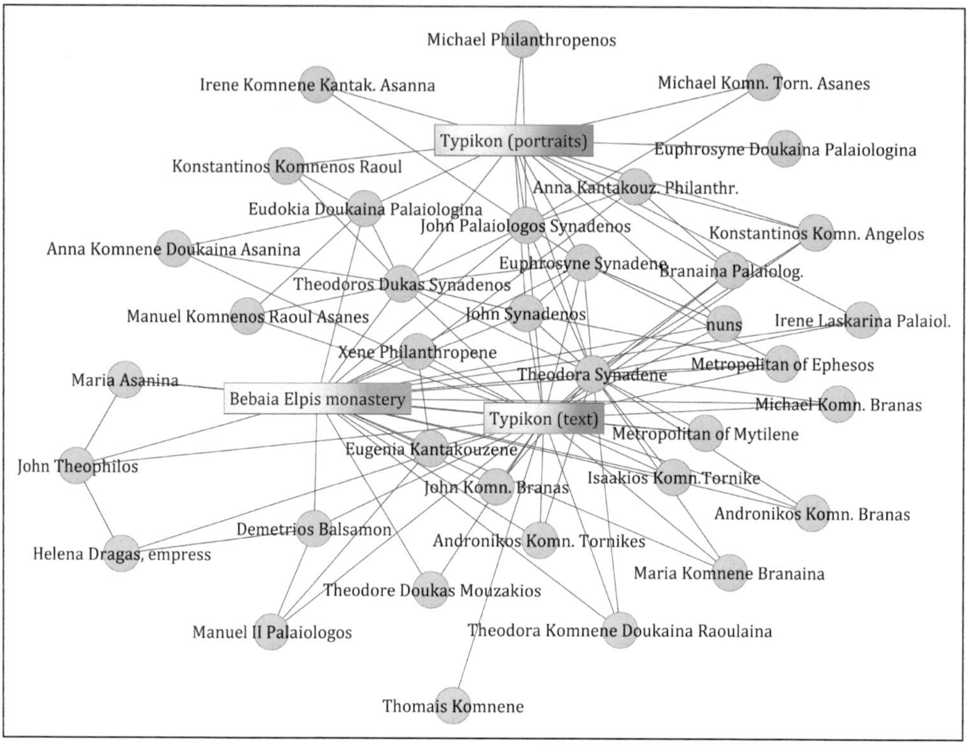

Figure 2.1. Lincoln *typikon* network, all.

before and after their monastic tonsure, while Euphrosyne appears both as a child and later in her role as abbess.

The history and dating of the manuscript, Oxford, Lincoln College, MS gr. 35 (ca. 1300–1355), are notably complex. Numerous scholars have examined its structure and proposed varying interpretations of its present form. Particularly valuable is the most recent description by Georgi Parpulov, which offers the most precise and comprehensive account of its contents to date.[47]

47 *Diktyon*: 48689; Spatharakis, *The Portrait in Byzantine Illuminated Manuscripts*, 190–206, and figs. 143–54; Hutter, "Die Geschichte des Lincoln College *Typikons*," 79–114. See also Hennessy, "The Lincoln College *Typikon*," 97–109; Gastgeber, "Das *Typikon* Lincoln College gr. 35," 95–110; Gaul, "Writing 'with Joyful and Leaping Soul,'" 243–71. On the manuscript description, see Coxe, *Catalogus codicum mss. qui in collegiis aulisque Oxoniensibus*, 18–19, Parpulov, "Lincoln College MS, Gr. 35." During a recent trip to Oxford and the Bodleian Library, I had the opportunity to consult the original manuscript and make my own observations. I plan to present a slightly different perspective on the composition and history of this codex in an upcoming article.

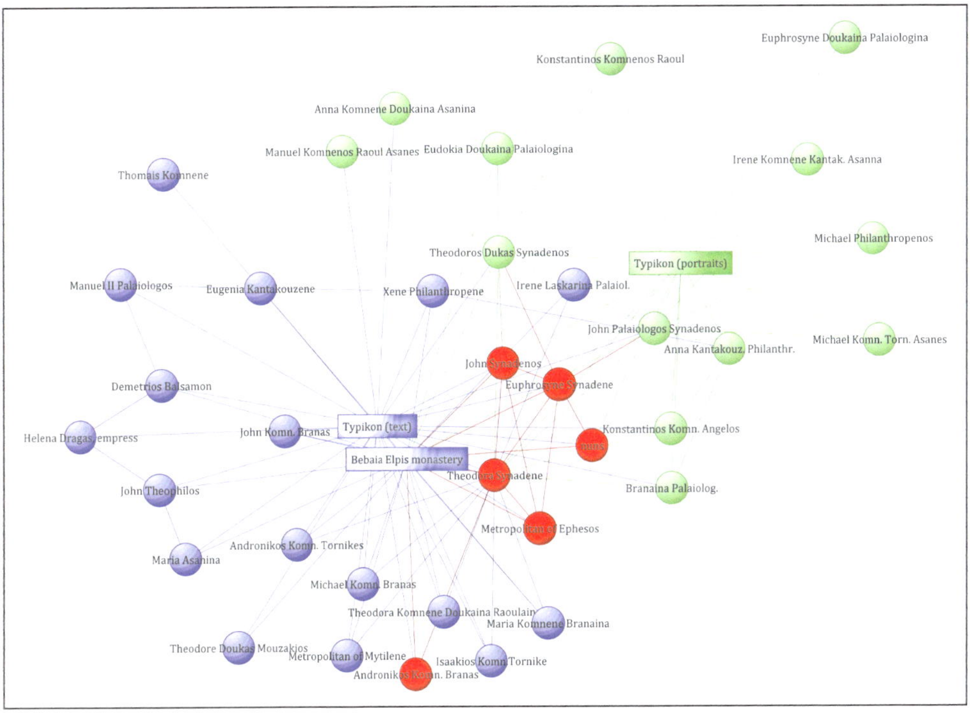

Figure 2.2. Lincoln *typikon* network, Newman Clustering Coefficient.

Scholarly research has identified two principal female scribes involved in the production of the manuscript, along with an additional female assistant. A fourth hand has also been recognized, responsible for later additions. The images appear to be the work of a distinct illuminator, though it remains uncertain whether this individual was one of the nuns portrayed on fol. 12r.[48]

The Lincoln College *typikon*—in both its text and illuminations—reflects the patronage network established by Synadene and her daughter, who held the *ktetorikon dikaion* (founder's rights) and oversaw the organization of a female monastic community. Like any foundation charter or devotional artifact, the *typikon* can be understood as a network of relational connections involving a range of agents. The complex web of relationships embedded within the Lincoln College *typikon* lends itself well to visualization and analysis through the methodologies of Social Network Analysis.

To illustrate Synadene's patronage as recorded in the Bebaia Elpis *typikon* (see Figure 2.1), we created a multi-mode ego-network with three categories of nodes: agents (persons), knowledge (i.e., the text and illuminations

48 Hutter, "Die Geschichte des Lincoln College *Typikons*," 90n52, 108.

of the *typikon*), and places (the monastery). In addition to kinship relations, we visualized all the agents mentioned in the text, even if they do not have their portrait in the *typikon*.

The network may seem densely interconnected at first glance, but further analysis allows for identifying further sub-structures.[49] The application of one of the most common algorithms for cluster detection, named after the physicist Newman, results in the identification of three clusters, which can be connected to the tight group of the first patrons (red) to the second generation (green) and later patrons (blue) (see Figure 2.2).

When it comes to central positions of individuals within this network graph, a non-surprising result is that Theodora Synadene has the greatest betweenness centrality (indicating intermediary potential, 0.0725), while her daughter and abbess, Euphrosyne, comes second in the rank (0.0425).

Conquering the Space: A Network of Female Foundations

The foundation of female monasteries required careful consideration of location. Founders often chose to establish them within cities or fortified areas, primarily for reasons of security—particularly in response to the threat of enemy attacks and other forms of instability. Access to water was another critical factor. It is therefore unsurprising that many nunneries in the Byzantine capital were situated near aqueducts and natural water sources and frequently incorporated cisterns within their enclosures.[50] Similarly, provincial nunneries prioritized proximity to water, recognizing that effective water management was essential for sustaining monastic life.[51]

In other instances, the size and location of available land played a decisive role in a founder's choice.[52] A common pattern was to establish a monastery on property already owned by the founder or their family. For example, the nunnery of Nea Petra was founded around 1271 near Velestinos in Thessaly by Anna/Anthousa Palaiologina and her husband, Nicholas Maliasenos. The land itself was an imperial gift to the Maliasenos family. The foundation document issued to both founders emphasizes that the site's tranquil

---

49 For the terminology used here, see the introduction.

50 Crow et al., *The Water Supply of Byzantine Constantinople*, 111–13 (maps 13–15); Ousterhout, "Water and Healing in Constantinople," 73 (Philanthropos Soter *hagiasma*); Talbot, "Holy Springs and Pools in Constantinople," 161–74.

51 Cf. Bénou, *Codex B*, pp. 100–1, no. 47 (1344), where the nun Aikaterina Amoirisa reaches an agreement with a neighbour regarding water rights and channels.

52 Talbot, "Founders Choices," 48.

and eremitical character further influenced their decision to establish the monastery there.[53]

Once the site was selected and the extent of the endowment determined, construction began on essential elements such as cells, courtyards, a surrounding wall, and a gate to provide residence, security, and seclusion for the nuns. Within the enclosed space, additional buildings could be erected as needed, often in significant numbers, as suggested by the detailed Ottoman survey of 1455.[54] Central to the foundation was the construction and adornment of the main church (*katholikon*), which required not only architectural investment but also the acquisition of icons, liturgical books, sacred vessels, and furnishings.[55] To ensure the monastery's long-term viability and financial independence, it was also endowed with income-generating properties and estates.[56]

Byzantine nunneries were primarily an urban phenomenon, with Constantinople serving as a prominent example of this characteristic, particularly in the late Byzantine period. Following the events of 1204, the number of nunneries declined significantly, and sources register little to no major building activity during this time. Nevertheless, a few convents under Greek sovereignty are known from the first half of the thirteenth century, including St. Antony in Nicaea, the Blachernitissa, and St. George in Arta.[57] The monastic landscape of Constantinople underwent dramatic transformation as many Orthodox churches were appropriated by Western monastic orders, who also constructed new buildings. Contemporary sources, such as the *Encomium of Gregory of Cyprus on Michael VIII*, depict a city marked by devastation and monastic decline following the Latin occupation and the events leading up to the restoration of Orthodox rule in 1261.[58]

53 Miklosich and Müller, *Acta et Diplomata graeca Medii Aevi sacra et profana*, vol. 4, p. 397, no. 28 (September 1271); Giannopoulos, "Αἱ παρὰ τὴν Δημητριάδα βυζαντιναὶ μοναί," 210–40.

54 İnalcık, *The Survey of Istanbul*, 320–22 (Lips Monastery).

55 *Patriarchal Register*, vol. 3, ed. Koder et al., p. 68, no. 184 (October 1351), lines 38–40.

56 On the financial aspects of foundations, see below, Chapter 3.

57 Acheimastou-Potamianou, "The Basilissa Anna Palaiologina of Arta and the Monastery of Vlacherna," 43–49; Parani, "'The Joy of the Most Holy Mother of God the Hodegetria,'" 113–45.

58 Gregory of Cyprus, *Ἐγκώμιον εἰς τὸν αὐτοκράτορα κυρὸν Μιχαὴλ Παλαιολόγον καὶ Νέον Κωνσταντῖνον*, col. 376.

Nikephoros Gregoras underscores the Latins' disregard for the numerous buildings destroyed by fire during their occupation of Constantinople. In his view, the city's recovery under Michael VIII marked a resurrection—life returning after a symbolic death.[59] A more nuanced perspective is offered by the historian George Pachymeres, who acknowledges that, despite the damage, some private structures remained in good condition after 1261. In contrast, David Jacoby has challenged the bleak portrayal found in Byzantine sources, distinguishing between the relatively well-maintained Venetian Quarter and the more severely affected areas under Latin imperial control.[60] Nonetheless, the city was clearly suffering from depopulation. Pachymeres recounts the presence of Izz al-Dīn Kaykāwūs II in Constantinople around 1261, portraying him wandering drunkenly through the deserted streets—a vivid testament to the capital's desolation at the time.[61]

The Byzantine initiative to reclaim and reassert control over Constantinople began under Michael VIII Palaiologos, who was hailed as a "New Constantine." This program of symbolic and physical restoration included the commissioning of a statue depicting the emperor holding the church of St. Sophia as well as the construction or restoration of key religious institutions, such as the churches of Theotokos Nikopoios and monasteries like St. Demetrios, St. George of Mangana, and Peribleptos. Michael VIII also enacted policies to facilitate the reoccupation of the city by allowing Byzantines to take possession of abandoned homes.[62] His successor, Andronikos II, continued this legacy, overseeing the renovation of major churches, including the Holy Apostles, St. Sophia, and the Theotokos of Blachernai. Like his predecessor, he was celebrated as a "New Constantine," particularly for his ecclesiastical initiatives.

According to the calculations of Vassilios Kidonopoulos and Alice-Mary Talbot of the newly established monasteries in Constantinople between 1261 and 1328, twelve—approximately one-third—were founded by women. Narrowing the focus to the period between 1282 and 1328, nine of the twenty-two monastic institutions that were restored had female patrons, while women were responsible for founding four out of the ten

---

59 Gregoras, *Roman History*, ed. Bekker et al., vol. 1, pp. 106, 107, 127; Puech, "La refondation religieuse de Constantinople," 351–62.

60 Jacoby, "The Urban Evolution of Latin Constantinople," 277–97. See now Mitsiou, "Die Netzwerke einer kulturellen Begegnung," 359–74.

61 Pachymeres, *History*, ed. Failler and Laurent, vol. 1, bk. 3, chap. 3, p. 235, lines 5–10.

62 Talbot, "The Restoration of Constantinople Under Michael VIII," 243–61.

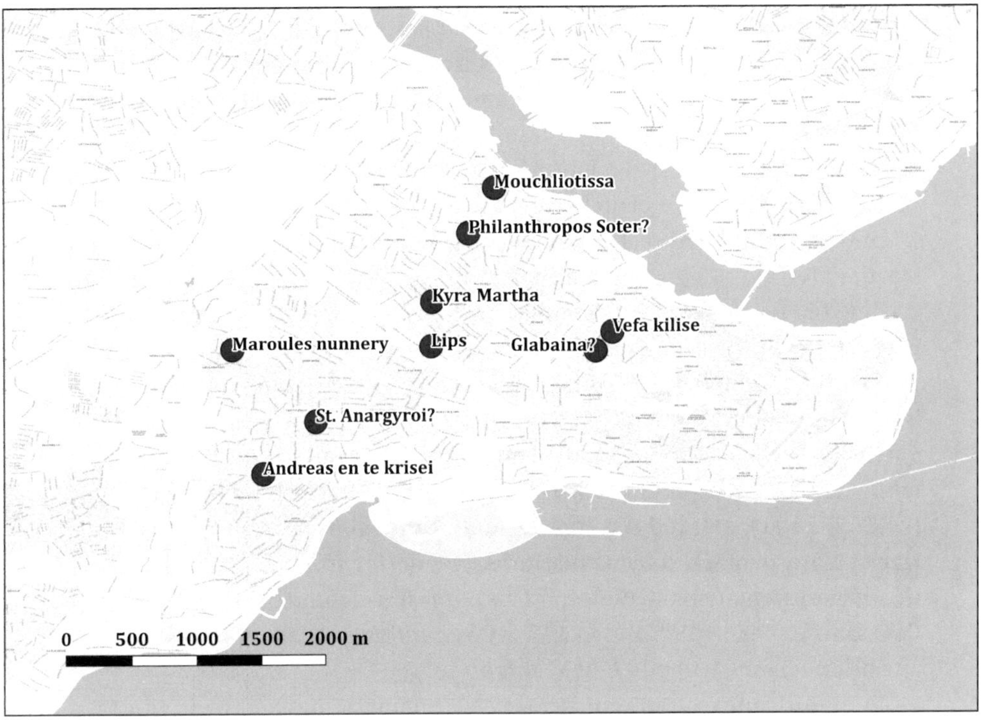

Map 2.1. Nunneries of Constantinople.

newly constructed monasteries (see Map 2.1). These figures underscore the significant role of women in the religious and urban revival of the Byzantine capital during the Palaiologan era.[63]

The *kyra* Martha Monastery was a prominent nunnery during the early Palaiologan period.[64] Founded in the late thirteenth century by Martha Tarchaneiotissa—an ardent supporter of the Arsenite movement and sister of Emperor Michael VIII. It became one of the largest female monastic communities in Constantinople by the fourteenth century. An Ottoman survey from 1455 records the Monastery of "Kir Martas" as comprising twelve one- and two-storey houses, wineries in its outer courtyard, two churches, a refectory, and fifty cells within its inner courtyard.[65] The precise location of

63 Talbot, "Building Activity in Constantinople Under Andronikos II," 329–43; Kidonopulos, *Bauten in Konstantinopel*, 232–42; Kidonopoulos, "The Urban Physiognomy of Constantinople," 101–5.

64 For the Constantinopolitan monasteries localized with certainty, see Kidonopulos, *Bauten in Konstantinopel*, 288–89.

65 İnalcık, *The Survey of Istanbul*, 323, 493.

the monastery remains debated. Raymond Janin, a leading authority on the topography of Constantinople, situates it near the Lips Monastery, south of the Church of the Holy Apostles. In contrast, Neslihan Asutay-Effenberger identifies it with the Bayezit Ağa Camii.[66] However, the 1455 Ottoman survey suggests a location near the Lips Monastery, making a site in or around the current Bali Paşa Camii plausible.[67]

A document dated to 1360 records unauthorized donations to the *kyra* Martha Monastery by a woman named Bryennissa alongside disputes concerning the improper use of a building within the complex. In 1402, a priest pledged never to serve again at the monastery, suggesting possible moral misconduct, though the document offers no explicit details.[68] Despite such issues, the nunnery maintained strong ties with elite Byzantine families, particularly the Palaiologoi and Kantakouzenoi. Around 1392, Helen Kantakouzene Palaiologina (1333–1397), wife of Emperor John V Palaiologos (r. 1354–1391), entered the convent under the monastic name Hypomone. Her entry was marked by a congratulatory letter from the statesman and theologian Demetrios Kydones.[69] The monastery endured until the Fall of Constantinople in 1453, and in 1455 it was still prominent enough to define an entire neighbourhood in the Ottoman survey.

A significant example of post-1261 monastic patronage is the Lips Monastery (now Feneri Isa Mosque), situated near the Church of the Holy Apostles.[70] Originally founded by the admiral Constantine Lips in 908 on the remnants of a sixth-century structure, the complex underwent substantial reconstruction between 1294 and 1301 under the patronage of Empress Theodora/Eugenia Palaiologina, the wife of Emperor Michael VIII

---

66 Laurent, "Kyra Martha," 296–320; Talbot, "Kyra Martha Nunnery," 1163; Effenberger, "Zu den Eltern der Maria Dukaina Komnene Branaina Tarchaneiotissa," 169–82; Effenberger, "Die Klöster der beiden Kyra Martha," 255–93; Asutay-Effenberger, *Die Landmauer von Konstantinopel-İstanbul*, 211–12.

67 İnalcık, *The Survey of Istanbul*, 323–25; Melvani, "The Monument of a Palaiologina and the Monastery of Kyra Martha," 161–74.

68 *Patriarchal Register*, vol. 3, ed. Koder et al., p. 256, no. 218 (1360), lines 81–84; Miklosich and Müller, *Acta et Diplomata graeca Medii Aevi sacra et profana*, vol. 2, p. 570, no. 687 (January 1402); Darrouzès, *Les regestes des Actes du patriarcat de Constantinople*, no. 3253; Kraus, *Kleriker im späten Byzanz*, 290.

69 Demetrios Kydones, *Epistulae*, ed. Loenertz, pp. 103–10, no. 222; Nicol, *The Byzantine Family of Kantakouzenos*, 35–38. See also Angelou, *Manuel Palaiologos*, 39–40.

70 Marinis, "The Monastery tou Libos"; Marinis, "Sacred Dimensions," 188; Kafescioğlou, *Constantinopolis/Istanbul*, 113–14; Kidonopulos, *Bauten in Konstantinopel*, 86–87; Ivanov, *In Search of Constantinople*, 259–66.

(d. 1303).[71] The empress endowed the monastery with extensive properties, including land, vineyards, buildings, and gardens amounting to approximately twenty thousand *modioi*. She also commissioned the construction of a second church dedicated to St. John Prodromos, which was appended to the south side of the original church. This new addition functioned as a mausoleum for members of the imperial family. The monastery likely became the final resting place of several prominent figures, including Theodora Palaiologina herself, Irene of Montferrat (d. 1324), Emperor Andronikos II (d. 1332), Constantine Palaiologos (d. 1306), and Irene of Brunswick, wife of Andronikos III (r. 1328–1341). The last known burial at the site was that of Anna of Moscow, the bride of John VIII Palaiologos, who died during a plague outbreak in 1417.

Whether the *typikon* was composed by an anonymous ghostwriter or directly authored by the founder herself is not the primary concern here. What is more significant is that, in the mid-fourteenth century, a perambulatory exonarthex was constructed around the south and west sides of the monastery to accommodate additional burial sites. The Ottoman survey of 1455 provides crucial details, recording 108 one- and two-storey houses as well as a single church within the monastery complex.[72] In addition to the Lips Monastery, the dowager empress also founded the Anargyroi Nunnery, located near Lips, although its precise location remains uncertain.

Another member of the imperial family, Theodora Raoulaina, is better known for her scholarly pursuits than for her role as a foundress. Her monastic name remains unknown. She founded the St. Andrew Monastery *In Krisei* (known as St. Andrew "By-the-Judgment"), which still survives today as Koca Mustafa Pasa Camii.[73] The monastery's history likely dates back to the sixth century, as the site had been occupied by the Monastery of St. Andrew near the Gate of Saturnin. The site was later transformed (certainly before 792) into a nunnery named "the Judgment" (*Krisis*). Emperor Basil I is credited with rebuilding it, and (following the period of Iconoclasm) it was rededicated to St. Andrew of Crete. For an extended period, until the mid-thirteenth century, no further information about the nunnery is available.

---

71 Melichar, *Empresses of Late Byzantium*, 94–102; Ivanov, *In Search of Constantinople*, 259–66.

72 İnalcık, *The Survey of Istanbul*, 320–22, 493–94. The added St. John Prodromos demonstrated an extraordinary brick decoration. See Ćirić, "Brickwork and Façade," 77–102.

73 Kafescioğlou, *Constantinopolis/Istanbul*, 225; Ivanov, *In Search of Constantinople*, 312–16.

Between 1282 and 1289, Theodora Raoulaina restored the nunnery and took up residence there.[74] Her foundation played a crucial role in ecclesiastical events following the renunciation of the Union of Lyons (1274). It also served as a place where prominent members of the imperial family took the monastic habit. In the Ottoman survey of 1455, the nunnery is listed as "Kızlar Manastırı," which included a gate and five one- and two-storey houses.[75]

The original structure followed the ambulatory type, featuring both an esonarthex and an exonarthex on its western side, though it underwent significant alterations during the Ottoman period. According to Wolfgang Müller-Wiener, the church restored by Theodora was a domed edifice with three apses, complemented by a tripartite domed narthex on the west. A cistern—one of the few surviving Byzantine elements—was located to the southeast of the church.[76]

The nunnery also housed a library that preserved part of the foundress's book collection. Located away from the bustling city centre and the imperial palaces, its placement raises questions regarding Theodora Raoulaina's motivations for choosing this specific site and church. One possible explanation lies in her staunch opposition to the Union of Lyons, making the restoration of a church dedicated to a saint associated with the Iconoclastic period symbolically significant. Alternatively, she may have selected the location due to familial landholdings in the area. Furthermore, the monastery gained religious importance as a pilgrimage destination, owing to its association with the burials of St. Andrew of Crete and Philaretos the Merciful.

The Monastery of St. Mary of the Mongols, also known as *tes Panagiotisses* or *Mouchliotissa* (present-day Kanlı Kilise), was founded at the end of the thirteenth or the beginning of the fourteenth century by Maria Palaiologina. A prominent member of the imperial family, Maria was the half-sister of Emperor Andronikos II Palaiologos (r. 1282–1328) and the widow of Abaqa, the second khan of the Mongol Ilkhanate in Persia.[77] After 1282,

74 Kidonopulos, *Bauten in Konstantinopel*, 9–10.

75 İnalcık, *The Survey of Istanbul*, 317, 491–92.

76 Müller-Wiener, *Bildlexikon zur Topographie Istanbuls*, 172–73.

77 *Patriarchal Register*, vol. 3, ed. Koder et al., p. 68, no. 184 (October 1351), lines 31–37. On the previous faulty assumption that Mouchliotissa was constructed in 1266–1267 by Maria Akropolitissa, see Schreiner, "Die topographische Notiz über Konstantinopel," 381–83. See also Bouras, "Η αρχιτεκτονική της Παναγίας του Μουχλίου στην Κωνσταντινούπολη," 37; Kafescioğlou, *Constantinopolis/Istanbul*, 199. On Maria Palaiologina see now Melichar, "Imperial Women as Emissaries, Intermediaries, and Conciliators," 103–28; Prazniak, *Sudden Appearances*, 55–78.

Maria Palaiologina acquired a group of buildings and a church in the Phanari district, converting them into the Monastery of Panagia ton Mougoulion ("Mother of God of the Mongols"). The *katholikon* is architecturally notable for its rare tetraconch plan crowned by a central dome and flanked by a tower and a narthex. However, a comprehensive architectural analysis is hindered by the many reconstructions and alterations the site has undergone over the centuries. Charalampos Bouras has suggested that the tripartite narthex may date to the thirteenth century—a period characterized by the addition of such elements, including narthexes and burial chapels.[78]

It is likely that the only original construction undertaken by Maria Palaiologina was the set of cells intended for the nuns. Some frescoes survive in the apse, narthex, and a two-chamber crypt, though their precise dating—whether late Byzantine or post-Byzantine—remains uncertain. The nunnery is located near the Monastery of Chora, where Maria is depicted as the nun Melania, reflecting her notable patronage.[79] Uniquely, Kanlı Kilise (St. Mary of the Mongols) was never converted into a mosque. Instead, Sultan Mehmed II endowed the church to the mother of Christodoulos, or Atik Sinan, the Greek architect of the Fatih Mosque, thereby preserving its Christian identity through the Ottoman period.[80]

Maria Doukaina Komnene Palaiologina Glabaina, daughter of Alexios Philanthropenos, was married to Michael Tarchaneiotes Glabas, *protostrator*. Following her husband's decision to take monastic vows, Maria herself entered the monastic life under the name Martha sometime between 1304 and 1321. Together, the couple founded the Monastery of Pammakaristos (present-day Fethiye Mosque), where Maria undertook the renovation of the chapel in which her husband was buried around 1310 (*terminus ante quem* 1321).[81] She may also have been the founder of the Glabaina nunnery in Constantinople, situated northwest of the Kyriotissa Monastery (modern Kalenderhane Camii).

Irene Choumnaina, later known by her monastic name Eulogia, stands out as the founder of both a female and a male monastery, constituting the most prominent example of a double monastery established by a woman in

---

78 Bouras, "Η αρχιτεκτονική της Παναγίας του Μουχλίου στην Κωνσταντινούπολη," 40; Ryder, "The Despoina of the Mongols and Her Patronage," 71–102.

79 Ivanov, *In Search of Constantinople*, 384–85.

80 van Millingen, *Byzantine Churches in Constantinople*, 276.

81 Kidonopulos, *Bauten in Konstantinopel*, 41–42. It may have been located at the site of Burmalı Minare Mosque. See Ivanov, *In Search of Constantinople*, 249.

the late Byzantine period. The daughter of the influential scholar and statesman Nikephoros Choumnos, she was born in 1291 and married John Palaiologos, son of Emperor Andronikos II, in 1303. Following her husband's death in April 1307,[82] Irene took monastic vows before 1310 and became known as Eulogia. Deeply committed to philanthropic endeavours, she directed significant resources toward charitable and religious causes.[83] Among her most notable undertakings was the renovation of the Monastery of Philanthropos Soter ("Merciful Saviour") in Constantinople, a project carried out with the assistance of her parents and most likely completed before 1320.[84] While the monastery has traditionally been associated with the Mangana complex,[85] recent scholarship—particularly the work of Nicholas Melvani—has challenged this identification. Melvani proposes that the monastery was instead located at the site of the Komnenian Kecharitomene and Philanthropos complex, near the Aetius Cistern.[86]

In any case, the foundation functioned as a double monastery, featuring a shared church and a common refectory.[87] Upon his death in 1327, Nikephoros Choumnos—having taken monastic vows under the name Nathaniel—was interred in the male section of the monastery.[88] Although the nuns resided in separate buildings, they likely participated in communal worship and dining—a practice that deviated from the typical arrangements of other double monasteries, where such shared spaces were often expressly avoided. According to Neilos Damilas, the interaction between the male and female communities was limited to the exchange of practical goods, such as

---

82 Irene Eulogia Choumnaina, *Correspondence*, ed. Constantinides Hero, 120–21; Stolfi, "La biografia di Irene-Eulogia Cumnena Paleologhina," 7.

83 Gregoras, *Roman History*, ed. Bekker et al., vol. 3, p. 238, lines 13–20; Savramis, *Zur Soziologie des byzantinischen Mönchtums*, 31–33.

84 Meyer, "Bruchstücke zweier τυπικά κτητορικά," 48; Talbot, "*Philanthropos*," 1386; Laurent, "Une princesse byzantine au cloître," 29–60.

85 Janin, "Les monastères du Christ Philanthrope à Constantinople," 135–50; Janin, *La géographie ecclésiastique de l'Empire byzantine*, 527–29; Kidonopulos, *Bauten in Konstantinopel*, 33–36.

86 Melvani, "The Duplication of the Double Monastery," 361–84.

87 Sinkewicz, *Theoleptos of Philadelpheia*, p. 220, lines 45–46, no. 9; Müller-Wiener, *Bildlexikon zur Topographie Istanbuls*, 109; Demangel and Mamboury, *Le quartier des Manganes et la première région de Constantinople*, 49–68; Kidonopulos, *Bauten in Konstantinopel*, 33.

88 Theodore Hyrtakenos, *Monody to Nikephoros Choumnos*, ed. Boissonade, 287. See also Laurent, "Une fondation monastique de Nicéphore Choumnos," 42–44; Stolfi, "La Biografia di Irene-Eulogia Cumnena Paleologhina," 10.

clothing, footwear, and other items produced through the monastic handicrafts of each community.[89]

High-ranking officials often played a central role in the establishment of monastic institutions particularly for the benefit of their immediate family; they typically selected sites near their residences. Before 1320, Phokas Maroules founded a monastery for his wife and daughters adjacent to his home at the Gate of St. Romanos.[90] This trend was not limited to the capital; provincial elites emulated Constantinopolitan precedents by founding monastic establishments within their own spheres of influence. A notable example is the now-ruined Lykousada Monastery near Phanarion in Thessaly, which was established between 1282 and 1289 by Hypomone, the wife of the *sebastokrator* John Doukas. Significantly, the monastery was granted stauropegial status, placing it directly under the jurisdiction of the Patriarch.[91]

Shifting financial dynamics in the late fourteenth century altered the profile of monastic founders. The decline of the traditional landowning aristocracy coincided with the rise of a new, mercantile elite—wealthy aristocrats engaged in trade—who increasingly assumed roles as patrons of monastic institutions. These individuals often redirected portions of their commercial capital toward the support of religious foundations. One of the most illustrative examples is George Goudeles and his establishment of the nunnery of St. Nicholas in the Forum Tauri of Constantinople. The history of this institution is reconstructed through a series of Goudeles' testaments, which survive solely in Latin translation. As a prominent *homme d'affaires* under Emperor Manuel II, Goudeles regularly updated his testaments to reflect changing decisions concerning the distribution of his wealth. Remarkably, seven such documents from 1465 alone are preserved in the Genoese archives.

---

89 Pétridès, "Le *typikon* de Nil Damilas," chap. 8, p. 101–3; Talbot, "*Neilos Damilas*," 1471–73.

90 *Patriarchal Register*, vol. 2, ed. Hunger et al., p. 276, no. 135 (May 1341), lines 25–35; Darrouzès, *Les regestes des Actes du patriarcat de Constantinople*, no. 2207; Kidonopulos, *Bauten in Konstantinopel*, 66; Failler, "Pachymeriana Novissima," 225–26; İnalcık, *The Survey of Istanbul*, 335, 497 (in the Top Yıkığı quarter). For the Gate of St. Romanos, see Janin, *Constantinople byzantine*, 420–21.

91 Lampros, "Ἀνέκδοτον χρυσόβουλλον τοῦ αὐτοκράτορος Ἀνδρονίκου τοῦ Παλαιολόγου," 116–19; Miklosich and Müller, *Acta et Diplomata graeca Medii Aevi sacra et profana*, vol. 4, pp. 369–71, no. 15 (August 1273); Lampros, "Νείλου Κωνσταντινουπόλεως σιγίλλιον περὶ τῆς μονῆς Λευκουσιάδος," 174–75; Belanidiotes, "Ἡ ἱερὰ μονὴ Λυκουσάδος," 162–64; Bees, "Fragment d'un chrysobulle du couvent de Lycousade," 479–86; Ostrogorsky, "Das Chrysobull des Despoten Johannes Orsini," 205–13; Koder and Hild, *Hellas und Thessalien*, 208–9.

A testament dated March 4, 1421—recently edited and thoroughly analyzed by Thierry Ganchou—offers critical insight into the foundation's administration.[92] It also suggests the existence of a *typikon* and likely an inventory associated with the nunnery.

The case of St. Nicholas is extremely interesting, as it demonstrates elements of both continuity and change. The nunnery was built in Constantinople and not in Pera, even though Goudeles had close ties with the Genoese colony. Moreover, it included a hospital and could support twenty-four (and later forty) nuns. The nunnery was founded for his daughter, Theodora, and his second wife, Anna. The foundation had clear commercial overtones, acting in some cases as a repository for Goudeles' money. The fact that two abbesses were appointed as joint heads of the community while the founder supported it financially mainly through his portfolios in public banks is eye-opening regarding innovative financing strategies.

Foundation and the Transformation of Space: The Case of Bebaia Elpis Nunnery

Monastic patronage offered women of means a unique avenue for agency within the constraints of Byzantine society. Although excluded from the formal priesthood and ecclesiastical teaching roles, women's material contributions to the Church were both significant and welcomed. In particular, women from imperial and aristocratic families played a vital role in the establishment and endowment of monastic institutions.[93] Through their foundations, they not only provided religious and charitable infrastructure but also shaped monastic life according to their personal ideals and values. These acts of patronage allowed them to assert authority over specific spaces and communities, subtly negotiating the boundaries of gender and power in late Byzantine society.

Therefore, it is essential to interpret the founding activities of these women within an alternative analytical framework: that of space. When examining the monastic landscape of Constantinople and its historical geography, Raymond Janin's foundational work remains a crucial reference. However, Janin did not distinguish between male and female monastic foundations, nor did he allocate them to separate categories or chapters. Similarly, in his important study on the buildings restored in Constantinople

92 Ganchou, "L'ultime testament de Géôrgios Goudélès," 346–53; Harris, "The Goudelis Family in Italy After the Fall of Constantinople," 168–79.

93 Koubena, "A Survey of Aristocratic Women Founders," 25–32.

between 1261 and 1328, Vassilios Kidonopoulos acknowledged the significance of female patronage in the post-recovery reconstruction process but did not offer a gendered analysis of the patrons. His primary focus remained on the architecture and topographical identification of these monuments. This highlights the need for a more nuanced approach that takes gender into account when reconstructing the spiritual and urban landscape of late Byzantine Constantinople.

However, the influence of gender studies and the discourse surrounding the social construction of the sexes have significantly contributed to the incorporation of spatial concepts into Byzantine monastic scholarship. Scholars such as Alice-Mary Talbot have raised critical questions regarding the gendering of space within monastic environments.[94] In her seminal article, "Building Activity in Constantinople Under Andronikos II: The Role of Women Patrons in the Construction and Restoration of Monasteries,"[95] Talbot directly addresses the same questions that this study seeks to explore.

One particularly illuminating case for examining the interplay between female patronage and the transformation of sacred space is the convent of Bebaia Elpis, which offers valuable insights into how women influenced and redefined monastic landscapes through their foundations.

The Topological Networks of Bebaia Elpis

Henri Lefebvre has argued that space is fundamentally a social construction, shaped by human practices and interactions.[96] Michel de Certeau further refines this perspective by distinguishing between fixed topographies and dynamic, socially produced spaces. He differentiates "place" as a site of stability and order, whereas "space" emerges through the movements, trajectories, and temporal activities that animate it. Space, in this sense, is a practiced place, shaped by intersecting elements, such as direction, time, and action.[97] Similarly, Pierre Bourdieu emphasizes that spatial organization carries social meaning, with elements like doorways and thresholds

94 Talbot, "Women's Space in Byzantine Monasteries," 113–27; Gilchrist has defined Gender Archaeology as follows: "Gender Archaeology classifies male and female activities, roles, relationships and cultural imagery according to the social and sexual divisions." Gilchrist, *Gender and Material Culture*, 2

95 Talbot, "Building Activity in Constantinople Under Andronikos II," 329–43.

96 Lefebvre, *La production de l'espace*; Shields, *Lefebvre, Love and Struggle*; Elden, *Understanding Henri Lefebvre.*

97 de Certeau, *L'Invention du Quotidien*. On Michel de Certeau, see Giard, *Michel de Certeau*; Dosse, *Michel de Certeau.*

functioning not merely as architectural features but as markers of social positioning and relational structure—connecting inner and outer realms, public and private, sacred and profane.[98]

This last point leads us to consider how patronage actively transforms space by reshaping the network of spatial relationships within a monastic complex. Specifically, the reconfiguration of connections between rooms—through the strategic placement of doors, thresholds, and axial alignments—alters not only the flow of movement but also the social and symbolic hierarchy embedded in the space. While traditional ground plans offer valuable representations of architectural space within a larger topographical context, they are limited in capturing the dynamic relationships between interior spaces. By contrast, converting these topographical layouts into topological network models enables a more nuanced understanding of how rooms interconnect and how spatial hierarchies are constructed and negotiated. Such models allow us to trace paths of circulation, access, and restriction, thus revealing the social logic inscribed in architectural design.

The value of topological representations for spatial orientation was first demonstrated in the 1930s with the design of the London Underground map. Faced with the complexity of representing a dense network of stations and transit lines, early topographical maps proved ineffective for passenger navigation due to their reliance on real-world scale and geography. In response, a topological map was introduced—one that abstracted spatial relationships and emphasized the connections between stations rather than their physical distances. This schematic approach, which underlies modern metro maps, prioritized clarity and usability over geographic accuracy, enabling more intuitive orientation within the network. Similarly, applying such topological principles to monastic architecture allows us to visualize and analyze spatial relationships—such as access, hierarchy, and circulation—beyond the constraints of scale or form.[99]

This kind of topological network facilitates a more nuanced understanding of "accessibility" and the symmetry within the spatial syntax of architectural environments—a concept introduced by Bill Hillier and Julienne Hanson in their seminal work *The Social Logic of Space* (1984). In such models, each room or discrete spatial unit is conceptualized as a node, with direct connections to other rooms represented by lines or edges. This

---

98 Bourdieu, *Esquisse d'une théorie de la pratique*; Bourdieu, *La domination masculine*. On Bourdieu, see Schwingel, *Pierre Bourdieu zur Einführung*.

99 On the appliance of network analysis in Archaeology, see Kohler, "Complex Systems and Archaeology," 93–123.

abstraction allows for the visualization and analysis of movement patterns, levels of access, and degrees of spatial segregation within a building. Utilizing Network Analysis software, these topological representations can be constructed and computationally analyzed, offering valuable insights into the organizational logic of monastic spaces and the ways in which patronage may have transformed spatial hierarchies and interactions.[100]

In previous studies, I have employed this method to investigate spatial organization and patronal impact within entire monastic complexes, including the Monastery of Sagmatas in Boiotia (ca. 1105/6) and the Lips nunnery in Constantinople.[101] The case of Sagmatas is particularly valuable due to the preservation of its additional monastic buildings and the full circuit wall, enabling a comprehensive topological analysis. By contrast, at the Lips nunnery, only the *katholikon* survives. Nevertheless, it was possible to apply a topological network model to the extant remains, reconstructing the spatial configuration of the Theotokos Church as it existed prior to the modifications introduced through the patronage of Theodora Palaiologina. This comparative approach highlights both the methodological adaptability and the interpretive potential of spatial syntax analysis in varied archaeological contexts.[102]

We can now apply the same methodological framework to the case of the convent of Bebaia Elpis. Scholars have proposed various locations for the site. Raymond Janin and others have situated it to the south of the Forum Tauri, near the Propontis, and thus south of the Mese. Alice-Mary Talbot, drawing on descriptions of adjacent properties, argued that Bebaia Elpis was more likely located in the Heptaskalon quarter, in the south-central part of the city. Alkmene Stauridou-Zaphraka and Kidonopulos offered a different hypothesis, placing the nunnery toward the southeastern end of the Valens aqueduct, near the Zeugma. More precisely, they situated it along the western slope of Constantinople's third hill, within the area formerly designated as the tenth district of the city.[103]

100 Hillier and Hanson, *The Social Logic of Space*, 223–41, 242–61.

101 Mitsiou, "Byzanz. Monastischer Raum und Raumordnung," 197–218. See also Mitsiou, "Byzantine Monastic Space," 175–98.

102 Mitsiou, "Female Monastic Space and Patronage in Late Byzantine Constantinople," 378–81, and plates 13–16.

103 Stauridou-Zaphraka, "Η Μονή Μωσελέ και η Μονή των Ανθεμίου," 66–92; Stauridou-Zaphraka, "Το Κοντοσκάλιο και το Επτάσκαλο," 1303–28; Kidonopulos, *Bauten in Konstantinopel*, 72. On Heptaskalon, see Preiser-Kapeller, "Heptaskalon und weitere Anlegestellen am Goldenen Horn," 101–2.

According to a more recent hypothesis, the main church of Bebaia Elpis may be identified with the Vefa Kilise Camii, a structure previously thought to be the Church of St. Theodore.[104] If this identification is correct, the core of the building can be dated to the tenth or eleventh century. It features a domed church with a narthex, and a cistern located to the south of the church may also belong to this early phase. In the first half of the fourteenth century, an exonarthex with three domes was added. These southern extensions were repurposed as burial spaces for the *ktetores* and their families. Although now only partially preserved, mosaics still adorn the domes of the exonarthex. At the same time, a portico was constructed along the church's south side, and remnants of a rectangular room—likely associated with a belfry tower—are still visible in this area.[105]

The architectural features of the Vefa Kilise Camii correspond closely with the descriptions found in its *typikon*. By 1392, both the church and its bell tower were reportedly at risk of collapse. Their restoration was undertaken by the nun Xene Philanthropene, who financed the repairs at a cost of two hundred *hyperpyra* (gold coins). This sum covered essential materials, such as tiles, nails, and plaster, as well as the wages for skilled labour and other necessary expenses.[106]

The *katholikon* of the nunnery is depicted in an illumination (fol. 11r) in the Lincoln College *typikon*, offering valuable insight into its architectural form and typology. The text of the *typikon* further complements this visual evidence, particularly in detailing the spatial organization within the *perioros* (enclosure) of the complex. It confirms the presence of several ancillary buildings beyond the church itself. The re-foundation of the nunnery included significant architectural enhancements, such as the addition of an exonarthex, a belfry tower, and mosaic decoration. The complex also contained monastic cells, a refectory, a cemetery chapel dedicated to St. Nicholas, storage facilities, and a bath. These new constructions, initiated by Synadene, were built on properties belonging to her aristocratic *oikos*, underscoring the connection between elite landownership and female monastic patronage.[107]

---

104 Effenberger, "Die Klöster der beiden Kyra Martha," 262–64; Müller-Wiener, *Bildlexikon zur Topographie Istanbuls*, 169; Ivanov, *In Search of Constantinople*, 240–43.

105 Müller-Wiener, *Bildlexikon zur Topographie Istanbuls*, 169.

106 *Typicon monasterii Theotoci Bebaias Elpidos*, ed. Delehaye, chap. 159, pp. 104–5; Talbot, "*Bebaia Elpis*," 1568; Talbot, "Female Patronage in the Palaiologan Era," 259–74.

107 Smyrlis, *La fortune des grands monastères byzantins*, 37.

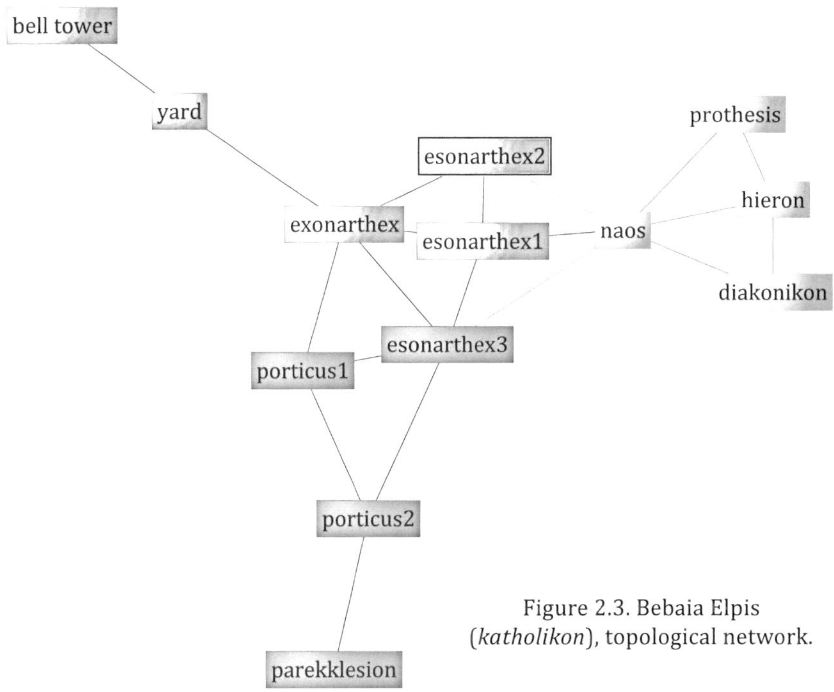

Figure 2.3. Bebaia Elpis (*katholikon*), topological network.

We constructed two topological networks using ground plans and architectural reconstructions featured in an article by Arnie Effenberger.[108] The first network focuses exclusively on the *katholikon*, visualizing the accessibility relationships among its various architectural components and highlighting areas of restricted or absent access (see Figure 2.3). In this model, we excluded later Ottoman interventions, such as the addition of the minaret, in order to preserve the integrity of the Byzantine spatial configuration.

In the subsequent analysis, we expanded our focus to the entire monastic complex, incorporating the details provided in the *typikon* regarding the extant buildings. While the precise spatial arrangement remains speculative, we propose that the various components of the complex were likely organized around a central courtyard, as no internal walls or courtyards are specifically mentioned in the sources. The cells, potentially housed in a two-storey structure, may have provided individual rooms for the nuns, with the prohibition of idle talk near a nun's cell suggesting a deliberate effort to maintain silence and separation. The bathhouse was likely situated near a water source—possibly the Valens aqueduct—where additional facilities,

108 Effenberger, "Die Klöster der beiden Kyra Martha," 287–88, 290, figs. 1, 2, and 4.

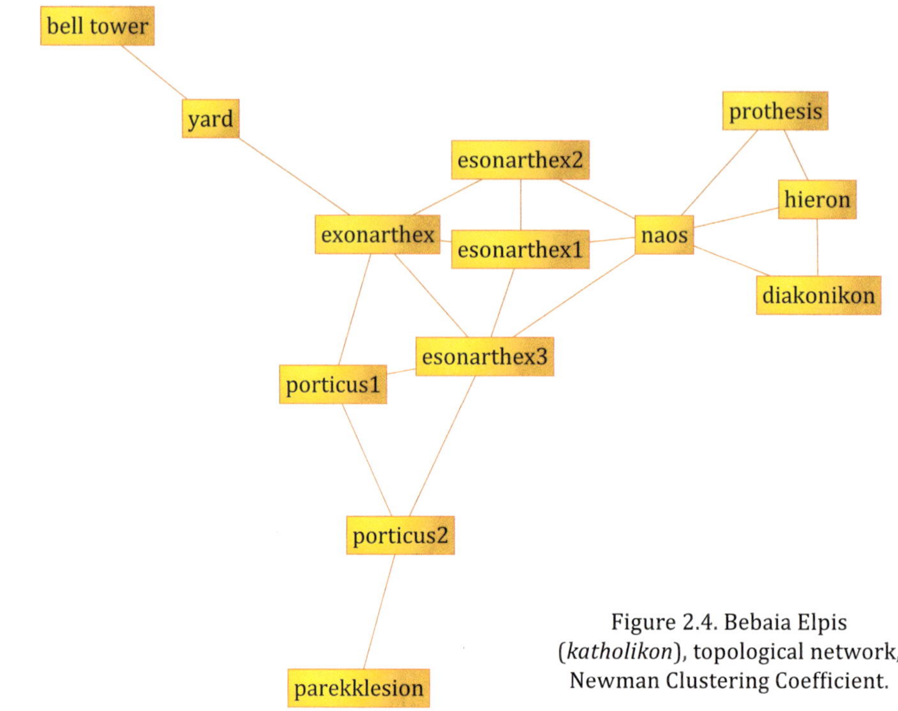

Figure 2.4. Bebaia Elpis (*katholikon*), topological network, Newman Clustering Coefficient.

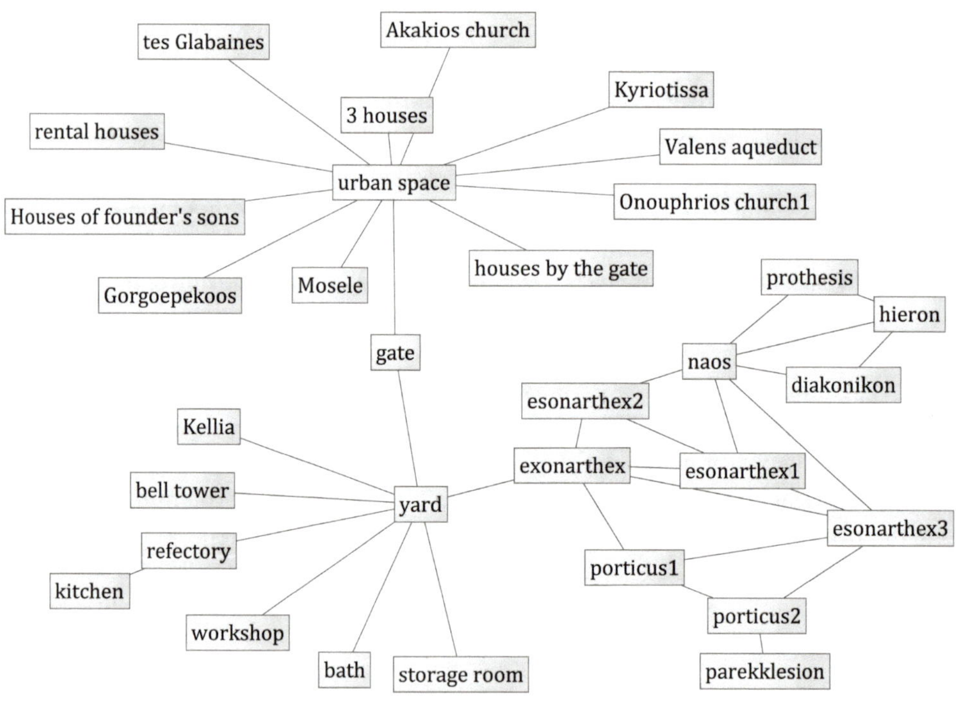

Figure 2.5. Bebaia Elpis (entire complex), topological network.

such as washrooms and a cistern, might have been located. The kitchen and refectory were probably positioned near one another, not far from the central church. Storage rooms, commonly located along the perimeter, are also indicated. Within the monastic enclosure, there were at least two vineyards and a garden. Additionally, in our analysis, we considered the surrounding urban space as a node that facilitates connectivity within the larger monastic network. Figures 2.4 and 2.5 illustrate the proposed configuration of the monastic complex and its spatial clusters, though these renderings should be regarded as approximations rather than definitive layouts.

Although this case study alone does not allow for definitive, gender-specific conclusions—a broader, systematic comparison of the spatial syntax of male and female monastic institutions would be necessary to draw such conclusions—it enables us to visualize and interpret the evolving interconnectivity of a monastic complex in the aftermath of its foundation. Monasteries and churches should be viewed as dynamic, spatial entities, continually reshaped by architectural additions and functional reconfigurations. Particularly significant are the internal and external modalities of connectivity. It is conceivable that the circuit wall included additional access points, possibly in

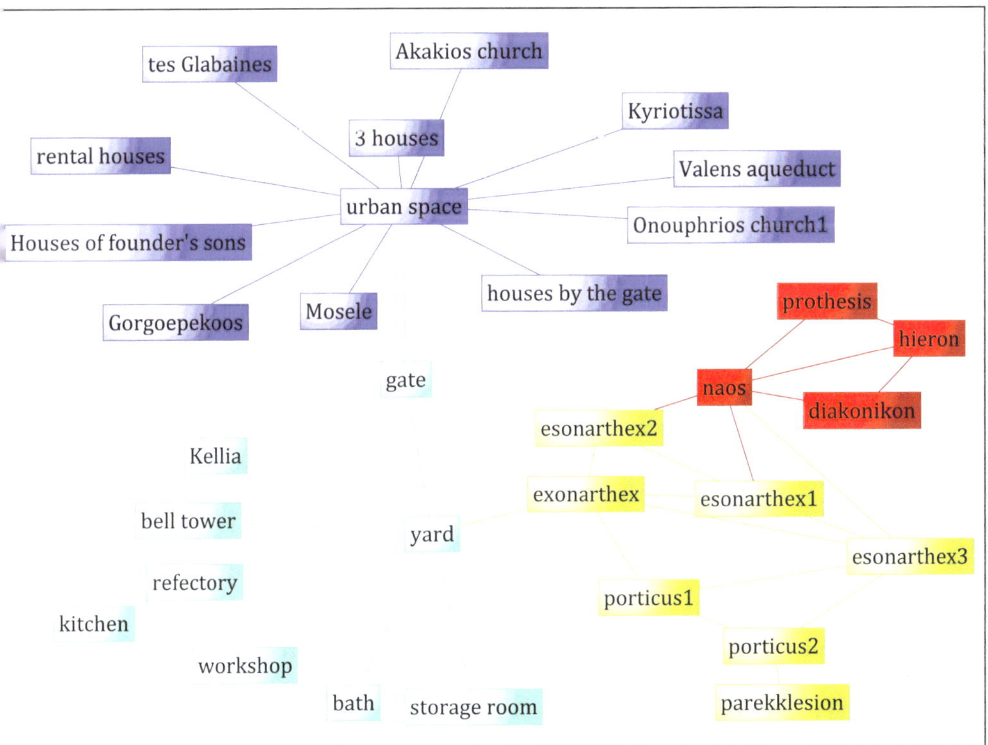

Figure 2.6. Bebaia Elpis (entire complex), topological network, Newman Clustering Coefficient.

the form of secondary entrances or subterranean passages. Further research into both newly founded and restored monastic institutions is essential for elucidating the intentions of their patrons, especially to assess whether they sought to create open and accessible environments or, conversely, to impose more restricted and hierarchical spatial structures. In the case of Bebaia Elpis, the spatial syntax—characterized by the formation of distinct and separate clusters—strongly suggests a model of controlled and limited accessibility.[109]

While a topographical reconstruction of the described arrangement of building suggests a densely packed monastic complex largely separated from the outside world, the space syntactic analysis de-composes the spatial arrangement in different clusters of rooms serving different purposes while also allowing for close control of movements (and their limitation) within the complex. This spatial "logic" correlates with the detailed prescriptions of movements and stays of members of the community according to their functions and hierarchical positions (see Figure 2.6).

Typika and the Organization of Monastic Life

Beyond establishing the legal and institutional status of a monastic foundation, *typika* primarily served to regulate the daily life of a convent. They outlined the internal organization of the community, codified interpersonal relations among the nuns, and governed the degree and nature of their interactions with the outside world.[110] The following summary focuses on key aspects addressed in these documents, including the roles of monastic officials, the liturgical schedule, and dietary regulations for the nuns.

Entrance to the Nunnery: Motives, Age, Numbers, and Gifts

Women entered convents for a variety of reasons. Most commonly, monastic vows were taken following the end of an engagement, the death of a spouse, or in anticipation of one's own death. In numerous cases, entry into the monastic life occurred with the mutual consent of both husband and wife, reflecting a deliberate and shared decision to embrace religious devotion.[111]

---

109 A gender-influenced difference between female and male monasteries was the depiction of female and not male saints in the refectory, *Patriarchal Register*, vol. 2, ed. Hunger et al., p. 278, no. 135 (May 1341), lines 47–49.

110 Galatariotou, "Byzantine Women's Monastic Communities," 263–90; Janin, "Le monachisme byzantine au Moyen Âge," 5–44; Konidares, *Νομικὴ θεώρηση τῶν μοναστηριακῶν τυπικῶν*, 75–162.

111 Miklosich and Müller, *Acta et Diplomata graeca Medii Aevi sacra et profana*,

A letter from Demetrios Chomatenos illustrates the normative expectations regarding spousal monasticism: he informs a female recipient that should her husband enter a monastery, she too would be required to follow suit, employing the term *melendytesei* (*μελενδυτήσει*), meaning "to put on the dark robe."[112] In other cases, entry into the monastic life was prompted by personal crises, such as an unhappy marriage, the death of a child, or as penance for criminal acts. Adulteresses and women guilty of murder were sometimes compelled to enter a convent as part of their moral and legal restitution.[113]

It should be emphasized that mothers were generally prohibited from abandoning their underage children in order to enter monastic life. In the first half of the thirteenth century, Patriarch Germanos II denied a request from the wife of a certain Xeros in Ikonion, citing her responsibility for several young children as the reason for his refusal.[114] Similarly, Neilos Damilas in 1399 explicitly forbade the entrance of women with children under the age of ten, although he made an exception if the child was a girl and could accompany her mother into the convent. For mothers with children over ten, entry into the monastery required a probationary period of three years, during which it would be assessed whether they could remain separated from their children.[115]

The case of the nun Melane, wife of Basil Basilikos,[116] poignantly illustrates how personal and familial circumstances could compel women to seek

vol. 2, p. 49, no. 360 (1383); Darrouzès, *Les regestes des Actes du patriarcat de Constantinople*, no. 2749; *Patriarchal Register*, vol. 3, ed. Koder et al., p. 256, no. 218 (1360), lines 81–82; Darrouzès, *Les regestes des Actes du patriarcat de Constantinople*, no. 2427; Miklosich and Müller, *Acta et Diplomata graeca Medii Aevi sacra et profana*, vol. 2, pp. 458–60, no. 622 (1401); Darrouzès, *Les regestes des Actes du patriarcat de Constantinople*, no. 3183. Cf. Justinian, *Novellae*, ed. Schöll and Kroll, no. 5, chap. 38, p. 621; Oltean, *Devenir moine à Byzance*, 153–56.

112 Demetrios Chomatenos, *Ponemata*, ed. Prinzing, p. 413, line 68, no. 138 (1222).

113 Oltean, *Devenir moine à Byzance*, 140–53, 181–96.

114 Germanos II, *Letters*, ed. Papadopoulos-Kerameus, vol. 1, pp. 465–66; Laurent, *Regestes*, no.1298. On Germanos II and translations of his works, see now Angold, *Germanos II*, 16–80.

115 Pétridès, "Le *typikon* de Nil Damilas," chap. 5, p. 100; Talbot, "*Neilos Damilas*," 1470. Konidares, *Νομική θεώρηση τῶν μοναστηριακῶν τυπικῶν*, 84.

116 The *πρωτοϊερακάριος* (protohierakarios) Basilikos, the emperor's first falconer, was of Persian (i.e., Seljuk) origin. On the brothers Basilikoi, who served at first the Seljuk sultan and later joined Michael VIII Palaiologos, see Shukurov, *The Byzantine Turks*, 121–22. Kubina incorrectly identifies Basilikos as being of Ottoman descent. Kubina, *Die enkomiastische Dichtung des Manuel Philes*, 79–80

solace and meaning in monastic life during the Byzantine period. Despite her noble lineage, considerable wealth, and her husband's prominent role at the imperial court, Melane was burdened by childlessness—a condition that led to deep feelings of regret and emotional anguish. Her inner turmoil, set against a backdrop of external privilege, is vividly expressed in a thirty-eight-verse poem composed by Manuel Philes, which captures the tension between worldly status and spiritual emptiness.[117]

Philes' poem, in which Melane's despair is poignantly expressed, underscores the profound psychological toll that childlessness could exact on a woman of high social standing in Byzantine society.[118] The work highlights how the inability to bear children could eclipse even the most advantageous economic and social circumstances. Beyond reflecting Melane's personal grief, the poem gestures toward the broader cultural expectations surrounding female fertility and motherhood, revealing how central these roles were to a woman's identity and perceived fulfillment. Subtly, the poem also attributes a measure of blame for Melane's childlessness to her foreign husband, thereby intertwining personal sorrow with latent cultural tensions.

Confronted with the unfulfilled dimension of her life, Melane sought refuge and spiritual purpose in the monastic vocation. For many Byzantine women in comparable circumstances, the convent offered a space for coping with personal loss, reorienting one's identity, and embracing a life of religious devotion. Melane's decision exemplifies a broader societal pattern in which childlessness—especially following the death of a husband—often led women to the cloister, where monastic life served both as consolation and as a means of redemption.

We can thus argue that while some women embraced the monastic habit out of genuine piety, for others, the convent functioned as a shelter and place of refuge. Many women donated their possessions to a monastery in return for care during illness and the assurance of a proper burial.[119] In some cases,

---

117 Manuel Philes, *Carmina*, ed. Miller, vol. 1, poem 180, p. 87; Rhoby, "Poetry on Commission in Late Byzantium," 281–82. On Philes, see Stickler, *Manuel Philes und seine Psalmenmetaphrase*, 10–36.

118 Similar expressions of pain can be found in the testament of the childless Maria Pakouriane from the end of the eleventh century. See now Chitwood, "The Testament of the Nun Maria," 97–126. Special prayers for pregnancy are attested early on in the Christian world. See the Coptic prayer from Upper Egypt (?), dated around the seventh century, in Gansell, "Prayer for Pregnancy," no. 174, pp. 292–93.

119 Cf. the case of Irene Apokaukissa, see Miklosich and Müller, *Acta et Diplomata graeca Medii Aevi sacra et profana*, vol. 2, pp. 509–10, no. 655 (1401); Darrouzès,

serious illness and the fear of imminent death prompted women to be tonsured even in male monasteries. One such case is that of Anna, daughter of the priest Theodore Limpos, who fell ill and died in the Monastery *ton Zaboulon* (commonly known as Vazelon) in Trebizond; she was tonsured as the nun Anysia by the monks and was buried there.[120]

A significant number of nuns entered the monastery at a very young age, sometimes even as infants.[121] Over time, church authorities established age limits for monastic entry, though these varied considerably. Basil the Great proposed sixteen or seventeen as the appropriate age.[122] The Council of Carthage (419) set the threshold at twenty-five (Canon 126), while the Quinisext Council (or *Concilium Trullanum*) (691) reduced it significantly to ten years (Canon 40).[123] In an effort to reconcile these divergent standards, Emperor Leo VI (Novel 6) ultimately endorsed the age of ten as the minimum requirement for taking the monastic habit.[124]

The *typika*, in turn, present discrepancies regarding age limits for entering a monastery. The Lips nunnery allowed individuals under twenty but older than sixteen to enter if they had spent their childhood in the monastery, while the Baionaia nunnery set the limit at thirteen.[125] Euphrosyne Synadene entered the Bebaia Elpis Monastery as a young girl simply because she accompanied her mother, who was also the foundress.

Most women were tonsured as nuns during widowhood. Theoleptos of Philadelphia,[126] the spiritual advisor to Irene Choumnaina, suggested that she take monastic vows to alleviate the "fire" or "heat" (*kaminos*) of

Les regestes des Actes du patriarcat de Constantinople, no. 3216; Talbot, "Old Age in Byzantium," 276–77.

120 Ouspenskij and Beneševič, *Ta Acta της Μονής Βαζελώνος*, trans. Petropoulos, p. 226.5–10, no. 70 (thirteenth century, second half).

121 *Patriarchal Register*, vol. 3, ed. Koder et al., p. 68, no. 184 (1351); Darrouzès, *Les regestes des Actes du patriarcat de Constantinople*, no. 2330.

122 *Council of Carthago*, ed. Joannou, Canon 126, pp. 397–98.

123 *Concilium Trullanum*, ed. Alberigo et al., Canon 40, p. 258.

124 Leo VI, *Novellae*, ed. Troianos, no. 6, pp. 60–63; Konidares, *Νομική θεώρηση των μοναστηριακών τυπικών*, 79–80.

125 *Typicon monasterii Lips*, ed. Delehaye, chaps. 17–18, pp. 115–16; Talbot, "*Lips*," 1270–71; Pétridès, "Le *typikon* de Nil Damilas," chap. 5, p. 100; Talbot, "*Neilos Damilas*," 1470.

126 On Theoleptos of Philadelphia see Salaville, "Un directeur spirituel à Byzance au début du XIVe siècle," 877–78; Constantinides Hero, "Theoleptos of Philadelphia," 27–38; Rigo, "Nota sulla dottrina ascetico-spirituale di Teolepto Metropolita," 165–200.

widowhood. The term *kaminos* likely refers to the burden of a sexually active woman living without a husband. In Choumnaina's case, psychological factors such as frustration or even depression also likely influenced her decision.

The *typika* framed the size of the monastic community based on its financial strength. In the twelfth century, the Kecharitomene *typikon* was allowed to have twenty-four nuns, excluding the abbess and six assistants. The number could be increased to thirty or forty nuns if finances permitted. At Lips, up to fifty nuns were admitted: thirty were responsible for the canonical hours and twenty for household duties.[127] At the Anargyroi nunnery, thirty nuns were admitted, with eighteen dedicated to hymnody and twelve responsible for general housekeeping duties. Generally, about sixty percent (three-fifths) of the personnel were assigned to hymnody, while forty percent (two-fifths) were assigned to other services.[128] Initially, Theodora Synadene assigned thirty nuns to her foundation; later, her daughter increased the number by adding twenty more.[129] If the demand exceeded the regulated number, the remaining nuns would be delegated to smaller nunneries (*kathisma*).[130]

Members of female monastic communities are rarely mentioned by name in historical sources, with epistolography being a notable exception. In his letters to the Philanthropos Soter community, Theoleptos of Philadelphia names the nuns Agathonike, Theodote, and Christophile. However, another nun, whom the abbess Irene "removed from the infidels," is left intentionally anonymous, likely for her protection.[131]

Founders usually regulated the so-called *apotage*, which involved a gift of part of one's property to the monastery. Canon 19 of the Seventh Ecumenical Council prohibited *apotage*. However, Novel 5 of Leo VI permitted

127 *Typicon monasterii Lips*, ed. Delehaye, chaps. 5–8, pp. 109–10; Talbot, "*Lips*," 1267.

128 *Typicon monasterii sanctorum Anargyrorum*, ed. Delehaye, chap. 60, p. 139; Talbot, "*Anargyroi*," 1292.

129 *Typicon monasterii Theotoci Bebaias Elpidos*, ed. Delehaye, chap. 23, p. 32, and chap. 147, p. 97; Talbot, "*Bebaia Elpis*," 1530 and 1564.

130 Sphrantzes, *Memorii*, ed. Grecu, chap. 18, §5, lines 1–3: "Λαβοῦσα δὲ μικρόν τι κάθισμα, συνέδραμον είς ὑποταγὴν τοσαῦται, ὅσαι ούκ ἂν ἐχώρησαν εΐς τε τὴν τοῦ Λιβὸς μονὴν καὶ τῆς Κυρα-μάρθας (sic!), ἡ δὲ ού πλείους ἢ δύο καὶ δέκα προσελάβετο." Sphrantzes specifically mentions the Lips and *kyra* Martha nunneries as being fully operational in the early fifteenth century.

131 Theoleptos of Philadelphia, *Letters*, ed. Constantinides Hero, pp. 38–68, no. 2.

such donations.[132] Emperor Alexios I Komnenos reiterated the prohibition of *apotage* in a Novel (1096), requiring that donations be recorded in the *brebion* (the monastery's register) and made known to the Patriarch. Some women preferred to make voluntary offerings to the nunnery, as evidenced in the cases of the Kecharitomene and Lips monasteries.[133]

Monastic Tonsure

The preparation stages (also known as novitiate) before taking final monastic vows were established by Justinian in Novels 5 and 123.[134] Canon 5 of the Council of Constantinople (861) set the duration of the novitiate at three years but allowed for exceptions in cases such as sickness or previous moral conduct.[135] The same synod also mandated the presence of an instructor or mentor, known as an *anadochos*, to guide the novice through this period.

In Kecharitomene, the novitiate period varied depending on a person's background. If the novice was an acquaintance of the founder, the length of the probationary period for the so-called *mikro schema* (or small monastic habit) was determined by the abbess, while the period for the *mega schema* (or great monastic habit) was only six months. However, if the novice was neither known to the community nor experienced in monastic asceticism, the novitiate lasted six months for the *mikro schema* and three years for the *mega schema*.

The novitiate could be shortened in cases of illness or impending death.[136] Female *typika* from Late Byzantium are mostly silent on this matter. However, in the Lips nunnery, a distinction is made between experienced and non-experienced women. For the experienced, the test period is

132 Leo VI, *Novellae*, ed. Troianos, no. 5, pp. 54–61.

133 Dölger, *Regesten der Kaiserurkunden des Oströmischen Reiches*, vol. 2, no. 1096; "Le *typikon* de la Théotokos Kécharitôménè," ed. Gautier, chap. 7, pp. 43–45; Jordan, "*Kecharitomene*," 672; *Typicon monasterii Lips*, ed. Delehaye, chap. 14, p. 114; Talbot, "*Lips*," 1269.

134 Justinian, *Novellae*, ed. Schöll and Kroll, no. 5, chap. 2, pp. 29–30 (a novitiate of three years); Justinian, *Novellae*, ed. Schöll and Kroll, no. 123, chap. 35, pp. 618–19 (the abbot decides). See also Konidares, *Νομικὴ θεώρηση τῶν μοναστηριακῶν τυπικῶν*, 88–97, with all the references to the texts of law. See also Oltean, *Devenir moine à Byzance*, 221–35.

135 *Council of Constantinople (Protodeutera)*, ed. Joannou, Canon 5, pp. 455–57; Konidares, *Νομικὴ θεώρηση τῶν μοναστηριακῶν τυπικῶν*, 90–91.

136 "Le *typikon* de la Théotokos Kécharitôménè," ed. Gautier, chap. 30, p. 77; Jordan, "*Kecharitomene*," 685.

only six months, while for the latter, it extends to one year. Regarding the *anadochos*, only Neilos Damilas explicitly mentions the necessity of a mentor for future nuns.[137]

The holy service of monastic tonsure took its final form in the ninth century and was included in the *euchologia* (prayer books) as the "Akolouthia of the Great and Angelic Schema."[138] The service was divided into two parts: the first involved the future monk or nun making a vow of virginity, obedience, and poverty, while the second part was the actual tonsure (*koura*) and the dressing of the monk or nun in monastic garments. The tonsure is typically performed by a priest, bishop, or abbot who is also a priest in male monasteries. Other sources confirm this procedure but also report deviations. For instance, a certain confessor named Theophilos was accused of tonsuring a nun in the monastery of *pinkernes* Theophilopoulos, despite being suspended from his duties as a priest and confessor.[139]

There are two *schemata*, or monastic habits, which represent different degrees of monasticism: the *mikro schema*, or Small Schema and the *mega schema*, or Great Schema. In the Small Schema, monks and nuns wore a tunic, a *mandyas* (cloak), and, for nuns, a veil that, in Late Byzantium, was often replaced by a head covering known as the *skepe*. Monks typically covered their heads with a *koukoulion* (hood), which was part of the common monastic habit. The Great Schema included a special garment called the *analabos* (a scapular with crosses) and a distinctive *koukoulion*, setting it apart from the small schema." The Great Schema is generally associated with a commitment to rigorous asceticism and greater isolation from the world. Additionally, monks and nuns in both schemata wore belts and leather shoes or sandals.[140] The regulations regarding shoes include gender-specific details:

---

137 *Typicon monasterii Lips*, ed. Delehaye, chap. 18, p. 116; Talbot, "*Lips*," 1270–71; Pétridès, "Le *typikon* de Nil Damilas," chap. 6, p. 100; Talbot, "*Neilos Damilas*," 1471–72.

138 Goar, *Euchologion sive Rituale Graecorum*, 407–14. About the "Small" and "Great Schema," see Konidares, *Νομικὴ θεώρηση τῶν μοναστηριακῶν τυπικῶν*, 111–16.

139 Miklosich and Müller, *Acta et Diplomata graeca Medii Aevi sacra et profana*, vol. 2, pp. 461–63, no. 205 (1401); Darrouzès, *Les regestes des Actes du patriarcat de Constantinople*, no. 2480. See Papagianne, "Οι κληρικοί των βυζαντινών γυναικείων μονών και το άβατο," 75–94. On *euchologia* in Byzantium, see the webpage of the "Euchologia-Project" at the Austrian Academy of Sciences, Institute for Medieval Research, Department of Byzantine Research (PI: Prof. Claudia Rapp).

140 Radle, "The Veiling of Women in Byzantium," 1072–76, 1079–80, 1084–85, 1087–89, 1108.

they should be suitable for women, meaning they must be high enough to cover the legs.[141]

The colour of monastic garments carried significant symbolism, especially in relation to the tonsure. According to Canon 45 of the Quinisext Council, nuns were required to wear a "black/dark garment" (*melan endyma*) upon taking their vows.[142] However, in practice, these monastic garments were often more brown or brownish in tone rather than pure black. This was mainly due to the limitations of dyeing technology until the late fourteenth century. High-quality black dyes were not widely available, and those that were—typically derived from the fruits of walnut, chestnut, or oak trees—resulted in garments that were gray, brown, or even bluish rather than true black. Moreover, achieving deeper, darker hues was costly, as it required a longer, more labour-intensive dyeing process involving multiple rounds of dye application.[143]

Canon 45 of the Quinisext Council indicates that some future nuns would enter the tonsure adorned in silks, various garments, and even with gold and jewels. The Synod condemned this practice, arguing:

> it is not lawful for her who has already of her own free will put away every delight of life, and has embraced that method of life which is according to God, and has confirmed it with strong and stable reasons, and so has come to the monastery, to recall to memory the things which they had already forgotten, things of this world which perisheth and passeth away.[144]

Nuns and monks would adopt a new monastic name, as the tonsure was regarded as a form of second baptism (even in the absence of water). This new name was chosen by the novice in consultation with the abbess. While the first letter of the new name was typically, though not always, the same as the initial of their lay name, this was not a strict requirement. In Late Byzantium, certain names were particularly popular, including Maria, Martha, Kallinike, Theodoule, Eulogia, Hypomone, Melania, Theoktiste, Xene, and others.[145]

---

141 So is mentioned in *Typicon monasterii Lips*, ed. Delehaye, chap. 36, pp. 125–26; Talbot, "*Lips*," 1276; cf. *Typicon monasterii Theotoci Bebaias Elpidos*, ed. Delehaye, chap. 98, p. 73; Talbot, "*Bebaia Elpis*," 1551; Talbot, *Varieties of Monastic Experience in Byzantium*, 72–73.

142 *Concilium Trullanum*, ed. Alberigo et al., Canon 45, p. 262; Ball, "Decoding the Habit of the Byzantine Nun," 25–52.

143 Finlay, *The Brilliant History of Color in Art*, 54.

144 *Concilium Trullanum*, ed. Alberigo et al., Canon 45, p. 262; Schaff, *The Seven Ecumenical Councils*, 498.

145 Talbot and McGrath, "Monastic Onomastics," 89–120.

The Abbess and the Other Officials

According to Talbot, the administrative structure of convents generally mirrored that of male monasteries. Both systems typically featured a twofold division of responsibilities: one group was assigned to choir duties, while another managed housekeeping tasks.[146] Within a nunnery, all members were expected to observe a strict internal hierarchy, headed by the superior. The process of electing this superior offers a rare insight into staff selection practices within Byzantine institutions, including nunneries.

Political theory identifies six primary modes of selecting individuals for positions of authority: election, assignment, co-optation, sortition (selection by lot), competition, and descent. Each method is based on different assumptions about equality or inequality. For example, sortition presumes equality either among the candidates themselves or between the decision-makers and the candidate pool. In contrast, methods such as descent, competition, and co-optation imply varying degrees of inequality, whether among the applicants or between those selecting and those being selected.

In the Kecharitomene *typikon*, the selection of a new superior involved a combination of selection methods. Initially, the current abbess and the nuns would choose three pious and intelligent candidates, writing each name on a separate slip of paper.[147] These were sealed and placed on the altar, where they remained until the abbess's death. Upon her passing, the priest—accompanied by the convent's protectress—would draw one of the sealed slips by lot (sortition) to determine the new superior. If the abbess died unexpectedly, the protectress would assist the nuns in the selection process. In such cases, she could help identify the three candidates, possibly including an outsider if needed—a practice reflecting co-optation. Ultimately, the final decision rested on the drawing of lots, combining both sortition and co-optation in a distinctive selection procedure.

At Bebaia Elpis, the election of the abbess involved the full participation of the monastic community. Although the *typikon* does not specify the precise method of selection, it required the nuns to assemble in the church and choose the candidate considered superior in every respect. The selection emphasized key qualities such as leadership, obedience, and experience, with particular attention to the candidate's demonstrated piety, prudence,

146 Talbot, "Monastic Experience," 11.

147 Gautier, "Le *typikon* de la Théotokos Kécharitôménè," chap. 11, pp. 47–51; Jordan, "*Kecharitomene*," 674–75.

and administrative ability.[148] While the description in the *typikon* remains somewhat vague, it is clear that preference was given to nuns with proven leadership and prior experience in monastic office. Once elected, the new abbess was required to present herself to the Patriarch, who would formally approve her appointment and bestow the pastoral staff, thereby validating the community's choice through higher ecclesiastical authority.

At the Lips nunnery, the election of a new superior was entrusted to a committee of choir sisters who were given one week to deliberate and reach a decision. Once the selection was made, the newly chosen superior, accompanied by the senior priest and twelve of the most respected nuns, would present themselves to the emperor. Upon their return to the nunnery, the priest would formally entrust the new superior with a box containing the *typikon*.[149] Similar procedures were observed in the Anargyroi nunnery, reflecting a consistent practice in the election of abbesses across the two different monastic communities.[150]

The *typika* not only outlined the duties of the superior but also established mechanisms for accountability in cases of misconduct. At the Lips nunnery, for example, the *typikon* encouraged harmonious relations between the abbess and the nuns.[151] However, if the abbess acted "in a manner unworthy of the *Typikon*," the nuns were instructed to report her to the spiritual father. Comparable regulations were in place at the Anargyroi nunnery, reflecting a broader concern with maintaining discipline and ethical leadership within monastic communities.[152]

At Bebaia Elpis, the *typikon* was explicitly placed in a position of authority above the abbess, underscoring that even the superior was subject to its regulations.[153] The abbess was instructed to "forget feminine weakness" and govern "if not 'like a man' (*Job* 38:3), then at least in a manly fashion." She was expected to avoid arrogance while nonetheless commanding the

148 *Typicon monasterii Theotoci Bebaias Elpidos*, ed. Delehaye, chap. 26, pp. 33–34; Talbot, *Bebaia Elpis*, 1530.

149 *Typicon monasterii Lips*, ed. Delehaye, chap. 7, p. 110; Talbot, "*Lips*," 1267.

150 *Typicon monasterii sanctorum Anargyrorum*, ed. Delehaye, chap. 59, pp. 138–39; Talbot, "*Anargyroi*," 1292.

151 *Typicon monasterii Lips*, ed. Delehaye, chap. 9, p. 111; Talbot, "*Lips*," 1268.

152 *Typicon monasterii Lips*, ed. Delehaye, chap. 10, p. 112; Talbot, "*Lips*," 1268; *Typicon monasterii sanctorum Anargyrorum*, ed. Delehaye, chap. 59, pp. 138–39; Talbot, "*Anargyroi*," 1292.

153 *Typicon monasterii Theotoci Bebaias Elpidos*, ed. Delehaye, chap. 13, p. 27; Talbot, "*Bebaia Elpis*," 1527.

respect of the nuns.[154] In turn, the nuns were required to practice obedience and refrain from taking any action without the abbess's permission. In dealing with misconduct, the abbess was to correct the faults of her sisters calmly and without anger, showing forgiveness and leniency "to the extent permitted to a male superior who is not a priest."[155]

Damilas adopts a relatively tolerant stance toward disobedient nuns, permitting expulsion only in cases involving those who are genuinely disruptive or malicious.[156] His *typikon* also outlines a tripartite leadership structure within the convent:

> Concerning the superior and the two nuns who have responsibility for the administration of the affairs of the convent, I am recording in the officially registered document how there should always be three of them. If one of them should die, the entire body of nuns—or a majority—should elect another who is capable of fulfilling her duties with fear of God and in all humility.

This structure reflects both an emphasis on shared governance and a clear procedure for leadership succession.[157]

At Lips, the abbess was required to consult the spiritual father when appointing the most important officials within the community. However, the "leading nuns" also had the authority to consult him independently on various matters and to keep him informed of appointments as they occurred. In contrast, Bebaia Elpis adopted a more democratic approach, requiring that monastic officials be selected through general election and voting. This procedure was intended to ensure transparency and to prevent the abbess from appearing to act improperly or in a manner contrary to apostolic tradition.[158]

The officials of the nunnery included the *oikonomos* (manager or steward), *ekklesiarchissa* (responsible for the church and its choir), *skeuophylakissa* (sacristan), *kelarissa* (cellarer), and *docheiareiai* (treasurers). In some cases—such as at Kecharitomene—the position of *oikonomos* could

---

154 *Typicon monasterii Theotoci Bebaias Elpidos*, ed. Delehaye, chaps. 34–35, pp. 38–39; Talbot, "*Bebaia Elpis*," 1533.

155 *Typicon monasterii Theotoci Bebaias Elpidos*, ed. Delehaye, chap. 32, p. 37; Talbot, "*Bebaia Elpis*," 1532.

156 Pétridès, "Le *typikon* de Nil Damilas," chap. 17, p. 108; Talbot, "*Neilos Damilas*," 1476–77.

157 Pétridès, "Le *typikon* de Nil Damilas," chap. 18, p. 108–9; Talbot, "*Neilos Damilas*," 1477.

158 *Typicon monasterii Theotoci Bebaias Elpidos*, ed. Delehaye, chap. 73, p. 60; Talbot, "*Bebaia Elpis*," 1544.

be held by a eunuch, though it was more commonly occupied by a nun. The primary responsibility of the *oikonomos* was to oversee the monastery's real estate and manage the financial accounts of those entrusted with the care of its lands. This role also included supervising maintenance and repairs, ensuring that the monastery's properties were efficiently administered and remained a reliable source of support for the community.[159]

The *skeuophylakissa* was entrusted with the preservation of the monastery's sacred utensils and household goods, maintaining a reliable inventory to prevent theft or embezzlement. She was also responsible for the storage and protection of important documents.[160] The *kelarissa* managed the community's essential supplies, especially food, and kept detailed records of all provisions entering the monastery.[161] The *ekklesiarchissa* oversaw the care of the church, ensuring it was properly cleaned, that icons were hung appropriately, and that lighting was maintained on both weekdays and feast days. She also maintained order during services and coordinated the synchronized kneeling during sacred rites. In addition, the church steward was present when any portion of the monastery's movable property was sold, underscoring her trusted role in matters of stewardship.

Additional key offices included the *docheiaireiai*, who oversaw various financial responsibilities within the monastery. One treasurer was in charge of distributing clothing to the nuns, while the other maintained the financial records.[162] At Kecharitomene, financial administration was notably organized around two distinct treasury boxes. The first box held coins—typically gold or electrum (a gold and silver alloy)—from the monastery's revenues as well as funds set aside for regular expenses. This box was jointly sealed by the abbess and the two treasurers. The second box was reserved for older currency, intended for use during times of financial difficulty. It was sealed by a broader group: the abbess, the *oikonomos*, the *skeuophylakissa*, and the two *docheiaireiai*, all of whom shared responsibility for the monastery's economic affairs.

The *epistemonarchissa* (prioress) was responsible for maintaining order during communal gatherings, particularly when the nuns assembled for

159 Gautier, "Le *typikon* de la Théotokos Kécharitôménè," chap. 14, pp. 55–59; Jordan, "*Kecharitomene*," 677–78.

160 Gautier, "Le *typikon* de la Théotokos Kécharitôménè," chap. 19, pp. 65–67; Jordan, "*Kecharitomene*," 680–81.

161 *Typicon monasterii Lips*, ed. Delehaye, chap. 24, p. 119; Talbot, "*Lips*," 1272.

162 Cf. Gautier, "Le *typikon* de la Théotokos Kécharitôménè," chap. 24, p. 69, and chap. 28, p. 75; Jordan, "*Kecharitomene*," 682 and 684.

chanting. She was expected to closely observe the behaviour of the sisters to ensure it aligned with their spiritual development. The *ergodotries* (literally "work givers") supplied materials to the working nuns for garment production, and once completed, the garments were delivered to the *docheiareia* of garments for distribution or storage. The *pyloros* (portière), who held the keys to the monastery, was tasked with guarding the entrance. No one was permitted to enter or exit the convent without the prior knowledge and approval of the abbess. This role was typically assigned to one of the older and more modest nuns, emphasizing the importance of discretion and vigilance.

Internal and External Connections—Daily Regime

External visitations were strictly regulated by the *typika*, as preserving the *abaton*—the sacred, secluded space of the convent—was essential. At Kecharitomene, female relatives were permitted to visit once or twice a year, and if a nun's mother was ill, she was allowed to stay overnight. Visits from male relatives were generally prohibited, with rare exceptions during feast days honouring the icon of the Theotokos Kecharitomene. Nuns were allowed to leave the convent to visit dying parents, but only if accompanied by two elderly nuns. In the Lips convent, relatives could meet the nuns only at the entrance and under the supervision of "respected" sisters. At Bebaia Elpis, young nuns were occasionally permitted to visit their families "for a short rest," but they too had to be escorted by two senior nuns and were required to return the same evening, after which the abbess would question them about the visit.[163]

Visitations by spiritual fathers and priests were also governed by the *typika*. At the Lips convent, the spiritual father was required to visit three days each month. During his stay, he lodged in small rooms located in the monastery's guesthouse and heard confessions in the morning, typically in the church's narthex.[164] In Bebaia Elpis, the spiritual father likewise held responsibility for hearing confessions, though in this case the practice could take place daily, reflecting a more continuous spiritual oversight.[165]

---

163 *Typicon monasterii Theotoci Bebaias Elpidos*, ed. Delehaye, chap. 77, p. 63; Talbot, "*Bebaia Elpis*," 1546.

164 *Typicon monasterii Lips*, ed. Delehaye, chaps. 11–12, pp. 112–13; Talbot, "*Lips*," 1268–69; cf. Pétridès, "Le *typikon* de Nil Damilas," chap. 9, p. 103; Talbot, "*Neilos Damilas*," 1473.

165 *Typicon monasterii Theotoci Bebaias Elpidos*, ed. Delehaye, chaps. 105–11, pp. 75–78; Talbot, "*Bebaia Elpis*," 1553–54.

The surviving fragment of the Philanthropos Soter *typikon* reveals that a coenobitic lifestyle—marked by communal living—was considered appropriate for both the nuns and monks of this double monastery. The community shared a common refectory and kitchen and participated collectively in manual labour. Nuns were not allowed to eat or work apart from the group, reinforcing the ideal of communal discipline and unity. Additionally, young girls could be admitted into the monastery, both for educational purposes and to ensure their safety.

This approach contrasts with the practices of other convents, where a clear division often existed between nuns engaged in ecclesiastical duties—typically the literate members—and those assigned to manual labour. In some aristocratic foundations, such as the Lips convent, women from the founder's family held a privileged status. They were sometimes granted special apartments and personal attendants, reflecting the influence of social hierarchy even within monastic settings.[166]

A significant portion of life in a nunnery was dedicated to liturgical duties.[167] The Lips *typikon* underscores that the primary responsibility of the nuns was the performance of the canonical hours. The hymnody was to follow the prescriptions of the liturgical *typikon* of St. Sabas, which was praised as being "both moderate and the royal road," reflecting a balanced and authoritative model for worship.[168]

The daily schedule in a nunnery was structured around the various Offices celebrated in the choir. Typically, these included the seven daytime Hours, the night Office of Vigils, and the daily celebration of the Divine Liturgy. On feast days, the liturgical observance was expanded, often including two celebrations of the Liturgy. While the exact timing of each Hour could vary according to the season, the structure and duration of the services differed between *typika*. To regulate the Daily Order of Prayer, monastic time followed the Jewish division into four principal hours: the First Hour at 6 a.m., when Matins were held; the Third Hour at 9 a.m.; the Sixth Hour at noon; and the Ninth Hour at 3 p.m. In the late afternoon, Vespers and Little Compline were sung, followed by the Midnight Office later in the evening.

166 *Typicon monasterii Lips*, ed. Delehaye, chaps. 40–41, pp. 128–29; Talbot, "*Lips*," 1278; Gkoutziokostas, "Observations on the Dating of the *Typikon*," 79–85.

167 Kouroupou and Vannier, "Commémoraisons des Comnènes dans le *typikon* liturgique," 41–69.

168 Cf. *Typicon monasterii Theotoci Bebaias Elpidos*, ed. Delehaye, chap. 79, p. 64; Talbot, "*Bebaia Elpis*," 1546–47; Wybrew, *The Orthodox Liturgy*, 137.

The *typika* of Byzantine nunneries consistently emphasize the central role of liturgical practice in monastic life. The regular celebration of the Divine Office was regarded as a fundamental spiritual duty for the nuns—a priority reflected in the strict regulations governing participation. For example, Damilas explicitly prescribed severe penalties for nuns who failed to attend parts of the Office, allowing exceptions only for those who were ill or elderly.[169] This insistence on full participation highlights the importance of communal worship as the core of monastic devotion.

At the Bebaia Elpis nunnery, the choir sisters—who were dedicated solely to the performance of church services—held a particularly important role within the community. These sisters were overseen by the *ekklesiarchissa*, an official whose responsibilities were intimately connected to the liturgical life of the convent. The qualifications for this position were notably rigorous, reflecting the vital role she played in upholding both the spiritual and musical integrity of the community. According to the *typikon* of Bebaia Elpis, the *ekklesiarchissa* was required not only to possess thorough knowledge of the ecclesiastical offices and rituals but also to be capable of singing and chanting in tune.[170] This requirement represents one of the earliest recorded instances where professional singing ability was explicitly stated as a prerequisite for a monastic office, underscoring the growing importance of musical proficiency in liturgical performance. The emphasis on such qualifications indicates a broader trend toward the specialization and professionalization of musical and liturgical roles within monastic life.

In the Byzantine monastic tradition, commemorations for deceased family members held an important place in the spiritual life of a nunnery. These observances typically involved liturgical services, memorial prayers, and the charitable distribution of bread at the monastery gates, serving both devotional and philanthropic purposes.[171] The Lips *typikon* provides detailed instructions for these commemorations, highlighting the enduring bond between the monastic community and the families of its benefactors.

According to the same *typikon*, the empress and her family were designated as the primary recipients of the Eucharistic offerings made during

---

169 Cf. *Typicon monasterii Lips*, ed. Delehaye, chaps. 4 and 30, pp. 109, 122–23; Talbot, "*Lips*," 1267, 1274; *Typicon monasterii sanctorum Anargyrorum*, ed. Delehaye, chap. 59, pp. 138–39; Talbot, "*Anargyroi*," 1292; Pétridès, "Le *typikon* de Nil Damilas," chaps. 10–12, pp. 104–6; Talbot, "*Neilos Damilas*," 1473–75.

170 *Typicon monasterii Theotoci Bebaias Elpidos*, ed. Delehaye, chaps. 49–56, pp. 46–50; Talbot, "*Bebaia Elpis*," 1536–39.

171 Krausmüller, "From Individual Almsgiving to Communal Charity," 111–26.

the monastery's liturgies.[172] These offerings, performed on the anniversaries of their deaths, were intended to ensure the continued remembrance and intercession for the souls of the empress, her ancestors, her mother, her son the emperor, his wife, and her other children. The document specifically instructs the nuns to include the empress in their prayers—not only during communal liturgical celebrations but also in their private devotions—underscoring the significance of these spiritual practices as a sustained link between the living monastic community and their deceased patrons.[173]

Furthermore, the Lips foundation was intended to serve as the final resting place for the empress and her family.[174] The *typikon* mandates that annual commemorations be held for all individuals buried within the monastery, thereby ensuring that their memory would be perpetually honoured. This tradition of burial and liturgical remembrance within the monastic setting was not merely an expression of personal piety; it also functioned as a means of reinforcing the enduring relationship between the monastic institution and the imperial household. The monastery thus operated simultaneously as a spiritual sanctuary and a dynastic memorial.

The inclusion of these commemorative provisions in the *typikon* underscores the central role of memorial practices in Byzantine religious life, especially within monastic communities. It reflects a deeply held belief in the efficacy of intercessory prayer for the dead and the necessity of maintaining their memory through ritual acts. Such practices were considered vital for the salvation of the souls of the departed and were instrumental in shaping the spiritual identity and social function of the convent.

At the Bebaia Elpis nunnery, the performance of memorial services was not merely a significant component of monastic life but the central function around which the entire institution was organized. The foundation's primary purpose was to ensure the regular, devout commemoration of the souls of the foundress and her family.[175] This focus underscores the profound interconnection between spiritual obligations and familial loyalty in the Byzantine monastic tradition. Through these commemorative practices, the nunnery served as a lasting spiritual legacy for the founder's lineage, binding monastic devotion to the memory and salvation of the aristocratic family it was designed to honour.

---

172 *Typicon monasterii Lips*, ed. Delehaye, chap. 30, p. 122–23; Talbot, "*Lips*," 1274.

173 *Typicon monasterii Lips*, ed. Delehaye, chap. 52, p. 135; Talbot, "*Lips*," 1281.

174 *Typicon monasterii Lips*, ed. Delehaye, chap. 42, p. 130; Talbot, "*Lips*," 1278–79.

175 Smyrlis, *La fortune des grands monastères byzantins*, 133–34.

According to the *typikon* of Bebaia Elpis, in addition to the customary commemorative services held on the Saturdays of Meatfare and Pentecost, special commemorations were required on the anniversary of the foundress's death. These memorial services were meticulously prescribed for a broad range of her relatives and later benefactors, ensuring that their souls would be perpetually remembered and prayed for within the monastic community.

The specific individuals included in these prayers were:

The foundress herself, whose memory was central to the spiritual activities of the nunnery.

Her parents, commemorated on **October 25**, emphasizing the importance of filial piety and the continuation of the family's spiritual legacy.

Her brother Michael/Manuel Komnenos Branas Palaiologos, commemorated on **June 6**.

Her other brother Andronikos/Arsenios Komnenos Branas Doukas Angelos, commemorated on **June 28**.

Her sister Maria/Mariamne Komnene Branaina Laskarina Doukaina Tornikina Palaiologina, commemorated on **September 16**.

The husband of her sister Isaak/Joasaph Komnenos Doukas Tornikes, commemorated on **January 8**.

Their son, Andronikos Komnenos Doukas Palaiologos Tornikes, commemorated on **July 3**.

Synadene's husband, commemorated on **February 6**.

Their daughter-in-law, Thomais/Xene, wife of the foundress's son, John Palaiologos, commemorated on **February 11**.

Sympentheros of Synadene, father-in-law of the foundress's son, the *protostrator* Theodore/Theodoretos Doukas Mouzakios, commemorated on **December 24**.

Their descendants:

Theodora/Theodosia Komnene Doukaina Raoulaina Palaiologina, daughter of Theodore Doukas Synadenos and granddaughter of the foundress, commemorated on **July 23**.

Other relatives:

Synadene's nephew, John/Joasaph Komnenos Doukas Angelos Branas Palaiologos, son of the Despoina of the Bulgars, commemorated on **August 8**.

Further commemorations:

Anonymous Metropolitan of Ephesos (exact date of death unknown).

Anonymous Metropolitan of Mytilene (exact date of death unknown).

John Theophilos, commemorated on **December 9**, and his wife **Maria Asanina**, commemorated on **November 24**.

Xene Philanthropene, commemorated on **February 13**, and her daughter **Eugenia Kantakouzene**, commemorated on **February 11**.[176]

No specific causes of death or ages are provided for the individuals commemorated. However, their generous donations to the nunnery are recorded. From the available data, we observed a higher mortality rate during the winter months, particularly in February. This trend is consistent with seasonal mortality patterns, where deaths typically rise in winter due to influenza and other respiratory illnesses.

Commemoration acts were seen as patronal privileges, reserved for benefactors who had established and supported the nunnery. This practice highlights the reciprocal relationship between the monastic community and its patrons; the latter provided material support, while the former ensured the spiritual well-being of the patrons and their families through continuous prayer and memorial services.

The emphasis on memorial services at the Bebaia Elpis nunnery reflects the broader Byzantine belief in the power of liturgical prayer to assist the souls of the deceased—a fundamental aspect of their spiritual worldview. It also underscores the deeply personal nature of monastic foundations, which often served not only as religious institutions but also as family memorials, preserving both the memory and the spiritual welfare of the patrons across generations.

The desire for perpetual remembrance—a key element of Byzantine monastic life—is evident in the practices surrounding the regular reading of the *typika* in various monastic foundations. These readings served not only as reminders of the founding principles and rules but also as acts of commemoration, ensuring that the memory of the founder and that the foundational intentions remained alive within the community.

In the Lips nunnery, the *typikon* was read three times a year during the dinner hour—a tradition consistent with practices in other independent monastic foundations. These specific occasions included the two patronal

---

176 *Typicon monasterii Theotoci Bebaias Elpidos*, ed. Delehaye, chaps. 113–19, pp. 80–82, and chaps. 135–44, pp. 91–94; Talbot, "*Bebaia Elpis*," 1555–56, 1561–62.

feasts (Theotokos and John Prodromos) and Easter. The *skeuophylakissa* at Lips was entrusted with safeguarding all paper documents, including the *typikon*. These documents were stored in sealed boxes to ensure their protection, underscoring the importance of preserving the physical embodiments of the monastery's spiritual and legal foundations.

At Bebaia Elpis, the *typikon* mandated the reading of the document in the refectory at the beginning of each month during mealtime—a practice that originated from the Evergetis. This monthly reading ensured that the monastic rules and the founder's intentions were consistently reaffirmed within the community, providing ongoing guidance and reflection.

These practices reflect the Byzantine monastic tradition's emphasis on the written word as a means of ensuring continuity, discipline, and remembrance. The regular reading of the *typikon* reinforced both the spiritual and administrative order within the monastery, serving as a perpetual act of commemoration. It aligned the daily lives of the monastics with the enduring memory of their benefactors and the foundational ideals of their community.

In the monastic life of Byzantine convents, manual labour was an essential part of the daily routine, complementing the liturgical and spiritual activities. The *typika* often delineated roles based on literacy, drawing a clear distinction between those engaged in choir duties and those considered illiterate. For instance, the *typikon* of Bebaia Elpis instructed illiterate nuns attending church services to recite simple yet spiritually meaningful prayers, described as "short but powerful phrases which are accepted by God in place of any other prayer."[177] This provision ensured that all nuns, regardless of literacy, could actively participate in the spiritual life of the convent. Moreover, the *typikon* emphasized that no manual labour should interfere with the time dedicated to holy services, underscoring the sanctity and inviolability of liturgical worship.

On the other hand, Theodora Synadene regarded manual labour as a necessary safeguard against idleness. She considered it not only a practical necessity but also a form of spiritual discipline. Her perspective highlights the belief that engaging in work was essential for maintaining a balanced and productive monastic life, which served as a defense against the distractions and spiritual perils associated with inactivity.[178]

---

177 *Typicon monasterii Theotoci Bebaias Elpidos*, ed. Delehaye, chap. 62, p. 53, lines 11–15; Talbot, "*Bebaia Elpis*," 1541.

178 *Typicon monasterii Theotoci Bebaias Elpidos*, ed. Delehaye, chap. 95, pp. 71–72; Talbot, "*Bebaia Elpis*," 1550–51.

At the Monastery of Baionaia, handiwork played a vital role, integrating both the spiritual and practical dimensions of monastic life. The nuns engaged in various forms of manual labour, including the production of garments. However, the *typikon* specified that these garments could not be made for their own family members. Instead, the nuns were permitted to sell them to monks and laypeople outside the monastery—a tradition that endured into modern times. In addition to garment production, the nuns also tended gardens, which formed an essential part of their daily responsibilities. Nonetheless, the more physically demanding gardening tasks and other strenuous labour were delegated to secular workers.

A letter by Maximos Neamonites (dating to the early fourteenth century) offers an unexpected glimpse into the practical realities of monastic life, particularly regarding the role of manual labour among nuns. The letter recounts the case of a woman who, following her husband's death, entered monastic life along with one of her daughters. Notably, the daughter supported them through wool work, highlighting a form of labour essential to their sustenance.[179] Although the letter does not delve deeply into their daily monastic routines, it sheds light on the significant role that such practical work played within the community. The focus of the letter—a request concerning the family's unmarried lay daughter—also illustrates how monastic labour was deeply intertwined with broader familial and social responsibilities, even after taking religious vows.

Diet, Bathing, and Sickness

Dietary regulations and fasting practices in Byzantine monasteries were carefully outlined in the *typika*, reflecting both moral principles and practical considerations.[180] These foundation documents governed not only the types of food permitted but also the frequency, timing, and manner of meals. The influential *typikon* of Kecharitomene stipulated that fish and cheese were allowed on Tuesdays, Thursdays, Saturdays, and Sundays. On Mondays, the diet consisted of legumes with oil and seasonal shellfish, while Wednesdays were limited to legumes with oil and vegetables. Similarly, the *typikon* of the Lips Monastery, drawing on the traditions of the *typikon* of St. Sabas, allowed three types of dishes—fish, cheese, and legumes—on

179 Mitrea, *A Late Byzantine Swan Song*, p. 92, lines 1–4, no. 4, and pp. 61–77 (analysis).

180 Dalby, *Tastes of Byzantium*, 93–97.

non-fast days (Tuesdays, Thursdays, Saturdays, and Sundays).[181] On fast days, the prescribed diet included legumes, vegetables, and seasonal shellfish (on Mondays) or simply vegetables and legumes (on Wednesdays and Fridays). The *typikon* also permitted dispensations from the regular dietary restrictions on feasts of the Lord and other major celebrations, demonstrating a degree of liturgical flexibility within the structured ascetic framework.

The *typikon* of the St. Sabas Monastery also influenced the dietary regulations of the nuns at Bebaia Elpis.[182] The nuns were instructed to observe strict moderation, defined as ceasing to eat "when one is still a little hungry," and to avoid treating food as "a pleasurable end in itself, but only a means of survival." This emphasis on restraint aimed to transcend bodily gratification and reinforce the ascetic ideals expected of monastic life. However, in contrast to this daily austerity, the foundress made a notable exception for the patronal feast, commissioning an "elegant and costly meal" valued at three *nomismata*.

With regard to the *trapeza* (refectory), the *typikon* of Kecharitomene instructed that, upon hearing the designated signal, the nuns were to enter the refectory in an orderly and reverent manner, following the conclusion of the Holy and Divine Liturgy. They were expected to do so without causing noise or disturbance. Any disruption to the peace and solemnity of the setting was to be addressed by the *trapezaria*, the monastic official responsible for overseeing the refectory. Persistent offenders were subject to further disciplinary action at the discretion of the abbess.

At the Lips Monastery, meals were taken at a common table with a prescribed seating order, and eating in secret was strictly prohibited.[183] Bebaia Elpis stipulated that a book should be read aloud during meals, and this was to be the only voice heard in the refectory; all others were to remain silent. The nuns were also instructed to keep their gaze fixed on the food before them, avoiding distraction or observation of others.[184] These regulations aimed to promote discipline, humility, and a sense of communal equality, thereby preventing favouritism and avoiding internal tensions.

---

181 *Typicon monasterii Lips*, ed. Delehaye, chaps. 13, 29, and 32, pp. 112, 123–24; Talbot, "*Lips*," 1275.

182 *Typicon monasterii Theotoci Bebaias Elpidos*, ed. Delehaye, chaps. 79–82, pp. 64–65; Talbot, "*Bebaia Elpis*," 1546–47.

183 *Typicon monasterii Lips*, ed. Delehaye, chap. 29, p. 122; Talbot, "*Lips*," 1274.

184 *Typicon monasterii Theotoci Bebaias Elpidos*, ed. Delehaye, chaps. 85–86, pp. 67–60; Talbot, "*Bebaia Elpis*," 1548. On women, nuns, and silence, see now Mitsiou, "Silence," 57–70.

Bathing practices at both the Lips and Bebaia Elpis were strictly regulated. Nuns were permitted to bathe only four times a year—"especially if they are young"—specifically before Lent, the Fast of the Holy Apostles (the earliest regulated Christian fast), the Dormition of the Mother of God, and Christmas.[185] As with dietary regulations, elderly nuns were allowed to follow their physician's advice. No restrictions applied to nuns who were ill, reflecting a measure of practical flexibility within the otherwise austere monastic framework.[186]

The *typika* offer detailed guidelines for the care of the sick within monastic communities. At the Lips nunnery, a weekly visit from a physician was mandated, with provisions for additional visits during Lent in cases of emergency. Notably, any treatment prescribed by the doctor required the approval of the spiritual father, underscoring the intersection of medical care and spiritual authority. The nunnery also maintained a hospital storehouse stocked with salves and bandages. Interestingly, the *typikon* makes special mention of nuns feigning illness, suggesting that both genuine and imagined sickness could be used to circumvent the community's strict daily discipline.[187]

In some cases, the preferential treatment afforded to sick nuns led to resentment among the rest of the community.[188] The *typikon* of Bebaia Elpis instructs that a "skilled and pious" physician should be summoned to examine the ill.[189] The nunnery was responsible for covering the cost of medical treatment and for adhering to the doctor's recommendations during the recovery process. These provisions reflect both the value placed on compassionate care and the potential for tension when communal equality appeared to be compromised.[190]

---

185 *Typicon monasterii Lips*, ed. Delehaye, chap. 34, p. 125; Talbot, "*Lips*," 1276; *Typicon monasterii Theotoci Bebaias Elpidos*, ed. Delehaye, chap. 101, p. 74; Talbot, "*Bebaia Elpis*," 1552.

186 *Typicon monasterii Theotoci Bebaias Elpidos*, ed. Delehaye, chap. 90, p. 70; Talbot, "*Bebaia Elpis*," 1549–50. On the health regulations in Bebaia Elpis, see also Volk, *Gesundheitswesen und Wohltätigkeit im Spiegel der byzantinischen Klostertypika*, 255–65.

187 *Typicon monasterii Lips*, ed. Delehaye, chaps. 33 and 35, pp. 124–125; Talbot, "*Lips*," 1275–76.

188 *Typicon monasterii Theotoci Bebaias Elpidos*, ed. Delehaye, chap. 92, pp. 70–71; Talbot, "*Bebaia Elpis*," 1550.

189 *Typicon monasterii Theotoci Bebaias Elpidos*, ed. Delehaye, chap. 90, p. 70; Talbot, "*Bebaia Elpis*," 1549–50.

190 *Typicon monasterii Theotoci Bebaias Elpidos*, ed. Delehaye, chaps. 90–94, pp. 70–71; Talbot, "*Bebaia Elpis*," 1549–50.

Beyond the *typika*, additional documentary sources shed light on the role of nunneries as shelters for the sick and elderly. For instance, in 1291, Kaliaba Anysia, a nun in Trebizond, composed her will while ill, illustrating the vulnerability of aging nuns and the support structures within their communities.[191] Female monastic institutions actively sought medical assistance when needed. A brief, four-line letter preserved in Milano, Biblioteca Ambrosiana, MS F 096 sup. (thirteenth century), fol. 33v, records that Nicholas Mesarites, Metropolitan of Ephesos, noted how nuns in his diocese had reached out to a doctor—likely Basil Megistos, who was probably a relative of his. Such documents highlight the practical responsiveness of Byzantine convents to issues of health and aging, complementing the normative prescriptions found in the *typika*.[192]

Convents also served as refuges for women suffering from psychological illness. One such case is that of Tzourakina, a woman who owned property near Kontoskalion in Constantinople and later lost her mental faculties. In 1402, the Patriarch, acting in his capacity as her legal guardian, arranged for the sale of her house. The proceeds—eighty-four hyperpyra—were allocated to the Monastery of St. Andrew *in Krisei*, which accepted Tzourakina into its care. This case illustrates the broader role of Byzantine nunneries as charitable institutions offering shelter not only to the physically ill and elderly, but also to those with mental health needs.[193]

As previously noted, female monasteries in Byzantium often served not only religious and charitable functions but also acted as places of punishment and moral correction. Women who had committed transgressions were sometimes required to enter monastic life as a form of atonement. One such case is that of Amarantina, a former sorceress who, having shown repentance, was enclosed in a nunnery before December 1351 as her sole punishment. Patriarch Kallistos I took personal pride in guiding both Amarantina and the broader clergy of Constantinople back to the path of God. Interestingly, despite her past, the emperor granted Amarantina one hundred hyperpyra, which she used to acquire an *adelphaton* (a form of monastic lodging) in the Mangana Monastery.[194] In another case, the Archbishop

191 Ouspenskij and Beneševič, *Τα Acta της Μονής Βαζελώνος*, trans. Petropoulos, pp. 229–30, no. 78 (1241).

192 *Diktyon*: 42764; Giarenes, *Ο βυζαντινός λόγιος Νικόλαος Μεσαρίτης*, 32; Nicholas Mesarites, *Epistulae*, ed. Cataldi Palau, 187–232.

193 Hunger, "Zu den restlichen Inedita des Konstantinopler Patriarchatsregisters," 66–68; Darrouzès, *Les regestes des Actes du patriarcat de Constantinople*, no. 3257.

194 *Patriarchal Register*, vol. 3, ed. Koder et al., pp. 76–80, no. 185 (1351); Darrouzès,

of Ohrid ruled that Chryse, a woman who had attempted to poison her husband, must enter the Monastery of the Holy Apostles in Epiros and perform the penance prescribed for murderers.[195] In her situation, the monastery also served as a refuge from a violent domestic life. These examples highlight the multifaceted role of nunneries as both instruments of ecclesiastical discipline and sanctuaries for women in distress.

Les regestes des Actes du patriarcat de Constantinople, no. 2331; Cupane, "Magie und Zauberei im späten Byzanz," 49–53. On Mangana Monastery, see Janin, *La géographie ecclésiastique de l'Empire byzantine*, 70–76.

195 See Demetrios Chomatenos, *Ponemata*, ed. Prinzing, p. 389, no. 121; cf. Mitsiou, "Mobile Criminals," 128–29.

Chapter 3

ECONOMIC NETWORKS OF FEMALE MONASTERIES

GENERAL CONSIDERATIONS

LATE BYZANTIUM PRESENTS a complex picture of both decline and resilience. While the period was marked by crises—such as the capture of Constantinople by the Latins in 1204, ongoing ecclesiastical disputes after 1261, and the accelerating expansion of the Ottoman Empire—it also witnessed significant adaptation and innovation. These challenges contributed to political instability and the decentralization of imperial authority.

In the agrarian economy, the *pronoia* system—the conditional grant of a specific amount of tax revenues from properties and peasant households, used by the Byzantine state especially from the twelfth/thirteenth centuries onwards—evolved further under the Laskarid dynasty and acquired a more hereditary nature during the Palaiologan era. Monasteries, bolstered by imperial land grants and fiscal immunities, expanded their holdings significantly, accumulating large estates and increasing their economic influence.[1]

The crises of the period triggered notable shifts in economic behaviour. As territorial losses to the Ottomans reduced the viability of traditional land-based income, many aristocratic landowners turned to commerce, adopting Western financial practices. This transformation gave rise to a new entrepreneurial class that Klaus-Peter Matschke and Franz Tinnefeld have termed *aristokratisches Unternehmertum* (aristocratic entrepreneurship).[2] Nevertheless, land ownership retained its central importance; in a pre-industrial context, land continued to be synonymous with power.[3]

Monastic land ownership in Byzantium primarily aimed at ensuring self-sufficiency. However, many male monasteries extended their activities beyond the mere preservation of their estates, actively seeking to expand

1 Smyrlis, *La fortune des grands monastères byzantins*; Smyrlis, "Τα μοναστήρια στο Ύστερο Βυζάντιο."

2 Matschke and Tinnefeld, *Die Gesellschaft im späten Byzanz*, 158–90. The term *aristokratisches Unternehmertum* designates the shifting of the interests of Byzantine aristocracy after the loss of their vast land properties due to the Ottoman expansion. While Byzantine nobility was previously not interested in participating in trading, it changed its attitude due to the circumstances and out of necessity.

3 Curtis, *Coping with Crisis*, 29–35.

their landholdings. Institutions such as the Great Lavra and the Monastery of Patmos participated in maritime trade and sold surplus agricultural products in both local and international markets.[4] Additionally, they often acted as creditors, providing loans to individuals in need of cash.

For female monastic communities, self-sufficiency was a more immediate and daily concern. Although some nunneries demonstrated entrepreneurial initiative, their engagement in financial activities was limited by structural constraints—namely, stricter regulations on the movement of nuns and a lack of access to influential social networks. As a result, it was essential for their founders to endow them with sufficient resources to ensure long-term sustainability. Given that most nunneries did not play a central role in economic development or innovation, any threat to their landholdings—whether political or financial—could have severe consequences for their survival.

Late Byzantine Nunneries: Finances and Management

The events of 1204 led to the abandonment of numerous Orthodox monasteries in territories that fell under Latin control. Monastic communities displaced by the Latin occupation relocated to regions governed by the emerging Greek successor states. Efforts were made to accommodate these displaced communities. For example, the Laskarid dynasty transferred the landholdings of Constantinopolitan monasteries in the Smyrna area to the Monastery of Lembos.[5]

However, the influx of monks and nuns into the Greek polities created significant spatial and demographic pressures. A document from Epiros, dated between 1224 and 1230, notes that due to the absence of female monastic institutions in the Arta region, nuns were "dwelling in the forecourts of churches in dilapidated shacks with space only for broken-down beds."[6]

Following the recapture of Constantinople in 1261, the city was reestablished as the imperial capital, necessitating substantial financial investment for its restoration.[7] While portions of these renovation expenses were cov-

4 Oikonomides, "The Monastery of Patmos and Its Economic Functions," 1–17; Nystazopoulou-Pelekidou, "Τὰ πλοῖα τῆς Μονῆς Πάτμου," 93–114.

5 The Pantokrator Monastery possessed the village of Bare in the area, which was later granted to Lembos. Miklosich and Müller, *Acta et Diplomata graeca Medii Aevi sacra et profana*, vol. 4, pp. 184–85, no. 105 (1194).

6 John Apokaukos, *Praxis on the Blachernitissa Monastery*, 17; Talbot, "Affirmative Action in the 13th Century," 405–6; Lampropoulos, *Ιωάννης Απόκαυκος*, 284–86.

7 Cf. Hilsdale, *Byzantine Art and Diplomacy in an Age of Decline*, 31–87.

ered by wealthy aristocrats and members of the imperial family, the overall strain on resources grew. By the fourteenth century, both newly founded and older monastic institutions had become smaller and increasingly struggled to sustain themselves.

The financial structures of Byzantine monasteries have garnered significant attention in modern scholarship, although the majority of research has focused on male monastic institutions.[8] This imbalance largely stems from the greater availability and richness of source material related to men's monasteries. In a recent survey, Kostis Smyrlis examined the wealthiest monastic foundations in Byzantium, classifying as *grandes* (great or rich) those that owned at least five thousand *modioi*—approximately five hundred hectares—of land.[9]

Among the wealthiest monastic institutions, only four were female aristocratic convents: Bebaia Elpis, Lips, Nea Petra, and Panagiotissa. Geographically, three of these were located within Constantinople, with Nea Petra being the sole example situated in the countryside. A shared characteristic among these affluent nunneries was their association with wealthy aristocratic patrons and close ties to the imperial family. Financial information for Bebaia Elpis and Lips is preserved in their *typika*, while Nea Petra is documented through archival sources. The economic status of Panagiotissa is discussed in a synodal act.

Bebaia Elpis

The endowment of the convent of Bebaia Elpis was relatively modest, comprising several plots of land and vineyards located in Constantinople and its surrounding regions.[10] In accordance with prevailing legislation and tradition, these properties were technically inalienable—a legal safeguard intended to preserve the integrity of large estates and ensure their continued viability as units of agricultural exploitation.[11] A notable feature of the initial endowment was the deliberate effort to concentrate the convent's

8 Talbot, "Personal Poverty in Byzantine Monasticism," 829–41.

9 Smyrlis, *La fortune des grands monastères byzantins*, 32–33.

10 *Typicon monasterii Theotoci Bebaias Elpidos*, ed. Delehaye, chaps. 120–24, pp. 82–85; Talbot, "*Bebaia Elpis*," 1556–58; Smyrlis, *La fortune des grands monastères byzantins*, 37.

11 On the inalienability of church and monastic property, see Konidares, *Το δίκαιον της μοναστηριακής περιουσίας*, 254–58; Papagianni, "Legal Institutions," vol. 3, pp. 1061–62; Smyrlis, "The State, The Land, and Private Property," 62; Curtis, *Coping with Crisis*, 24–25.

holdings around key locations rather than maintain a dispersed portfolio of assets. Bebaia Elpis owned an estate and a village near Constantinople, another village near Herakleia, and seven vineyards.

Table 3.1. Bebaia Elpis Nunnery—list of properties.

	Principal Endowment of the Nunnery	**Value and Comments**
1	Half of Synadene's entire ancestral estate of Pyrgos	This may have included arable land or a vineyard. The other half was kept by Synadene for herself and her daughter
2	The village of Ainos[12] near Parapolia	Valued at 400 *hyperpyra*: 200 were donated as her ancestral property and 200 were donated by her son
3	Vineyard of ___ *modioi* at Selokaka[13]	
4	Vineyard of ___ *modioi* together with its houses near St. Nicholas Mesomphalos[14]	400 *hyperpyra* Purchased years earlier from a man named Kaligas as barren land, where Synadene later planted vines
5	Vineyard of ___ *modioi* near Kosmidion[15]	Donated by Synadene's nephew, John (Joasaph) Palaiologos Angelos Branas
6	Vineyard of ___ *modioi* in Kosmidion	John (Joasaph) Palaiologos Angelos Branas gave this vineyard in exchange for "adelphata" for his wife, from which eight *hyperpyra* were paid annually as *telos* to the monastery of Kosmidiotes
7	Village of Morokoumoulou[16] near Herakleia	The landed property of Diakephalaios is also located there
8	Vineyard of ___ *modioi* in the village of Kanikleion[17]	Donation for the salvation of Thomais Palaiologina Kantakouzene, daughter-in-law of Synadene

12 Külzer, *Ostthrakien*, 242.

13 Külzer, *Ostthrakien*, 634.

14 Külzer, *Ostthrakien*, 549.

15 Külzer, *Ostthrakien*, 471–73.

16 Külzer, *Ostthrakien*, 538.

17 Külzer, *Ostthrakien*, 435.

Properties Kept by Synadene for Herself and Her Daughter		Value and Comments
1	Half of the estate of Pyrgos	
2	Village of Kanikleion in Parapolia	Ancestral estate
3	Garden called Gymnou near the convent in Constantinople	Synadene's daughter decided upon the garden's fate
4	A large vineyard close to Kyriotissa	Theodore, Synadene's son, the *protostrator*, gave it to her
5	The houses around the large vineyard very close to Kyriotissa, on the public road	Theodore, Synadene's son, the *protostrator*, gave it to her

Later Additions		Value and Comments
1	John Theophilos left 300 *hyperpyra* for an estate to be purchased for the convent	The heir of John's property first gave 100 *nomismata* to the monastery, and the nuns handed over the garden at Blanga. The nuns received the remaining 200 *hyperpyra* because of the difficulties they faced due to the siege by the Turks Donation for commemoration of the anniversaries of the deaths of John Theophilos and his wife[18] These transactions were recorded by the great sacristan of the Great Church, Demetrios Balsamon, on February 11, 1397
2	Courtyard of Anna Kantakouzene, sister of Eugenia Kantakouzene	300 *hyperpyra* Cleared and turned into a wheat-field
3	Donation of gold by Eugenia Kantakouzene	In 1398
4	Restoration and repair of the church and bell tower	200 *hyperpyra*, of which 70 *hyperpyra* came from the sale of the house of Marachas Eugenia Kantakouzene added 130 *hyperpyra* Manuel II gave Eugenia Kantakouzene the house in 1400
5	Vineyard close to Kyriotissa in Constantinople	100 *hyperpyra* The garden of St. George was planted and restored as a vineyard; it joined the large vineyard of the convent

18 *Typicon monasterii Theotoci Bebaias Elpidos*, ed. Delehaye, chap. 8, pp. 102–3.

The convent's foundress, Synadene, contributed half of her ancestral estate in Pyrgos to the monastery,[19] while retaining the other half for her own "maintenance and modest comfort" as well as for her daughter, Euphrosyne. According to the *typikon*, these retained properties were to be transferred to the convent upon their deaths, with the exact terms of the donation left up to Euphrosyne's discretion.

To provide a clearer picture of Bebaia Elpis's endowment, Table 3.1 presents a breakdown of the convent's original assets, the properties retained by the foundress, and those later added, many of which were recorded in the *typikon* by Euphrosyne, reflecting her role in expanding the monastery's economic base.

Maps 3.1 and 3.2 illustrate the locations of the nunnery's properties in Constantinople and its surrounding hinterland. Over the course of a generation, the nunnery of Bebaia Elpis gradually expanded its membership from the original thirty to fifty nuns.[20] This growth was likely supported by external contributions, including entrance gifts, *adelphata* (fellowships granted in return for substantial donations), and other forms of benefaction. During the Ottoman siege of Constantinople in the late fourteenth century, such donations—both monetary and in land—proved especially vital.

Some of these contributions may have come from Eugenia Kantakouzene Philanthropene, the (new) foundress, whose entrance gifts possibly formed part of her overall support. Tonsured at an early age, Eugenia reportedly dedicated "all her fortune" to the convent.[21] At a time of financial hardship, she repurposed part of the convent's property, transforming a yard into a wheat field and a garden into a vineyard to help sustain the community.

While the original endowment of Bebaia Elpis included a combination of arable land, vineyards, and villages, later developments indicate a strategic shift in focus toward vineyard cultivation within the city itself.

The *typikon* does not always provide precise figures regarding property prices and revenues.[22] Nevertheless, by comparing its information with contemporary data, certain conclusions can be drawn. For instance, the purchase of a garden in the Blanga district for one hundred *hyperpyra*

19 Külzer, *Ostthrakien*, 606. Pyrgos is a settlement ca. twelve kilometres northeast of Constantinople, three kilometres southeast of Peteinochori (today Kemerburgaz).

20 *Typicon monasterii Theotoci Bebaias Elpidos*, ed. Delehaye, chap. 146, p. 96; Talbot, "*Bebaia Elpis*," 1564.

21 *Typicon monasterii Theotoci Bebaias Elpidos*, ed. Delehaye, chap. 159, pp. 104–5; Talbot, "*Bebaia Elpis*," 1568.

22 Morrisson and Cheynet, "Prices and Wages in the Byzantine World," 815–78.

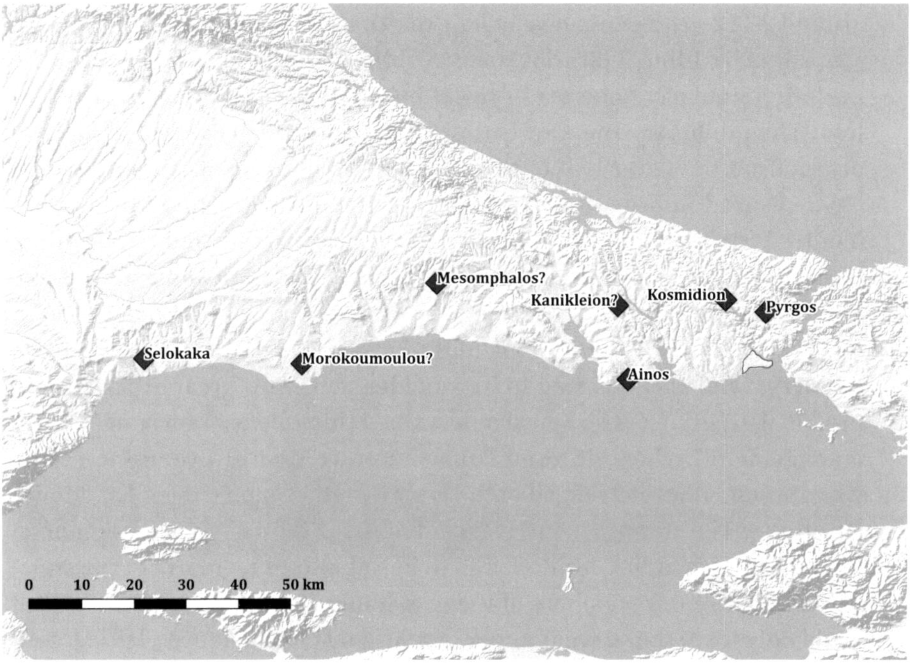

Map 3.1. The properties of Bebaia Elpis nunnery outside Constantinople.

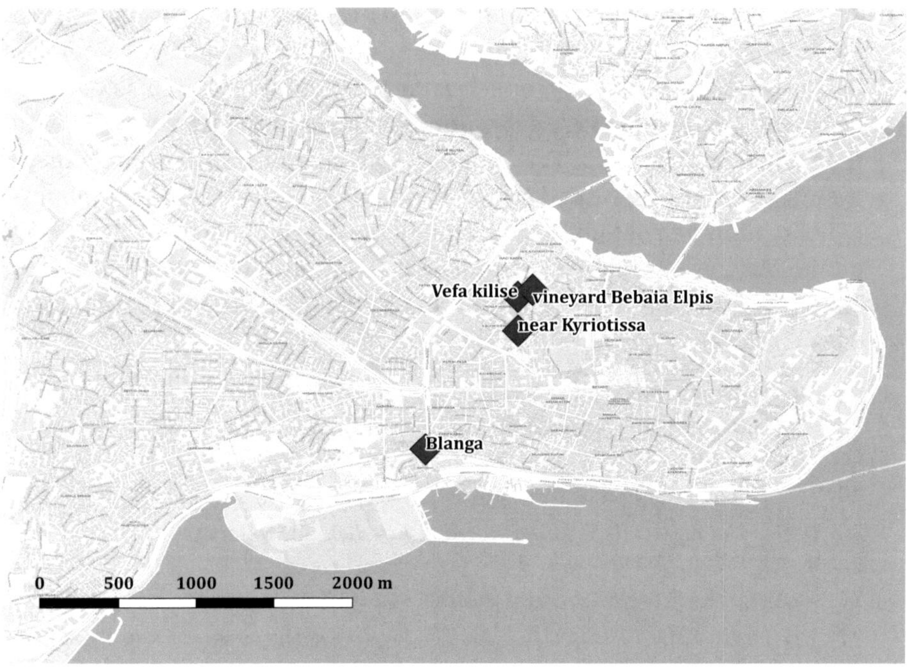

Map 3.2. The properties of Bebaia Elpis nunnery in Constantinople

around 1342 represents nearly half the cost of a similar property in the same area by 1400, indicating a noticeable increase in land value over the period.[23] Similarly, the sum of three hundred *hyperpyra* bequeathed by John Theophilos for the acquisition of an estate aligns with known land prices from the latter half of the fourteenth century. This amount would have covered approximately twelve *modioi* of land.[24] In addition, two hundred *hyperpyra* were designated for the restoration and repair of the church and its bell tower, reflecting typical construction and maintenance costs of the time.

The *oikonomos* held responsibility for all financial matters within the nunnery[25] and was required to be an older nun with "great experience in practical affairs." Kostis Smyrlis describes this role as a form of "hybrid management," which differed from the more typical Byzantine model where estates were managed exclusively by either monastic or lay administrators.[26] The steward's duties included the careful documentation of all financial transactions, with records to be submitted regularly to the superior and the senior members of the community. While the steward herself could only leave the convent under exceptional circumstances, lay external managers were appointed to oversee the administration of the nunnery's estates.[27]

The detailed recording of all actions related to the legacy of John Theophilos—amounting to three hundred *hyperpyra*—by Demetrios Balsamon, *skeuophylakissa*, or sacristan, of the Great Church, is particularly noteworthy. In 1397, Balsamon documented the transactions with the following statement: "For future security and the explanation of these events, they were recorded by my hand, the great sacristan of the most holy Great Church of God [Hagia Sophia], the deacon Demetrios Balsamon, on the eleventh day of the month of February, fifth indiction of the year 6905."[28] According to the *typikon*, this act of documentation was likely

---

23 Miklosich and Müller, *Acta et Diplomata graeca Medii Aevi sacra et profana*, vol. 2, p. 394, no. 578 (June 1400); Darrouzès, *Les regestes des Actes du patriarcat de Constantinople*, no. 3137.

24 Morrison and Cheynet, "Prices," 832.

25 *Typicon monasterii Theotoci Bebaias Elpidos*, ed. Delehaye, chaps. 54–55, pp. 48–49; Talbot, "*Bebaia Elpis*," 1538–39.

26 Smyrlis, "The Management of Monastic Estates," 249.

27 *Typicon monasterii Theotoci Bebaias Elpidos*, ed. Delehaye, chap. 55, p. 48; Talbot, "*Bebaia Elpis*," 1538–39.

28 Gastgeber, "Das *Typikon* Lincoln College gr. 35," 96–100.

intended to safeguard the fund from potential mismanagement. In fact, the Patriarchate exercised close oversight over changes to the *typika* and *brebia* of nunneries, as these foundational documents were archived under its authority.

Lips

Theodora Palaiologina endowed her monastic foundation, the Lips nunnery, with an extensive array of properties, including land, vineyards, buildings, and gardens, totaling approximately twenty thousand *modioi*. This endowment was intended to provide for a community of fifty nuns along with twenty-one hospital staff and twelve patients. The sources of these assets varied; a portion came from her mother and son, another from her dowry, while additional holdings were personally acquired by the empress. One property was offered as an entrance gift.

Within Constantinople, the Lips nunnery owned approximately twenty-three buildings, not including its mills. It also held significant land in Galata, Blanga, and other parts of the capital, comprising 237 *modioi* of vineyards and ninety-eight *modioi* of gardens. Beyond the city, the nunnery's possessions included three estates, five villages, and numerous parcels of land, vineyards, gardens, mills, and apartments located across Thrace, western Macedonia, Bithynia, Pergamon, and the Smyrna region. A detailed list of the properties held by the Lips nunnery is presented in Table 3.2 below.[29]

In contrast to the centralized landholdings of Bebaia Elpis, the properties of the Lips nunnery were geographically dispersed across multiple regions and Constantinople (see Maps 3.3 and 3.4 below).

This difference in spatial organization influenced administrative practices; while Bebaia Elpis employed a female steward, the broader distribution of the Lips estate required a more mobile and externally oriented administrator. Following the precedent set by the Kecharitomene convent, Theodora Palaiologina appointed a male or eunuch steward to manage the holdings—an example of the lay management model commonly adopted by Byzantine nunneries.[30]

29 *Typicon monasterii Lips*, ed. Delehaye, chaps. 43–49, pp. 130–34; Talbot, "*Lips*," 1279–80.

30 Smyrlis, "The Management of Monastic Estates," 249.

Table 3.2. Lips Nunnery—list of properties.

	Donations of the Empress	Value and Comments
1	Estate (*ktema*) Kastellou in theme of Pergamon	350 gold pieces (*hyperpyra*)
2	Part of the estates of Achilleion and Barys	Worth 300 gold pieces (*hyperpyra*) Included in this amount was a fish pond (*vivarium*)
3	The mill of Thermene near the estates of Achilleion and Barys	From the property of the same ancestral estates
4	Vineyard of Emporianos	Purchased by Theodora Palaiologina
5	A vineyard of 32 *modioi* near the *ktemata* (near Anaia?)	Part of *zeugelateion* called Kythrina
6	A garden of 20 *modioi*	Part of *zeugelateion* called Kythrina
7	A smaller garden of 10 *modioi*	Part of *zeugelateion* called Kythrina
8	Arable land of 390 *modioi*	Part of *zeugelateion* called Kythrina
9	A double mill near Anaia	Part of *zeugelateion* called Kythrina — operated all year round
10	Vineyards of 145 *modioi*	Part of *zeugelateion* called Kythrina — some acquired by purchase, others through improvements and maintenance
11	Gardens of 150 *modioi*	Part of *zeugelateion* called Kythrina
12	Arable land of 350 *modioi*	Part of *zeugelateion* called Kythrina
13	Fourteen houses for rent	Part of *zeugelateion* called Kythrina
14	Arable land of 500 *modioi* near Kordoleon in the *katepanikion* of Smyrna	Purchased from Abalantos
15	Arable land of 2000 *modioi* in the vicinity of Philopation[31] near Constantinople	
16	The houses of Batrachonites and Gabras in the Kynegoi quarter, Constantinople	Buildings in Constantinople obtained by purchase
17	Workshop near the Kynegos Gate	Buildings in Constantinople
18	The [house] of Chabaron near Blachernai	Buildings in Constantinople
19	The [houses] at Tzochareia [near?] the Imperial Gate	Buildings in Constantinople purchased from a Syrian tar-maker named Maphre

31 Külzer, *Ostthrakien*, 587–88.

	Donations of the Empress	Value and Comments
20	The houses of John Eulogios behind the Latin church of the exceedingly Holy Mary	
21	The houses of the *archon tes thymeles* (magistrate of the stage) near the houses of John Eulogios	
22	The [houses] of Sampson near the houses of nos. 20 and 21	
23	The guard house at the Beautiful Gate	

	Properties Donated to the Hospital	Value and Comments
1	The village of Nymphai[32] in the vicinity of Constantinople	Dependent peasants and arable land amounting to 260 *nomismata* A portion of 600 *nomismata*
2	Two mills near Aphameia	Worth 32 *nomismata* A portion of 600 *nomismata*
3	Skoteinon village in the region of Macedonia[33]	308 *nomismata*: 138 *nomismata* from dependent peasants 70 *nomismata* from four mills 100 *nomismata* from arable land of 2600 *modioi* A portion of 600 *nomismata*
4	A vineyard of 300 *modioi* at Lopadion	Part of the estates of Lachanas
5	Arable land of 860 *modioi* at Lopadion	Part of the estates of Lachanas
6	A winter mill at Lopadion	Part of the estates of Lachanas
7	A half share in another mill at Lopadion	Part of the estates of Lachanas
8	Houses at Lopadion	Part of the estates of Lachanas

32 Külzer, *Ostthrakien*, 550–51.

33 Soustal, *Makedonien, südlicher Teil*, 995–96: northeast of Berroia.

	Donations of the Empress's Mother	Value and Comments
1	The village of Ennakosia[34] near Constantinople	95 gold pieces from dependent peasants
2	The village of Plakos[35]	66 *nomismata* from dependent peasants
3	The properties at the village Kalon Neron (lit. Good waters)[36]	58 *nomismata*
4	Abandoned land amounting to 500 *modioi* in Ennakosia, Plakos, Kalon Neron	18 *nomismata*
5	Another abandoned property of 1400 *modioi* in the vicinity of Ennakosia, below the paved road	42 *nomismata*
6	A mill in the village of Ennakosia	8 *nomismata*
7	The pier in the village of Ennakosia	10 *nomismata*
8	Arable land of 700 *modioi* in the vicinity of Martinakion[37]	28 *nomismata* **Total: 344 *nomismata***
9	Arable land of 3000 *modioi* in the neighbourhood of St. Anna[38]	
10	Arable land of 200 *modioi* near Empyrites at Palatitzia[39]	
11	Two mills at Kamelogephyron[40]	
12	Two other mills in the village of Apodroungarion[41] in the theme of Selymbria	

34 Külzer, *Ostthrakien*, 349–50.

35 Külzer, *Ostthrakien*, 597: in the southern part of Küçükçekmece Gölü.

36 Külzer, *Ostthrakien*, 431: one kilometer north of Küçükçekmece (modern Soğuksu Çiftlik).

37 Külzer, *Ostthrakien*, 517: in close proximity to Küçükçekmece Gölü.

38 Külzer, *Ostthrakien*, 252: in close proximity to Küçükçekmece Gölü.

39 Külzer, *Ostthrakien*, 558–59: in close proximity to Empyrites located at the Küçükçekmece Gölü.

40 Külzer, *Ostthrakien*, 279–81, esp. at 280: Kamelogephyron was a bridge of the river Barbyses in the hinterland of Constantinople.

41 Külzer, *Ostthrakien*, 255.

	Properties of the Convent Located in Constantinople, Nikomedeia, and Skoutari	Value and Comments
1	A vineyard of 125 *modioi*	
2	Gardens of 40 *modioi* in different locations	
3	Another garden of 15 *modioi* at Blanga	
4	Another called Dzefre of 40 *modioi*	
5	A vineyard of 112 *modioi* at Galata	
6	Garden of 3 *modioi* at Galata	
7	A vineyard of 237 *modioi*	
8	Gardens of 98 *modioi*	
9	Six mills reconstructed near the monastery of Pantepoptes and outside at the wall of the Phanar	
10	Houses of Tzochareia	Purchase from Nikolezos
11	Two further houses at Beautiful Gate	Purchase from Chrestine
12	Ten further houses in the area of Blachernai	
13	House with an upper floor in the area of the Blachernai palace, near the houses of Niketiates	
14	Half of the field of Diabatenos including 112 olive trees	
15	Half of the field of Magistros including 210 olive trees	
16	Olive trees at Nikomedeia	Conveyed to the convent by the recessor (*apographeus*) Cheilas
17	The small convent of the recessor (*apographeus*) dedicated to the Great martyr St. George, called Trapeza in Skoutari	Entrance gift of the nun Tzakalina

The responsibilities of the lay steward included appointing local administrators for individual estates, supervising agricultural activities such as fieldwork and viticulture, preventing theft or damage, and ensuring the upkeep of buildings. Although he was allowed to confer with the abbess—always in the presence of senior nuns—he was not permitted to reside within the monastery and was required to leave before the midday meal.[42]

42 *Typicon monasterii Lips*, ed. Delehaye, chaps. 25–26, pp. 119–20; Talbot, "*Lips*," 1272–73.

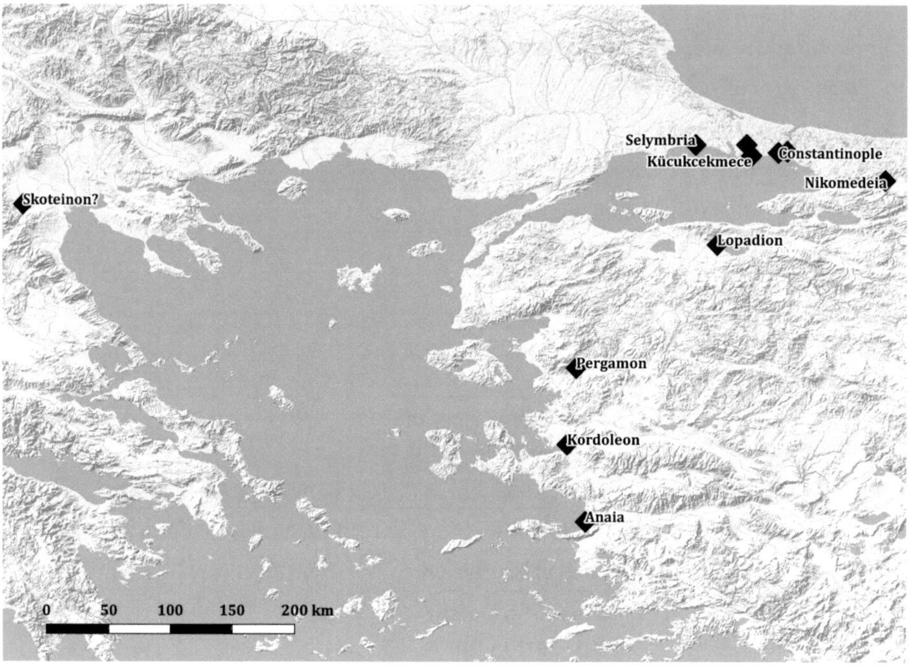

Map 3.3. The properties of Lips nunnery in Asia Minor and Greece.

The alienation of immovable property was strictly prohibited, and movable goods could only be pawned under exceptional circumstances, such as enemy incursions or a significant decline in revenues.[43] Entrance gifts were not obligatory; however, as illustrated in Table 3.2, some foundations, such as the small convent of St. George "called Trapeza" in Skoutari (Chrysopolis),[44] originated as entrance gifts—this one from the nun Tzakalina. Other offerings, including property, money, sacred vessels, or furnishings donated "by anyone with pious intentions," were also accepted and valued.

A final observation concerns the financial difficulties the Lips nunnery likely encountered shortly after the death of its foundress in 1303. Its holdings in Asia Minor probably fell into Turkish hands within a short period, causing considerable economic strain. In such a context, further private donations would have been essential to sustain the institution.

The case of the Lips nunnery also illustrates how monastic foundations could function as mechanisms for preserving familial wealth. Instead of

43 *Typicon monasterii Lips*, ed. Delehaye, chap. 43, p. 130; Talbot, "*Lips*," 1279; Stolte, "Law for Founders," 126–27: *res sacrae* were *extra commercium*.

44 Janin, *Les églises et les monastères des grands centres Byzantins*, 26.

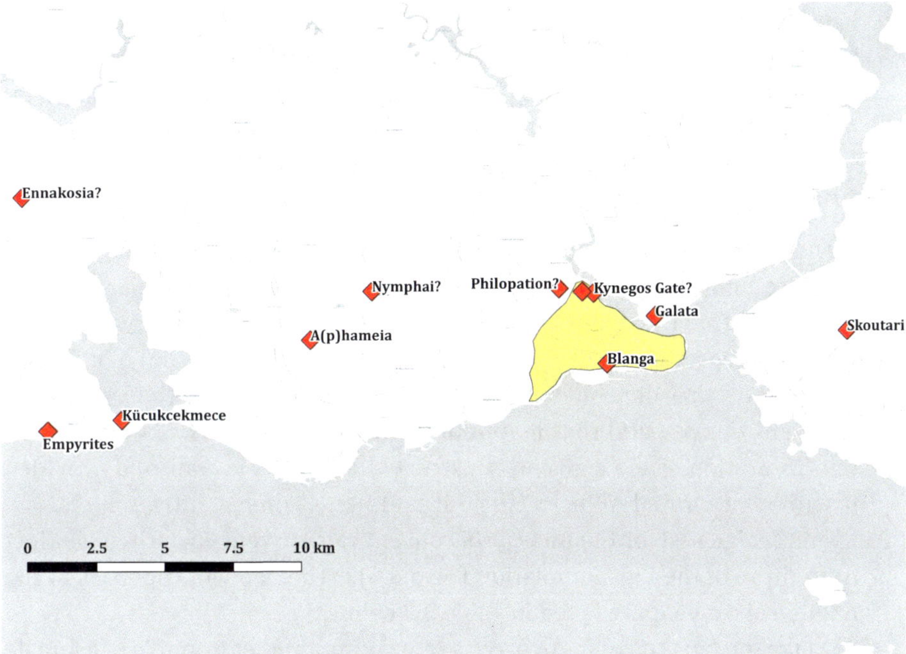

Map 3.4. The properties of Lips nunnery in Constantinople and Thrace.

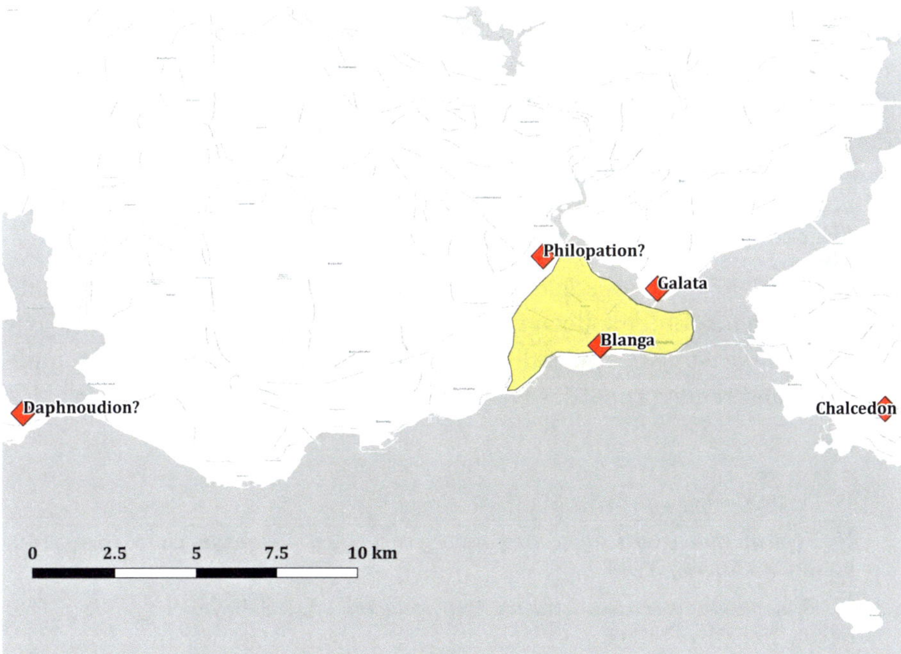

Map 3.5. The properties of Anargyroi Monastery.

being divided among heirs or sold, the extensive estates of Theodora Palaiologina were consolidated within a monastic institution. This arrangement effectively prevented their fragmentation, ensuring the unity and continued use of family assets under ecclesiastical stewardship.[45]

Anargyroi

Anargyroi, the second monastic foundation of Theodora Palaiologina, was likewise endowed with properties in Constantinople and other regions. However, some of its landholdings remain unknown due to lacunae in the manuscript preserving the *typikon*, specifically on fols. 66v and 67r. Palaiologina notes that the convent had lost its properties during the Latin occupation of the city and that its buildings were left in ruins. She undertook the restoration of the convent, constructed a protective wall, and provided it with consecrated objects "since it had none." Importantly, the endowments designated for the Anargyroi convent were to remain entirely distinct from those of the Lips foundation (Map 3.5).[46] The known properties of the Anargyroi convent are listed in Table 3.3 below.[47]

Like the Lips convent, Anargyroi represents another example of a female monastic institution employing the traditional model of lay management. Financial oversight was entrusted to a male steward—either a eunuch or an individual belonging to the category of "otherwise respectable men." While he was not permitted to reside within the convent, he was required to make regular visits on designated days. His responsibilities included maintaining detailed records of all financial transactions and receiving payments from the convent in both currency and goods.[48]

Theotokos tes *Panagiotisses*

Maria Palaiologina—the foundress of the nunnery *ton Mougoulion*—established the institution following the purchase of buildings and land for four thousand *hyperpyra*. The endowment comprised bakeries, churches, vineyards, and rental properties within Constantinople, collectively generating

45 Curtis, *Coping with Crisis*, 25.

46 *Typicon monasterii sanctorum Anargyrorum*, ed. Delehaye, chap. 61, p. 140; Talbot, "*Anargyroi*," 1293.

47 *Typicon monasterii sanctorum Anargyrorum*, ed. Delehaye, chap. 58, p. 138; Talbot, "*Anargyroi*," 1291.

48 *Typicon monasterii sanctorum Anargyrorum*, ed. Delehaye, chap. 59, p. 139; Talbot, "*Anargyroi*," 1292.

Table 3.3. Anargyroi Monastery—list of properties.

	Properties	Value and Comments
1	The [monastery?] at Oulas in the Thrakesian theme	It also possessed a *chrysobull* determining its properties
2	A piece of arable land of 640 *modioi* in Constantinople	
3	A vineyard of 65 *modioi*	
4	A garden with pasturage in Blanga	
5	Arable land of 1,000 *modioi* in Philopation	
6	The estate of St. Leontios in Daphnoudion[49]	Included the pasturage, the *panegyris*, and land called the Apotheke
7	Dependent peasants (*paroikoi*) at Marnakiou in Chalcedon	40 *nomismata*
8	Arable land of 452 *modioi*	
9	The vineyard of Ampeles of 9 *modioi*	
10	The vineyard of Aoinares, of 18 *modioi*	
11	A field of 30 *modioi* at Galata	
12	The field of Barelina of 10 *modioi* at Galata	With a bath and *ptochoi proskathemenoi*
13	240 olive trees in different places at Charax	
14	Arable land of 250 *modioi* at Charax	
15	Four *paroikoi* at Charax	Worth six *nomismata*

an annual income of approximately three hundred *hyperpyra*. Beyond the city, the monastery also owned villages, a *zeugelateion* (arable land), vineyards, and residences in areas such as Rhaidestos and Medeia.

The financial stability of the nunnery began to decline shortly after the deaths of Maria Palaiologina (after 1307) and her daughter Theodora (before 1351), when Isaakios Palaiologos Asanes, Maria's son-in-law, assumed the role of *ephoros* (overseer) of the institution. A critical misstep under his administration was the excessive increase in the number of nuns—thirty-three of whom were external/lay appointees (*ἀδελφαί ἐξωτερικαὶ κοσμικαί*) and additional nuns. This expansion appears to have been driven by his aim to collect *apotage* donations—entry fees given

49 Külzer, *Ostthrakien*, 323–24.

upon joining the monastery—which he hoped would yield a sum of two thousand *hyperpyra*.[50]

Nea Petra

Nea Petra was an aristocratic foundation established by the Maliasenoi family in Thessaly. In contrast to Lips and Bebaia Elpis, information about Nea Petra's economic foundation derives not from a *typikon* but from a now-lost cartulary that contained forty-two documents dated between 1215 and 1276. This documentary evidence offers a vivid account of the complexities of monastic foundation and aristocratic patronage as well as the financial opportunities present in the peripheral regions of the Byzantine Empire.

The convent was founded around 1271–1272 by Anna/Anthousa Palaiologina, the niece of Emperor Michael VIII.[51] Along with her husband, she donated a range of assets to the patriarchal nunnery, including buildings, agricultural land, mills, *zeugelateia*, and *metochia* (dependent estates). The initial parcel of land was purchased from a certain Michael Archontitzes, and, notably, the inhabitants of the nearby village of Dryanoubaina agreed to assume responsibility for the annual tax payments, thereby freeing the convent from fiscal obligations.

Shortly thereafter, the Maliasenoi acquired additional vineyards and landholdings from local peasants at very low prices, often structuring the transactions to appear as donations. The documentation makes clear that the majority of these acquisitions occurred between September 1271 and 1272, during a time of crisis marked by the ongoing conflict between Epiros and Constantinople and a prolonged regional famine.[52]

The endowment of Nea Petra generally included lands and *metochia* in Dryanoubaina,[53] while the properties later acquired for the nunnery con-

---

50 *Patriarchal Register*, vol. 3, ed. Koder et al., pp. 66–76, no. 184 (October 1351), lines 79–85; Darrouzès, *Les regestes des Actes du patriarcat de Constantinople*, no. 2330; Thomas, *Private Religious Foundations in the Byzantine Empire*, 261; Smyrlis, *La fortune des grands monastères byzantins*, 68–69. This is a special reference to the existence of external/lay appointees in Late Byzantium. Their exact relationship to the nunnery is not clear.

51 Smyrlis, *La fortune des grands monastères byzantins*, 65–68; Giannopoulos, "Αἱ παρὰ τὴν Δημητριάδα βυζαντιναὶ μοναὶ," 210–40; Ostrogorsky, *Pour l'histoire de la féodalité byzantine*, 93–99; Koder and Hild, *Hellas und Thessalien*, 224–25.

52 Teleles, *Μετεωρολογικά φαινόμενα και κλίμα*, does not include this famine, as his research was based solely on historiographical sources.

53 Koder and Hild, *Hellas und Thessalien*, 150.

sisted of *staseis* (settlements or groups of holdings), as well as vineyards, farmland, and one *zeugelateion* (plowland) in the area of Brasta (see Table 3.4). Among these, vineyards were the most significant and frequent type of acquisition.[54] Importantly, Nea Petra was located near the male Monastery of Makrinitissa, which had been founded by the Maliasenoi family shortly before 1215 and granted *stauropegial* status in 1256.[55] As Angeliki Laiou has noted, the development of both Makrinitissa and Nea Petra exemplifies the broader trend of consolidating small, fragmented landholdings into larger, more economically viable monastic estates.[56]

The nunnery of Nea Petra enjoyed exemption from all taxes and obligations with the sole exception of *kastroktisia*: a corvée duty related to the construction of fortifications.[57] A legal dispute arose between Nea Petra and the *pronoia* holder Marmaras over the *zeugelateion* in Brasta. While Nea Petra leased this land to its peasants and collected rent, Marmaras claimed that Brasta fell within the bounds of his *pronoia* in Tyrnabos and attempted to collect rent from it as well. In July 1277, the *pinkernes* Manouel Komnenos Raoul adjudicated the case in favour of the nunnery, relying on witness testimony, and forbade Marmaras from interfering in the property.[58] The eventual transformation of Nea Petra into a male monastery may reflect its inability to attract or sustain a sufficiently large female monastic community or perhaps the inadequacy of its economic resources to support long-term female habitation. The properties associated with the convent of Nea Petra are listed in Table 3.4.

---

54 Miklosich and Müller, *Acta et Diplomata graeca Medii Aevi sacra et profana*, vol. 4, pp. 391–92, no. 26 (1271), pp. 393–96, no. 27 (1271), pp. 396–99, no. 28 (1271), pp. 399–402, no. 29 (1271), pp. 402–4, no. 30 (1271), pp. 404–7, no. 31 (1271), pp. 407–9, no. 32/1 (1272), pp. 410–11, no. 32/2 (1272), pp. 412–14, no. 33 (ca. 1272), pp. 330–32, no. 1 (1272), and pp. 333–36, no. 2 (1274); Smyrlis, *La fortune des grands monastères byzantins*, 65–67; Stefec, "Beiträge zur Urkundentätigkeit epirotischer Herrscher," 249–370.

55 Koder and Hild, *Hellas und Thessalien*, 210–11. Melvani sets the foundation between 1205 and 1209. Melvani, *Late Byzantine Sculpture*, 108. On Maliasenoi, see Puech, " L'aristocratie et le pouvoir à Byzance," vol. 1, p. 14.

56 Laiou, "The Agrarian Economy," 325.

57 Laurent, *Regestes*, nos. 1392, 1394, 1397, 1402, 1403, 1411, 1412; Dölger and Wirth, *Regesten der Kaiserurkunden des Oströmischen Reiches*, vol. 3, nos. 1989, 1999a, 2011, 2012, and 2031a.

58 Miklosich and Müller, *Acta et Diplomata graeca Medii Aevi sacra et profana*, vol. 4, pp. 419–20, no. 37 (1277); Bartusis, *Land and Privilege in Byzantium*, 410–11; Nystazopoulou-Pelekidou, *Βυζαντινή διπλωματική*, 60–61.

Table 3.4. Nea Petra Nunnery—list of properties.

	Properties	Value and Comments
1	Epano Dryanoubaina	It was the location of the nunnery
2	Kato Dryanoubaina	It included land in the valleys and mountains, as well as vineyards, lands, and mills
3	Stasis of Zoe Melanchrene, daughter of Stephan Syropoulos in theme of Dryanoubaina	5 *hyperpyra* even though its real price was more than double or triple this sum[59] - Zoe received a portion from the payment of an *adelphaton* The stasis included: - a vineyard - the nearby vineyards - orchards and 3 more arable pieces of land in Palatia - a *choraphion* in Plateos Lithou - 2 vineyards in Dryanoubaina - 2 houses
4	Metochion Portarea close to Nea Petra	3 *litrai* of wax to be given by the nunnery to the bishop of Demetrias, Michael Panaretos
5	Metochion Epaliropatou	4 *litrai* of wax to be given to the bishop of Demetrias, Michael Panaretos
6	Metochion Hesychastareion	Stauropegial
7	Metochion St. Nicholas Xylopas	Included a mill, fruit trees
8	Mill?	26 ducats even though its real price was more than double this sum
9	Mill site in Velestinos[60]	Given by the bishop of Demetrias, Michael Panaretos
10	Vineyard of Martinos in Velestinos	1 *olokotinarea almyriotiken*[61] sold for only 10 *hyperpyra* even though its real price was more than double this sum
11	Vineyard of Nikolaos Bardas in Velestinos, close to Martinos's vineyard	*Posoumenon* 1 *olokotinarea almyriotiken* sold for 10 *hyperpyra* even though its real price was more than double this sum

59 This mention refers to the principle of *laesio enormis* (abnormal harm, excessive injury), where the sale price is half of the "just price" of the land. Maniatis, "Organization, Market Structure, and Modus Operandi," 311–12n180.

60 Koder and Hild, *Hellas und Thessalien*, 133.

61 *Olokotinarea* is a term for the common Byzantine *modios* of forty *litrai*. Schilbach, *Byzantinische Metrologie*, 60–61.

Properties		Value and Comments
12	Vineyard of John Katzidones in Velestinos	Sold by the brother of Katzidones Konstantinos *Posoumenon* 1 *olokotinarea almyriotiken* Sold for 7 ὑπέρπυρα παρά τρίτον (6²/₃) even though its real price was more than double this sum
13	Vineyard of Konstantinos Katzidones in Velestinos	Sold to the *ktetor* for 8 *hyperpyra* even though its real price was more than double this sum
14	Vineyard in St. George ton Kanalion in Velestinos	2 *olokotinareas* Sold to the *ktetores* for 15 *hyperpyra*
15	Property of Archontitzes in Dryanoubaina	12 *hyperpyra*
16	Arable land (*zeugelateion*) of Brastoi	Subject of a dispute with *pronoia* holder Marmaras (see above)
17	Hagioi Apostoloi tou Megalostomou	Vineyards, land, *ptochoi* (=peasants with no personal land and means of cultivation), i.e., children and relatives of Eunostos

Our sources offer only a partial picture of the financial operations of the great monasteries. What is clear, however, is that these institutions functioned primarily as landowners, with their wealth concentrated in assets such as houses, arable land, vineyards, and gardens, most of which were secured at the time of their foundation. In many cases, additional properties were donated by the foundress's relatives.

Theodora Palaiologina acknowledged that some individuals contributed to nunneries out of vanity. Nonetheless, the more socially and theologically acceptable motive for such acts was the salvation of the donor's soul and those of their kin. These intentions were often commemorated through inscriptions on church walls. A notable example is found in the hermitage dedicated to St. John near Zoupena (St. Anargyroi), close to Geraki (Peloponnese), where a dedicatory inscription records the nun Euphrosyne Glyka's plea for divine remembrance and forgiveness on the Day of Judgment.[62] Similarly, in 1482, the nun Kataphyge Skoularopoulos donated her private properties to the monastery of Vazelon explicitly for the salvation of her soul and the remission of her sins.[63]

62 Drandakes, "Τὸ Παλιομονάστηρο τῶν Ἁγίων Σαράντα στή Λακεδαίμονα καὶ τὸ ἀσκηταριό του," 135.

63 Ouspenskij and Beneševič, *Ta Acta της Μονής Βαζελώνος*, trans. Petropoulos, p. 187, no. 7 (1482); Janin, *Les églises et les monastères des grands centres Byzantins*, 283–86.

The cartulary of the Vazelon Monastery also preserves records of donations made by Eudokia/Eudoxia Taronitissa,[64] Anysia Papagenakopoulos, and two additional nuns in the mid-fifteenth century.[65] A close analysis of these documents suggests that the donations took place within specific familial and socio-political contexts. Eudokia Taronitissa, the sister of a priest, mirrored her brother's pious act—his donation of the family property known as *stasis Aitherissa*—by contributing her own share of the same estate to the monastery. In another case, Anysia Papagenakopoulos bequeathed all her properties to Vazelon in response to a personal crisis: her children had been taken captive by the Turks. Significantly, the document stipulates that if her sons were to return, they would be entitled to reclaim their share of the family estate.[66]

Other donations and sales to nunneries were occasionally made in exchange for basic necessities such as food, housing, and shelter. In the first half of the thirteenth century, for instance, an individual named Planites donated his family property in Mantaia to the Lembos Monastery. This arrangement was confirmed by his relatives, Basil Planites and the nun Anysia Planitissa, under the explicit condition that the monastery would provide Anysia with the means for her subsistence.[67]

Further insight into such transactions comes from Codex B of the Monastery of John Prodromos in Serres, which documents monastic property dealings in rural contexts. In July 1275, Abbess Marina Sgouraina of the convent of Megalos Taxiarches, along with her community of five nuns, donated a parcel of dry land to Abbot Ioannikios Kaloudes for the purpose of constructing a chapel. Additionally, the nuns sold a vineyard for ten *hyperpyra*,

64 Ouspenskij and Beneševič, *Ta Acta της Μονής Βαζελώνος*, trans. Petropoulos, pp. 218–19, no. 60 (1275).

65 On the nun Anysia, see Ouspenskij and Beneševič, *Ta Acta της Μονής Βαζελώνος*, trans. Petropoulos, pp. 241–43, no. 100 (1344). On Margarita/Makrina Kalliepopoulos, see Ouspenskij and Beneševič, *Ta Acta της Μονής Βαζελώνος*, trans. Petropoulos, pp. 274–75, no. 123 (1415). On Makaria Sagmataba, see Ouspenskij and Beneševič, *Ta Acta της Μονής Βαζελώνος*, trans. Petropoulos, p. 306, no. 185 (mid-fifteenth century).

66 Ouspenskij and Beneševič, *Ta Acta της Μονής Βαζελώνος*, trans. Petropoulos, p. 242, no. 100 (1344); Pahlitzsch, "Zum Loskauf von griechischen Gefangenen und Sklaven," 136.

67 Miklosich and Müller, *Acta et Diplomata graeca Medii Aevi sacra et profana*, vol. 4, pp. 86–88, no. 32 (1257).

designating the proceeds for the *lychnokaia* (λυχνοκαΐαν; the lighting of lamps) and for the general support of the community's welfare.[68]

In September 1304, the nun Magdalene donated a mill with year-round operations to the Monastery of John Prodromos in Serres.[69] Prior to 1318, the nun Kleptoulia endowed the Monastery of Esphigmenou with vineyards located in Krousobon (Strymon).[70] Numerous other women made similar contributions to Athonite monasteries, including nuns such as Paraskeue,[71] Athanasia,[72] and Kallinika[73] along with unnamed nuns from Lemnos. A notable case from 1445 involves the nun Nymphodora, who transferred her entire estate to the Monastery of Xeropotamou on the condition that she would be provided with sustenance for the remainder of her life.[74] This donation represents a clear instance of *adelphaton*—a contractual arrangement by which benefactors received lifelong support in exchange for material contributions. Such arrangements were not only vital for the subsistence of individual monks and nuns but also played a crucial role in bolstering the financial sustainability of female monastic communities.[75]

The Patriarchal Register of Constantinople serves as a key source for understanding the practice of *adelphata*. One illustrative example involves the nuns of the Monastery of Evergetidos tes Sebastokratorisses, who were obliged to supply a quantity of wine to Demetrios Palaiologos Kallistos as part of the *adelphaton* arrangement for his father.[76] This obligation implies

68 Bénou, *Codex B*, pp. 21–23, no. 1 (July 1275). On the correct date of the document, see Kresten and Schaller, "Diplomatische, chonologische und textkritische Beobachtungen," 184–91. On the monastery, see Soustal, *Makedonien, südlicher Teil*, 443–44.

69 Bénou, *Codex B*, pp. 44–45, no. 13 (1301). On the correct date of the document, see Kresten and Schaller, "Diplomatische, chonologische und textkritische Beobachtungen," 210.

70 *Actes d'Esphigménou*, ed. Lefort, p. 108, no. 14 (1318), lines 195–97.

71 *Actes de Lavra*, ed. Guillou et al., vol. 3, p. 62, no. 136 (1355), lines 32–33.

72 *Actes de Lavra*, ed. Guillou et al., vol. 3, p. 63, no. 136 (1355), lines 81–82.

73 *Actes de Lavra*, ed. Guillou et al., vol. 3, p. 219, Appendix 18 (1415), line 30 (forged document).

74 *Actes de Xéropotamou*, ed. Bompaire, p. 216, no. 30 (1445), lines 17–23; Soustal, *Makedonien, südlicher Teil*, 503.

75 Smyrlis, *La fortune des grands monastères byzantins*, 138–45; Magdalino, "Adelphaton," 19; Euangelatou-Notara, "ΑΔΕΛΦΑΤΟΝ. ΨΥΧΙΚΟΝ," 164–70; Laiou, "Economic Activities of Vatopedi in the Fourteenth Century," 71–72.

76 Miklosich and Müller, *Acta et Diplomata graeca Medii Aevi sacra et profana*, vol. 2, pp. 430–31, no. 601 (October 1400); Darrouzès, *Les regestes des Actes du patriarcat*

that the nuns not only had access to wine production but also managed it at a scale sufficient to fulfill such commitments. Moreover, the evidence suggests that *adelphata* were not exclusively granted by male monasteries; female monastic communities could also both provide and receive such arrangements. Broadly defined, *adelphaton* refers to a contractual relationship wherein individuals—including nuns—made donations or endowments to monastic institutions in exchange for material support, sustenance, or a place within the monastic community. This practice reveals the intersection of spiritual motives and pragmatic concerns within the economic structures of Byzantine monasticism.

One such example is the case of Amarantina, who paid one hundred *hyperpyra* to the Mangana Monastery—an amount consistent with typical *adelphaton* arrangements in the fourteenth century.[77] Similarly, the nun Sikile held *adelphata* at the Monastery of St. Demetrios of the Palaiologoi.[78] This case underscores the role of legal proxies, or *epitropoi*, in representing *adelphataria* (recipient of *adelphaton*).[79] For instance, in January 1400, the *protonotarios* and hymnographer George Eugenikos received an *adelphaton* consisting of twenty *meters* of wine and ten *hyperpyra*, followed by an additional ten *hyperpyra* in the summer of the same year. A comparable arrangement is documented in the Lincoln College *typikon*, which references the *adelphata* of the wife of John (later Joasaph) Palaiologos Angelos Branas, acquired in exchange for a vineyard. These examples illustrate the transactional nature of *adelphata*, often involving land or monetary contributions in return for long-term material support.[80]

In these cases, the nuns held *adelphata* as *exomonitai* (non-members of the monastery), entitling them to material support without full integration into the monastic community. In contrast, Theognosia Mauriane possessed

---

de Constantinople, no. 3161; Janin, *La géographie ecclésiastique de l'Empire byzantine*, 184; Talbot, "Old Age in Byzantium," 276–77.

77 Konidares, *Νομικὴ θεώρηση τῶν μοναστηριακῶν τυπικῶν*, 59.

78 Miklosich and Müller, *Acta et Diplomata graeca Medii Aevi sacra et profana*, vol. 2, pp. 325–26, no. 535 (January 1400); Darrouzès, *Les regestes des Actes du patriarcat de Constantinople*, no. 3091.

79 Cf. Konidares and Manaphes, "Επιτελεύτιος βούλησις καὶ διδασκαλία τοῦ οἰκουμενικοῦ πατριάρχου Ματθαίου Α΄," p. 491, line 732, and p. 492, line 743; Darrouzès, *Les regestes des Actes du patriarcat de Constantinople*, no. 3066; Talbot, "Testament of Matthaios I," 1648.

80 *Typicon monasterii Theotoci Bebaias Elpidos*, ed. Delehaye, chap. 122, p. 84; Talbot, "*Bebaia Elpis*," 1557.

adelphata at the Monastery of Andrew *in Krisei*, where she served as abbess, thus holding the status of *esomonitissa* (a full member). According to the agreement she had secured with the monastery, Theognosia was permitted to bequeath one *adelphaton* upon her death. She sought to appoint a new recipient for this *adelphaton* and arranged for two individuals who lived in her cell to retain the same rights within the monastery after her death. However, Patriarch Matthew I in 1400 ruled this arrangement to be impossible. He clarified that *adelphata* were considered goods consecrated to the saint, and that beneficiaries of *adelphata* had to be nuns who remained within the monastery. If these individuals were to leave, they would forfeit their right to any benefits associated with the *adelphaton*.[81]

There were also male recipients of *adelphata* in nunneries, such as the father of Demetrios Palaiologos Kallistos. Serving as *ephoros* of the monastery of Evergetidos tes Sebastokratorisses, he was entitled to receive the *boutziatikon* (a customary payment).[82] When the nuns were unable to fulfill this obligation, he was instead compensated with an *adelphaton* from the monastery.[83]

Adelphata were often closely tied to a nunnery's wine surplus. Vineyards and rental properties—frequent sources of monastic income—encouraged a degree of entrepreneurial activity. By around 1400, many documents explicitly reference the possession of vineyards or gardens, suggesting that such assets were significant components of a nunnery's economy.[84] The cultivation and management of these properties typically required the hiring of

81 Miklosich and Müller, *Acta et Diplomata graeca Medii Aevi sacra et profana*, vol. 2, pp. 353–54, no. 552 (1400); Darrouzès, *Les regestes des Actes du patriarcat de Constantinople*, no. 3107.

82 The *boutziatikon* was a tax on wine production. See Miklosich and Müller, *Acta et Diplomata graeca Medii Aevi sacra et profana*, vol. 2, pp. 379–80, no. 567 (August 1400); Darrouzès, *Les regestes des Actes du patriarcat de Constantinople*, no. 3124.

83 Miklosich and Müller, *Acta et Diplomata graeca Medii Aevi sacra et profana*, vol. 2, pp. 430–31, no. 601 (October 1400); Darrouzès, *Les regestes des Actes du patriarcat de Constantinople*, no. 3161; Macrides, "The Transmission of Property in the Patriarchal Register," 179–88; Janin, *La géographie ecclésiastique de l'Empire byzantine*, 184.

84 Gardens could be a profitable business producing a high income. Miklosich and Müller, *Acta et Diplomata graeca Medii Aevi sacra et profana*, vol. 2, pp. 368–69, no. 559 (March 1400); Darrouzès, *Les regestes des Actes du patriarcat de Constantinople*, no. 3115. Flowers, and especially roses, could be sold to perfumeries (*myrepsika ergasteria*). Therefore, the presence of nunneries close to the market places of Constantinople is not a coincidence. On the other hand, thorny rose hedges were a natural boundary preventing intruders in a land property.

labourers, indicating that even contemplative communities were engaged in practical economic management.[85]

In other cases, nunneries relied on their *paroikoi* for both labour and income. A fiscal reassessment (*apographe kai apokatastasis*) conducted in 1302 provides insight into the economic structure of the female nunnery of Kantakouzene in the theme of Thessaloniki. The assessor, Demetrios Apelmene, confirmed that the assigned *paroikoi* were obligated to fulfill their customary labour duties for the convent. Despite these periodic corvées, the nunnery's overall income remained modest, generating just four *hyperpyra* annually, along with limited in-kind revenues, such as wine and cheese.[86]

In addition to vineyards and gardens, nunneries also generated income through rental properties and workshops. A notable example comes from September 1306, when Anna Doukopoulina Mesopotamitissa formalized her *protage* in a legal document, designating the nunnery of St. Anargyroi *tes Parathyrou* as her hereditary possession.[87] Among the assets endowed to the convent was an orchard located near the Hippodrome in Thessaloniki.[88] Anna transferred the rights to this property to Leon Paulos, who intended to construct houses on the land. In return for development rights, Leon agreed to pay a *telos* of six *kokkia hyperpyra* to the nunnery, derived from the rental profits generated by the houses over a period of twenty-five years.

---

85 Miklosich and Müller, *Acta et Diplomata graeca Medii Aevi sacra et profana*, vol. 2, pp. 499–501, no. 650 (May 1401); Darrouzès, *Les regestes des Actes du patriarcat de Constantinople*, no. 3211; Miklosich and Müller, *Acta et Diplomata graeca Medii Aevi sacra et profana*, vol. 2, pp. 501–2, no. 651 (May 1401); Darrouzès, *Les regestes des Actes du patriarcat de Constantinople*, no. 3212; Miklosich and Müller, *Acta et Diplomata graeca Medii Aevi sacra et profana*, vol. 2, pp. 506–9, no. 654 (June 1401); Darrouzès, *Les regestes des Actes du patriarcat de Constantinople*, no. 3215.

86 *Actes de Lavra*, ed. Guillou et al., vol. 2, pp. 120–21, no. 24 (1302); Dölger, "Aus dem Wirtschaftsleben eines Frauenklosters in der byzantinischen Provinz," 353–54. Dölger assumed that the document ended in Lavra through Ignatios Kalothetos who had brought the nunnery under his possessions. The otherwise unknown nunnery of Kantakouzene must have been located close to Athos. See Soustal, *Makedonien, südlicher Teil*, 1043–44. On the type of document "*apographe kai apokatastasis*," see Pelekidou, *Βυζαντινή διπλωματική*, 60.

87 *Actes de Xénophon*, ed. Papachryssanthou, p. 100, no. 7 (1306); Maniate-Kokkine, "Γυναίκα καὶ "ἀνδρικὰ" οἰκονομικὰ προνόμια," 440–44; Saradi-Mendelovici, "A Contribution to the Study of the Byzantine Notarial Formulas," 72–73. *Protage* (*protagai* in plural) signifies a signature cross at the beginning of the document.

88 The Hippodrome quarter was located south of the port of Kassandra, at the southeast part of Thessaloniki. See Vickers, "The Hippodrome at Thessaloniki," 25–32; Soustal, *Makedonien, südlicher Teil*, 137, 153–54.

The arrangement concerning the orchard near the Hippodrome illustrates a broader pattern in which nunneries entered into leasing and rental agreements to secure long-term revenue. Under the original terms, after the initial twenty-five-year lease, Leon Paulos was given the option to settle his obligations through a one-time payment of twelve *hyperpyra*, effectively ending his financial responsibilities to the nunnery. However, by June 1336, the situation had shifted. Irene, the widow of Leon Paulos, sold the properties—including those derived from the orchard—to the priest-monk Ignatios Syrriares for fifty-eight *hyperpyra*. Significantly, this later transaction was witnessed by the abbess Hypomone, while the *ktetor* (founder or patron) was no longer mentioned. This absence suggests a possible change in the management or legal oversight of the nunnery's assets, potentially reflecting evolving administrative practices or a transition in the monastic leadership.[89]

The complex legal and property history of the land originally belonging to Syrgis[90]—later donated by Anna of Savoy to the nunnery of St. Anargyroi in Thessaloniki—highlights the fluid and often contested nature of property ownership in the Byzantine period. Anna's donation was a characteristic expression of aristocratic piety and patronage, aimed at supporting monastic institutions. However, the later fate of this property underscores the impact of broader political and military upheavals. From a document dated in March 1415, we hear that in 1370/71 Manuel II Palaiologos granted the same garden and courtyard to the *basilissa* Kantakouzene, possibly Isabelle of Lusignan. This act likely served a political purpose, reflecting Manuel's strategy to reinforce alliances with influential families amid instability perhaps during his travels or in preparation for a shift in imperial power dynamics.[91]

Following the Battle of Maritsa in 1371, the Byzantine state engaged in widespread appropriation of properties to reward military service,[92] suggesting that this estate was likely confiscated during that period. By 1384, however, ownership had shifted once more, with the property ultimately

---

89 *Actes de Xénophon*, ed. Papachryssanthou, pp. 179–83, no. 24 (1336).

90 Dölger, *Regesten der Kaiserurkunden des Oströmischen Reiches*, vol. 5, no. 3074. This is Sire Guz de Lusignan, *strategos* of West, city administrator of Serres (1341–1342) and Armenia (1342–1344). See Maniate-Kokkine, "Γυναίκα καὶ "ἀνδρικὰ" οἰκονομικὰ προνόμια," 441n135.

91 *Actes de Lavra*, ed. Guillou et al., vol. 3, pp. 163–66, no. 163 (1415); Dölger, *Regesten der Kaiserurkunden des Oströmischen Reiches*, vol. 5, no. 3346.

92 Smyrlis, "The State, The Land, and Private Property," 66–72.

granted to the monastery of Nea Mone in Thessaloniki. This transfer reflects the dynamic redistribution of land in response to military, political, and monastic interests in the late Byzantine period.[93]

In 1415, the nuns of the Anargyroi convent filed a legal complaint over the loss of a courtyard they claimed as theirs by virtue of Anna of Savoy's original donation. This dispute highlights the continued economic and symbolic significance of monastic property, particularly in a period of political instability and financial constraint. The case was adjudicated by the *katholikoi kritai* (general judges), who acknowledged the substantial investments and improvements made by the Monastery of Nea Mone.[94] Their decision to divide the courtyard between the two institutions reflects a pragmatic compromise, aimed at preserving the economic viability of both monastic communities while recognizing their respective claims.

This ruling reflects a broader legal norm in Byzantine land law: improvements made to land often conferred certain rights to those who had invested in its development.[95] In disputes over ownership, the principle of *epidosis*—that labour and investment could justify partial or full claims to land—was frequently decisive. In the case of the Anargyroi nunnery, this legal logic was central to the decision to divide the courtyard with Nea Mone, whose contributions to the property were acknowledged by the *katholikoi kritai*. Notably, the contested courtyard likely included a wider complex of income-generating assets, such as rental houses and workshops. These were essential for the financial sustainability of the nunnery, which relied heavily on revenues from urban and agricultural properties to maintain its community and fund charitable obligations.

The grant of the courtyard to Kantakouzene likely followed the confiscation of the estate by the state—a practice not uncommon in times of fiscal or military crisis. This allowed the emperor to redistribute valuable property, often as *pronoia*, to secure loyalty or reward service. Over time, the same plot was granted to successive holders, eventually passing to Nea Mone via a *chrysobull* issued in memory of John Kantakouzenos, the grandfather of Manuel II. This sequence of transfers underscores the instability

93 Janin, *Les églises et les monastères des grands centres Byzantins*, 350; Laurent, "Le métropolite de Thessalonique Gabriel," 241–55.

94 *Actes de Lavra*, ed. Guillou et al., vol. 3, pp. 165–66, no. 163 (1415); Bartusis, *Land and Privilege in Byzantium*, 556–58.

95 Justinian, *Novellae*, ed. Schöll and Kroll, no. 64, chap. 2, p. 338.

of land tenure during the late Byzantine period, particularly in urban centres like Thessaloniki.[96]

While the connection to the Kantakouzenoi is unmistakable, several links in the property's transmission remain unclear. What is evident, however, is that the courtyard—along with its associated houses and workshops—represented a consistently profitable asset. Over time, it served the financial interests of multiple parties: the St. Anargyroi nunnery, Kantakouzene, a series of lesser-known *pronoia* holders, and eventually the monastery of Nea Mone. For the nunnery of St. Anargyroi, this property was not directly managed or exploited in agricultural terms; rather, it conformed to a widespread, urban monastic practice. Instead of overseeing the site's development, the nunnery received a *telos* (rental or usage fee) from the income produced by the buildings and commercial structures that were erected there. This arrangement allowed the monastery to benefit financially without assuming the risks or responsibilities of property development.[97]

The case of Xene Soultanina stands out as an intriguing departure from the usual monastic property transactions. As the widow of Alexios Soultanos Palaiologos, Xene not only inherited her husband's estate but actively petitioned for a *pronoia*—a type of land grant typically reserved for military service or aristocratic families—worth the *posotes* (lit. amount)[98] of one hundred *hyperpyra* in the region of Berroia. This *pronoia* had previously been awarded to her late husband, Alexios, and later transferred to their son, Demetrios. The fact that Xene, as a widow, was able to secure this grant for herself in 1344 underscores the fluidity and sometimes personal nature of *pronoia* transactions during the late Byzantine period.[99]

The circumstances surrounding her petition have been extensively discussed.[100] Setting aside the remarkable case of a nun receiving a *pronoia*, I would like to focus on the sum of one hundred *hyperpyra*. This amount corresponds to what Soultanina, as a nun, could have received from a monastery

---

96 Dölger, *Regesten der Kaiserurkunden des Oströmischen Reiches*, vol. 5, no. 3180a.

97 Smyrlis, "The Management of Monastic Estates," 252.

98 On the special meaning of *posotes* in relation to *pronoia*, see Bartusis, *Land and Privilege in Byzantium*, 242–51.

99 *Actes de Vatopédi*, ed. Bompaire et al., vol. 2, p. 190, no. 89 (1344); Dölger, *Regesten der Kaiserurkunden des Oströmischen Reiches*, vol. 5, no. 2896. The monogram of Palaiologina is to be seen on the decoration of St. Sabas *tes Kyriotissas* in Berroia, see Papazotos, *Η Βέροια και οι ναοί της*, 57–58.

100 Bartusis, *Land and Privilege in Byzantium*, 319–20; Maniate-Kokkine, "Γυναίκα καὶ "ἀνδρικὰ" οἰκονομικὰ προνόμια," 431–35.

as an *adelphaton* during this period. However, she opted to obtain a *pronoia*, likely because an *adelphaton* required the donation—and thus the loss—of a land asset to the monastery in exchange for cash or goods. In contrast, a *pronoia* grant was a hereditary asset that she could later dispose of at her discretion. By choosing the *pronoia*, Soultanina could pass it on to other family members and heirs, as it was considered her *gonikon* (private property). This allowed her entire family to benefit from her hereditary grant.

Private Property of Nuns

Up to this point, the general picture is that nuns were landowners who held private property and managed it according to their own discretion.[101] While the Desert Fathers prohibited private property, the fifth Novel of Leo VI established a key principle allowing monks and nuns to own private property and freely dispose of possessions acquired after entering the monastery.[102] This decision builds upon earlier legislation by Justinian, with the notable addition of provisions regarding the handling of assets acquired later.[103]

In general, the *typika* express ambivalent views on private property. Some completely rejected any form of personal possession, while others imposed more moderate restrictions. The *typikon* of Neilos Damilas did not forbid nuns from having personal property but emphasized that they should not become attached to material objects.[104]

Monks and nuns of aristocratic origin were often reluctant to renounce their landowning past. Theoleptos of Philadelphia, the spiritual father of Irene Choumnaina, foundress of the Monastery of Philanthropos-Soter, reprimanded her for her inability to detach herself from her family's affairs. He wrote: "If you cling to your dowry and retain houses and farms, and if

---

101 Talbot, "Personal Poverty in Byzantine Monasticism," 829–41.

102 Leo VI, *Novellae*, ed. Troianos, no. 5, pp. 54–60.

103 For the legal aspects of private property held by monks and nuns, see Konidares, *Το δίκαιον της μοναστηριακής περιουσίας*, 19–20; Konidares, *Νομική θεώρηση τῶν μοναστηριακῶν τυπικῶν*, 156–62; Simon, "Vertragliche Weitergabe des Familienvermögens in Byzanz," 183–96; Macrides, "Dowry and Inheritance in the Late Period," 89–98. Generally, see Laiou, "Family Structure and the Transmission of Property," 51–75.

104 Pétridès, "Le *typikon* de Nil Damilas," chap. 2, p. 97; Talbot, "*Neilos Damilas*," 1468.

any other earthly possessions remain yours, how can you say with Paul, 'the world has been crucified to me,' while the world lives and thrives in you?"[105]

During the political and financial crises of the late Byzantine period, the ability to sell land and other assets—often to monastic institutions—provided nuns with a crucial source of financial security. Around 1260, the nun Giagoupaina in Trebizond sold a piece of land in St. Theodore to the Monastery of Vazelon.[106] In 1330, Xene Indanina Sarantene and her sister, the nun Sophrosyne Sarantene, along with their *protagai*, signed a bill of sale for private assets near Pelorygion/Strymon to the Monastery of Zographou for five hundred *hyperpyra*. This land, adjacent to Zographou's property, was part of the dowry of their deceased sister Anna, and they acted as her representatives.[107] In 1326, Anysia Platyskalitissa sold two houses in Thessaloniki to the Monastery of Chilandar for forty *hyperpyra*.[108] In 1355, Thamar sold a vineyard of two *modioi* in Lemnos to Kakkabiotissa.[109] Additionally, the 1264 *praktikon* of the village of Avion on the Latin-held Island of Kephalenia records a field as belonging to the nun Mastrangelena.[110]

Epigrammatic references on sales or donations made by nuns without a connection to a specific nunnery are a common phenomenon. In some documents from Serres, portions of land are listed with names such as "the nun of Stamenare"[111] or "a portion of land from nun Blandymerine."[112]

Similarly, in the Patriarchal Register, most nuns who appeared before the synodic court defended their rights to private property independently of their convents. The nun Marina, sister of Euphrosyne *tou Chytou* and owner

105 Theoleptos of Philadelphia, *Letters*, ed. Constantinides Hero, p. 78, no. 3.

106 Ouspenskij and Beneševič, *Τα Acta της Μονής Βαζελώνος*, trans. Petropoulos, pp. 200–201, no. 37 (1260).

107 *Actes de Zographou*, ed. Regel et al., pp. 64–68, no. 28 (1330). See new edition Pavlikianov, *The Medieval Greek and Bulgarian Documents of the Athonite Monastery*, pp. 310–17, no. 32 (1330); Maniate-Kokkine, "Γυναίκα καὶ "ἀνδρικὰ" οἰκονομικὰ προνόμια," 429–30, 462–63.

108 *Actes de Chilandar*, ed. Petit and Korablev, pp. 218–20, no. 106 (1326). On the transactions of immovable property in Thessaloniki, see Patlagean, "Transactions immobilières à Thessalonique," 133–44.

109 *Actes de Lavra*, ed. Guillou et al., vol. 3, p. 61, no. 136 (1355), line 10; cf. Haldon, "Limnos, Monastic Holdings and the Byzantine State," 161–215; Kondyli, "Tracing Monastic Economic Interests and Their Impact," 129–50.

110 Tzannetatos, *Πρακτικόν τῆς Λατινικῆς Ἐπισκοπῆς Κεφαλληνίας*, p. 33, line 58.

111 Bénou, *Codex B*, p. 193 no. 117 (fourteenth century).

112 Bénou, *Codex B*, p. 199, no. 120 (fourteenth century), line 18.

of a house in Constantinople (1351), had her rights represented in court by her brother-in-law, George Phoster.[113] In 1359, a nun named Aspietina sold a vineyard for 120 *hyperpyra* to a man named Manuel Pazykes.[114] In another case, Magistrina versus Triphyllina, we learn that Bryennissa, a cousin of Triphyllina, became a nun at the end of her life. She left part of her possessions to the imperial Monastery of *kyra* Martha[115]—possibly the monastery where she was tonsured. Additionally, Pheronike Aspietissa also owned a vineyard.[116]

The nun Hypomone Chrysokephalina Kaukanina owned one-third of a shop at the Kynegos Gate, which she inherited from her grandson.[117] Zenobia Phialitissa bequeathed a house in the area of Eugeniou to her grandson.[118] In another case, the nun Petraliphina served as the administrator of her brother-in-law Maurommates' allotment. However, she neglected her duties, damaging the trees on the land and diminishing its value, ultimately leading to the abandonment of the lot.[119]

Documents of sale involving nuns also appear in Serres. In 1328, Andronikos Lypenares, his son Manuel, and his daughter Irene sold a vineyard of

113 *Patriarchal Register*, vol. 3, ed. Koder et al., p. 230, no. 216 (January 1359), lines 9–30; Darrouzès, *Les regestes des Actes du patriarcat de Constantinople*, no. 2409.

114 *Patriarchal Register*, vol. 3, ed. Koder et al., p. 234, no. 217 (January 1359), lines 11–13; Darrouzès, *Les regestes des Actes du patriarcat de Constantinople*, no. 2410.

115 *Patriarchal Register*, vol. 3, ed. Koder et al., p. 256, no. 218 (November 1360), lines 81–84; Laurent, "Kyra Martha," 296–320; Talbot, "Kyra Martha Nunnery," 1163; Effenberger, "Die Klöster der beiden Kyra Martha," 255–93; Asutay-Effenberger, *Die Landmauer von Konstantinopel-İstanbul*, 211–12.

116 Miklosich and Müller, *Acta et Diplomata graeca Medii Aevi sacra et profana*, vol. 2, p. 363, no. 557 (1400); Darrouzès, *Les regestes des Actes du patriarcat de Constantinople*, no. 3113.

117 Miklosich and Müller, *Acta et Diplomata graeca Medii Aevi sacra et profana*, vol. 2, 358–59, no. 555 (March 1400); Darrouzès, *Les regestes des Actes du patriarcat de Constantinople*, no. 3111.

118 Miklosich and Müller, *Acta et Diplomata graeca Medii Aevi sacra et profana*, vol. 2, 564–65, no. 684 (December 1401); Darrouzès, *Les regestes des Actes du patriarcat de Constantinople*, no. 3247.

119 Miklosich and Müller, *Acta et Diplomata graeca Medii Aevi sacra et profana*, vol. 2, pp. 497–99, no. 649 (May 1401); Darrouzès, *Les regestes des Actes du patriarcat de Constantinople*, no. 3210; Kazhdan, "The Italian and Late Byzantine City," 16. According to the historian Doukas, there was a tremendous lack of firewood during the siege of Constantinople by Bayezit. See Doukas, *Historia*, ed. Grecu, bk 13, ch.7, p. 79, lines 12–14; Bernicolas-Hatzopoulos, "The First Siege of Constantinople by the Ottomans," 39–51.

one *stremma* to the nun Mariamne *tou Blakou* for eighteen *nomismata*.[120] One year later, in 1329, the same individuals sold another vineyard of one *stremma* in the same area to Mariamne.[121] Additionally, in 1328, Mariamne purchased another vineyard of two *stremmata* in Kontarion, this time from Theodore Basilikiotes and his wife, Kale.[122]

Nuns possessed not only land, houses, and vineyards but also holy icons.[123] From these icons (or the lands associated with them) they could generate significant profits. However, great profit often brings complications. For example, in 1316, an ecclesiastical court ruled against Marinia Euphrosyne's claim to half of the income from a wonderworking icon.[124]

In many instances, nuns (whether mothers or sisters of a deceased person) defended their own rights as well as the rights of their grandchildren or nieces and nephews.[125] This is evident in the cases of Euphemia Petraliphina in April 1330[126] and Eleodora Sarantene Tzympinissa from Thessaloniki in 1348.[127] A similar situation is recorded in 1397, when the nun Hypomone

120 Bénou, *Codex B*, pp. 104–7, no. 50 (May 1328).

121 Bénou, *Codex B*, pp. 107–9, no. 51 (July 1329).

122 Bénou, *Codex B*, pp. 109–11, no. 52 (December 1328).

123 On this issue, see Oikonomides, "The Holy Icon as an Asset," 35–44.

124 *Patriarchal Register*, vol. 1, ed. Hunger and Kresten, pp. 274–78, no. 35 (April 1316); Darrouzès, *Les regestes des Actes du patriarcat de Constantinople*, no. 2064; Oikonomides, "The Holy Icon as an Asset," 40; cf. the case of Athanasia Gabraina, Miklosich and Müller, *Acta et Diplomata graeca Medii Aevi sacra et profana*, vol. 2, pp. 513–15, no. 658 (July 1401); Darrouzès, *Les regestes des Actes du patriarcat de Constantinople*, no. 3219. On the case of the nun Eugenia Chrysolorina, see Miklosich and Müller, *Acta et Diplomata graeca Medii Aevi sacra et profana*, vol. 2, pp. 565–66, no. 685 (28 December 1401); Darrouzès, *Les regestes des Actes du patriarcat de Constantinople*, no. 3248; Oikonomides, "The Holy Icon as an Asset," 40–41.

125 See Leo VI, *Novellae*, ed. Troianos, no. 48, pp. 174–76, which permitted the presence of a woman as a witness only in female affairs, such as childbirth. Cf. *Πεῖρα sive Ἐπιτομὴ νόμων*, ed. Zepos and Zepos, bk. 60, chap. 25, p. 217. On the judicial status of women see Beaucamp, "La situation juridique de la femme à Byzance," 145–76; Beaucamp, *Le statut de la femme à Byzance*, vol. 1, pp. 35–45, and vol. 2, pp. 21–31; Buckler, "Women in Byzantine Law About 1100 A.D.," 391–416. On the Medieval West, see Brundage, "Juridical Space," 147–56.

126 *Patriarchal Register*, vol. 1, ed. Hunger and Kresten, pp. 562–66, no. 100 (December 1329); Darrouzès, *Les regestes des Actes du patriarcat de Constantinople*, no. 2153; *Patriarchal Register*, vol. 1, ed. Hunger and Kresten, pp. 578–84, no. 102 (April 1330); Darrouzès, *Les regestes des Actes du patriarcat de Constantinople*, no. 2156.

127 *Patriarchal Register*, vol. 2, ed. Hunger et al., pp. 412–14, no. 152 (December 1348); Darrouzès, *Les regestes des Actes du patriarcat de Constantinople*, no. 2304.

Kaloeidina sought to ensure the proper execution of her daughter's testament, as her son-in-law, Theodore Kaloeidas, appeared unable to fulfill this responsibility.[128]

In each of these cases, a written will of the deceased family member is central to the discussions of the Synod, while the nuns (whether mothers or sisters) act as executors of their wishes.[129]

The Poverty of Nunneries and Nuns

The struggle to maintain financial stability was a significant aspect of life in many convents, affecting both the well-being of the nuns and the functioning of their religious communities. While some affluent women and nuns could rely on their possessions as a safeguard for the future, others were compelled to sell or donate land to wealthier monasteries, including those on Mount Athos. In return, they often received an annual stipend or secure accommodation in a nunnery for the remainder of their lives.

The nun Eupraxia Sabentzina owned a house in Constantinople, which she donated to the Monastery of Lavra around 1342.[130] At the end of the thirteenth century, the widow Zoe Syropoulina explained her decision to sell her ancestral property—including three vineyards and four fields—to the nunnery of Nea Petra, where she planned to take monastic vows. Syropoulina cited her desperate circumstances: she was poor, childless, homeless, and lacked sufficient food.[131] Byzantine texts often portray a kind of psychological hardship that accompanied physical poverty and deprivation, which frequently drove women to seek refuge or support from powerful individuals or institutions, such as monasteries and nunneries.

Financial hardship also led nuns and their families to mortgage property in exchange for loans. The nun Eulogia Petzikopoulos and her mother,

128 Miklosich and Müller, *Acta et Diplomata graeca Medii Aevi sacra et profana*, vol. 2, pp. 347–52, no. 549–50 (October 1397); Darrouzès, *Les regestes des Actes du patriarcat de Constantinople*, nos. 3061 and 3063.

129 The nun Martha Baropolitissa managed the money her nephew earned from the sale of his family's houses. Miklosich and Müller, *Acta et Diplomata graeca Medii Aevi sacra et profana*, vol. 2, pp. 447–48, no. 613 (November 1400); Darrouzès, *Les regestes des Actes du patriarcat de Constantinople*, no. 3173. On sale transactions in Constantinople during this period, see Papagianne, "Η αγορά των ακινήτων στην Κωνσταντινούπολη," 145–55.

130 *Actes de Lavra*, ed. Guillou et al., vol. 3, p. 24, no. 123 (1342), lines 114–15.

131 Miklosich and Müller, *Acta et Diplomata graeca Medii Aevi sacra et profana*, vol. 4, pp. 394, no. 27 (1271), lines 24–27.

Martha/Melane, owned land and houses in the Paramonou Quarter of Thessaloniki. Around 1325, they secured a loan of fifty *hyperpyra* from the Monastery of Chilandar. Two years later, unable to repay the debt, Eulogia sold the mortgaged properties to the monastery for 140 *hyperpyra*—an amount that covered the cancellation of the original debt and included an additional payment of ninety gold coins.[132]

When the risk of impoverishment became too great, nuns, monks, and even laypeople sometimes assumed control of nunneries in an effort to improve their financial standing. The nun Martha Syriana, for example, secured the *ephoreia* and *dioikesis* as well as the *ktetorikon dikaion*, of the Pausolype Monastery for the remainder of her life after making substantial improvements to the nunnery. The previous holder of these rights, the nun Kallinike, had already agreed to the arrangement. However, Syriana was obligated to repair the church and enhance the monastic properties as part of the agreement.[133]

In another instance, the nun Theodoule Tzouroulene rebuilt a church that had fallen into disrepair. During her absence, a neighbour, Kavallarios Kontostephanos, encroached on the property and planted a vineyard on the land surrounding the church. After his expulsion, Patriarch Matthew I granted Theodoule the *ktetoreia* and *ephoreia* of the church, formally recognizing her rights over it.[134]

When funds were scarce or when faced with pressure from wealthier monasteries, some nunneries resorted to selling parts of their property. The six nuns of the Taxiarchai Nunnery in the Serres region granted a piece of non-arable land to the Monastery of Prodromos for the construction of a *monydrion* dedicated to St. John Chrysostom. A few years later, they sold a vineyard to the same monastery for ten *hyperpyra* to cover their basic living expenses and lighting costs.[135]

Another indicator of potential poverty within monastic institutions was the transformation of female monasteries into male ones, and vice versa.

---

132 *Actes de Chilandar*, ed. Petit and Korablev, pp. 230–35, no. 112 (1327); Janin, *Les églises et les monastères des grands centres Byzantins*, 363, 404, and 415.

133 Miklosich and Müller, *Acta et Diplomata graeca Medii Aevi sacra et profana*, vol. 1, pp. 454–55, no. 200 (January 1365); Darrouzès, *Les regestes des Actes du patriarcat de Constantinople*, no. 2476; Stolte, "Law for Founders," 128–29.

134 Miklosich and Müller, *Acta et Diplomata graeca Medii Aevi sacra et profana*, vol. 2, pp. 395–99, no. 579 (June 1400); Darrouzès, *Les regestes des Actes du patriarcat de Constantinople*, no. 3138.

135 Bénou, *Codex B*, pp. 21–23, no. 1 (July 1275).

A notable example is the male Monastery of Blachernitissa in Epiros, which was vacated by its monks to accommodate fugitive nuns, owing to an insufficient number of nunneries.[136] Similarly, a monastery in Didymoteichon, initially inhabited by monks, was converted for female use but soon fell into disrepair. The nuns were eventually relocated to other convents, prompting the *ktetor*—who was concerned about further financial deterioration—to petition the Patriarch and the Synod for permission to restore the monastery to its original male status.[137]

Female monastic communities were often more susceptible to poverty than their male counterparts due to their limited engagement with the external world. The restricted mobility of nuns impeded their ability to manage and oversee monastic properties effectively. Additionally, their comparatively narrower social networks curtailed access to influential benefactors and consistent financial support. These vulnerabilities were well understood by the Byzantines, who sought to mitigate them through charitable donations.

In his 1325 testament, Theodore Sarantenos, founder of the Prodromos Monastery in Berroia, stipulated that a substantial annual provision of grain and wine be allocated to impoverished female monastic communities. His wife, Eudokia Angelina Komnene, was similarly noted for her charitable activities, including the distribution of food and clothing to the poor in Berroia.[138] Likewise, the monk Gregory Isbes bequeathed fifty *hyperpyra* to an unnamed nun in his will.[139] The testament of Patriarch Isidore I Boucheir (r. 1347–1350) further illustrates this pattern of support: he directed that the wine and grain stores of the Great Church be divided into three portions—one for the clergy, one for impoverished nuns, and one for his assistants, both monastic and lay.[140]

In July 1339, the nun Hypomone, widow of the *sakellarios* Mourmouras, along with her family, donated the Monastery of St. George Kryonerites—comprising 244 *modioi* of land—to the Prodromos Monastery near Serres. Documentary evidence indicates that the monastery had originally been founded by Mourmouras and his wife, who possessed the full rights

136 John Apokaukos, *Praxis on the Blachernitissa Monastery*, 17; Talbot, "Affirmative Action in the 13th Century," 405–6.

137 *Patriarchal Register*, vol. 2, ed. Hunger et al., p. 190, no. 127 (May 1340); Darrouzès, *Les regestes des Actes du patriarcat de Constantinople*, no. 2199.

138 *Actes de Vatopédi*, ed. Bompaire et al., vol. 1, p. 358, no. 64 (1325).

139 *Actes de Docheiariou*, ed. Oikonomides, p. 207, no. 34 (1361), lines 6–8.

140 *Patriarchal Register*, vol. 2, ed. Hunger et al., p. 440, no. 156 (February 1350), lines 188–94.

of a *ktetor* (*τέλειαν δεσποτείαν καὶ κυριότητα*).[141] Despite the donation, the Mourmouras family retained the right to receive a siteresion, including provisions of food and firewood. The donation was formally ratified by the metropolitan of Serres; thus, the monastery of Kryonerites, designated as a *metochion*, was duly recorded in the official inventory of assets.[142]

This charter offers valuable insight into the quantities of food and provisions deemed necessary for sustaining monastic life. A comparable testament from the fifteenth century further illuminates such practices. In 1421, George Goudeles stipulated in his will that each of the forty nuns residing in the Convent of St. Nicholas was to receive annually one *modios* of grain—approximately 322.3 to 234 kg., or roughly 650 g. per day—along with twelve *metra* of wine (with one *metron* equivalent to 10.25 litres), and firewood valued at one *hyperpyron* (corresponding to approximately 712.5 kg.).[143]

George Goudeles, who was actively engaged in trade with the Genoese, provided substantial financial support to the Convent of St. Nicholas, with this support being primarily funded through the proceeds of his commercial enterprises. In addition to monetary aid, he endowed the convent with a variety of income-generating assets, including vineyards, gardens, workshops, and properties—referred to as *luoghi*[144]—in Genoa, Constantinople, Pera, and other locations.

The financial condition of nuns and their communities is occasionally illuminated through indirect or unexpected sources. One such example is the case of the double Monastery of Athanasios, addressed in a patriarchal *sigillion* dated 1383.[145] This document includes an excerpt from the *typikon*, which outlines the internal organization of the monastic community, including regulations concerning diet and discipline. Although the two communities—male and female—resided in separate quarters, they shared a common abbot and operated within a unified financial framework. The nuns occupied

141 Bénou, *Codex B*, p. 282, no. 162 (1339); cf. Guillou, *Les archives de Saint-Jean-Prodrome sur le Mont Menecee*, pp. 112–13, no. 34; Smyrlis, *La fortune des grands monastères byzantins*, 264; Soustal, *Makedonien, südlicher Teil*, 443–44.

142 Bénou, *Codex B*, pp. 285–86, no. 163 (July 1339?), and pp. 287–88, no. 164 (July 1339?).

143 Ganchou, "L'ultime testament de Géôrgios Goudélès," p. 348, lines 28–31; Schilbach, *Byzantinische Metrologie*, 98.

144 Felloni, *Amministrazione ed etica nella Casa di San Giorgio*, 3–4.

145 Miklosich and Müller, *Acta et Diplomata graeca Medii Aevi sacra et profana*, vol. 2, p. 80, no. 375 (March 1383); Darrouzès, *Les regestes des Actes du patriarcat de Constantinople*, no. 2754; cf. Fusco, "L'encomio di Teoctisto Studita per Atanasio I di Costantinopoli," p. 121, lines 16–20, chap. 14.

Table 3.5. Athanasios Double Monastery—list of properties.

	Male Monastery — Properties	**Value and Comments**
1	Vineyards inside the monastery	2485 *hyperpyra*
2	Oil press	200 *hyperpyra*
3	The vineyard of Anapnoas and the garden which a certain Hierakina pawned. They should be divided in *dimoira* and *trita*.	
4	The fields of St. Theodore	
5	Vineyards of St. Theodore	264 *hyperpyra*
6	Part from *telos* of Pinakidion	80 *hyperpyra*. From this amount, the nuns should have received 23. The rest was divided in *dimoira* and *trita*.
7	The fields of the watermill in Pinakidion (?) to be divided in *dimoira* and *trita* between monks and nuns	
8	Fields *tou Barangou* in Pinakidion	The rest—*in modioi tes metras* — of the part of the nunnery (cf. female monastery, no. 8, below).
9	3 horses used at the watermills in Pinakidion (?)	
10	3 *zeugaria*	
11	Vineyards of Pinakidion	
12	Fields in Mitylene	
	Female Monastery — Properties	**Value and Comments**
1	Vineyards near the monastery and a vineyard together with fields by the Golden Gate[146]	1076 *hyperpyra*
2	Bakery in Constantinople	100 *hyperpyra*
3	The vineyard of Anapnoas and the garden pawned to a certain Hierakina which should be divided in *dimoira* und *trita*	
4	The fields of Monasteriotes[147]	
5	The vineyards of Monasteriotes	240 *hyperpyra*. Like the monks, they received 132 *hyperpyra*, while 108 *hyperpyra* were paid to them due to a debt
6	A watermill in Pinakidion (?)	Rent: 40 *hyperpyra*
7	The fields of the watermill were divided in *dimoira* and *trita* (cf. male monastery, no. 7, above)	
8	The field *tou Barangou* in Pinakidion	78 *modioi tes metras*
9	A horse used at the watermill	
10	A *zeugarion*	
11	Buildings in *Mikra Pyle* in Constantinople[148]	
12	A field in Rhaidestos	

146 On Golden Gate, see Asutay-Effenberger, *Die Landmauer von Konstantinopel-İstanbul*, 54–71.

147 Monasteriotes may have been the father-in-law of a certain Sebasteianos and *oikeios* of the emperor, *Patriarchal Register*, vol. 2, ed. Hunger et al., pp. 390–99, no. 150 (October 1348); Darrouzès, *Les regestes des Actes du patriarcat de Constantinople*, no. 2300.

148 Janin, *Constantinople byzantine*, 297.

a subordinate position, relying on the monks for the management and provision of their material needs.[149]

Difficulties emerged soon after the death of Athanasios. The monks, tasked with sustaining both their own community and the nuns, became overburdened, which led to a decline in their productivity and overall economic output. As a result, the monastery faced significant financial hardship. In response, Neilos Kerameus and the Synod in 1383 resolved to formally separate the two communities and to divide their assets accordingly.[150]

Given that the monastic community of men was significantly larger than that of the women, the division of landholdings followed the principle of a two-to-one ratio, in accordance with Justinianic law. While vineyards and other fixed assets were to be apportioned based on their assessed value, arable land was divided using the traditional categories of *dimoira* (two-thirds) and *trita* (one-third), reflecting the demographic and administrative structure of the monastery (see Table 3.5).[151]

The document begins by enumerating the possessions located closest to the monastery, gradually progressing to those situated farther afield. It first references the vineyards within the monastic enclosure, followed by the workshops in Constantinople, which included an oil press and a bakery. The inventory then turns to more distant holdings, concluding with properties in Mytilene and Rhaidestos. The final section addresses and resolves the monastery's outstanding debts. Among these properties, the vineyard of Anapnoas—likely situated in Thrace, outside Constantinople—is of particular note.[152] In September 1394, the nun Eugenia appears to have sold this vineyard to her son, the priest-monk Theophanes.[153] Similarly, the estate of Pinakidion and its associated holdings—including land, water mills, vineyards, horses, and *zeugaria* (yoke teams or plough oxen)—were also located beyond the city limits.[154]

---

149 The expression *κοινὴν δὲ καὶ τὴν τροφὴν* should not be understood as common meals but much more as a common diet. For a relevant discussion in the monastery of Christos Philanthropos, see Trone, "A Constantinopolitan Double Monastery of the Fourteenth Century," 86; Gregoropoulos, *Θεολήπτου Φιλαδελφείας τοῦ Ὁμολογητοῦ*, 95–108.

150 Miklosich and Müller, *Acta et Diplomata graeca Medii Aevi sacra et profana*, vol. 2, pp. 80–83, no. 375 (March 1383); Darrouzès, *Les regestes des Actes du patriarcat de Constantinople*, no. 2754; Boojamra, *Church Reform in the Late Byzantine Empire*, 166.

151 Miklosich and Müller, *Acta et Diplomata graeca Medii Aevi sacra et profana*, vol. 2, p. 82, no. 375 (March 1383).

152 Janin, *La géographie ecclésiastique de l'Empire byzantine*, 512.

153 Hunger, "Zwei byzantinische Urkunden der späten Palaiologenzeit," p. 305, lines 5–6, no. 2.

154 Eustathios of Thessalonike, "Adversus implacabilitatis accusationem," p. 111,

Closer to the city was the vineyard of St. Theodoros. The arable land in Mytilene was linked to the *metochion* of St. Theophano, which belonged to the Monastery of Athanasios on the island.[155] If this identification is correct, it implies that the synodic ruling of 1331—mandating the return of the *metochion* to the Metropolis of Methymna—was never fully implemented. The bulk of the monastery's debt, amounting to 250 *hyperpyra*, was assigned to the monks, while the nuns were responsible for only 24.5 *hyperpyra*.[156]

According to the synodic decree, the monks received assets valued at three thousand *hyperpyra*, whereas the nuns were allotted property worth two thousand *hyperpyra*. As I have argued in a previous article, the Monastery of Athanasios was actively engaged in Black Sea trade, a factor that may have contributed to both its indebtedness and the subsequent tensions between the male and female communities.[157]

Preliminary Conclusions

In conclusion, nunneries in the late Byzantine period were markedly more susceptible to poverty than male monasteries. The few that attained relative wealth were typically established by members of the aristocracy, the imperial family, or, in later periods, affluent merchants, such as George Goudeles. Unlike many male institutions, female monasteries rarely succeeded in becoming significant landowners—a limitation that curtailed their social influence and institutional power. This pattern was also reflected in the lives of individual nuns. Wealthy women who entered monastic life often retained ownership of their personal assets, including dowries and family estates.[158] Rather than dedicating these resources to the communal benefit of their convents, they frequently preserved them for personal or familial use. Consequently, transactions involving nuns, nunneries, or monasteries were often shaped more by economic considerations than by purely spiritual motivations.

---

lines 74–75, no. 14; Janin, *La géographie ecclésiastique de l'Empire byzantine*, 516.

155 *Patriarchal Register*, vol. 1, ed. Hunger and Kresten, p. 608, no. 106 (April 1331), lines 30–31; Darrouzès, *Les regestes des Actes du patriarcat de Constantinople*, no. 2164.

156 Miklosich and Müller, *Acta et Diplomata graeca Medii Aevi sacra et profana*, vol. 2, p. 83, no. 375 (March 1383); Darrouzès, *Les regestes des Actes du patriarcat de Constantinople*, no. 2754.

157 Mitsiou, "Das Doppelkloster des Patriarchen Athanasios I," 87–106.

158 Laiou, "The Role of Women in Byzantine Society," 238–39.

Chapter 4

FEMALE MONASTIC NETWORKS OF ART AND KNOWLEDGE

IN LATE BYZANTIUM, both rural and urban nuns contributed gifts of piety and commissioned portraits accompanied by inscriptions or epigrams. These intertwined texts and images often imitated stereotypical motifs and adhered to existing patterns of representation. On a different level, female monastics supported literate circles by patronizing intellectuals and commissioning manuscripts. These activities enabled them to become part of more complex networks of artistic and scholarly production. Additionally, late Byzantine nuns used images and texts to depict themselves, express their desires, and record their thoughts.

Female Monastics and Art

Artistic objects frequently represent the donations of patrons or founders. Anna Komnene Raoulaina Strategopoulina, for example, donated manuscripts, liturgical vessels, and other treasures to the Krataios nunnery in Constantinople in the late thirteenth century.[1] Empress Theodora Palaiologina similarly donated liturgical books and vessels to the Lips and Anargyroi nunneries. Additionally, she commissioned textile furnishings for her tomb at Lips.[2]

Art objects could also serve as material expressions of thanksgiving for healing miracles or assistance in difficult situations. These specific individual donations were votive in nature, praising God, the Virgin Mary, and the saints for their help. For instance, Empress Helen/Hypomone Palaiologina commissioned a silver cross, which is now housed in the Monastery of Dionysiou.[3] An inscription at the base of the obverse vertical arm identifies this cross as a votive offering: "Votive offering from the Lady Helena

1 For the Krataios nunnery, see Janin, *La géographie ecclésiastique de l'Empire byzantine*, 510–11.

2 Talbot, "Empress Theodora Palaiologina, Wife of Michael VIII," 299 and 301; Melichar, *Empresses of Late Byzantium*, 92–93.

3 Loverdou-Tsigarida, "Cross of the Empress Helena Palaiologina," no. 9.23, pp. 346–47; Talbot, "Female Patronage in the Palaiologan Era," 269; Evans,

Palaiologina, Mistress of the Romans, wife of Emperor Manuel Palaiologos, daughter of Constantine Dragaš, Prince of Serbia."[4] On the front of the cross is depicted the Crucifixion of Christ, while the reverse features the Baptism of Christ. Katia Loberdou-Tsigarida identifies similarities with the so-called "Cross of Constantine the Great," which is associated with a member of the Palaiologoi. However, this cross is dated prior to Palaiologina's entry into the monastery in 1448. This explains why the identity markers on the cross refer to her as empress, wife, and daughter rather than as a nun.

In Vatopedi, there is an icon of the Virgin Dexiokratousa (holding the Christ Child in her right arm), dated to the first half of the fourteenth century. This icon, along with a corresponding icon of Christ, originally formed a diptych.[5] The original inscription has been obscured by later additions. It was commissioned by Anna Philanthropene, as attested by an epigram written on the now much-damaged silver gilt frame. Fortunately, the text can be adequately reconstructed, as it was also recorded in Hagion Oros, Vatopediou, MS 1037, fol. 25v (thirteenth century).[6] The donor has recently been identified as Anna Philanthropene Kantakouzene Komnene Palaiologina Bryennissa, granddaughter of Theodora Synadene, the foundress of Bebaia Elpis. Her portrait, along with that of her husband, Michael Philanthropenos, is preserved in the Lincoln College *typikon* (Lincoln College, MS gr. 35, fol. 4).[7] The silver frame, the epigram, and possibly the icon itself were gifts to the convent. The epigram may have been composed by Manuel Philes, the most prominent poet of his time.[8]

Byzantium, 122–23. For the text of the inscription, see Millet et al., *Recueil des inscriptions chrétiennes de l'Athos*, p. 159, no. 461.

4 Effenberger, "Ein byzantinisches Emailkreuz mit Besitzerinschrift," 116 (Lips Monastery).

5 Loberdou-Tsigarida, "Βυζαντινή μικροτεχνία," pp. 492–93, fig. 437; Tsigaridas and Loberdou-Tsigarida, *Ιερά Μεγίστη Μονή Βατοπαιδίου*, pp. 357–60, figs. 313–14.

6 *Diktyon*: 19181; Eugenios, *Περιγραφή ἔμμετρος τῆς ἐν Ἄθῳ ἱερᾶς καὶ σεβασμίας Μεγίστης Λαύρας τοῦ Βατοπεδίου*, 21. English translation from Talbot, "Female Patronage in the Palaiologan Era," 260–61. See also Rhoby, *Byzantinische Epigramme auf Ikonen und Objekten der Kleinkunst*, pp. 91–94, no. Ik 26.

7 See Kiilerich, "Attire and Personal Appearance in Byzantium," 439–51, 479–511 (illustrations).

8 Carr, "Donors in the Frames of Icons," pp. 193–94, fig. 2, and pp. 196–97n45; cf. on frames and revetments, Peers, *Sacred Shock*, 101–31.

Similarly, Eulogia Komnene Palaiologina requested from Philes a long epigram with a votive character.[9] Modern scholars have focused on the miracle-working presence of the Virgin and on several elements of a standard miracle account. Eulogia Palaiologina was cured of numerous maladies through the assistance of the Virgin, not by her doctors. The poem refers specifically to a *sostron*: a silver gilt frame or revetment.[10] However, the verses are precious due to the personal information they provide about the life of an unfortunate aristocratic woman. The poem describes the painful journey that led her to take monastic vows. Eulogia, daughter of a *megas stratopedarches* and niece of Andronikos II, had poor health since her childhood. She admits that she was easily susceptible to disease, sometimes being on the verge of dying. No mention of a specific illness is made. Constant health problems formed an obstacle to any marriage plans, leaving her with monastic life as her only option. Her decision was therefore a thanksgiving action, which also saved her from a social dead-end.

Some nuns and donors were "monumentalized" through portraits and inscriptions or by the combination of both in a sacred space. Sharon Gerstel suggested that in Byzantium "the use of monumental decoration as a primary source for the space women occupied in the church was common."[11] Monumental painting offers interesting material on the external appearance of nuns and the way they chose to be depicted. On the other hand, the inscriptions reveal the names of female monastics who left their mark on monuments in the countryside and the cities.

Modern scholars have turned their attention to the study of nuns in the periphery of Byzantium; more accurately, they have focused on their involvement in the donation and patronage of village churches. Sophia Kalopissi-Verti has collected dedicatory inscriptions and donor portraits in churches of thirteenth-century Greece. From her data, we can infer that of seventy-nine inscriptions and portraits, only five (6%) mention exclusively women, while thirty-four (43%) were commissioned by both men and women. Additional material from other regions informed later studies by Sophia Kalopissi-Verti, Sharon Gerstel, and Alice-Mary Talbot. Geographically, we can

9 Manuel Philes, *Carmina*, ed. Miller, chap. 1, poem 168, pp. 77–78.

10 On *sostron*, see Talbot, "Epigrams of Manuel Philes on the Theotokos tes Peges," 152–53.

11 Brooks, "Women's Authority in Death," 317–32; Papamastorakes, "Επιτύμβιες παραστάσεις κατά τη μέση και ύστερη βυζαντινή περίοδο," 285–304.

detect clusters in the representation of nuns in monuments in the Peloponnese, Crete, and Rhodes.[12]

Kalopissi-Verti acknowledged that "the woman who participates in a donation is not mentioned only as wife but also as sister or mother." This attitude is exemplified in the inscription of St. George in Longanikon in Lakonia (1374/75); one of the founders (priest and notary Basil Kourteses) is mentioned with two female relatives, i.e., his mother (nun Maria/Martha) and his sister (nun Magdalena).[13]

Sole female donors in villages are usually nuns or widows.[14] It is no surprise that these identities often coincide. The wall paintings of the cave church of Ai-Giannakes in Zoupena (Lakonia) reveal two phases (eleventh and thirteenth centuries). In the last phase of the hermitage, an inscription dated to this period is located to the right of St. Basil and reads: "Remember, Lord, the soul of your servant, the nun Euphrosyne Glyka. Forgive her on the Day of Judgment."[15] Adjacent to the figure of St. Catherine is the inscription of the name of a laywoman, Kale Alype.

By setting their names and images among the saints, the nun-donors hoped for closeness to the sacred and acceptance of their supplications. As mentioned earlier, it is a general tendency to depict nuns together with family members. A dedicatory inscription on the south part of the western wall names the nun Kataphyge Alexena and her children as responsible for the foundation and decoration of the church of Hagia Triada near Psinthos on the island of Rhodes (1407/8).[16] The widow and nun Kataphyge, dressed in monastic garments and depicted in a three-quarters pose, presents a model

---

12 A search on similar material from Asia Minor and Epiros has not added any further names of nuns. For Middle-Byzantine Macedonia and Thrace see Zarras, *Ideology and Patronage in Byzantium*.

13 Feissel and Philippidis-Braat, "Inventaires en vue d'un recueil des inscriptions historiques," no. 78, pp. 339–40; Chassoura, *Les peintures murales byzantines des églises*, pp. 18–24, fig. 12; Gerstel and Kalopissi-Verti, "Female Church Founders," 209.

14 Gerstel and Talbot, "Nuns in the Byzantine Countryside," 486; Gerstel and Kalopissi-Verti, "Female Church Founders," 195–212.

15 Drandakes, "Ο σπηλαιώδης ναός του Άι-Γιαννάκη στη Ζούπενα," 81–82; Gerstel, *Rural Lives and Landscapes in Late Byzantium*, 148.

16 Christophorake, "Χορηγικές μαρτυρίες στους ναούς της μεσαιωνικής Ρόδου," pp. 460–61, plate 181a; Bitha, "Ενδυματολογικές μαρτυρίες στις τοιχογραφίες της μεσαιωνικής Ρόδου," pp. 435, 445, fig. 2: ια, plate 171γ; Gerstel and Talbot, "Nuns in the Byzantine Countryside," 486; Gerstel, *Rural Lives and Landscapes in Late Byzantium*, 70, 101.

of her church to Christ. It appears that after her husband's death, Kataphyge built the church to serve as the final resting place for both herself and her husband.[17]

An intriguing female monastic portrait has survived in Crete: the nun Martha, depicted in the Koimesis Church at Alikambos (1315), is shown in a kneeling position, gazing towards the enthroned Virgin on her right. Her supplication, positioned to the left of Martha, reads: "Remember the servant of God, Martha the nun." Martha is dressed in a brown *himation* (robe) and a black cloak, with her head covered by a turban of brown or a light colour.[18]

The names of some nuns and donors of village churches are preserved only in inscribed texts. The nun Kallinike is one of the donors mentioned in the Church of Archangel Michael in Polemitas (Mesa Mane, Peloponnese) (1278).[19] A painted inscription on the north wall above the entrance door records the names of about twenty-nine donors and their donations. However, Kallinike's exact contribution is not specified. Additionally, her name appears after the date in the first part of the inscription, without any mention of her affiliation with a nunnery. This suggests she may have resided in the village or maintained close ties with her family and the local community. Gerstel argues that she was related to other families in Polemitas and asserts a possible connection to the Chapel of St. Nicholas, located near the Church of Archangel Michael.[20]

St. Theodore Church in Ano Poula Kepoulas (Mesa Mane) (thirteenth century) bears testimony to the nun Kyriake, daughter of Leon Ropounges. The poorly written inscription indicates that the monk Euthymios Lekousas was the primary builder of the church. The same monk appears in a portrait as an older man and in two additional inscriptions on the south wall of the church.[21] Kyriake's figure stands in a supplicating gesture next to St. Theodore Teron. She is wearing brown clothes and a white head covering. In her hands, she holds a scroll with a red cord.[22] The monument is connected with

---

17 Bolanakes, "Ναός Αγίας Τριάδας Ψίνθου," 825–26; Archontopoulos and Papabasileiou, "Ρόδος," no. 53, p. 209.

18 Gerstel, *Rural Lives and Landscapes in Late Byzantium*, 68, 149.

19 Kalopissi-Verti, *Dedicatory Inscriptions and Donor Portraits*, 71 (text of the incription), 73 (a list of all the donors); Gerstel, *Rural Lives and Landscapes in Late Byzantium*, 102, 147 (fig. 76).

20 Gerstel, *Rural Lives and Landscapes in Late Byzantium*, 147.

21 Gerstel, *Rural Lives and Landscapes in Late Byzantium*, 140.

22 Drandakes, "Ο Ταξιάρχης τῆς Χαροῦδας καὶ ἡ κτητορικὴ ἐπιγραφή του," 287–88; Drandakes, "Ἔρευναι εἰς τὴν Μάνην," 127. Kalopissi-Verti (*Dedicatory Inscriptions

the village of Kounos and its church, St. Kyriake, located below Ano Poula. We can presume that the nun Kyriake Ropounge had family ties to the monk Euthymios and to the village of Kounos.[23]

An inscription in St. Basil Pediadas in Crete (1291) lists a nun among the donors of the St. John Church.[24] Her name has not survived, but she may have been a relative of Nicholas Tzyanontopoulos, who is also mentioned in the same inscription. Among the donors of the single-aisled Church of St. Marina (1300) in the village of Mournes (in Rethymnon, Crete) is the nun Eugenia, mother of the three brothers Koudoumniakos.[25] In Crete, there are many examples of nuns donating together with other village members for the restoration of small churches.[26] Other inscriptions on the same island are funerary, such as the one for the nun Euphrosyne Drakontopoula (uncertain reading) in the Church of St. John at Stilos (1271 or 1280).[27]

On the island of Chalke, northwest of Rhodes, stands the small Church of Theotokos Enniameritissa. A dedicatory inscription mentions the financial support of two nuns, Agnese and Magdalena, for the completion of the wall paintings. This occurred on August 11, 1367, just a few days before the feast of the church on August 23. Other donors included a deacon and two laymen. Maria Sigala, who has studied the monument, argued that the nuns either belonged to a nunnery, came from Rhodes, or were anchorites.[28] The area is well known for its hermitages and the special form of anchoritism. If these nuns were anchorites, then we need to reevaluate our perception of female monasticism as solely an urban coenobitical phenomenon. Hermitages for women may have existed in other areas as well, such as on Mount Skollis in Achaia (Peloponnese). According to Myrto Georgopoulou-Verra,

---

and Donor Portraits, 106) has offered an incomplete reading of the text. In her study, *Rural Lives and Landscapes in Late Byzantium* (141–42), Gerstel included the better reading of the incription by Katsafados, "Νέα στοιχεία για τις αφιερωτικές επιγραφές," 275–88.

23 Gerstel, *Rural Lives and Landscapes in Late Byzantium*, 140.

24 Kalopissi-Verti, *Dedicatory Inscriptions and Donor Portraits*, 93.

25 Gerola, *Monumenti veneti nell'isola di Creta*, vol. 4, pp. 490–91; Albani, "Οι τοιχογραφίες του ναού της Αγίας Μαρίνας στον Μουρνέ της Κρήτης," 211–22.

26 On the nuns Kataphyge and Eugenia in the Saviour's church at Blithias (1358–1359), see Gerola, *Monumenti veneti nell'isola di Creta*, vol. 4, p. 438; Spatharakis, *Dated Byzantine Wall Paintings of Crete*, 106–7.

27 Gerola, *Monumenti veneti nell'isola di Creta*, vol. 4, p. 428.

28 Sigala, "Η Παναγία η Οδηγήτρια η Ενναμερίτισσα στη Χάλκη της Δωδεκανήσου," 329–81.

the small churches of St. George and Theotokos (in the cave of Portes) include iconographic elements that suggest the existence of a female monastic community.[29]

Contrary to those in villages, female donor portraits in Constantinople were more elaborate. The most outstanding example is the portrait of Maria/Melania of the Mongols in the esonarthex (inner narthex) of the Chora Monastery (Kariye Camii).[30] In this mosaic, the image takes precedence over the text. Scholars have speculated about the reasons for Melania's prominent position, concluding that her lavish donations of golden textiles and an eleventh-century gospel manuscript with a new binding played a significant role.

This information is recorded in a fourty-eight-line epigram by Manuel Philes, copied in two columns on two pages inserted at the end of the donated manuscript.[31] Maria asserts that these gifts were offered to the Virgin in gratitude for her salvation from myriad dangers. Another theory is it may connect to a personal ailment of Maria/Melania, as her depiction lies beneath the image of the woman with the issue of blood.[32] However, her donations may have been even more lavish and precious than the epigram suggests, especially considering that her portrait was placed near that of the twelfth-century restorer of Chora. Her figure stands next to the entrance to the *naos*, to the left of the figures of Christ and the Virgin. Isaakios Komnenos stands on the right side of the Virgin. Maria of the Mongols, wearing a tall headdress and a dark mantle, is depicted in a kneeling position with her hands extended in supplication to Christ.[33]

29 Georgopoulou-Verra, "Βυζαντινά μονύδρια και ασκηταριά στην περιοχή του όρους Σκόλλις," 120, 122.

30 Connor, *Women of Byzantium*, 309–16.

31 Sherry, "The Poem of Maria Komnene Palaiologina to the Virgin," 181–82; Asdracha, "A Brief Commentary to the Verses of Supplication to the Virgin," 183–84; Ivanov, *In Search of Constantinople*, 385. This scene can be found also in amulets made of hematite. See the piece mentioned by Gansell, "Amulet Portraying the Woman with the Issue of Blood," no. 165, pp. 283–84, and dated to the tenth-twelve centuries.

32 Cf. Studer-Karlen, "Walking Through the Narthex," 50n80, 63n131; Ivanov, *In Search of Constantinople*, 385.

33 Underwood, *Kariye Djami*, 33, 45–48, 65–70, 96–100 (also for the architectural features of this part of the inner narthex); Teteriatnikov, "The Place of the Nun Melania," 163–80; Ivanov, *In Search of Constantinople*, 384, with mistakes on her biography.

Another Constantinopolitan monument, the Pammakaristos (Fethiye Camii) bears witness of a dedicatory epigram by an aristocratic nun.[34] The *protostrator* Michael Tarchaneiotes Doukas Glabas (who died between 1305 and 1308) and his wife Maria Doukaina Komnene Branaina Palaiologina Tarchaneiotissa constructed the *parekklesion* (chapel) at the beginning of the fourteenth century.[35] After his death, Maria/Martha Tarchaneiotissa added the epigrams and its mosaics.[36] On the apse of the chapel survives a verse inscription running along the arch. It consists of three verses with the motivation for the donation: "Martha the nun set up this thank-offering to God in memory of Michael Glabas her husband who was a renowned warrior and bore the title of Protostrator."[37]

Tombs of nuns—as was also the case with male monastics—were located in the main church of a monastery. This was a prestigious position reserved for the founder and members of their family. *Parekklesia*, a common feature in Palaiologan architecture, often featured large-scale painted programs, typically including a portrait. However, these portraits did not depict the deceased but rather the individual as a living person. Tomb portraits also represented the patron(s), and in larger group portraits additional family members were included.

Even in a rural context, funerary portraits visualized the agency of women. A funerary portrait of the nun Martha Archontokephalene is found in the Church of the Saviour in Kakodiki (Crete).[38] The figure wears brown clothes and is depicted in the position of a deceased person, with hands

---

34 Rhoby, *Byzantinische Epigramme auf Ikonen und Objekten der Kleinkunst*, 307. For Pammakaristos, see Kidonopulos, *Bauten in Konstantinopel*, 80–86; Belting et al., *The Mosaics and Frescoes of St. Mary Pammakaristos*, 3–42; Janin, *La géographie ecclésiastique de l'Empire byzantine*, 208–13; Effenberger, "Zu den Gräbern in der Pammakaristoskirche," 170–96; Asutay-Effenberger, "Zum Datum der Umwandlung der Pammakaristoskirche in die Fethiye Camii," 32–41.

35 Effenberger, "Zur Restaurierungstatigkeit des Michael Dukas Glabas Tarchaneiotes," 79–93; Ivanov, *In Search of Constantinople*, 356–66. Tarchaneiotes commissioned by Philes also an epigramm on an icon of John the Baptist. See Pietsch-Braounou, *Beseelte Bilder*, 182–84.

36 Ivanov, *In Search of Constantinople*, 362.

37 A slightly revised version of the English translation by Underwood, "Notes on the Work of the Byzantine Institute in Istanbul," 298n17. For the Greek text and further bibliography, see Rhoby, *Byzantinische Epigramme auf Ikonen und Objekten der Kleinkunst*, 402–3; Ivanov, *In Search of Constantinople*, 364.

38 Gerstel and Talbot, "Nuns in the Byzantine Countryside," 486, fig. 6; Gerstel, *Rural Lives and Landscapes in Late Byzantium*, 148–49.

crossed over the body. Vines are depicted on the white background. Her monastic garments bear a resemblance to those in the portrait of Kataphyge Alexena in Rhodes.[39] In the small Church of Ai-Giannakes in Mystras (ca. 1375), the *ktetorissa* (foundress) Kale/Kallinike Kabasalea is painted with her children, depicted both as a laywoman and as a nun. This is a double portrait of a funerary character.[40]

The most prominent examples, however, come from Constantinople. Theodora Palaiologina and members of her family were buried in the Prodromos Church, in the nunnery of Lips. The empress gave written instructions about her own burial place and those of her family members:

> The body of my daughter is buried to the right of the entrance to the church of [St. John] the Forerunner. My tomb and that of my honored mother (for I cannot bear to be separated from her even after my death) should be built after the intervening door. In the future any of my children or sons-in-law, who request during their lifetime to be laid to rest here, shall be suitably buried. The same shall apply to my grandsons and granddaughters, daughters-in-law, and the husbands of granddaughters, for all of whom there are to be annual commemorations. The opposite side, on your left as you leave for the old church of the Virgin, will be totally reserved for whatever purpose desired by my son the emperor.[41]

Theodora commissioned *περιταφίους στέγας* (an arch or canopy) to surmount her tomb, which may resemble the archivolt from the Lips nunnery (now in the Istanbul Archaeological Museum, Inv. Nos. 4570, 4355).[42] In the south church of the nunnery, twelve masonry tombs and two ossuaries were discovered.[43] Cyril Mango and Ernest J. W. Hawkins identified the tombs of Theodora Palaiologina and her daughter in the arcosolia of the south church, with Theodora's tomb in the eastern arcosolium and her daughter's tomb in the western one. Mango and Hawkins observed remains of mosaic

---

39 Bitha, "Ενδυματολογικές μαρτυρίες στις τοιχογραφίες της μεσαιωνικής Ρόδου," 445.

40 Drandakes, "Ὁ Ἀϊ-Γιαννάκης τοῦ Μυστρά," 78 and fig. 27; Papamastorakes, "Επιτύμβιες παραστάσεις κατά τη μέση και ύστερη βυζαντινή περίοδο," 298; Kalopissi-Verti, "Δωρεές γυναικών στην υστεροβυζαντινή περίοδο," 253, fig. 9; Parani, "Negotiating Gender Identity Through the Visual Arts," 432–35.

41 *Typicon monasterii Lips*, ed. Delehaye, chap. 42, p. 130; Talbot, "*Lips*," 1278.

42 Talbot, "Empress Theodora Palaiologina, Wife of Michael VIII," 298–99; Shawcross, "In the Name of the True Emperor," 221; Melvani, *Late Byzantine Sculpture*, 14.

43 Macridy, "The Monastery of Lips and the Burials of the Palaeologi," 269–71; Marinis, "The Monastery tou Libos," 179; Marinis, "Tombs and Burials in the Monastery tou Libos," 147–66.

decoration on the back walls of these spaces. In the middle of the eastern arcosolium was a standing figure of Theodora with her hands folded over her breast. An illegible inscription accompanied the composition.[44]

A nun in the convent of Lips, Maria Palaiologina, established a tomb for herself in the monastery. William H. Buckler, who firstly published the relief, spoke of a nun Maria Palaiologina, while Hans Belting and André Grabar identified the figure with Virgin Mary.[45] According to Titos Papamastorakes, we should accept the original opinion of Buckler. Palaiologina commissioned also an epigram for her own tomb; it was inscribed on a sculpted relief panel. The tomb slab was probably inserted on the back wall of an arcosolium niche; this was the position normally reserved for the execution of painted portraits.[46] The poem is written at the centre of the panel in the first person, while at left her figure turns in a three-quarter pose towards the inscribed text.[47] Maria Palaiologina wears a mantle, a tunic, and shoes. An epigram explains that she took her monastic vows probably in Lips nunnery after her husband (a *sebastos*) died. Maria Palaiologina has still not been identified. Buckler proposed five possible candindates.[48] Andreas Rhoby has rejected all proposed names on various grounds; he proposed that Maria was an unknown member of the Palaiologoi family who lived in the first half of the fourteenth century.[49] While the epigram can be attributed to Manuel Philes, the style of the inscribed funerary panel, according to Nicholas Melvani, indicates a date in the last quarter of the thirteenth century.[50]

Images of nuns survive as part of the decoration of three tombs in the *parekklesion* and in the outer narthex of the Chora Monastery (Kariye

---

44 Mango and Hawkins, "Additional Notes," 301–3; Marinis, "The Monastery tou Libos," 182–83.

45 Buckler, "The Monument of a Palaiologina," pp. 521–26, table 10. According to Firatli, the stele was an antiquarian purchase "but in 1917 was to be found in Atmeydan (Forum of Arkadios)". Firatli, *La sculpture byzantine figurée au Musée Archéologique d'Istanbul*, no. 115, p. 67. See also Belting, *Das illuminierte Buch in der spätbyzantinischen Gesellschaft*, no. 267, p. 79; Grabar, *Sculptures byzantines du Moyen Âge*, nos. 128 and 129, table 110a.

46 Melvani, *Late Byzantine Sculpture*, 65; Marsengill, *Portraits and Icons*, p. 241, and no. 176.

47 Papamastorakes, "Επιτύμβιες παραστάσεις κατά τη μέση και ύστερη βυζαντινή περίοδο," 285–304; Talbot, "Epigrams in Context," 80–81, fig. 9 and translation.

48 Buckler, "The Monument of a Palaiologina," 524.

49 Rhoby, *Byzantinische Epigramme auf Stein*, 631.

50 Melvani, *Late Byzantine Sculpture*, 233.

Mosque). One significant testimony is Tomb D in the southwest wall of the *parekklesion*. The double funerary portrait on the back wall of the niche includes the great *konostavlos* Michael Tornikes and his wife, depicted both as laypeople and, on the soffits of the niche, as monastics (monk Makarios and nun Eugenia).[51] Eugenia wears a black mantle, a dark tunic, and a flat-topped hat (*analabos*). Unfortunately, Tornikes' wife is only attested in this inscription and only by her monastic name.[52] The *terminus ante quem* for the tomb is the year 1328 (the death of Tornikes). A twenty-four-line epigram glorifies the deceased constable (*konostavlos*) only, although nun Eugenia was also buried there.[53]

The funerary portraits of Tornikes and his wife in both lay and monastic garments depict in colours and lines the transition from one state to another. For members of aristocratic families, adopting monastic dress marked an enormous change, and both written and pictorial sources refer to this drastic transformation. A document related to John/Joasaph Maliasenos described the passage from an aristocratic appearance to the monastic (angelic) habit as follows: "he...replaced those soft tunics, the various and diverse formations (of cloths) with the rough worn garment (of the life according to God)" (my translation).[54]

On the north wall of the *parekklesion*, Tomb C includes portraits of three women and a man. The woman on the far right has been identified by Paul Underwood as a nun. She wears a tunic or dress of light yellowish-brown with dark brown folds and over it a long mantle of dark brown. Prominent is a "light yellowish-brown headdress that fits tightly around her face and covers her shoulders. Her face, on plaster that rises in relief, seems to be a restoration, but her hands appear to be unrestored."[55] The depicted persons cannot be identified; however, the monograms on the mantle of the central

---

51 Underwood, *Kariye Djami*, 276–80; Weißbrod, *"Hier liegt der Knecht Gottes,"* 96–97 (on *parekklesion* D), 130–34 (on the double portraits); Brooks, "Sculpture and the Late Byzantine Tomb," 96; Brooks, "Commemoration of the Dead," 297–300.

52 Schmalzbauer, "Die Tornikioi in der Palaiologenzeit," 131–32.

53 Rhoby, *Byzantinische Epigramme auf Stein*, 643–50, no. TR68; Melvani, *Late Byzantine Sculpture*, 17–18, 91; Melvani, "The Last Century of the Chora Monastery," 1219–39; Ivanov, *In Search of Constantinople*, 408.

54 Miklosich and Müller, *Acta et Diplomata graeca Medii Aevi sacra et profana*, vol. 4, p. 337, no. 3 (after 1274).

55 Underwood, *Kariye Djami*, 272–76, esp. 275; Brooks, "Commemoration of the Dead," 296; Brooks, "The History and Significance of Tomb Monuments," 26–27.

female figure indicate that they belonged to a branch of the Palaiologos-Asanes family. This tomb should be dated to around 1330.

Finally, a female monastic figure is represented in Tomb E in the outer narthex of the Chora (around 1340).[56] She is part of a group portrait with a male descendant of the Palaiologos and Asanes families, identified through the monograms decorating the dresses. Six figures are depicted on the niche's black wall, while the jambs feature portraits of a monk on the left and the nun Athanasia on the right. Athanasia wears a long brown tunic, a brown mantle, and a black headdress. An inscription provides information about her death and suggests that she was related to the *ktetor*, Theodore Metochites. Underwood has convincingly identified the nun Athanasia as Irene Raoulaina Palaiologina, related to Metochites through her marriage to Constantine Palaiologos Porphyrogennetos.[57] The Chora nun portraits elucidate the roles under which a nun could be included in the art program of a monument: either as a donor or as a member of a family—usually an aristocratic one—buried there. In none of these cases is a nunnery named, which highlights the significance of being buried with their husbands and children in a family grave. The focus of such portraits is on the laywomen rather than the monastic figures.

Devotion, donation, and death (the three Ds) facilitated the presence of female monastic portraits, and sculpture is no exception. Sculpture and nuns were primarily connected through death, as demonstrated by the sarcophagus of St. Theodora in Arta (located in the narthex).[58] The latest interpretation links this funerary monument to Anna Kantakouzene, wife of Nikephoros, son of the saint. According to Branislav Čvetković, Anna commissioned the sarcophagus around 1296 to promote the cult of her mother-in-law.[59] Čvetković identified the figures depicted on the sarcophagus as Anna and her son Thomas. However, other scholars argue that the figures are St. Theodora and her son Nikephoros, or even Theodora and her husband Michael

56 Underwood, *Kariye Djami*, 280–88; Brooks, "Commemoration of the Dead," 301–4.

57 Underwood, *Kariye Djami*, 284–86; Brooks, "Commemoration of the Dead," 303.

58 Orlandos, "Ὁ τάφος τῆς Ἁγίας Θεοδώρας," 105–15; Grabar, *Sculptures byzantines du Moyen Âge*, 144–45; Pazaras, *Ανάγλυφες σαρκοφάγοι και επιτάφιες πλάκες της μέσης*, 42, 50, 79–80, 170–72, 174–75; Studer-Karlen, "Mise en scene multiple et lecture simultanée," 79–94. On Theodora as an emissary, see Melichar, "Imperial Women as Emissaries, Intermediaries, and Conciliators," 107–11.

59 Čvetković, "The Investiture Relief of Arta, Epiros," 103–12; cf. Melvani, *Late Byzantine Sculpture*, 65, 105.

II, deliberately presented on a smaller scale. The identification with Anna and her son Thomas is not entirely convincing, and many scholars continue to associate the figures with the *despotissa* Theodora (d. 1270) and her son Nikephoros.[60]

My reluctance to accept the idea promoted by Čvetković is based on two main points. First, the female figure is depicted in imperial attire with symbols of power. According to Čvetković, "the *basilissa* is wearing an open crown with a long-decorated veil, falling down on her shoulders." However, the veil is actually a *kalyptra* (head cover) used instead of the *prependoulia*, which is the usual depiction for imperial persons who have taken monastic vows.[61] Second, a sarcophagus typically features a depiction of the saint. The assumption that the sarcophagus of Theodora depicts individuals other than the saint herself contradicts the essence of a saint's cult.

If this figure is indeed the saint *despotissa*, then it shows that art and nuns remained connected through sanctity. In contrast to several cases from Late Antiquity and middle Byzantine periods, Theodora of Arta is the only canonized female saint from Late Byzantium.[62] After her death, icons featuring her portrait would likely have been commissioned. In her icons, St. Theodora is depicted in imperial attire and as a nun with a *skepe* (head cover).[63]

Her cult, however, remained confined to the boundaries of the Despotate of Epiros. In contrast, icons of the Iconoclast St. Theodosia became extremely popular, with her relics housed in a monastery in Constantinople.[64] Notable are five icons from Sinai and her portrait in the Triumph of Orthodoxy icon (now in the British Museum), dated to the late fourteenth century. During the Palaiologan period, St. Theodosia is depicted frontally; she holds a cross and wears a tall or flat-topped hat.[65]

60 Papadopoulou, *Η Βυζαντινή Άρτα και τα μνημεία της*, 53–54; Brooks, "Sculpture and the Late Byzantine Tomb," 100.

61 Moutsopoulos, *Οι βυζαντινές εκκλησίες της Άρτας*, 182–89, esp. 186.

62 On St. Theodora, see Talbot, "Life of St. Theodora of Thessalonike," 159–63; cf. Melicharová, "Crown, Veil and Halo," 315–44. Another holy woman (*hosia*) was the godmother of Sphrantzes; however, she was never canonized.

63 Talbot, "Literati and the Revival of Hagiography in the Early Palaiologan Period," 435–46.

64 On the Monastery of Theodosia (Gül Camii and Ayakapı Mescidi) in Constantinople, see Effenberger, "Theodosia von Konstantinopel," 121–34; Schaeffer, *Die Gül Camii in Istanbul*; Müller-Wiener, *Bildlexikon zur Topographie Istanbuls*, 97, 140–43.

65 Mouriki, "Portraits of St. Theodosia in Five Sinai Icons," 213–19; Galavaris, "Two Icons of St. Theodosia at Sinai," 313–16; Cormack, "Icon of the Triumph of Orthodoxy," 129–30. See also Baltogianne, "Εικόνα της Αγίας Θεοδοσίας της

A special category of art products is the so-called *koutroubia* of St. Demetrios. Many of these lead ampullae feature a depiction of St. Demetrios on one side and St. Theodora of Thessaloniki on the reverse. St. Theodora is shown as a nun with a cloak covering most of her face. The coexistence of both saints is certainly intriguing. These moulded lead ampullae were widely distributed, having been found in various regions of the Balkan Peninsula, particularly in Bulgaria. An interesting example is a *koutroubion* included in a mosaic icon of St. Demetrios, dated to the fourteenth or fifteenth century and now housed in the Museo Civico in Sassoferrato near Ancona. This icon was incorporated into a wooden frame and covered with a metal frame by its owner, the Italian humanist Niccolò Perotti (1429/30–1480), who was also the secretary of Bessarion.[66]

Few images of nuns appear in illuminated manuscripts. The Codex Sinai, St. Catherine Monastery, MS gr. 61 (ca. 1274),[67] contains a portrait of the nun Theotime on fol. 256v. Theotime, wearing a brown cape, a *himation* (robe), and a *skepe* (head covering), prostrates herself before the Virgin. Due to its small size, the Psalter was probably a private devotional book rather than an aristocratic votive donation.[68]

The last testimony of nuns in an illuminated manuscript comes from the monastery *ton Hodegon* in 1449/50. A certain Methodios produced a luxurious manuscript (Sankt-Petersburg, Rossijskaja Nacional'naja biblioteka, MS Ф. No. 906 (Gr.), gr. 243) containing the works of monk Isaiah.[69] The forty-eight illuminations depict female saints—primarily the Desert Mothers—and the everyday life in a nunnery.[70] On fol. 25, a female figure in monastic

---

Κωνσταντινουπολίτισσας στη Νάξο," 219–21, for two additional representations of St. Theodosia in icons.

66 Bakirtzis, "Κουτρούβια μύρου από τη Θεσσαλονίκη," 523–29; Foskolou, "Blessing for Sale?" 60–62; cf. Mitsiou, "Ευλογίες," 195–229; Evans, *Byzantium*, no. 139, pp. 209–12.

67 *Diktyon*: 58436; Ball, "Greek Psalter," no. 34, 176–77. On the Psalters in Byzantium, see Cutler, *The Aristocratic Psalters in Byzantium*, no. 52, pp. 99–103; Parpulov, "Ornament and Status," 101–16.

68 Kalopissi-Verti, "Δωρεές γυναικών στην υστεροβυζαντινή περίοδο," 253; Evans, *Byzantium*, no. 202, pp. 343–44. On illuminated manuscripts of the thirteenth century, see Toumpouri, "Changes and Innovation," 171–206.

69 *Diktyon*: 57315; Granstrem, "Каталог греческих рукописей ленинградских хранилищ," 143–44; Ganchou, "Héléna Notara Gateliousaina d'Ainos," 148–49; Politis, "Eine Schreiberschule im Kloster τῶν Ὁδηγῶν," 270n88.

70 Likhačeva, "Роль бытовых реалий и пейзажа в миниатюрах рукописи," 229–42; Likhačeva, *Византийская миниатюра*, tables 50–55.

garment is shown with a spinning wheel. Vera Likhačeva emphasized the illuminator's imagination and the limited palette of colours used (black, brown, and a few others such as green).

The depiction of female monastic bodies and the attached inscriptions provided a voice to Byzantine women; they became the visual and written manifestations of their identity. However, by including themselves in a church pictorial program or an illuminated manuscript, they became part of a complex network of these artifacts.

In a previous chapter, we applied network analytical methods to understand textual testimonies of foundation as a network of patronage. The base of these examples was the *typikon* of Bebaia Elpis.[71] At this point, we will focus on the network of illuminations included in the first folios of the codex. Hutter argued that the surviving copy was intended for special occasions, while an unillustrated copy (made of paper) served the everyday needs of the convent. The illuminations were added around 1330–1335 by Theodora's daughter.[72]

Euphrosyne Synadene "constructed" a family *album* of direct kinship, including her grandparents, parents, brothers, sisters, and their offspring.[73] Additionally, on fol. 12r it contains a unique representation of the entire monastic community,[74] reminiscent of a similar depiction at the *Hortus Deliciarum*: an encyclopedia for nuns composed by the abbess Herrad of Hohenburg in

71 Cutler and Magdalino, "Some Precisions on the Lincoln College *Typikon*," 179–98; Spatharakis, *The Portrait in Byzantine Illuminated Manuscripts*, 190–206; Hutter, "Die Geschichte des Lincoln College *Typikons*," 79–144; Patlagean, *Ο ελληνικός Μεσαίωνας*, 196–207; Yota, "L'image du donateur dans les manuscrits illustrés byzantins," 286.

72 Hutter, "Die Geschichte des Lincoln College *Typikons*," 105–11. See also Connor, *Women of Byzantium*, 268–308.

73 Cutler and Magdalino, "Some Precisions on the Lincoln College *Typikon*," 179–98; Hutter, "Die Geschichte des Lincoln College *Typikons*," 79–114; Hutter, *Corpus der byzantinischen Miniaturenhandschriften*, pp. 56–62, figs. 201–21 and tables 6–18; Brooks, "Poetry and Female Patronage in Late Byzantine Tomb Decoration," 237–48. Marsengill argues that the portrait of Constantine and Irene may resemble the original panel portrait of Synadene's parents at their tomb. Marsengill, *Portraits and Icons*, 237–40 On the clothes of the male family members and officials, see Woodfin, *The Embodied Icon*, 154–58.

74 Hennessy argues that the miniatures with the persons in monastic garments were painted at the time of the opening of the convent. Hennessey, "The Lincoln College *Typikon*," 107–8. For recent approaches to the manuscript, see Gastgeber, "Das *Typikon* Lincoln College gr. 35," 95–110; Gaul, "Writing 'with Joyful and Leaping Soul,'" 243–71.

Sainte-Odile in Alsace (twelfth century).[75] In the Lincoln *typikon*, the various subgroups are depicted with subtle tones of colour in their garments, while the abbess holds the symbol of her power: a staff. Five small girls (novices) are shown in the foreground, two with white headscarves and three in brown. The depiction conveys severity and austere gestures, yet there is an effort to highlight the uniqueness of each person through small facial details.

The first twelve folios of the codex depict the foundress and family members, including her parents, Constantine Palaiologos and Irene, as well as three of her children and their spouses. The first portrait of Theodora Synadene shows her with her husband, John, in luxurious garments. However, on fol. 7r, Synadene, her husband, and their young daughter, Euphrosyne, are shown in monastic attire. John is identified as the monk Ioakeim and Theodora as the nun Theodoule. Synadene wears a typical black mantle and a tall, flat-topped headdress while holding her daughter's hand, evidently offering her to Theotokos. Euphrosyne, who is known to have been tonsured at a very young age, is depicted as a novice in a brown gown.

Unlike Western practice,[76] it is uncommon in Byzantium to identify nuns working as illuminators. Nonetheless, in the case of the Lincoln *typikon* a female artist may have created the portraits based on sketches or family portraits kept in the family archives of the Synadenoi. The depicted luxurious garments, though, were not a monastic product despite the existence of female weavers and embroiderers.[77] The monastic craftmanship consisted mostly of low-cost and profitable everyday products which they could sell in local markets. The nuns of Baionaia were not allowed, for example, to manufacture garments for their family members but could sell them to external monks and laymen. In this double monastery, both monks and nuns created clothes for each other.[78]

75 Grabar, *L'art byzantin*, p. 234, plates 41a-b and 42a-b. The original has been destroyed and only a later copy has survived.

76 Cf. Hamburger, *Nuns as Artists*; Hamburger and Suckale, "Between This World and the Next," 76–108.

77 Johnstone, *The Byzantine Tradition in Church Embroidery*, 57–64.

78 Pétridès, "Le *typikon* de Nil Damilas," chap. 8, p. 101–3; Talbot, "*Neilos Damilas*," 1471–73. On the monastery, see Psilakes, *Μοναστήρια και ερημητήρια της Κρήτης*, 521–24.

Networks of Female Literacy and Knowledge

The text of the Lincoln *typikon* was probably copied by nuns and commissioned by a woman. It represents the symbolic or social capital of the aristocratic patroness, which then became part of her foundation. According to Pierre Bourdieu, symbolic capital is related to knowledge. These two terms can be connected to specific social markers, such as literacy and education, the production of literary works, and manuscripts (acquisition, donation, commission, copying).[79]

Since women in Byzantium could not hold public office, education was not considered essential for their upbringing. They mostly had access to primary education (*hiera grammata*), which focused on gaining reading and writing skills. After the eleventh century, and especially during the Palaiologan period, examples of highly educated women, such as Anna Komnena and Theodora Raoulaina, became more common.[80] However, even in the upper society, these women remained exceptions to the rule.[81]

The literacy of Byzantine women has been assessed based on their ability to sign their names.[82] 1.8% of women signing documents in the thirteenth century was literate, while 16% were literate in the fourteenth century. However, signatures such as that of Anna Doukopoulina Mesopotamitissa in September 1306 contain orthographic errors;[83] similarly, the signatures of Xene Indanina Sarantene and Sophrosyne Sarantene in 1330 are not flawless, indicating inexperienced hands.[84] Insecurity is also evident in imperial signatures, such as that of Irene Doukaina in the Kecharitomene

79 Bourdieu, "Ökonomisches Kapital, kulturelles Kapital, soziales Kapital," 183–98; Erler, "Das Buch als soziales Symbol." On social markers, see Reuter, "Nobles and Others," 85–98. On the Byzantine example, see Laiou, "The Role of Women in Byzantine Society," 254–57; Grünbart, "Paideia Connects," 19–21.

80 On Raoulaina, see below in this chapter. Anna Komnena's handwriting is being now identified at the manuscript San Lorenzo de El Escorial, Real Biblioteca, MS gr. Ω-II–13 (*Diktyon*: 15079), which contains the homilies of John Chrysostom and Cyril of Alexandreia. See Pérez Martín, "L'Escorial Ω-II–13 (gr. 530) et sa copiste Anna" (to be published). Until recently, the manuscript was erroneously dated in the thirteenth century. See De Andrés, *Catálogo de los códices griegos de la Real Biblioteca*, 168; Schreiner, "Kopistinnen in Byzanz," 37.

81 Nikolaou, *Η γυναίκα στη μέση βυζαντινή εποχή*, 185–213.

82 Saradi-Mendelovici, "A Contribution to the Study of the Byzantine Notarial Formulas," 72–79.

83 *Actes de Xénophon*, ed. Papachryssanthou, p. 100, no. 7 (1306); Maniate-Kokkine, "Γυναίκα καὶ "ἀνδρικὰ" οἰκονομικὰ προνόμια," 440–44.

84 Laiou, "The Role of Women in Byzantine Society," 254–57.

typikon (twelfth century). However, a lack of perfect writing skills does not equate to illiteracy. These aristocratic women could function as administrators of their properties, dealing with specific types of texts, such as financial records. Their ability to operate financial transactions and maintain accounting documents is beyond doubt.[85] Such qualifications would have been useful in a nunnery, which operated under principles similar to those of an (aristocratic) household (*oikos*).[86]

Nunneries in Late Byzantium could function as educational institutions. The focus was on ensuring an adequate number of literate nuns to handle basic administrative and liturgical duties. Some nuns were educated before entering the nunnery, while others acquired these skills either from a young age within the nunnery or at a later stage. For instance, the Philanthropos Soter convent accepted young girls for both educational purposes and security reasons.[87]

In Bebaia Elpis, young girls intending to become nuns were instructed by the *ekklessiarchissa* in reading and chanting.[88] At the same time, abbesses needed to be educated to fulfill their duties effectively.[89] Learning activities included not only reading but also listening to specific types of texts. The *typikon* had to be read aloud once a month or three times a year, while during meals, one nun was responsible for reading aloud edificial texts.[90]

The possession or lack of education led to an internal division of nuns into two groups, as we have already explored above: those responsible for the liturgy (*ekklesiastikai*) and those engaged in manual work (*domestikai*). Generally, 60% (three-fifths) of the personnel in convents were assigned to hymnody, while 40% (two-fifths) performed other services. The *typikon* of Bebaia Elpis mandated that literate nuns participate in chanting, while

85 Waring, "Byzantine Monastic Libraries in the Eleventh and Twelfth Centuries," 122.

86 Late antique monasteries already resembled households, and their architecture can be considered a form of domestic architecture. See Brooks Hedstrom, "The Archaeology of Monastic Households," 185–203.

87 Theoleptos of Philadelphia, *Letters*, ed. Constantinides Hero, p. 60.362–67, no. 2.

88 *Typicon monasterii Theotoci Bebaias Elpidos*, ed. Delehaye, chap. 53, p. 47; Talbot, "*Bebaia Elpis*," 1538.

89 *Typicon monasterii Theotoci Bebaias Elpidos*, ed. Delehaye, chap. 25, p. 33; Talbot, "*Bebaia Elpis*," 1530.

90 *Typicon monasterii Theotoci Bebaias Elpidos*, ed. Delehaye, chap. 85, p. 67; Talbot, "*Bebaia Elpis*," 1548.

illiterate nuns were limited to saying small prayers.[91] In their monastic cells, educated nuns were expected to read, while illiterate monastics relied on their ability to pray and recite psalms by heart after hearing them repeatedly in the church. Teaching was foreseen for some nuns of the convent. Neilos Damilas also encouraged literate nuns to teach their less educated sisters.

The reading habits of nuns and their monastic communities cannot be precisely elucidated. Damilas advised the nuns of Baionaia to read works by Maximos the Confessor and an oration by St. Zosimas, suggesting that manuscripts of these texts were likely part of the convent's library.[92] Some *typika* also reference books available in convents. In addition to the Pentateuch, Psalter, and New Testament, significant texts included the *typikon* of St. Sabas, works by John Klimax, ascetic treatises by St. Basil, and writings by Gregory of Nazianzos.[93]

Annemarie Weyl Carr argued that female "learning did not go beyond the narrow limits of devotional and sacred literature to embrace the secular realm of grammar and classical thought."[94] This view is supported by evidence of private ownership of manuscripts containing sacred texts. For instance, the nun Euphrosyne Pegene owned the illuminated Tetraevangelion (Hagion Oros, Stauroniketa, MS 56) from the thirteenth century.[95] Similarly, the literary output of nuns primarily consisted of hymnographic[96] and hagiographic works.

---

91 *Typicon monasterii Theotoci Bebaias Elpidos*, ed. Delehaye, chap. 62, p. 53; Talbot, "*Bebaia Elpis*," 1540–41.

92 Pétridès, "Le *typikon* de Nil Damilas," chap. 2, pp. 96–97; Talbot, "*Neilos Damilas*," 1468; Talbot, "Bluestocking Nuns," 614.

93 Talbot, "Bluestocking Nuns," 613n51.

94 Carr, "Women and Monasticism in Byzantium," 8 and 10.

95 *Diktyon*: 30117; Vogel and Gardthausen, *Die griechischen Schreiber des Mittelalters und der Renaissance*, 123; Lambros, *Catalogue*, vol. 1, p. 79: "Εὐφροσύνη μοναχὴ τοὔνομα ἡ Πηγηνή". See also Demus, "Studien zur byzantinischen Buchmalerei des 13. Jahrhunderts," pp. 78–79, plate 3. Pegene may have been a nun in a Zoodochos Pege nunnery, although this is only an assumption.

96 Only one female hymnographer is known in Late Byzantium, i.e., Palaiologina from the St. Theodora convent in Thessaloniki. In the late fourteenth to early fifteenth century, she composed canons on St. Demetrios and St. Theodora. See Sphrantzes, *Memorii*, ed. Grecu, bk. 18, chap. 2, §32, lines 20–24; Talbot, "Bluestocking Nuns," 607; Beck, *Kirche und theologische Literatur im byzantinischen Reich*, 797; Rapp, "Figures of Female Sanctity," 328. For Byzantine female hymnographers, see Catafygiotou-Topping, "Women Hymnographers in Byzantium," 98–111; Riehle, "Authorship and Gender (and) Identity," 245–62; Mullett, "Aristocracy and Patronage in the Literary Circles of Comnenian Constantinople," 173–201; Nikolaou, *Η γυναίκα στη μέση*

In this context, we should also consider the significant number of catechetical and edifying works addressed to nuns and written by male authors. These texts aimed to strengthen the faith of female monastics to help them avoid sin and suppress their passions. They often presented varied and sometimes contradictory ideas about the appropriate knowledge nuns should seek and receive. Frequently, the authors acted as spiritual fathers to their recipients, whether individual nuns or entire nunneries. The tradition of spiritual guidance from male figures to nuns and abbesses has deep roots in Byzantine monasticism. For instance, Theodore of Stoudios corresponded with numerous nuns and nunneries, offering advice on monastic life.[97] In Late Byzantium, this tradition continued, occasionally incorporating contemporary issues.

The monk Mark (ca. 1260) was the spiritual father of Eulogia, sister of Michael VIII, to whom Mark addresses part of his work.[98] The thirteenth-century manuscript Città del Vaticano, Biblioteca Apostolica Vaticana, MS Chig. R.V. 033 (gr. 27) contains 239 titles, which can be divided into five different texts.[99] Significant in this manuscript are not only the anthologies with citations from various authors but also a dedicatory letter to Eulogia.[100] Moreover, a sermon (*Λόγος πρὸς εὐγενεστάτην ψυχήν*) was addressed to Eulogia prior to her tonsure (after 1257). This sermon serves as a kind of short monastic rule.[101] For his compilation, Mark used various authors, most of whom were later associated with hesychastic theology, while no secular authors are mentioned. Feminine inflections are rarely found, as his spiritual advice derives from general principles about the monastic life.

The role of spiritual fathers is uniquely illuminated in the correspondence of Irene Choumnaina with Theoleptos of Philadelphia and her second

βυζαντινή εποχή, 206–9. In modern times, nun Theotekne (Hagiostephanitissa) in Meteora has composed hymns that have been approved by the Church and can be used in the Liturgy.

97 Cf. Theodore of Stoudios, *Epistulae*, ed. Fatouros, pp. 505–6, no. 375; Rigo, "La direction spirituelle des moniales à Byzance," 283–300. On Western female spirituality, see Spearing, *Medieval Writings on Female Spirituality*, vii-xii.

98 Rigo, "Principes et canons pour le choix des livres," 175–76; Roelli, *Marci monachi opera ascetica*, 11*–14* (introduction).

99 *Diktyon*: 65214; De'Cavalieri, *Codices graeci Chisiani et Borgiani*, 44–65; Roelli, *Marci monachi opera ascetica*, 33* (introduction).

100 Roelli, *Marci monachi opera ascetica*, 3–105.

101 Roelli, *Marci monachi opera ascetica*, 107–35, 157–79; Cunningham, "Messages in Context," 83–98.

spiritual father. The metropolitan of Philadelphia, although residing in his see in Western Asia Minor, maintained contact with Irene and her monastic community in Constantinople, acting as a caregiving spiritual father by sending letters and homilies (*katecheseis*).[102] He requested that Irene and the nuns frequently read his letters. At least three individuals served as bearers of these epistles: Kydonates, Karbones, and the monk Niphon.[103]

The surviving letters reveal challenges for the leadership qualities of Irene Choumnaina. On some occasions, she did not know how to handle situations, displaying impatience, insecurity, unhappiness, and great doubts about her abilities as abbess. Theoleptos attempted to teach his spiritual daughter how to remain calm, how to behave in the church and during meals, and to avoid speaking too much. Additionally, he advised her to learn and recite by heart the Gospel, the *Apophthegmata Patrum*, and their Lives.[104]

Irene/Eulogia struggled to leave behind the life she once knew: the palace, honours, wealth, and the love of her parents and relatives.[105] Her worldly concerns often drained her energy for monastic life. While she was sufficiently ascetic, she was also authoritarian and intolerant of disobedient nuns. For instance, she once wanted to readmit a repentant nun who had left the monastery of her own accord, despite her spiritual father's skepticism.[106] Inside the nunnery, aggression manifested in fights between the nuns. On one occasion, Choumnaina refrained from reporting a problem she faced with a nun to avoid distressing Theoleptos. However, the nun sought forgiveness and guidance from him. Shortly before his death in 1322, Theoleptos sent his spiritual testament,[107] a compilation of his discussions with Irene and the nun Agathonike.

After Theoleptos's death, Choumnaina sought new spiritual advisors, hoping to find someone who could replace him.[108] By around 1335, it appeared she had finally succeeded. A collection of twenty-two letters has survived, including eight of hers and fourteen from her new spiritual father.

---

102 On a much more restricted model for the spiritual father, see Pétridès, "Le *typikon* de Nil Damilas," chaps. 9 and 15, pp. 103, 107; Talbot, "*Neilos Damilas*," 1473, 1476.

103 Theoleptos of Philadelphia, *Letters*, ed. Constantinides Hero, p. 70, no. 3.

104 Theoleptos of Philadelphia, *Discourses*, ed. Sinkewicz, p. 104, no. 1.

105 Theoleptos of Philadelphia, Letters, ed. Constantinides Hero, p. 78, no. 3.

106 Theoleptos of Philadelphia, *Letters*, ed. Constantinides Hero, p. 58, no. 2.

107 Sinkewicz, *Theoleptos of Philadelpheia*, pp. 352–82, no. 23.

108 Previale, "Due Monodie inedite di Matteo di Efeso," 26–31.

However, the identity of this person is a matter of dispute. He may have been Ignatios the Philosopher[109] or Gregory Akindynos. The new spiritual father was reluctant in his interactions with Irene, often accepting her suggestions with great difficulty. One particular issue was her desire for him to visit the monastery regularly—a request he initially rejected. He argued that many female saints in the past rarely met their spiritual fathers, with some seeing them only once a year or even just once in their entire lives.[110] Irene, in turn, argued that she could not leave the monastery and remained enclosed, not even attending royal weddings and funerals due to a lack of means for such expensive and grand occasions.[111] Under the pressure of her pleas, the spiritual father eventually agreed to visit her in the monastery six times a year.

Regarding her literacy, the letters reveal spelling mistakes, poor handwriting, and difficulties in expressing her thoughts clearly. Her spiritual father tried to comfort her by stating:

> As for what you wrote to me about your inability to express your thoughts clearly in writing...this does not happen to you alone—who surpass all contemporary women in education by a royal cubit, as they say—but it seems also to happen occasionally even to men who have reached the peak of Hellenic learning and rhetorical skill, and probably no one can escape this [difficulty] all the time.[112]

Works by Nikephoros Choumnos and Theoleptos of Philadelphia were in her possession. Book exchanges occurred between Irene and her second spiritual father; she desired copies of his various writings, while he requested works by Theoleptos and Nikephoros Choumnos. It is further known that after the death of Theoleptos, Irene commissioned a manuscript of his works.[113] Moreover, the letters to and from her second spiritual father (1332–1338)

---

109 Cf. Rigo, "La direction spirituelle des moniales à Byzance," 283–300. Neophytos Prodromenos, a known anti-Palamite, is the main scribe, whereas Matthew Blastares may have copied the fols. 83r–156v. Martínez Manzano, "Prontuario para una abadesa," 311–322.

110 Irene Eulogia Choumnaina, *Correspondence*, ed. Constantinides Hero, pp. 78–82, no. 16.

111 Irene Eulogia Choumnaina, *Correspondence*, ed. Constantinides Hero, pp. 72–78, no. 15.

112 Irene Eulogia Choumnaina, *Correspondence*, ed. Constantinides Hero, p. 56, no. 10.

113 The Città del Vaticano, Biblioteca Apostolica Vaticana, MS Ottob. gr. 405 (fourteenth century, first half) (*Diktyon*: 65648) belonged to Irene and was copied from her own file. See Feron and Battaglini, *Codices manuscripti graeci Ottoboniani Bibliothecae Vaticanae*, 216.

are preserved in a single manuscript, San Lorenzo de El Escorial, RB, MS gr. Φ. III. 11 (230) (fols. 235r–254v). This codex also contains medical, astronomical, philosophical, and theological texts as well as the letters of Gregory Akindynos and a letter to Matthew Kantakouzenos by an anonymous friend of John Kyparissiotes.[114] The same anonymous author sent to Choumnaina his works, an "insignificant gift, appropriate for philosophers, though not for emperors."[115]

Gregory Palamas, an opponent of Choumnaina, sent a treatise to a certain nun, Xene, in 1346–1347 to instruct young nuns.[116] Xene, who had spent many years in the convent, was a supporter of Palamas. The first part of the treatise discusses topics such as life, soul, virginity, and poverty. In the second part, Palamas addresses major passions, mourning, and the divine light. It is only in the first part that Gregory Palamas refers to Xene and the young nuns who needed his advice. Palamas's interest in female monastics is also evident in the case of his sisters. While residing in the Skete of Berroia, he arranged for them to be transferred from Constantinople to Berroia to oversee their ascetic practices.[117]

The fourteenth-century manuscript Paris, Bibliothèque nationale de France, MS gr. 1372 (fols. 155r–170v) contains the letters of Jacob, Metropolitan of Chalcedon (1351–1370), who participated in the Hesychastic synod of 1351. He is depicted on fol. 5v of Paris, BnF, MS gr. 1242 (fourteenth century) alongside other metropolitans, the Patriarch, and Emperor John Kantakouzenos.[118] The forty letters (dated 1350–1360) were collected by his spiritual daughter, Eulogia. The metropolitan exhorted her to regard his letters as a rule and canon, recommending a life of solitude, obedience, sacramental practices, repetition of the Jesus Prayer, reading, and repentance.[119]

Around 1390, a nun named Eugenia sought the spiritual guidance of Nathaniel, the metropolitan of Pentapolis, who was then in Constantinople. Nathaniel responded with a letter composed of a prologue and fifteen

114 Congourdeau, "Nicolas Cabasilas et Matthieu Cantacuzène," 85–98.

115 *Diktyon*: 15184; Constantinides Hero, "An Unknown Letter," 280n1.

116 Gregory Palamas, *Letter to nun Xene*, ed. Chrestou, 193–230; Rigo, *Mistici bizantini*, 555–91.

117 Philotheos Kokkinos, *Logos on Gregory Palamas*, ed. Tsames, p. 456, chap. 20.

118 *Diktyon*: 50984; cf. Rigo, "Le lettere di Giacomo metropolita di Calcedonia alla monaca Eulogia," 195–201; Rigo, *Mistici bizantini*, 595–604; Laurent, "La direction spirituelle à Byzance," 64–84; Preiser-Kapeller, *Der Episkopat im späten Byzanz*, 74–75.

119 Rigo, *Mistici bizantini*, 595.

short chapters that addressed issues of everyday monastic conduct, such as prayer, silence, and handiwork. He urged Eugenia to consider his letter a rule (*στάθμη, ὑποτύπωσις*) and a canon (*κανών*). By following his instructions, Eugenia would become part of *ταῖς τῶν ὁσίων γυναικῶν χορείαις* (the group of holy women). This spiritual advice from the Hesychast metropolitan evidently found a degree of dissemination, as it was copied into at least eight manuscripts.[120]

The second book of monk Isaiah should also be dated to the end of the fourteenth century.[121] This work is known through the Russian translation by Theophanes the Recluse, based on the manuscript in the Sankt-Petersburg, RNB, MS Φ. No. 906 (Gr.), gr. 243. The first part of Isaiah's work includes 140 *Apophthegmata* of Holy Fathers, presented as Sayings of the Desert Mothers, featuring figures such as Sara, Synkletike, Melania, Theodora, and Matrona. This section is referred to as the *Meterikon*.[122] Following this initial part, the work includes seven letters of Isaiah on various issues. The manuscript tradition of the second book of Isaiah is divided into two groups. The first group, containing the original redaction of the text, begins with the phrase *Βίβλος καλλίστη μοναχῆς Ἀγγελίνας* ("The most beautiful book of the nun Angelina") and is transmitted only in the Hagion Oros, Panteleeimonos, MS 578 (6085) (seventeenth century) manuscript.[123] The second group of manuscripts is dedicated to Helen Notara Gateliousaina,[124] to which the Sankt-Petersburg, RNB, MS Φ. No. 906 (Gr.), gr. 243 belongs. This luxurious codex was written in 1449/50 by Methodios in the Hodegon Monastery and includes, as already mentioned, depictions of the Desert Mothers.[125]

Porfiri Uspenskij dated the work to the tenth century,[126] while other scholars placed it at the beginning of the thirteenth century, identifying

---

120 Rigo, "Il metropolita di Pentapolis Natanaele a Costantinopoli," 697–707.

121 Rigo, *Mistici bizantini*, 607–15; Rigo, "Principes et canons pour le choix des livres," 176–78.

122 Rapp, "Figures of Female Sanctity," 326–27.

123 *Diktyon*: 22717; Lambros, *Catalogue*, vol. 2, p. 400.

124 Ganchou, "Héléna Notara Gateliousaina d'Ainos," 141–68.

125 Granstrem, "Каталог греческих рукописей ленинградских хранилищ," 143–44; Ganchou, "Héléna Notara Gateliousaina d'Ainos," 148–49. On Methodios, see Politis, "Eine Schreiberschule im Kloster τῶν Ὁδηγῶν," 270n88. Likhačeva, "Роль бытовых реалий и пейзажа в миниатюрах рукописи," 229–42; Likhačeva, *Византийская миниатюра*, tables 50–55.

126 Uspenskij, *Vostok christianskij*, vol. 2, p. 134.

Theodora Angelina with the daughter of Isaakios II Angelos.[127] However, Antonio Rigo has recently questioned this identification, dating the work to the second half of the fourteenth century, and his argumentation is convincing. Angelina is referred to as "nun Angelina" or "nun Theodora Angelina the Phokaitissa." Isaakios II's daughter was named Euphrosyne,[128] making it improbable that she would be called "Phokaitissa." Rigo suggests that the attribute Phokaitissa likely refers to her hometown (Phokaia) or a monastery where she resided.[129] This hypothetical convent (Phokas convent?) might have been an unknown foundation established by a member of the Phokas family.[130] By reassessing these historical and textual connections, Rigo provides a more plausible context for Theodora Angelina's identification and the origins of her monastic affiliation. This new perspective allows for a clearer understanding of her role and identity within the Byzantine monastic landscape.

The last testimonies come from George/Gennadios Scholarios, who corresponded with Simonis/Sophrosyne Asanina Palaiologina. The letters were written after 1457/58,[131] indicating that Sophrosyne entered the monastery at a very young age without having been previously married.[132] Sophrosyne was educated, which allowed her to correspond with Gennadios.[133] In her letters, she requested to meet Scholarios and sought his advice on reading materials. Gennadios recommended two books to her: his own treatise "On the First Service of God" (Περὶ τῆς πρώτης τοῦ Θεοῦ λατρείας) and the

---

127 Hausherr, "Note sur l'inventeur de la méthode hésychaste," 180n1; Hausherr, "Le Métérikon de l'abbé Isaïe," 286–301; Gouillard, "Une compilation spirituelle du XIIIe siècle," 81–82; Beck, *Kirche und theologische Literatur im byzantinischen Reich*, 645–46; Thiermeyer, "Das Meterikon," 303–5.

128 Hiestand, "Die erste Ehe Isaaks II. Angelos," 204.

129 Rigo, "La direction spirituelle des moniales à Byzance," 295–97.

130 In 1397–1398, a certain Psepharas Georgios donated a manuscript to a certain Phokas Monastery. See Kitchin, *Catalogus codicum mss. qui in Bibliotheca Aedis Christi*, 16. On the other hand, the family name Phokas is attested in the thirteenth and fourteenth centuries.

131 Gennadios Scholarios, *Letter to Sophrosyne*, ed. Petit et al., 234–35; Gennadios Scholarios, *Letter to Simonis*, ed. Petit et al., 502–3. On Scholarios, see now Blanchet, *Georges-Gennadios Scholarios*. The dating derives from a mention of Gennadios Scholarios, *On the First Service of God*, ed. Petit et al., 236–64; Zeses, *Γεννάδιος Β' Σχολάριος*, 308–9.

132 Gennadios Scholarios, *Letter to Sophrosyne*, ed. Petit et al., p. 234, lines 9–12.

133 Gennadios Scholarios, *Letter to Sophrosyne*, ed. Petit et al., p. 234, line 6; Gennadios Scholarios, *Letter to Simonis*, ed. Petit et al., p. 502, lines 11–12.

"Asketikon" of St. Basil.[134] He sent his treatise, which was originally written for monks, with the suggestion that Sophrosyne focus on the points relevant to women.[135] However, he did not explicitly mention which points these were. From the correspondence, it is evident that Simonis/Sophrosyne Asanina Palaiologina maintained an intellectual and spiritual relationship with Scholarios. This relationship highlights her level of education and her active engagement in theological and monastic discourse—an exceptional case that underscores the presence of educated women in the Byzantine monastic tradition.

Apart from spiritual guidance, Palaiologan nunneries needed various texts to support their religious and administrative functions. One such manuscript is Oxford, Bodleian Library, MS Cromwell 22, dating to around 1314/15.[136] This manuscript is a homiliary (a collection of homilies), and it was specifically intended for a nunnery. The colophon of the manuscript is signed by a priestmonk named Mark. Barbara Crostini Lappin has analyzed its contents, concluding that Bodleian, MS Cromwell 22 was meant to be used by the abbess of the nunnery. Unlike other writers of his time, Mark did not deem certain topics unsuitable for a female audience, showing a progressive approach to the education and spiritual needs of nuns.

Crostini Lappin also connected the manuscript to the nunnery of Trichinareai on Mount Auxentios and the Evergetis Monastery. If this connection is accurate, it suggests that the well-known middle Byzantine nunnery of Trichinareai was still active at the beginning of the fourteenth century. This connection underlines the enduring influence of earlier monastic traditions and the continued relevance of such manuscripts in the spiritual life of later Byzantine nunneries.[137]

The codex Firenze, Biblioteca Nazionale Centrale, MS Magliabecchi Conv. B.1.1214 (Olivieri 50) (fourteenth century)[138] includes the Lives, or *vitae*, of only female saints. Certain *vitae* were the works of well-known Palaiologan authors such as Nikephoros Kallistou Xanthopoulos, John Staurakios,[139]

134 Gennadios Scholarios, *Letter to Sophrosyne*, ed. Petit et al., p. 234, line 24.

135 Gennadios Scholarios, *Letter to Sophrosyne*, ed. Petit et al., p. 234, line 18.

136 *Diktyon*: 47812.

137 Crostini Lappin, "A Fourteenth-Century Homiliary for Nuns," 35–68. For Trichinareai, see Belke, *Bithynien und Hellespont*, 1051–52.

138 *Diktyon*: 16927. For the manuscript's description, see Delehaye, "Vita sanctae Olympiadis et Narratio Sergiae de eiusdem Translatione," 406–8.

139 Kountoura-Galake, "Ιωάννης Σταυράκιος," 379–94.

Constantine Akropolites, and the monk Makarios. Due to the benediction formula "mother, bless" (*εὐλόγησον μῆτερ*) (fol. 12v), we can deduce that the manuscript was used in a nunnery.[140]

A similar case is represented by Hagion Oros, Koutloumousiou, MS 208 (fifteenth century).[141] The codex contains the funerary *akolouthia* (*τῶν κεκοιμημένων*) with a (non-authentic) work of John Chrysostom, works of St. Basil, followed by sixteen Lives of female saints and one male (Stephen the Younger), which are organized as a *menologion*. The original number of saints' Lives would have been higher, judging from some lacunae in the codex. A text entitled "Instruction about the salvation of the soul and the patience to be read aloud in the gatherings of monks and to nuns" (fols. 39r–46v)[142] indicates that the codex could have been used in a convent.

The production and accumulation of books by Byzantine monasteries is not well-documented in detail,[143] but some insights can be gathered from specific instances. Founders often played a crucial role in establishing monastic libraries by donating collections of books. For example, Neilos Damilas included a detailed list of forty-one books in the *typikon* of his foundation, which likely were intended for the nunnery. His inventory (dated to 1417) consisted of gospels, liturgical books, ascetical treatises, and theological works.[144]

Damilas, a bibliophile, emphasized the importance of preserving the convent's collection by forbidding external lendings, stating: "if they are damaged, you have no one to restore them."[145] This protective measure highlights the value and scarcity of books during that period. Additionally, he mandated that the personal books of the nuns should remain within the

140 Rapp, "Figures of Female Sanctity," 319–20.

141 *Diktyon*: 26237; Lambros, *Catalogue*, vol. 1, p. 297; Ehrhard, *Überlieferung und Bestand der hagiographischen und homiletischen Literatur*, vol. 3, pp. 907–8.

142 Ehrhard, *Überlieferung und Bestand der hagiographischen und homiletischen Literatur*, 907; Rapp, "Figures of Female Sanctity," 320n44.

143 Carr, "Women and Monasticism in Byzantium," 13; Volk, "Die byzantinischen Klosterbibliotheken von Konstantinopel, Thessalonike und Kleinasien," 10–13; Wilson, "The Libraries of the Byzantine World," 53–80; Waring, " Byzantine Monastic Libraries in the Eleventh and Twelfth Centuries "; Cavallo, *Η ανάγνωση στο Βυζάντιο*, 153–98. See also the articles in Shawcross et al., *Reading in the Byzantine Empire and Beyond*. On Western women and their relations to manuscripts, see, for example, Hand, *Women, Manuscripts and Identity in Northern Europe*.

144 Lampros, "Das Testament des Neilos Damilas," 585–87; Talbot, "*Neilos Damilas*," 1478–79; Caseau, "Objects in Churches," 549–79.

145 Pétridès, "Le *typikon* de Nil Damilas," chap. 20, p. 109; Talbot, "*Neilos Damilas*," 1477.

convent, further ensuring that the library's resources were safeguarded and available for the community's use.

This practice of keeping personal books within the monastery underscores the communal approach to knowledge and education in Byzantine nunneries. It also reflects the broader monastic values of resource conservation and shared intellectual and spiritual enrichment.

Anna/Antonia Komnene Raoulaina Strategopoulina made a significant donation to the nunnery of Krataios, presenting a parchment manuscript of 319 folios (Hagion Oros, Pantokratoros, MS 6), which dates back to the fourteenth century.[146] This manuscript, as noted extensively on fol. 3v, contained essential panegyrical readings for feast days and Lent, as well as saints' Lives, though only two *vitae* were dedicated to female saints: Gregory of Cyprus' *Logos on St. Marina* and the *Vita* of St. Irene of Chrysobalanton. This selection made the manuscript particularly valuable for the liturgical needs of the nunnery.

In addition to this manuscript, the *ktetorissa* (founder) Anna Raoulaina contributed other important items to the convent, including additional books, sacred vessels, and holy heirlooms. Such contributions would have greatly enriched the spiritual and liturgical life of the nunnery, providing the necessary resources for worship and devotion. This act of donation reflects the tradition of monastic patronage, where founders and benefactors played a crucial role in equipping monastic communities with the tools required for their religious practices and daily lives.

The scribes (*οἱ γεγραφότες*) invested significant time and effort in compiling the diverse material found within the manuscript donated by Anna/Antonia Komnene Raoulaina Strategopoulina to the nunnery of Krataios. This extensive collection included works from various notable sources, such as John Chrysostom, Gregory of Nyssa, Andrew of Crete, John of Damascus, Nikephoros Blemmydes, Gregory of Cyprus, and Nikephoros Choumnos.[147]

Given the laborious process of gathering and transcribing these texts, the scribes emphasized the importance of treating the holy and wondrous book with the utmost caution and care. They especially directed this admonition towards the future users of the manuscript, particularly the nuns,

146 *Diktyon*: 29025; Lambros, *Catalogue*, vol. 1, p. 94; Ehrhard, *Überlieferung und Bestand der hagiographischen und homiletischen Literatur*, vol. 1, p. 436, and vol. 3, p. 216.

147 Lambros, *Catalogue*, vol. 1, p. 94; Taxidis, "L'éloge de saint Eudocime par Constantin Acropolite," 5–44.

underscoring the sacred nature of the content and the effort involved in its creation.[148]

This careful preservation was crucial for maintaining the integrity and longevity of the manuscript, ensuring that it could continue to serve as a vital resource for liturgical and devotional practices within the nunnery.

The Krataios library holds significant historical interest, particularly highlighted by a revealing note found in fol. 78r-v of the fifteenth-century manuscript Città del Vaticano, BAV, MS Vat. gr. 677. The scribe recounts the challenges encountered in locating the Athanasian Creed (*ἔκθεσις πίστεως*) due to the deliberate destruction of its records by opponents of the Union. According to the scribe, the Creed had been nearly eradicated, with only two known testimonies remaining: one in a Psalter from the Krataios convent and another in a codex at the Mangana Monastery. In an effort to preserve the Creed, an anonymous individual transcribed it based on the Krataios Psalter. However, by the time the scribe penned his note, these testimonies, too, had been destroyed, indicating the systematic effort to eliminate this particular theological text.[149]

The Città del Vaticano, BAV, MS Vat. gr. 604 manuscript (fourteenth-fifteenth century)[150] provides valuable insights into the intellectual and religious currents of its time, being a private asset of Demetrios Kydones. The manuscript is notable for including both anti-Palamite and Unionist works, reflecting the contentious theological debates of the period. The involvement of prominent scholars, such as Prochoros Kydones, Manuel Kalekas, and Isidore of Kiev, whose hands have been identified in the manuscript, further underscores its significance.

One of the scribes (probably Manuel Kalekas) utilized two "old manuscripts" from the convent *tes megales Doukaines* in Constantinople.[151] These manuscripts contained Proklos's sermon on the Transfiguration (fol. 37v) and a marginal note on John Chrysostom's sermon on the same issue (fol. 39v).[152] This indicates that at the end of the fourteenth century, the convent's library was accessible to both Unionist and anti-Palamite scholars.

---

148 Lambros, *Catalogue*, vol. 1, p. 94.

149 *Diktyon*: 67308; Devreesse, *Codices Vaticani graeci*, 132; Stefec, "Zur Schnittdekoration kretischer Handschriften," 501–33.

150 *Diktyon*: 67235.

151 Mercati, *Notizie di Procoro e Demetrio Cidone, Manuele Caleca e Teodoro Meliteniota*, 261n4; Talbot, "Bluestocking Nuns," 610. On this nunnery, see Janin, *La géographie ecclésiastique de l'Empire byzantine*, 330.

152 Devreesse, *Codices Vaticani graeci*, 5.

The luxurious eleventh-century Stoudite Psalter, Città del Vaticano, BAV, MS Vat. gr. 752 (fol. 2r), includes a note indicating its association with a Pantanassa (Queen of All) monastery.[153] Robert Devreesse proposed that this might refer to the male Monastery of Pantanassa in Mistras, which dates to the fifteenth century.[154] However, further options cannot be dismissed. Two potential monastic connections for the Psalter include the Pantanassa in Baionaia or of *tes Pantanasses* nunnery in Constantinople. The latter was founded in the twelfth century as an imperial establishment; it became a significant pilgrimage site, especially for Russian travelers during the fourteenth and fifteenth centuries. Its imperial foundation and historical significance lend credence to the possibility that the Psalter could have belonged to this nunnery. The exact provenance of the Psalter remains uncertain, but these possibilities highlight the rich tapestry of monastic and religious life in the Byzantine world and the diverse paths through which such a manuscript might have travelled.

The Lips nunnery likely owned an eleventh-century parchment codex containing works of Dionysios Areopagites (Città del Vaticano, BAV, MS Vat. gr. 1787). According to a note on fol. 4v, an anonymous male donor stated that he drafted the *typikon* for the nunnery at the behest of Empress Theodora Palaiologina.[155] To further support the spiritual development of the nuns, this anonymous ghostwriter gifted the codex, which was likely from his private collection. This nunnery is linked to the so-called Palaiologina group: a collection of manuscripts named after the monogram of a female member of the Palaiologos dynasty that appears in a thirteenth century Gospel Book (Città del Vaticano, BAV, MS Vat. gr. 1158). Initially, Hugo Buchthal and Hans Belting attributed a group of fifteen deluxe codices to Theodora Raoulaina.[156] This initial group comprised seven Gospel Books, three Lectionaries, three Psalters, a New Testament, and a Praxapostolos. However,

153 *Diktyon*: 67383; Devreesse, *Codices Vaticani graeci*, 268: "Βιβλείω τῆς Παντανάσσου"; Parpulov, *Toward a History of Byzantine Psalters*, 122–26, 130–33; Crostini and Peers, *A Book of Psalms from Eleventh-Century Constantinople.*

154 Janin, *La géographie ecclésiastique de l'Empire byzantine*, 215–16; Majeska, *Russian Travelers to Constantinople in the Fourteenth and Fifteenth Centuries*, 377–79.

155 *Diktyon*: 68416; Canart, *Codices Vaticani graeci*, 135; Talbot, "Empress Theodora Palaiologina, Wife of Michael VIII," 299n40.

156 *Diktyon*: 67789; Buchthal and Belting, *Patronage in Thirteenth-Century Constantinople*, 100–21. See also Pérez Martín, "Irene Cumno y el 'taller de la Paleologuina,'" 223–34.

subsequent scholars identified Theodora Palaiologina, wife of Michael VIII, as the patroness of these codices.[157]

Robert S. Nelson and John Lowden expanded the group by adding the fourteenth-century Lips *typikon* (London, British Library, MS Addit. 22748)[158] and several other manuscripts to the known collection. They also questioned the attribution of all manuscripts to a single patron due to the increasing number of new attributions, the significant proportion of Lectionaries, and the production of these manuscripts extending into the fourteenth century. Nonetheless, it remains that at least three manuscripts of the Palaiologina group were commissioned by women: the original Palaiologina Gospel book (Città del Vaticano, BAV, MS Vat. gr. 1158), the Lips *typikon*, and the Gospel Firenze, Biblioteca Medicea Laurenziana, MS Plut. VI.28 (1285).[159]

Nuns in Byzantine society often had connections to manuscripts through male ownership or male actions, reflecting the intertwined nature of religious and familial relationships in manuscript preservation and transmission. An illustrative example is found in the Tetraevangelion Hagion Oros, Iviron, MS 5 (mid-thirteenth century).[160] A notice on an unnumbered folio records the death of Maria/Martha Spanopoulou on March 8, 1387.[161] Maria was the mother of the manuscript's owner, highlighting the familial linkage in the manuscript's history. This example underscores the broader

157 Nelson and Lowden, "The Palaeologina Group," 59–68; Talbot, "Empress Theodora Palaiologina, Wife of Michael VIII," 302; Kalopissi-Verti, "Δωρεές γυναικών στην υστεροβυζαντινή περίοδο," 245; Nicol, *The Byzantine Lady*, 33–47; Maxwell, "Another Lectionary of the "Atelier" of the Palaiologina," 47–54.

158 *Diktyon*: 39019. According to Talbot, "Empress Theodora Palaiologina, Wife of Michael VIII," 301 it is "a deluxe codex, probably the original version of the *typikon*"; see also Nelson and Lowden, "The Palaeologina Group," 65–67, with plates 9, 11, and 13.

159 *Diktyon*: 16015; Talbot, "Female Patronage in the Palaiologan Era," 269–70. For further manuscripts of the Scriptures owned by and/or produced for convents, see Carr, "Women and Monasticism in Byzantium," 11–12.

160 *Diktyon*: 23602; Lambros, *Catalogue*, vol. 2, pp. 1–2; Yota, "L'image du donateur dans les manuscrits illustrés byzantins," 282–83; Belting, *Das illuminierte Buch in der spätbyzantinischen Gesellschaft*, 35–37; Belting, "Die Auftraggeber," 165–66.

161 Lambros, *Catalogue*, vol. 2, p. 2: "*Τῆ κ΄ Μαρτήου ίνδ. ζ΄ ϛωϟε΄* (1387) *έκυμιθι υ μητέρα μου ονομαν της Μαρία μετανομαζόμενη το καλογερικόν της Μαρθα μοναχη*." See Yota, "L'image du donateur dans les manuscrits illustrés byzantins," 283; Belting, "Die Auftraggeber der spätbyzantinischen Bildhandschrift," 149–76. Martha must have belonged to the Spanopoulos family, since a further notice reports the birth of a certain John Spanopoulos.

phenomenon where women's connections to significant religious texts were often mediated through male relatives or associates.

The commission of manuscripts in Byzantine society indeed fostered a rich network of knowledge and relationships among patrons, copyists, and recipients. A poignant example of this is found in a panegyrical volume (Istanbul, Patriarchike Bibliotheke, MS Panagias 11) commissioned in 1360 by the nun Eirenarchia "for the repose of her son, the monk Theodoulos." This codex, copied by the monk Jacob, reflects the collaborative efforts and the devotion involved in such projects.[162]

A scribal note within the manuscript provides further insights into its journey and the connections between the individuals involved. Initially, Eirenarchia and Jacob donated the codex to the imperial monastery of St. Basil.[163] This gesture signifies their intention to honour the memory of Theodoulos within a respected religious institution. However, the historical upheavals of the time—specifically the Ottoman capture of Herakleia Pontike—led to the manuscript's relocation. Jacob's note indicates that it was subsequently donated to the Prodromos monastery in Sozopolis (Thrace).[164]

The establishment of knowledge networks in Byzantine society was significantly influenced by the patronage of literati and the scholarly relations they cultivated. Empress Helen/Hypomone Kantakouzene Palaiologina stands out as a notable example of female patronage in this intellectual and cultural milieu. Helen, the well-educated daughter of John VI Kantakouzenos, demonstrated her literary talent early on by composing *epinikioi logoi* celebrating her father's victory.[165] Her education and literary output facilitated the creation of a network of patronage encompassing prominent scholars and intellectuals of her era. Two of the most notable figures within

---

162 *Diktyon*: 33646; Vogel and Gardthausen, *Die griechischen Schreiber des Mittelalters und der Renaissance*, 156.

163 The St. Basil Monastery may have also been the known nunnery in Constantinople refounded by Gregory Antiochos in the middle of the twelfth century. See Janin, *La géographie ecclésiastique de l'Empire byzantine*, 59–60.

164 Athenagoras (Metropolitan), *Κατάλογος τῶν χειρογράφων τῆς ἐν Χάλκῃ Μονῆς τῆς Παναγίας*, 243; Papadopoulos-Kerameus, "Ἡ ἐν τῷ νησίῳ Σωζοπόλεως βασιλικὴ μονὴ Ἰωάννου τοῦ Προδρόμου," 670; Kouroupou and Géhin, *Catalogue des manuscrits conservés dans la Bibliothèque du Patriarcat Oecuménique*, 63–67; Euangelatou-Notara, *Χορηγοί–κτήτορες–δωρητές*, pp. 88 and 240, no. 260; Soustal, *Thrakien*, 454–56.

165 Demetrios Kydones, *Epistulae*, ed. Loenertz, pp. 340–41, no. 389. On Kydones' letters to the empress, see Kianka, "The Letters of Demetrios Kydones to Empress Helena," 155–64; Tinnefeld, *Die Briefe des Demetrios Kydones*, 63–64.

her network were her teacher Demetrios Kydones and the historian and philosopher Nikephoros Gregoras.[166]

Helen's patronage extended beyond mere intellectual engagement; it also included material support. Before entering the *kyra* Martha nunnery, Helen distributed her wealth generously. Among the recipients of her beneficence was Demetrios Kydones, who expressed his gratitude in a letter. This correspondence not only thanked Helen for her gifts but also provided a poignant account of the empress's trials and tribulations. Kydones depicted the bitter life of the empress and the numerous difficulties she had faced, highlighting her resilience and fortitude.

An intriguing aspect of this correspondence is the involvement of Manuel II Palaiologos, Helen's son. Manuel confirmed that he had read Kydones' epistle to his mother,[167] indicating that the scholarly and personal exchanges facilitated by Helen's patronage were known and valued at the highest levels of Byzantine society. This interaction between the empress, her scholarly correspondents, and her son underscores the intricate web of relationships and knowledge exchange fostered through female patronage in the Byzantine Empire.

The most impressive example, however, is the nun Theodora Raoulaina, a female scholar, patron, author, bibliophile, and copyist.[168] The *protovestiaria* Raoulaina renovated the Monastery of St. Andrew *in Krisei*, where she brought her personal library. Raoulaina's only known work is the *Life of the Graptoi* (*Vita Theophanis et Theodori Grapti*, *BHG* 1793).[169] This *Vita* bears testimony to the books she had at her disposal, referencing works from Homer's Iliad, Hesiod, Aeschylus and Euripides, Herodotus, Plato, and

166 Guilland, *Correspondance de Nicephore Gregoras*, pp. 144–47, no. 42. See also Manolova, "Discourses of Science and Philosophy in the Letters," 220.

167 Demetrios Kydones, *Epistulae*, ed. Loenertz, pp. 103–10, no. 222; Manuel II Palaeologos, *Letters*, ed. Dennis, p. 65, no. 23; Leonte, "A Late Byzantine Patroness," 345–53.

168 On Raoulaina, see Constantinides, *Higher Education in Byzantium in the Thirteenth and Early Fourteenth Centuries*, 43–44; Fryde, *The Early Palaeologan Renaissance*, 180–81. For the title *protovestiaria*, see Margarou, *Τίτλοι και επαγγελματικά ονόματα γυναικών στο Βυζάντιο*, 102–4. Interestingly, she may have been portraited in the Blachernai Church in Arta. See Parani, "'The Joy of the Most Holy Mother of God the Hodegetria,'" 113–45.

169 The work exists in Athens, Ethnike Bibliotheke tes Ellados, MS Metochion Pan. Taphou 244, fols. 129–53 (fourteenth century) (*Diktyon*: 6641); Theodora Raoulaina, "Vita Theophanis et Theodori Grapti," ed. Papadopoulos-Kerameus, 185–223; Sode, *Jerusalem—Konstantinopel—Rom*, 199–201.

Dionysios of Halicarnassus. She also quotes the Proverbs and the Scriptures, though patristic works are not included.[170]

Raoulaina is a well-known copyist. Around 1280, she copied the Orations of Aelius Aristides (Città del Vatican, MS Vat. gr. 1899)[171] and the Simplicius commentaries on Aristotle's Physics (Moscow, Gosudarstvennyj Istoričeskij Musej, MS Mus. Sobr. 3649).[172] In this role, she belongs to a small group of female scribes. Other known female copyists from the Palaiologan period include the nun Maria[173] and the calligrapher Irene, daughter of Theodore Hagiopetrites.[174]

The *protovestiaria* was an avid collector of books, with a personal library that included manuscripts of classical and ecclesiastical significance. Her collection featured the works of Demosthenes and other rhetoricians, writings by Gregory of Cyprus, the *Ethics* of St. Basil, a treatise on harmonics, and a variety of other texts.[175] Additionally, the famous, tenth-century Thucydides

---

170 Talbot, "Old Wine in New Bottles," 20–21; Nervo, "Teodora Raoulena," 152–61; Matschke and Tinnefeld, *Die Gesellschaft im späten Byzanz*, 319.

171 *Diktyon*: 68528; Turyn, *Codices graeci Vaticani saeculis XIII et XIV*, 63–65; Canart and Peri, *Sussidi bibliografici per I manoscritti greci della Biblioteca Vaticana*, 656; Gamillscheg, *Repertorium der griechischen Kopisten*, vol. 3, p. 85, no. 206. See also Kugeas, "Zur Geschichte der Münchener Thukydideshandschrift," 594; Pérez Martín, *El patriarca Gregorio de Chipre*, 35–36; Zorzi, "Una copista, due copisti, nessuna copista?" 259–82; Nousia, "Theodora Raoulaina's Autograph Codex Vat. gr. 1899," 339–59.

172 Harlfinger, "Einige Aspekte der handschriftlichen Überlieferung," 267. On the eight twelve-syllable verses in Città del Vaticano, BAV, MS Vat. gr. 1899 (*Diktyon*: 68528) and in Moscow, GIM, MS Mus. Sobr. 3649 (*Diktyon*: 43621), where Raoulaina is mentioned as the scribe, see Fonkič, "Zametki o grečeskich rukopisjach Sovietskich chranilišč," 134.

173 She copied the Moscow, GIM, MS Sinod. gr. 343 (Vlad. 268) (thirteenth century) (*Diktyon*: 43968). The parchment manuscript contains liturgical formulas (*Akolouthiai*) to Baptism and to the monastic tonsure. See Vladimir (Archimandrit), *Sistematičeskoe opisanie rukopisei Moskovskoj Sinodalnoj biblioteki*, 386–87; Lampros, "Ἑλληνίδες βιβλιογράφοι καὶ κυρίαι κωδίκων," 243–44; Vogel and Gardthausen, *Die griechischen Schreiber des Mittelalters und der Renaissance*, 288; Schreiner, "Kopistinnen in Byzanz," 36–37; Carr, "Women and Monasticism in Byzantium," 5–6.

174 Carr, "A Note on Theodore Hagiopetrites," 287–90; Nelson, *Theodore Hagiopetrites*, 25; Schreiner, "Kopistinnen in Byzanz," 38.

175 Gregory of Cyprus, *Letters*, ed. Kotzabassi, p. 154, no. 12, and p. 157, lines 1–4, 10–11, no. 17, and p. 158, lines 18–20, 22–24, no. 17, and p. 159, no. 18; Leone, *Maximi Monachi Planudis Epistulae*, p. 103, lines 11–12, and p. 104, lines 8–10, no. 68; Constantinides, *Higher Education in Byzantium in the Thirteenth and Early Fourteenth Centuries*, 140. On the letters of Gregory of Cyprus, see Chrysostomides, "To

manuscript (München, Bayerische Staatsbibliothek, MS gr. 430) was part of her collection.[176] In 1300/1, Raoulaina donated to Lavra a twelfth-century manuscript containing Theophylaktos of Ohrid's commentaries on the Four Gospels (Paris, BnF, MS Coisl. gr. 128).[177] A note in the manuscript records that the monks were requested to offer prayers on behalf of the donor.

Raoulaina participated energetically in a book exchange with other scholars and, like the *sebastokratorissa* Irene in the twelfth century,[178] had a circle of protégés. She sent a mathematic treatise to Constantine Akropolites, who was not impressed by its quality.[179] Nikephoros Choumnos sent her Aristotle's *Meteorologika* with the comments of Alexander of Aphrodisias.[180] Her correspondence is reflected in the letter collections of many Palaiologan scholars, including Gregory of Cyprus, Maximos Planoudes (ca. 1255–1305), Manuel Holobolos (ca. 1245–1310/14), Nikephoros Choumnos and probably also Constantine Akropolites.[181]

---

corpus των επιστολών του Γεωργίου-Γρηγορίου Κυπρίου"; Riehle, "Epistolography, Social Exchange and Intellectual Discourse," 225. Raoulaina was his spiritual child. Pachymeres criticized her attachment to the Patriarch. Pachymeres, *History*, ed. Failler and Laurent, vol. 3, bk. 3, chap. 10, p. 151, line 9.

176 *Diktyon*: 44878; Kugeas, "Zur Geschichte der Münchener Thukydideshandschrift," 594, 608. This codex includes a notice on the death of Theodora on December 6, 1300. See Kugeas, "Zur Geschichte der Münchener Thukydideshandschrift," 590: "+ἐκοιμήθη ἡ ἁγία κυρία μου ἡ μοναχὴ κυρὰ Θεοδώρα Ῥαούλαινα Καντακουζηνὴ Κομνηνὴ ἡ Παλαιολογίνα ἡ ἐξαδέλφη τοῦ εὐσεβεστάτου βασιλέως κυροῦ Ἀνδρονίκου ἐν ἔτει ϛωθ ἰνδ. ιδ κατὰ τὴν ϛ′ τοῦ Δεκεμβρίου μηνὸς ὥρα ζ′ τῆς αὐτῆς νυκτός." Pérez Martín, *El patriarca Gregorio de Chipre*, 270.

177 *Diktyon*: 49272; Devreesse, *Catalogue des manuscrits grecs*, 122; Euangelatou-Notara, *Χορηγοί—κτήτορες—δωρητές*, 99–100; see also the dedicatory notices in De Montfaucon, *Bibliotheca Coisliniana olim Segueriana sive Manuscriptorum omnium Graecorum*, 201. On her library, see now Taxidis, "Public and Private Libraries in Byzantium," 470.

178 Jeffreys, "The *Sebastokratorissa* Irene as Patron," 177–94.

179 Constantine Akropolites, *Epistole*, ed. Romano, pp. 155–56, no. 60; Constantinides, *Higher Education in Byzantium in the Thirteenth and Early Fourteenth Centuries*, 78, 109, 140, and appendix no. 60.164.

180 Riehle, *Die Briefsammlungen des Nikephoros Chumnos*, p. 332, no. B76; Leone, "Le epistole di Niceforo Chumno," p. 77, no. 76; Riehle, "Funktionen der byzantinischen Epistolographie," 108, 159; Riehle, "*Καί σε προστάτιν ἐν αὐτοῖς τῆς αὐτῶν ἐπιγράψομεν σωτηρίας*," 299–315.

181 On Raoulaina and Planoudes, see Leone, *Maximi Monachi Planudis Epistulae*, pp. 79–80, no. 65; Kugeas, "Zur Geschichte der Münchener Thukydideshandschrift," 602–3; Lampros, "Ἑλληνίδες βιβλιογράφοι καὶ κυρίαι κωδίκων," pp. 415–18; Taxides, *Μάξιμος Πλανούδης*, 74–77; Pérez Martín, *El patriarca Gregorio de Chipre*,

Theodora Raoulaina had a very close relation to Gregory of Cyprus (ca. 1241–1290), who may have already been supported by Raoulaina's mother and son, Theodore Mouzalon.[182] Their friendship is attested in historical sources as well as in the twenty-nine letters of the Patriarch adressed to her, most of them dated during Gregory's patriarchate. Despite her literacy, Gregory occasionally used a simplified style in his letters, which caused a reaction from Raoulaina, who felt insulted by this "priestly" (πρεσβυτερικά)—as she called it—style. Unfortunately, the existing data do not support such an accusation. Nevertheless, it is notable that their correspondence refers to gifts and manuscripts but does not delve into scientific topics.

In conclusion, educated nuns were capable of reading edifying texts, but there were limitations on the works recommended to them by spiritual fathers or by the *typika*. Spiritual fathers advised the nuns to read texts of ecclesiastical content or monastic tradition, such as the *Apopthegmata Patrum* and the works of St. Basil. Profane literature was not considered appropriate for the edification of female monastics. Only few women could escape illiteracy and even been acknowledged as scholars on their own merit.

270n48; Grünbart, *Formen der Anrede im byzantinischen Brief*, 183, 185, 187, 290; Talbot, "Old Wine in New Bottles," 20–21; Rizzo Nervo, "Teodora Raoulena," 147–62. On Raoulaina, Holobolos, and Choumnos, see Treu, *Manuelis Holoboli Orationes*, 552; Treu, "Manuel Holobolos," 538–59; Riehle, "Funktionen der byzantinischen Epistolographie," 108, 159.

182 After the death of Theodora's mother, Gregory of Cyprus sent both to her and her sister, Anna, a condolence letter. See Gregory of Cyprus, *Letters*, ed. Kotzabassi, p. 145, no. 1. On the kinship relation of Raoulaina to Theodore Mouzalon, see Samara, *Θεόδωρος Μουζάλων*, 22–24.

Chapter 5

FEMALE MONASTICISM AND THE CHURCH

THE ROLE OF female monasticism within the Byzantine Church from the thirteenth to the fifteenth centuries can be examined from multiple angles. This chapter primarily focuses on the involvement of nuns in the ecclesiastical controversies of the thirteenth century, employing modern methodologies such as Social Network Analysis. This approach enables us to visualize and quantify the influence of female monastics in the broader social dynamics of Byzantium. A secondary objective is to explore the Church's stance toward female monastic communities and assess how decisions made by ecclesiastical authorities affected these communities—particularly in the aftermath of the Fourth Crusade in 1204 and the Union of Lyons in 1274.[1]

Ecclesiastical Controversies and Female Networks

The thirteenth, fourteenth, and fifteenth centuries witnessed several momentous ecclesiastical events, including the Arsenite Schism (1265–1310), the failed attempts at union with the Latin Church (1274 and 1438/39),[2] and the Hesychast controversy (in the 1330s and 1340s). These developments cannot be fully understood when viewed solely through an ecclesiastical

1 Gill, *Byzantium and the Papacy*; Nicol, "The Greeks and the Union of the Churches," 454–80; Nicol, "The Byzantine Reaction to the Second Council of Lyons," 113–46; Roberg, *Die Union zwischen der griechischen und der lateinischen Kirche*; Roberg, *Das Zweite Konzil von Lyon*; Evert-Kappesowa, "La société byzantine et l'Union de Lyon," 28–41; Evert-Kappesowa, "Une page de l'histoire des relations byzantino-latines: Le clergé byzantin et l'Union de Lyon," 68–92; Evert-Kappesowa, "Une page de l'histoire des relations byzantino-latines," 297–317; Evert-Kappesowa, "Une page de l'Histoire des relations byzantino-latines: 2. La fin de l'Union de Lyon," 1–18; Puech, "The Byzantine Aristocracy and the Union of the Churches," 45–54; Beaucamp, "Les femmes et l'église," 362–63.

2 Blanchet, *Georges-Gennadios Scholarios*; Blanchet, "L'église byzantine á la suite de l'union de Florence," 79–123; Kiousopoulou, "Ἡ κοινωνικὴ διάσταση τῆς σύγκρουσης," 25–36; van Dieten, "Der Streit in Byzanz und die Rezeption der Unio Florentina," 160–80; Gounarides, "Πολιτικές διαστάσεις της συνόδου Φεράρας-Φλωρεντίας," 107–29; Demacopoulos, "The Popular Reception of the Council of Florence," 37–53; Chrysos, "Η Ανατολή συναντά τη Δύση," 49–62.

lens, as they were deeply intertwined with political and social dynamics. Although each occurred under distinct historical circumstances—by the late thirteenth century, the Byzantine Empire remained a significant power, whereas by the fifteenth century it had become a mere shadow of its former self—they share notable commonalities. Chief among these is the active involvement of women, particularly nuns.

In Byzantium, women frequently played active roles in religious controversies. A prominent early example is their passionate involvement in the Iconoclastic conflict, which established a precedent for female engagement in theological disputes for generations to come. The memory of those who resisted Iconoclasm was preserved and celebrated during the Palaiologan period, with scholars such as Constantine Akropolites chronicling the lives of iconophile saints. Among them, St. Theodosia emerged as a symbolic embodiment of Orthodoxy by the late thirteenth century. It is thus unsurprising that Theodora Raoulaina—a staunch Arsenite and anti-Unionist nun—chose to author the *Life of the Graptoi* (*Vita Theophanis et Theodori Grapti*), further reinforcing this legacy of female theological resistance.

The controversies of the late Byzantine period were marked by significant complexity and fluidity. As the political and ecclesiastical landscape evolved, many participants altered their positions, at times aligning themselves with previously opposing factions, as numerous cases after 1282 illustrate. Nevertheless, some individuals remained unwavering in their convictions, often at great personal cost—including exclusion from the Orthodox community.

The Arsenite Schism

The Arsenite Schism was the first major ecclesiastical controversy of the late Byzantine period in which women—especially nuns—played a significant role.[3] The conflict began in 1265 with the deposition of Patriarch Arsenios, but it soon evolved into a broader movement marked by strong anti-Palaiologan sentiment. The catalyst was Emperor Michael VIII Palaiologos's blinding of the legitimate heir, John IV Laskaris—an act that prompted Arsenios to excommunicate the emperor. In response, and with no reconciliation in sight, Michael VIII convened a synod that ultimately deposed the unyielding

3 On the Arsenites, see Gounarides, *Τὸ κίνημα τῶν Ἀρσενιατῶν*; Sykoutres, "Περὶ τὸ σχίσμα τῶν Ἀρσενιατῶν," 267–332, 15–44, 107–26. See also Puech, "L'aristocratie et le pouvoir à Byzance," vol. 2, pp. 411–34; Tinnefeld, "Das Schisma zwischen Anhängern und Gegnern," 143–65.

patriarch. The backlash from Arsenios's supporters, however, was unexpectedly intense and endured for decades, continuing until 1310.[4]

The Arsenite Schism has often been linked to the perceived neglect of the population in Asia Minor following the recapture of Constantinople in 1261, and it is closely associated with the legacy of the Laskarid dynasty. Lacking centralized leadership, the Arsenite movement fragmented into competing factions, including those led by figures such as Hyakinthos and John Tarchaneiotes. While some groups, like the one headed by Theodore Manouelites, were willing to reconcile with the official Church after 1282 (the death of Michael VIII), others persisted in their opposition until the Schism's eventual resolution in 1310. In the years following 1282, the Arsenites increasingly sought to establish a parallel ecclesiastical structure, conducting liturgies in their own churches with their own clergy, effectively forming an alternative Church alongside the official one.[5]

The presence of women, and particularly nuns, in the discussions surrounding the Arsenite Schism is clearly evident in the source material. Theodora Raoulaina, one of the most prominent female figures of the period, joined the Arsenite cause along with the rest of the Raoul family. Female members of the Tarchaneiotes family,[6] such as the nuns Maria and Theodora Tarchaneiotissa, were also ardent supporters of the deposed Patriarch Arsenios.

Vincent Puech identifies personal and dynastic motives behind Tarchaneiotissa's involvement in the movement against Michael VIII. Firstly, there was Maria/Martha's animosity towards her sister, Irene/Eulogia. As Puech correctly notes, "one can think that the two sisters of the emperor, having entered into different families, maintained a rivalry."[7] Similarly, Theodora Raoulaina aligned with the political commitments of the family into which she married.

Puech further speculates that Maria/Martha sought to play an intermediary role between the Laskaris and Palaiologos families. It is important to remember that the Tarchaneiotes, Nestongos, and Raoul families supported Michael VIII in his bid for the regency (*symbasileia*), despite being candidates for the same role themselves. These families also objected to the blinding of the young John IV Laskaris, which was done on the advice of Irene/

---

4 Laurent, "La fin du schism arsénite," 285–313.

5 Gounarides, *Τὸ κίνημα τῶν Ἀρσενιατῶν*, 70–71, 121–59.

6 On the Tarchaneiotes family, see Leontiades, *Die Tarchaneiotai*, 61–77.

7 Puech, "L'aristocratie et le pouvoir à Byzance," vol. 2, p. 416. Translation my own.

Eulogia. On the other hand, their kinship with Michael VIII's political opponents[8] suggests that the Arsenites (at least among the aristocratic families) were more focused on gaining imperial power than on restoring ecclesiastical order.

The Unions of Lyons (1274) and Ferrara-Florence (1438/39)

Since the Schism between the Orthodox and Catholic Churches in 1054, as well as the Crusades and the capture of Constantinople in 1204, Byzantines and Latins had viewed each other with suspicion and prejudice.[9] After the recapture of Constantinople from the Latins in 1261, Emperor Michael VIII sought to leverage the possibility of a Church union to secure papal approval for his return to the capital and to prevent renewed Western crusading attempts against the Byzantines. However, the Union—concluded at Lyons in 1274—mobilized several conservative segments of Byzantine society against both the policy and the emperor.[10]

The reaction to the proclaimed union began soon after the return of the representatives from the West. George Pachymeres describes it as a schism affecting the entire Church. In addition to the initial group of opposition known as the Arsenites, a second group emerged: the anti-Unionists. This group included people "whose knowledge was confined to the hoe and the axe, and others with knowledge but excessively zealous in their advocacies."[11] The motto "do not touch, do not be affected" (*μὴ ἅψῃ, μηδὲ θίγῃς*), which had already been used by the Arsenites, became widely adopted once again.[12]

Female participation in the anti-Union faction became evident soon after 1274. Unionists depicted their activities in a negative light. A synodal

---

8 On the marriage of Andronikos Tarchaneiotes to a daughter of John Doukas and his escape to the lands of his father-in-law, see Leontiades, *Die Tarchaneiotai*, 64–65.

9 Kolbaba, *The Byzantine Lists*; Kolbaba, *Inventing Latin Heretics*; Kolbaba, "The Orthodoxy of the Latins in the Twelfth Century," 199–214; Kolbaba, "Byzantine Perceptions of Latin Religious 'Errors,'" 117–43; Pérez Martín, "Le conflit de l'Union des Églises," 411–22; Constantinides, "Byzantine Scholars and the Union of Lyons," 86–93.

10 Darrouzès and Laurent, *Dossier grec de l'Union de Lyon*; Puech, " L'aristocratie et le pouvoir à Byzance," vol. 2, pp. 434–53.

11 Pachymeres, *History*, ed. Failler and Laurent, vol. 2, bk. 5, chap. 13, pp. 511–13. English translation by Gill, *Byzantium and the Papacy*, 163.

12 Pachymeres, *History*, ed. Failler and Laurent, vol. 2, bk. 5, chap. 23, p. 511, lines 15–16. For Pachymeres' perspective on the issue of Church Union, see Lampakes, *Γεώργιος Παχυμέρης*, 87–89.

document from February 1277 detailed the resistance against the Union in Constantinople, outlining the involvement of various groups. It began with the imperial family and the senate, then moved to bishops and metropolitans, church office holders, priests, and finally monks and the laity. The document particularly mentioned the high number of women involved and lamented that "this evil" had even reached them.[13] Similarly, Constantine Meliteniotes sharply criticized "women who were obsessed with fame and were advocating for religious issues." After 1282, these women actively participated in various synods that deposed Unionist metropolitans and imposed punishments on members of the clergy and laity.[14]

The expression "women mad after fame" likely refers to Irene/Eulogia Kantakouzene Palaiologina. Once the favoured sister of Michael VIII, Irene/Eulogia supported him throughout his bid for the throne. She brought him the news of Constantinople's recapture in 1261 and advised in favour of deposing John IV Laskaris.[15] However, the Union significantly altered her relationship with her brother, leading her to become a staunch anti-Unionist.[16]

Pachymeres presents Irene/Eulogia and Theodore Mouzalon as key instigators of the policy shift after 1282. They were instrumental in persuading Andronikos II to renounce the Union and return to Orthodoxy.[17] Additionally, Irene/Eulogia convinced Michael VIII's wife, Theodora Palaiologina, that praying for her husband's soul was futile, as he was destined for eternal damnation.[18]

The anti-Union movement between 1274 and 1282 achieved significant success in attracting supporters within the palace and among the patriarchal clergy. Relatives of the emperor were openly opposed to his policy. Ogerio

13 Darrouzès and Laurent, *Dossier grec de l'Union de Lyon*, p. 465, lines 4–9, no. 16 (1277).

14 Constantine Meliteniotes, *Λόγοι ἀντιρρητικοὶ δύο*, ed. Orphanos, p. 116, lines 6–7.

15 Pachymeres, *History*, ed. Failler and Laurent, vol. 1, bk. 2, chap. 35, p. 225, lines 12–16.

16 On Irene/Eulogia Palaiologina, see Papadopulos, *Versuch einer Genealogie der Palaiologen*, no. 29, 18–19.

17 Pachymeres, *History*, ed. Failler and Laurent, vol. 3, bk. 7, chap. 2, p. 23, lines 19–20. For a different opinion, see Gregoras, *Roman History*, ed. Bekker et al., vol. 1, bk. 6, chap. 1, p. 159, line 17, and p. 160, line 1. See also Pseudo-Sphrantzes, *Chronicle*, ed. Grecu, bk. 1, chap. 4, p. 170, lines 3–4. On Mouzalon, see Samara, *Θεόδωρος Μουζάλων*, with an edition of his letters and other works.

18 Pachymeres, *History*, ed. Failler and Laurent, vol. 3, bk. 7, chap. 3, p. 25, lines 8–12; Talbot, "Empress Theodora Palaiologina, Wife of Michael VIII," 297–98; Mitsiou, "Regaining the True Faith," 77–96.

Boccanegra, *protonotarios* of Michael VIII, reported in a letter to Marco and Marchetto, *latores litterarum* of Pope Nicholas III (May-June 1278), about the challenges the emperor faced in implementing the Union. He specifically mentioned the imperial female relatives who were particularly resistant, including Michael's sister Maria/Martha Tarchaneiotissa (widow of Nikephoros Tarchaneiotes), her daughter Theodora (widow of the great *stratopedarches* Balanidiotes), and his niece Theodora Raoulaina, daughter of Irene/Eulogia, all of whom had been ardent followers of Arsenios. They were imprisoned, and their properties were confiscated.[19] Irene/Eulogia and her daughter, Theodora Raoulaina, were exiled to the fortress of St. Gregory in the Gulf of Nikomedeia.[20]

On the other hand, female opposition to the Union of Ferrara-Florence of 1438/39—arranged in the hope of provoking a new crusade to save Byzantium from the Ottomans—seems less dynamic compared to that of the thirteenth century (or at least is less prominent in the sources). Only Doukas mentions the behaviour of nuns—notably supporters of Gennadios—who in 1452 protested against the Unionist liturgy in St. Sophia. He describes it as follows:

> Those nuns, who considered themselves to be pure and dedicated to God in Orthodoxy, with common resolve and in accord with their teacher Gennadios, and with the abbots and the confessors and the remaining priests and laymen, cried aloud the *anathema*. The Article of Union of the Council and those who had acquiesced in the past and who acquiesce in the present and will acquiesce in the future, they anathematized.[21]

Doukas also criticized these nuns in another context. While addressing the anti-Unionists' claim that the altars had become pagan through their use by Catholics, he reported: "I saw with my own eyes a nun who had taken sacred vows not only eating meat and covering her body with barbarian dress but

---

19 See Dölger and Wirth, *Regesten der Kaiserurkunden des Oströmischen Reiches*, vol. 3, no. 2038a; Loenertz, "Memoire d'Ogier, protonotaire, pour Marco et Marchetto," chap. 13, p. 554; Geanakoplos, *Emperor Michael Palaeologos and the West*, 324; Gill, *Byzantium and the Papacy*, 170; Papadopulos, *Versuch einer Genealogie der Palaiologen*, no. 22, pp. 13–14 and no. 28, p. 18.

20 After 1282, the Unionists were also exiled there. Pachymeres, *History*, ed. Failler and Laurent, vol. 3, bk. 7, chap. 35, p. 117, lines 21–26; Gregoras, *Roman History*, ed. Bekker et al., vol. 1, bk. 6, chap. 2, p. 171, lines 2–3. For the Fort of St. Gregory, see Foss, *Survey of Medieval Castles of Anatolia*, 68; Belke, *Bithynien und Hellespont*, 582.

21 Doukas, *Historia*, ed. Grecu, chap. 36, §4, p. 317, lines 12–16; Magoulias, *Dukas*, 204; Gill, *The Council of Florence*, 384.

also making an offering to the false prophet and shamelessly confessing his unholy faith [i.e., Islam]"[22] Doukas questions the purity that the anti-Unionist nuns preached and demanded, portraying them as preferring Muslims over Latins. Additionally, Demetrios Palaiologos, the brother of John VIII, attempted to seize power in Constantinople in 1442 with the support of anti-Unionists and Turks, although his attempt ultimately failed.[23]

Nothing is known about the exile or imprisonment of nuns following the Union Council of 1438/39. Additionally, very few women from the imperial family or high aristocracy were involved in the anti-Unionist faction. Those who did show any anti-Unionist sentiments often quickly reversed their position. For example, Helen Dragaš, mother of John VIII and Constantine Palaiologos, was influential in shaping her sons' opinions on many important matters. While in Italy, the pope urged the emperor to appoint a patriarch after consulting with archpriests rather than relying solely on the opinion of his mother, who had been a nun since 1426/27.[24] In 1445, she supported the anti-Unionists by refusing to pray for the Unionist Patriarch, but she later changed her stance.[25]

In reality, it seems that the Union of Florence was accepted by the majority of the Byzantine aristocracy, many of whom had family members who had chosen monastic life.[26] A possible reason for this acceptance may be the shift in their socio-economic circumstances since the thirteenth century. After the loss of substantial portions of the Empire, the wealth of the aristocracy increasingly depended on commercial activities rather than land and property, especially in the West. Several prominent aristocratic women became trading partners with the Venetians and Genoese.[27]

The lower classes were likely the main supporters of the anti-Unionists, although shifts between groups were possible over time. Isidore of Kiev claimed that he had not only the majority of the senate on his side but also "the lower classes of the race, the bulk of the populace, a foolish people, and

---

22 Doukas, *Historia*, ed. Grecu, chap. 36, §6, p. 319, lines 28–31; Magoulias, *Dukas*, 206.

23 Nicol, *The Last Centuries of Byzantium*, 360.

24 Sylvestros Syropoulos, *Les "Mémoires,"* ed. Laurent, bk. 10, chap. 24, p. 510, lines 13–16.

25 John Eugenikos, *Τοῦ νομοφύλακος Ἰωάννου διακόνου τοῦ Εὐγενικοῦ τῷ δεσπότῃ παραμυθητικόν*, ed. Lampros, p. 59, lines 21–15; Gill, *The Council of Florence*, 369; Kiousopoulou, *Βασιλεύς ἤ οικονόμος*, 184. On Helen Dragaš and her attitude towards the Union, see Petanovič, *Elena*, 143–64.

26 Gill, *The Council of Florence*, 390.

27 Mitsiou, "Aspekte der Wirtschafts- und Sozialgeschichte," 32–42.

in no way sensible, who, to put it plainly, readily, alas, accepted the betrayal (at least in part) of their own faith for human considerations."[28] Contrary to Doukas's testimony, Isidore referred to a small group of eight anti-Unionist monks around Gennadios—a claim also supported by Theodore Agallianos.[29] It is evident that, due to numerous adverse political circumstances and the looming Ottoman threat, the anti-Unionist movement of the fifteenth century was less vigorous than it had been in the thirteenth.

The Hesychast Controversy

Between the two unions with the Latin Church, Byzantium experienced another significant ecclesiastical turmoil during the Hesychast movement of the fourteenth century. Women, especially nuns, played an active role in this period.[30] Philotheos Kokkinos refers to a considerable number of women, some of imperial descent, who supported the orthodox position, although he does not mention any female opponents of Hesychasm. However, there were indeed notable women who opposed Hesychasm. Theodora/Theodosia Palaiologina, the *tsarina* of Bulgaria, was an opponent of Palamas,[31] as was Simonis, the wife of the Serbian ruler (1299–1321) and later a nun.

The Register of the Patriarchate records instances where the *ktetorikon dikaion* was revoked from abbesses due to their involvement in ecclesiastical controversies. In 1354, Patriarch Philotheos Kokkinos ordered the

---

28 John Eugenikos, *Letters*, ed. Lampros, p. 196, line 25, and p.197, line 1, no 22.

29 Isidore of Kiev, "Letter to Nicholas V," in Pertusi, *La caduta di Costantinopoli*, p. 92; Theodore Agallianos, *Sermones*, ed. Patrineles, p. 97, lines 238–41; Blanchet, *Georges-Gennadios Scholarios*, 442; Theodore Agallianos, *Contra Latinos*, ed. Blanchet, 122–30.

30 On Hesychasm, see generally Meyendorff, *Byzantine Hesychasm*. Hesychasm developed through monastic practices around *hesychia* (quietness and peacefulness) ending up to mean a specific way of praying in order to envision the Holy Spirit. The biggest supporters were Palamas and Athonite monks. Among its opponents can be listed many scholars and intellectuals. The theological controversy had severe political dimensions until the final prevalence of Palamism.

31 John Kantakouzenos, *History*, ed. Schopen, vol. 1, pp. 12, 186, 208, 430, and vol. 2, p. 222; Gregoras, *Roman History*, ed. Bekker et al., vol. 1, bk. 9, chap. 1, pp. 390–91; Mercati, *Notizie di Procoro e Demetrio Cidone, Manuele Caleca e Teodoro Meliteniota*, 223; Fatouros and Krischer, *Johannes Kantakuzenos*, vol. 1, pp. 213, 266–67, and vol. 2, p. 202; van Dieten, *Nikephoros Gregoras*, vol. 2, pp. 102–94; Papadopulos, *Versuch einer Genealogie der Palaiologen*, 71; Dölger, *Regesten der Kaiserurkunden des Oströmischen Reiches*, vol. 4, nos. 2303 and 2679; Oikonomides, "Theodora δέσποινα τῶν Βουλγάρων in a Prostagma," 209–10.

expulsion of nun Angelina Senacheirina from the patriarchal monastery of *kyr David* in Philadelphia, citing that "she had harmed the souls of the nuns and had engaged in unacceptable behavior."[32]

It remains unclear what specific accusations were made against this nun, but connections with anti-Palamite circles cannot be ruled out. Kokkinos appointed Makarios Chrysokephalos, the metropolitan of Philadelphia, as the *ephoros* of the nunnery.[33] Similarly, in 1360/61, the nun Maroulina from the Barangiotissa Monastery in Constantinople was identified as a follower of Barlaam and Akindynos—two prominent anti-Palamite figures. Rather than working for the benefit of the nuns' souls, Maroulina (according to the document) harmed both her own soul and those of the other nuns.[34] As a result, she lost her rights as *ephoros* of the nunnery.

The most prominent female adversary of Gregory Palamas was Irene Choumnaina Palaiologina, the daughter of Nikephoros Choumnos and daughter-in-law of Andronikos II.[35] After being widowed, Irene took monastic vows and renovated the Monastery of Philanthropos Soter in Constantinople. Highly educated, she supported Gregory Akindynos—likely her second spiritual father after Theoleptos of Philadelphia—to whom she remained loyal until the end of her life.[36]

Abbess Irene Choumnaina was accused by the followers of Palamas of attempting to act as a *didaskalos* (teacher),[37] a role for which she was, in contrast, praised by Nikephoros Gregoras and Matthew of Ephesos.[38]

---

32 *Patriarchal Register*, vol. 3, ed. Koder et al., p. 100, no. 191 (March 1354), lines 4–9; Darrouzès, *Les regestes des Actes du patriarcat de Constantinople*, no. 2359.

33 *Patriarchal Register*, vol. 3, ed. Koder et al., p. 100, no. 191 (March 1354), lines 12–20.

34 *Patriarchal Register*, vol. 3, ed. Koder et al., pp. 516–18, no. 258 (February 1361), lines 29–33; Darrouzès, *Les regestes des Actes du patriarcat de Constantinople*, no. 2433.

35 For the list of the Antipalamites given by John Kyparissiotes, see Mercati, *Notizie di Procoro e Demetrio Cidone, Manuele Caleca e Teodoro Meliteniota*, 222–23. On Kyparissiotes, see Gioffreda, "Giovanni Ciparissiota e il Contra Nilum Cabasilam," 87–106.

36 Gregory Akindynos, *Letters*, ed. Constantinides Hero, p. 18, lines 8–29, no. 6, and p. 214, lines 94–102, no. 50.

37 Gregory Palamas, *Orationes antirrheticae contra Acindynum*, ed. Chrestou et al., p. 468, lines 13–16, and p. 468, lines 32–469; Gregory Palamas, *Contra Barlaam et Acindynum*, ed. Chrestou et al., p. 99, lines 13–15.

38 Gregoras, *Roman History*, ed. Bekker et al., vol. 3, bk. 29, chaps. 21–24, pp. 238–40, lines 2 and 7; Reinsch, *Die Briefe des Matthaios von Ephesos*, p. 136, lines 5–8, no. 32.

Described as a "Jezebel" by Palamas but regarded as a strong woman by her supporters,[39] Choumnaina's case highlights the ambiguous status of female pedagogy in these religious controversies. One faction would readily disparage the practice to tarnish the reputation of their opponents, even when members of their own side were known to engage in it as well.

Since the dawn of Christianity, the expression of theological views by women has often been linked to heretical groups in the eyes of religious authorities, and the period under discussion is no exception. The anti-Palamites, for instance, accused their opponents of Messalianism, claiming that both Gregory Palamas and Isidore Boucheir had connections with known Bogomils, such as the nun Irene Porine from Thessaloniki. Allegedly, Irene had converted citizens of Thessaloniki to Bogomilism and also influenced people on the Holy Mountain and in Trnovo through her disciples.[40]

Irene Porine and the nun Agathe were condemned in 1344 at a synod on Mount Athos. Both were followers of the Bogomil monk George of Larissa (1337–1344),[41] who was allegedly a friend of Palamas and Isidore. George of Larissa fled Thessaloniki for Mount Athos before 1338 and was expelled from there in 1344 or 1345. Porine met Isidore and Palamas around 1325/26 in Thessaloniki, where Isidore tutored a mixed group of monks and laypeople. He was accused of teaching strange doctrines and of not abstaining from food and drink at the prescribed times.[42] Similarly, Gregoras accused the Bogomils, including George of Larissa and Joseph of Crete, of spending most of their time drinking strong wine and feasting.[43]

Akindynos described Porine and her followers in the following manner:

> Their leader and goddess, as it were, was found to be Porine, a minister to them of all infamy and abomination. Isidore visited her more than anyone else and spent his time watching her, as if she were a divine rule, while she was saying and doing everything possible and nodding and dancing and drinking and being constantly intoxicated, and he praised her as a prophet-

---

39 Gregory Palamas, *Letters*, ed. Chrestou, p. 323, lines 15–17, no. 1; Gregory Akindynos, *Letters*, ed. Constantinides Hero, p. 246, lines 88–103, no. 60.

40 Kallistos I, *Life of St. Theodosios*, ed. Zlatarski, 19–20; Werner, "Spätbogomilisch-adamitische Spekulationen und Praktiken in religions-historischer Sicht," 41.

41 Rigo, "L'assemblea generale athonita del 1344 su un gruppo," 480, 484, 495; Gones, *Τὸ συγγραφικὸν ἔργον τοῦ οἰκουμενικοῦ πατριάρχου Καλλίστου Α΄*, 86.

42 Cf. *De Gregorio Palama*, ed. Migne, cols. 881–82; Meyendorff, *Introduction à l'étude de Grégoire Palamas*, 54.

43 Nikephoros Gregoras, *Antirrhetika*, ed. Beyer, chap. 1.2, p. 131, lines 2–15; Meyendorff, *Introduction à l'étude de Grégoire Palamas*, 57n69.

> ess together with the sage Palamas. And now they are so attached to her, just as to the 'lower divinity,' or rather, just as the pious to the 'all-transcendent' divinity.[44]

This passage presents Porine as a leader and teacher with significant influence over a group of lay and monastic men, without explaining how or why this situation arose. Nothing is mentioned about her nunnery or the reasons behind her influential position in monastic communities in Thessaloniki and Athos. This may have been of little importance to Akindynos or Gregoras, who were primarily focused on propagandistically linking the corruption of Palamite doctrine to the scandalous behaviour of a morally compromised woman. Similarly, the Palamites, as we have seen, employed the same strategy when targeting Choumnaina.

Women and Ecclesiastical Controversies: Patterns of Behaviour

In her significant article titled "Les femmes et l'église: droit canonique, idéologie et pratiques sociales à Byzance,"[45] Beaucamp provides a comprehensive examination of the role of women in defending the faith. After discussing the praise of Pulcheria as the "light of Orthodoxy"[46] and Theodora as the "guardian of faith,"[47] she briefly touches on the nuns of the Palaiologan period. Beaucamp rightly highlights the accusation against Irene Choumnaina for attempting to act as a *didaskalos* (teacher)—a common charge also echoed in George Metochites' ironic remarks about Irene/Eulogia Palaiologina's supposed profound knowledge.[48] In the fourteenth century, Philotheos Kokkinos criticized Constantinopolitan women in general as "superficial, credulous, and vain," condemning their "intemperance of tongue."[49] This perspective aligns with earlier ecclesiastical restrictions, such as the Council

---

44 Gregory Akindynos, *Letters*, ed. Constantinides Hero, p. 222, line 6 and 77, no. 52.

45 Beaucamp, "Les femmes et l'église," 349–70.

46 Gregory of Nyssa, *Oratio funebris in Flacillam imperatricem*, ed. Heil et al., p. 480, line 21; Holum, *Theodosian Empresses*, 23–24; James, *Empresses and Power in Early Byzantium*, 14–15; Angelidi, *Pulcheria*, 117–21.

47 Garland, *Byzantine Empresses*, 103.

48 George Metochites, *Historia Dogmatica*, ed. Cozza-Luzi, chap. 28, p. 39, line 2. On George Metochites, see Samori, "A Self-Portrait of an Unyielding Unionist," 67–103, who is preparing a new critical edition and commentary of the "Dogmatic History."

49 Philotheos Kokkinos, *Logos on Gregory Palamas*, ed. Tsames, p. 172, chap. 122, lines 16–22.

of Laodicea,[50] influenced by the New Testament, which forbade women from entering the altar, and the Quinisext Council, which later prohibited them from talking during ecclesiastical services.[51]

Regarding this last point, Judith Herrin argued that:

> Such a firm denial of the public expression of Christian faith (the prohibition to participate actively in the church) by women could only drive them into other forms of devotion. Of course, they could attend the liturgy as onlookers, but it was in more intimate relations with the holy, such as icon veneration, that they found a way of proving their commitment. Their pursuit of Christian ideals could still be followed in domestic contexts, both within the home and in social work and welfare, but it was always an individual one, peripheral to the ordered ecclesiastical life of the church. While many female Byzantine saints displayed a dedication to the relief of poverty and illness, the contrast between their activity and the great variety of fields open to their male equivalents reveals what very limited possibilities existed for women.[52]

The Byzantines indeed had their own interpretations for women's involvement in Church affairs. John Chrysostom argued that the exclusion of women from the priesthood often led them to become more active in church elections, where they sought to influence outcomes and impose their views on local bishops. This activism was coupled with a sense of *parresia*, or "outspokenness," which sometimes took on a negative connotation as "license of tongue." Chrysostom observed that women felt emboldened to criticize even the highest Church authorities, addressing them more harshly than a master would speak to a slave. This suggests a tension between the perceived appropriate roles for women in ecclesiastical life and the realities of their active participation and leverage.[53]

In the thirteenth century, George Metochites provided a psychological interpretation of the motives driving Irene/Eulogia Palaiologina, a prominent anti-Unionist nun. According to Metochites, her energetic and assertive stance was rooted in her inherent character, which was further shaped by her aristocratic upbringing and education. Before taking monastic vows,

---

50 Cf. *Council of Laodicea*, ed. Joannou, Canon 11, p. 135, and Canon 44, p. 148.

51 *Concilium Trullanum*, ed. Alberigo et al., Canon 70, p. 275; Ohme, *Das Konzil Quinisextum*, 260–62, 118–19; Konidaris, "Die Rechtsstellung," 131–43; Herrin, "'Femina Byzantina,'" 116, 120.

52 Herrin, "'Femina Byzantina,'" 120.

53 John Chrysostom, *De sacerdotio*, ed. Malingrey, bk. 3, chap. 9, p. 162, line 28, and p. 164, line 44.

Irene/Eulogia was deeply involved in secular matters as the sister of the emperor. After entering the monastic life, she redirected her focus toward ecclesiastical and spiritual concerns.[54] Metochites perceived her determination and strong will as a manifestation of her sense of aristocratic entitlement, which persisted even after she became a nun. This explanation suggests that her noble background and prior engagement in worldly affairs influenced her assertive approach within the Church, reflecting a continuation of her earlier attitudes rather than a transformation.

These contemporary explanations demonstrate that true conviction or piety alone cannot be considered sufficient motives for women's roles in ecclesiastical controversies; questions of influence and imitation must also be considered. Many women may have simply followed the will of others, such as their spiritual fathers, or aligned themselves with the positions of their husbands or male relatives. For instance, Empress Theodora Palaiologina adhered to her husband's views. After the restoration of Orthodoxy, she was compelled by the Council of Blachernai (1283) to affirm her orthodoxy.[55] However, when an influential woman—often a nun—joined a particular faction, her female and, frequently, male relatives would often follow her example and directives. For example, the nun Eulogia Palaiologina encouraged her daughter, Maria Kantakouzene, to invite the Mamluk Sultan Baibars I to oppose Michael VIII, and the *tsarina* of Bulgaria ultimately followed her mother's instructions.[56]

Late Byzantine sources emphasize the involvement of widows and nuns in major Church events, particularly in the struggle against the Union. The female relatives of Michael VIII mentioned in Ogerios' report were nuns who became active members of the opposition. Since widows traditionally enjoyed more freedoms than married women in Byzantine society, many (particularly from the aristocracy) chose to take monastic vows. The established connection between these women and their spiritual fathers could

---

54 George Metochites, *Historia Dogmatica*, ed. Cozza-Luzi, p. 37, line 7, and p. 38, line 12. During the Second Iconoclasm, Theodore of Stoudios sent a letter of praise to the widow of a nobleman who helped persecuted monks. Theodore of Stoudios, *Epistulae*, ed. Fatouros, p. 259, no. 143.

55 Mitsiou, "Regaining the True Faith," 77–96 (new edition and English translation); cf. Pétridès, "Chrysobulle de l'impératrice Théodora," 25–28; Petit, "La profession de foi de l'imperatrice Théodora," 286–87; John Eugenikos, *Oratio ad imperatorem Constantinum Palaeologum*, ed. Lampros, p. 130, line 2, and p. 131, line 3.

56 Pachymeres, *History*, ed. Failler and Laurent, vol. 2, bk. 6, chap. 1, p. 545–47, lines 14–24; Gill, *Byzantium and the Papacy*, 164.

influence their thoughts and actions.[57] After 1438–1439, the Unionist historian Doukas expressed particular frustration with the fanatical nuns who surrounded Gennadios.

While the women of the uneducated majority remained anonymous, nuns of imperial and aristocratic descent often succeeded in making their names known.[58] These nuns were members of the Kantakouzenoi, Raoul, and Tarchaneiotes families, which belonged to the so-called *dynatoi* ("the powerful"). Their roles in political and church events are documented in the written sources of the period, which were primarily interested in these social groups.

Prior to the upheaval surrounding the Union of Lyons, many nuns of aristocratic descent had aligned with the Arsenites, becoming familiar with opposition tactics. Consequently, it is not surprising that nuns in the Josephite groups (the supporters of Patriarch Joseph I, who had resigned because of his resistance against the Union in 1275) adopted similar methods to those used by the Arsenites. For instance, Arsenite nuns provided protection to movement leaders, such as Martha Palaiologina, who supported Hyakinthos financially. Similarly, Irene/Eulogia offered refuge to the Josephites. A half-century later, Choumnaina sheltered Akindynos during the Palamite controversy. In some instances, women played crucial roles in strategic decisions. According to George Metochites, Irene/Eulogia was the one who compelled Patriarch Joseph to take an oath before the conclusion of the Union.[59]

With the exception of the Ferrara-Florence Council, the imperial response to disobedient female relatives is generally well-documented. After failing to convince the clergy, monks, and populace of Constantinople with arguments, Michael VIII—determined to maintain peace with the Latin Church—resorted to harsher measures to discipline recalcitrant aristocrats. The typical actions included imprisonment and confiscation of property.

---

57 In Late Byzantium, only rarely spiritual mothers are mentioned, for example the godmother of Sprantzes. Nevertheless, the context and meaning are different, as these spiritual mothers are the abbesses of female communities and not their confessors.

58 Laiou, "The Role of Women in Byzantine Society," 250–53.

59 George Metochites, *Historia Dogmatica*, ed. Cozza-Luzi, chap. 27, p. 37, lines 5–6. See also Laurent, "Le Serment anti-latin du Patriarche Joseph Ier," 396–407; Laurent, *Regestes*, no. 1401; Darrouzès and Laurent, *Dossier grec de l'Union de Lyon*, pp. 303–5, no. 2. Pachymeres, however, attributes the oath of Joseph to Job Iasites. Pachymeres, *History*, ed. Failler and Laurent, vol. 1, bk. 5, chap. 16, p. 489, lines 26–28.

Public humiliation was another tactic, as demonstrated by the case of Manuel Holobolos and his niece in October 1273. Notably, Holobolos' anonymous niece was also accused of engaging in magical practices.[60]

On the other hand, Makarios of Pisidia reports that Patriarch Joseph I expelled Arsenite nuns from their monastic communities in Constantinople during severe winter conditions.[61] Other followers of Arsenios were imprisoned, and many left Byzantium to spread negative propaganda about the Palaiologoi abroad.

During the Hesychast controversy, abbesses were removed from the administration of nunneries, and other nuns were anathematized. According to Gregoras, Irene Choumnaina was persecuted for her involvement in the controversy, though the exact details are unclear. An analysis of private documents from the monastery of Prodromos in Serres suggests that she left Constantinople and her monastery before 1355 and lived for a time in the Serres region, where she owned private land.[62] At some point, she returned to Constantinople and likely died around 1355. Gregoras was asked to write her obituary, but no such work has survived. However, he did claim that miracles occurred at her grave, indicating that her beliefs were considered correct. Nevertheless, as an ardent supporter of the heretics, she could not be accepted and venerated as a saint by the official Church.

Way(s) of Action

The sources provide insight into the methods employed by the opposition during religious controversies. Between the thirteenth and fifteenth centuries, the strategies of the opposition largely remained consistent. Monks engaged in propaganda within their own monastic communities and utilized pamphlets and other writings to disseminate their ideas more broadly. During the disputes over the Church Union and the Arsenite Schism, the rebels also avoided the official Church institutions in favour of their own assemblies.

The wealthier and more influential members of the opposition groups provided financial support and offered shelter and protection to those sought by the authorities. Additionally, through their networks of kinship,

---

60 Pachymeres, *History*, ed Failler and Laurent, vol. 2, bk. 5, chap. 20, p. 501–5, lines 20–24; Bydén, "'Strangle Them with These Meshes of Syllogisms,'" 133–57.

61 Eustratiades, "Ὁ πατριάρχης Ἀρσένιος ὁ Αὐτωρειανός," 93.

62 Guillou, *Les archives de Saint-Jean-Prodrome sur le Mont Menecee*, pp. 142–44, no. 46; Bénou, *Codex B*, pp. 311–13, nos. 173–77 and 201.

they could mobilize foreign political powers against Byzantium, exerting external pressure on the emperor.

According to Gregoras, only a small fraction of the anti-Unionists were willing to suffer and become martyrs for their beliefs. He claimed that the majority consisted of troublemakers who disguised themselves as monks and travelled to regions outside the Byzantine Empire, where they incited unrest.[63] Donald Nicol has argued that significant disturbances were indeed caused, as fanatical monks and professional agitators stirred up trouble among local populations. They advised the common people to avoid visiting churches, to minimize their interactions with priests, and to reject baptism administered by Unionist clerics. In this way, they disrupted the daily functions of the Church.[64]

After his deposition in 1282 and during his exile, the Unionist Patriarch John Bekkos lamented the actions of certain women, saying, "What can one say when women and children still in the nursery, when men whose knowledge is limited to agriculture or manual labour cry criminal to anyone who so much as whispers about the Union of the Churches?" He complained that "children at school, women chatting over their distaffs and spindles, farmers and labourers, all of them now have only one subject in the forefront of their minds and conversations—the Procession of the Holy Spirit from the Son."[65] On another occasion, Bekkos complained that "men, women, old and young, [of] all sorts and conditions...thought this peace [in the Church] to be a division and not a union."[66]

No doubt the populace did not grasp all details of the complex theological differences with the Latin Church. In many cases, their instigators—primarily monks—were also inadequately educated on theological matters. However, this ignorance did not hinder their effectiveness; the arguments they used to incite the people were far more persuasive than abstract theological debates. They simply warned the masses of the peril to their souls if they betrayed the faith of their ancestors.

---

63 Gregoras, *Roman History*, ed. Bekker et al., vol. 1, bk. 5, chap. 2, p. 127, line 18, and p. 128, line 14.

64 Darrouzès and Laurent, *Dossier grec de l'Union de Lyon*, p. 465, no 16.

65 John Bekkos, *De Depositione Sua (Oratio 2)*, ed. Migne, col. 984; English translation of the passages by Nicol, "The Byzantine Reaction to the Second Council of Lyons," 124–25. To John Bekkos, see Xexakes, "Ἰωάννης Βέκκος καὶ αἱ θεολογικαὶ ἀντιλήψεις αὐτοῦ"; Gounarides, "Ιωάννης Βέκκος εχθρός Ρωμαίων," 29–40.

66 John Bekkos, *De Depositione Sua (Oratio 1)*, ed. Migne, cols. 952–53.

Case Study: Theodora Raoulaina and the Arsenite Network

Meanwhile, educated women who demonstrated an understanding of the theological stakes in these controversies were often heavily reprimanded. As previously mentioned, Bekkos struggled to explain how the "evil" of religious controversy had spread to the female population.[67] Modern tools, however, can shed light on this phenomenon. I will focus on one of the female figures in this complex social environment: Theodora Kantakouzene Palaiologina Raoulaina.

Theodora was born around 1240 in the Empire of Nicaea. Her first husband, the *protobestiarios* George Mouzalon, was brutally murdered in 1258 at the Sosandra Monastery.[68] In 1261, Theodora married John Raoul as her second husband.[69] Many members of the Raoul family were Arsenites and, as a result, faced punishment and imprisonment. After John's death in 1274, Theodora became a nun. She was imprisoned with her mother in Nikomedeia but returned to Constantinople after 1282, where she played a significant role in the restoration of Orthodoxy and the integration of the Arsenite faction led by Theodore Manouelites into the official Church. Along with her mother and sister Anna, Raoulaina participated in the Synod of Adramyttion in 1284, which convened to determine the fate of those involved in the Union.[70] After 1285, as we have already mentioned, she renovated the Monastery of Andrew *in Krisei*,[71] where she also transferred the body of Arsenios.[72]

As a widow of aristocratic descent, Theodora Raoulaina actively participated in the ecclesiastical controversies of her time. On one hand, she was a nun and the founder of monasteries (Andrew *in Krisei* and Aristene).[73]

---

67 Darrouzès and Laurent, *Dossier grec de l'Union de Lyon*, p. 465, lines 7–9, no. 16.

68 Mitsiou, "The Monastery of Sosandra," 665–83.

69 On the Raoul family, see Fassoulakis, *The Byzantine Family of Raoul-Ral(l)es*, 1–6.

70 Pachymeres, *History*, ed. Failler and Laurent, vol. 3, bk. 7, chap. 31, p. 97, line 14, and p. 99, line 8. Acheimastou-Potamianou, "Η ζωγραφική της Άρτας στο 13° αιώνα και η μονή της Βλαχέρνας," 185–86; Acheimastou-Potamianou, *Η Βλαχέρνα της Άρτας*, 120. Acheimastou-Potamianou identified the three female figures in the wall painting with procession of Theotokos Blacherna in Blachernai Monastery in Arta with Anna Palaiologina, Eulogia Palaiologina, and Theodora Raoulaina.

71 Gregoras, *Roman History*, ed. Bekker et al., vol. 1, bk. 6, chap. 2, p. 167, lines 17–21, and bk. 6, chap. 4, p. 178, line 19, and p. 179, line 2; Talbot, "The Restoration of Constantinople Under Michael VIII," 257.

72 Pachymeres, *History*, ed. Failler and Laurent, vol. 3, bk. 7, chap. 31, pp. 95–99.

73 For the Monastery of Aristene, see Janin, *La géographie ecclésiastique de l'Empire byzantine*, 51; Talbot, "The Restoration of Constantinople Under Michael VIII," 257; Kidonopulos, *Bauten in Konstantinopel*, 14–16.

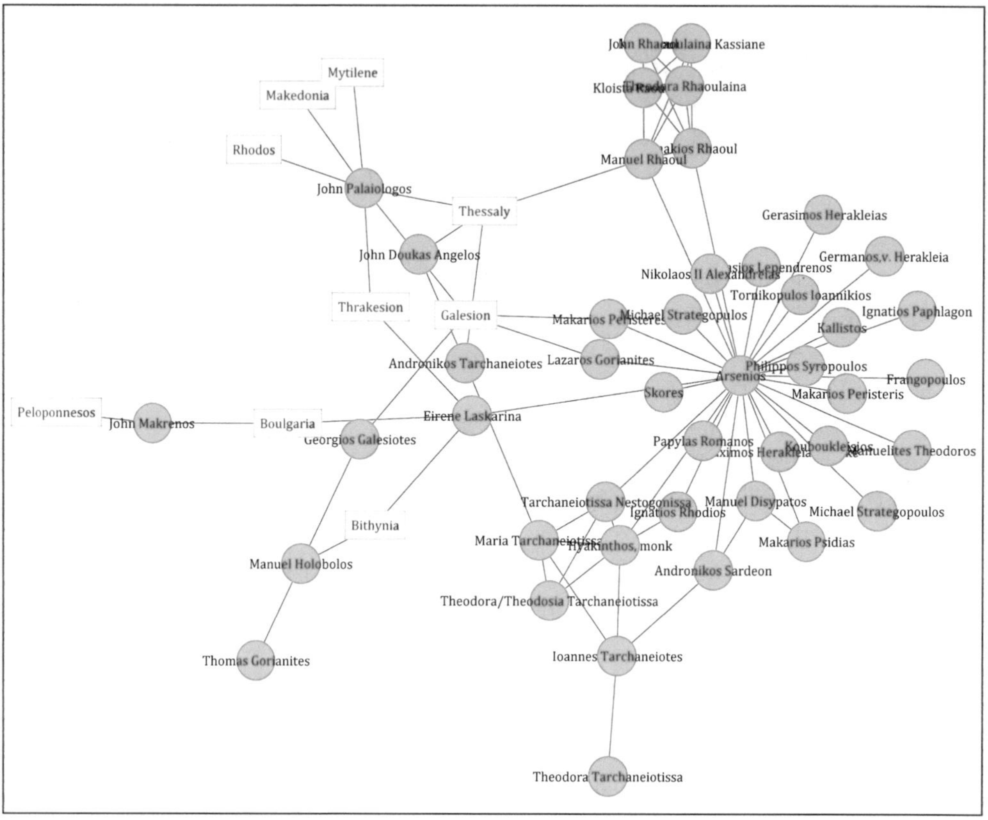

Figure 5.1. Theodora Raoulaina and the Arsenites: the network.

On the other hand, she was a scholar, author, bibliophile, and copyist. She exemplified an Arsenite, who maintained relationships not only with anti-Unionists but also with imperial and patriarchal authorities. For the purpose of our study and due to the complexity of the material, we have focused on the Arsenite network around the year 1280 and the connections of Raoulaina. Our information derives from various sources of the period, including Latin and Greek documents as well as the *PLP* and various more recent studies. Below is a network graph illustrating the connections of the Arsenite movement during the Union of Lyons (see Figure 5.1).

In this network, we have categorized nodes into two classes: important agents (fifty-one in total) and geographical locations (ten in total) related to the Arsenite movement. This classification allows us to reconstruct and evaluate the network on multiple levels, particularly focusing on individual nodes, their positions, and their relevance. According to the results, Raoulaina is connected with only some members of the movement.

Furthermore, we can conclude that the Arsenites were organized into clusters of different size, with only few nodes strongly connected between these sub-groups. Regarding Theodora Raoulaina, her significance within the Arsenite network stems from her position in a dense kinship cluster of nodes around her. However, from a structural perspective, she lacked the potential to act as a key broker within the network.

Female Monastic Communities and the Church (Thirteenth to Fifteenth Centuries)[74]

The relations between female monastic communities and the official Church were not always strained. Outside of periods of religious controversy, the Patriarchate and local bishops generally fulfilled their duties towards the nunneries as outlined in the canons and laws. Even during the period when the Patriarchate was in exile, the Church endeavoured to support endangered monastic communities and provide refuge to nuns who had fled from Latin-controlled territories. While the authorities' interference in the internal affairs of self-governed monasteries and nunneries was limited, Church officials retained the right to oversee the moral conduct of monks and nuns as well as the financial well-being of their institutions.

In previous chapters, we discussed the detrimental effects of the Fourth Crusade on female monastics. However, this situation improved after the recapture of Constantinople in 1261. Both written sources and archaeological evidence reveal a new phase of female monasticism characterized by the establishment or re-establishment of nunneries by prominent aristocratic women, such as Theodora Palaiologina. Consequently, the latter half of the thirteenth century and the early fourteenth century emerged as a flourishing period for female monastic foundations.

After 1261, it becomes much easier to trace the processes related to the establishment of nunneries, such as their financial backing, the lives of the women within them, and their relationships with the ecclesiastical hierarchy. Canons and laws stipulated that, like all monasteries, nunneries were under the authority of the local bishop and, in Constantinople, the Patriarch.[75]

---

74 What follows is an abridged version of my article, Mitsiou, "Female Monastic Communities in Byzantium and the Role of Silence," 105–14.

75 On the canonical and legal framework, see Konidares, *Νομικὴ θεώρηση τῶν μοναστηριακῶν τυπικῶν*, 177–78.

Many were designated as patriarchal, stauropegial,[76] or imperial, granting them a privileged status.

This tendency is well documented in the *typika*, where founders and refounders frequently sought to assert the independence of their nunneries. For example, the Bebaia Elpis *typikon* reflects this intention:

> Even he who is the most holy patriarch at the time should take only that which he is commanded to take by the holy canons, he should be content with these things alone and perforce keep his hands off the rest, that is whatever does not lead to the edification and support [of the convent], but to its ruin and destruction.[77]

The patriarchal rights implied here include those of visitation and spiritual correction, as outlined by the Novel of Alexios I Komnenos (1096). This decree granted the Patriarch the authority to investigate all monasteries under his jurisdiction—including independent institutions—in order to address moral failings or deviant behaviour, even based on rumours.[78] Additionally, the Patriarch had the right to inspect even the free monasteries to ensure they were not being mismanaged by their administrators.[79]

The reasons behind Synadene's strong rejection of patriarchal intervention in Bebaia Elpis may be linked to the reputation of Patriarch Niphon (1310–1314), about whom Nikephoros Gregoras had little praise. Gregoras criticizes Niphon for his lack of education and his affinity for money and business. These accusations are supported by official documents, which

---

76 On the stauropegial monasteries, see Herman, "Das bischöfliche Abgabenwesen im Patriarchat von Konstantinopel," 451–52; Herman, "Ricerche sulle istituzioni monastiche byzantine," 353–55; Soule, "The Stauropegial Monastery," 147–67; Kazhdan and Talbot, "Stauropegion," 1946–47; Darrouzès, *Les regestes des Actes du patriarcat de Constantinople*, 186, 193.

77 *Typicon monasterii Theotoci Bebaias Elpidos*, ed. Delehaye, chap. 16, p. 29; Talbot, "*Bebaia Elpis*," 1528.

78 When a nun from Andrew *in Krisei* became pregnant by a priest-monk from the Hodegon Monastery, he purchased an abortifacient from the doctor Gabrielopoulos. The priest-monk may have been the nunnery's confessor despite the distance between Andrew *in Krisei* (near the Stoudios Monastery) and Hodegon (close to Saint Sophia). The pregnancy and abortion became known during the trial against the doctor, which involved charges of sorcery. Mitsiou, "Das Leben der Kirche von Konstantinopel," 214–20. On abortions in Byzantium, see Cupane and Kislinger, "Bemerkungen zur Abtreibung in Byzanz," 21–49.

79 Balsamon, *Commentary on Canon 19*, ed. Zepos and Zepos, pp. 346–48; Dölger, *Regesten der Kaiserurkunden des Oströmischen Reiches*, vol. 2, no. 1076; Konidares, *Νομικὴ θεώρηση τῶν μοναστηριακῶν τυπικῶν*, 178.

indicate that Niphon redirected revenues from metropolitans and archbishoprics to the Patriarchate. Gregoras is particularly critical of Niphon's decision to use the income from two female monasteries, *tou Pertze* and Krataios under the guise of renovation and maintenance costs. Niphon utilized their resources for a period, potentially diverting funds to support institutions he had established, such as the St. Apostoloi in Thessaloniki. Krataios was founded by Anna/Antonia Komnene Raoulaina Strategopoulina after 1293 and was located to the north or northwest of Christos Philanthropos Soter and east of the Basilike market.[80] The nunnery *tou Pertze* has recently been identified with the Latin convent *Percheio*, situated near the Patriarchate.[81] Gregoras emphasizes that Niphon spent extended periods residing in both convents, suggesting that these were not mere visitations. The duration of these stays, combined with information about the possessions of *tou Pertze*, indicates that both nunneries were sufficiently wealthy to meet the Patriarch's demands during his stays. Later testimonies suggest that both convents continued to be under the control of Niphon's successors.[82]

In contrast to Theodora Synadene, other foundresses had differing views on the role of the Patriarch. For example, in chapter 3 of the Lips *typikon*, regarding the election of the abbess, we read "how she is to be elevated to her lofty position of authority and leadership by patriarchal blessing and installation."[83] In the same chapter, Theodora Palaiologina declares:

---

80 Kidonopulos, *Bauten in Konstantinopel*, 36–37; Majeska locates the nunnery close to and east of the church of St. Barbara (which has not survived). Majeska, *Russian Travelers to Constantinople in the Fourteenth and Fifteenth Centuries*, 384–85.

81 Martin et al., " Un acte de Baudouin II en faveur de l'abbaye Cistercienne," 211–23; Saint-Guillain, "Sainte-Marie du Perchay," 593–603; Saint-Guillain, "Propriétés et bienfaiteurs de l'abbaye constantinopolitaine," 9–40; Tsougarakis, *The Latin Religious Orders in Medieval Greece*, 61–67, 288, 293; Janin, *La géographie ecclésiastique de l'Empire byzantine*, 396–97; Kidonopulos, *Bauten in Konstantinopel*, 61–62. The opinion that the Cistercian nuns of Percheio received a former Byzantine monastery and its possessions located in Thrace, Bithynia, and Constantinople has to be reevaluated. Guillaume Saint-Guillain argued that the founder of the nunnery was Guilelmus or another member of the family *du Perchay*.

82 Gregoras, *Roman History*, ed. Bekker et al., vol. 1, bk. 7, chap. 9, p. 260, line 10, and p. 261, line 1; van Dieten, *Nikephoros Gregoras*, vol. 2, 198–99.

83 *Typicon monasterii Theotoci Bebaias Elpidos*, ed. Delehaye, chap. 21, p. 31; Talbot, "*Bebaia Elpis*," 1530; cf. *Typicon monasterii Lips*, ed. Delehaye, chap. 6, p. 110; Talbot, "*Lips*," 1267. The description can find a parallel in the Life of Irene of Chrysobalanton. See Rosenqvist, *The Life of Saint Irene*, 26–30.

> After choosing her in this way with the help of God, next you should take her and go to the most holy patriarch; and she is to accompany you. Then, after she has received from him the blessing and grace of authority as well as the pastoral staff, as is customary for the patriarch at such installations, you should return to the convent with great joy and cheer, and with God's assistance you will behave towards each other in the prescribed manner.[84]

The *procheirisis* (ordination)—a ceremony in which the abbot received the pallium and his pastoral staff—is well documented in the *euchologia*, or prayer books.[85] However, we lack information on how this procedure might have been adapted for the ordination of a woman as abbess or what specific documents may have been produced in such cases.[86]

It is also recorded that Patriarch Gerasimos, on an unspecified date, confirmed the election of the newly appointed abbess of the renovated convent of Maroules. As was customary, the abbess was escorted to the nunnery by the nuns, who carried torches. The doorkeeper of the Patriarchate, George Sigeros, was able to pinpoint the location where this event took place.[87]

Patriarchal intervention was crucial for confirming the status of a nunnery and affirming the founders' rights. Patriarch John Kalekas and the Synod certified the rights of the nun Agathonike over the small Monastery (*monydrion*) of *tes Kryoneritisses*.[88] Her uncle, monk Theodosios, had built this monastery in Herakleia at his own expense and effort for her and her mother, Anastasia, who was also a nun. All three were refugees from Asia Minor.

The case of the nunnery of Maroules, dating to 1341, provides further insight into this issue. As already argued in this book, the *domestikos* had constructed a nunnery intended for his wife and daughters sometime after 1305 but before 1320.[89] Some time after his death, his son, John Synadenos, sought to convert the nunnery into a male monastery, presenting forged documents.

---

84 *Typicon monasterii Theotoci Bebaias Elpidos*, ed. Delehaye, chap. 26, pp. 33–34; Talbot, "*Bebaia Elpis*," 1530.

85 Goar, *Euchologion sive Rituale Graecorum*, 490–92; De Meester, *De monachico statu iuxta disciplinam Byzantinam*, 237–38.

86 Darrouzès, *Recherches sur les ΟΦΦΙΚΙΑ de l'église byzantine*, 162–63.

87 *Patriarchal Register*, vol. 2, ed. Hunger et al., p. 280, no. 135 (May 1341), lines 83–87; Darrouzès, *Les regestes des Actes du patriarcat de Constantinople*, no. 2207.

88 *Patriarchal Register*, vol. 1, ed. Hunger and Kreseten, p. 586, no. 103 (1330); Darrouzès, *Les regestes des Actes du patriarcat de Constantinople*, no. 2157.

89 Kidonopulos, *Bauten in Konstantinopel*, 65–67; Janin, *La géographie ecclésiastique de l'Empire byzantine*, 196, 336; Darrouzès, *Les regestes des Actes du patriarcat de Constantinople*, no. 2207; Talbot, "A Comparison of the Monastic Experience," 7–8.

These charters were later exposed as fraudulent through the testimony of the priest-monk Theodoretos and a later admission by Maroules' wife.[90]

It is important to follow the jurisprudence applied by the Synod which searched for solid testimonies and proof. The fraudulent documents appear to have been a secondary issue in the final decision. The primary concern was to establish beyond doubt that the monastery founded by Maroules was originally intended for women. The following evidence was considered:

- An abbess had been elected and resided in the nunnery for many years.
- John Synadenos had constructed an *eukterion* (unconsecrated church) and a chapel for his mother near the monastery.[91]
- Most significantly, the monastery's refectory (*trapeza*) initially depicted female saints, but John Synadenos later replaced these with male saints.[92]

This evidence made it clear to the synodic court that the Maroules Monastery had originally been a female establishment, with nuns having lived and been tonsured there.[93]

Patriarch John XIV Kalekas and the Synod both affirmed that, according to the Holy Fathers, converting a female monastery into a male one was forbidden.[94] This decision was based on the principle that the original purpose

---

90 *Patriarchal Register*, vol. 2, ed. Hunger et al., p. 276, no. 135 (May 1341), lines 25–35; Darrouzès, *Les regestes des Actes du patriarcat de Constantinople*, no. 2207.

91 Kidonopulos assumed incorrectly that the wife of Maroules became abbess in this monastery. Kidonopulos, *Bauten in Konstantinopel*, 66.

92 Figures of saints were generally a part of the iconography of refectories together with scenes such as the Hospitality of Abraham, the Wedding at Cana, the Multiplication of the Loaves and Fishes, and the Last Supper. See Talbot, "Mealtime in Monasteries," 111. See also Orlandos, *Μοναστηριακὴ Ἀρχιτεκτονική*, 43–60; Popović, "The 'Trapeza' in Cenobitic Monasteries," 281–303; Rapp, "Figures of Female Sanctity," 332. On the differences between the depiction of male and female saints, see Maguire, *The Icons of Their Bodies*, 28–32. On the function of female saints' depictions in Cypriote churches, see Connor, "Female Saints in the Church Decoration of the Troodos Mountains," 211–28.

93 *Patriarchal Register*, vol. 2, ed. Hunger et al., p. 278, no. 135 (May 1341), lines 49–52; Darrouzès, *Les regestes des Actes du patriarcat de Constantinople*, no. 2207.

94 *Patriarchal Register*, vol. 2, ed. Hunger et al., p. 280, no. 135 (May 1341), lines 91–96; cf. Theodore of Stoudios, *Epistulae*, ed. Fatouros, p. 784–85, no. 526. On the nunnery of Prodromos called the Nea Petra in Thessaly, which was converted into a male monastery, see Miklosich and Müller, *Acta et Diplomata graeca Medii Aevi sacra*

of the foundations should be preserved. However, in some instances, such conversions were tolerated. The Patriarchate generally did not respond immediately but acted only after receiving requests from individuals with a personal stake in the matter.[95]

The period's sources illuminate the patriarchs' interest in the nuns and the welfare of their communities, allowing us to reconstruct the social and economic networks of the nunneries. Much of the Patriarchate's involvement in managing nunneries was related to financial matters. Lay patrons, primarily *ephoroi* (protectors), were responsible for the *systasis* (maintenance) and *beltiosis* (improvement) of monasteries. However, they often failed to meet their obligations, as we have seen in the case of the monastery *tes Panagiotisses* and its *ephoros* Isaakios Palaiologos Asanes.[96]

Founders and protectors often sought to derive financial profit from the revenues of monasteries. Nunneries could own a variety of assets, including houses, land, vineyards, and gardens, each serving as a potential source of income. For example, the monastery *tes Panagiotisses* (after 1282) owned bakeries, churches, vineyards, and rental properties in Constantinople, generating revenues of three hundred *hyperpyra*. After Patriarch Neilos decided to separate the double monastery of Athanasios, the female portion was endowed with assets worth approximately two thousand *hyperpyra*, including bakeries, houses, land, vineyards, and livestock.[97] Neilos took great care to safeguard the rights of the nuns and ensure their continued security.

In various sources from the thirteenth and fourteenth centuries, we can identify efforts by patriarchs and emperors to provide financial support to nunneries. For instance, according to Patriarch Gregory of Cyprus (around 1283), the nuns of the monastery of *tou Pertze* received five hundred *modioi* of grain from John Theologites, the apographeus (recessor) of the themes of Thrace and Macedonia, based on a *prostagma*, or an imperial decree. However, Gregory reported to Theodore Mouzalon, the great logothetes, that the *apographeus* had improperly divided the grain between the Patriarchate

---

et profana, vol. 4, p. 339, no. 3 (September 1274/11 December 1282); Dölger and Wirth, *Regesten der Kaiserurkunden des Oströmischen Reiches*, vol. 3, no. 2031a.

95 *Patriarchal Register*, vol. 2, ed. Hunger et al., p. 282, no. 135 (May 1341), lines 115–26. The synodal court decided that neither the wife of Maroules nor the daughters nor their relatives still living in the monastery should try to interfere in the administration of the monastery.

96 See above, pp. 95–96.

97 Mitsiou, "Das Doppelkloster des Patriarchen Athanasios I," 87–106.

and the nuns, whereas he was supposed to allocate all one thousand *modioi* to the Patriarch.[98]

Nunneries often faced significant financial challenges. Patriarchs, such as Isidore I, specifically addressed these concerns. In his testament (1347–1350), Isidore I divided the existing wine and grain supplies of the Great Church into three parts: one part for the clergy, a second for the poor nuns, and a third for his helpers (monks and laymen).[99]

Internal issues within nunneries often prompted intervention from the Patriarch or local Church authorities, as illustrated by the case of the nunnery of Gerontiou in Thessaloniki.[100] Gregory of Cyprus instructed the Great *chartophylax* of Thessaloniki and the abbots of Akapniou and Chortaites to investigate accusations made by the nuns against the convent's abbess, a sister of *kyr* Mourinos. Allegedly, she had shown disrespect towards the Patriarch.[101]

The spiritual correction of nuns was a significant responsibility for the patriarchs. They used their catechetical work to remind monastics of the attitudes and behaviours appropriate for individuals dedicated to God. Athanasios I frequently issued general instructions for monks and nuns, mandating that his testament (dated sometime between 1303 and 1305)[102] be read on the fifteenth of every month—the day of monastic tonsure—in all the monasteries of the Byzantine Church. In his discourse, he emphasizes the importance of preventing women from entering male monasteries.

---

98 Gregory of Cyprus, *Letters*, ed. Eustratiades, pp. 91–92, no 115; Darrouzès, *Les regestes des Actes du patriarcat de Constantinople*, nos. 1519 and 1483.

99 *Patriarchal Register*, vol. 2, ed. Hunger et al., p. 440, no. 156 (February 1350), lines 188–94; Patedakes, "Οι διαθήκες των πατριαρχών της πρώιμης Παλαιολόγειας περιόδου," 69; Helfer, "Das Testament des Patriarchen Isidoros," 76–83.

100 Gregory of Cyprus, *Letters*, ed. Eustratiades, pp. 135–36, no. 144; Darrouzès, *Les regestes des Actes du patriarcat de Constantinople*, nos. 1530 and 1531; Janin, *Les églises et les monastères des grands centres Byzantins*, 358.

101 Only Hagion Oros, Megistes Lavras, MS B 39 (thirteenth century) (*Diktyon*: 27091) provides Mourinos's name. The *protovestiarites* Demetrios Mourinos fought against the Bulgars of the usurper Lachanas in 1279 and in return became governor of Thessaloniki. In a *chrysobull* of Andronikos II, he is named Demetrios, *pansebastos sebastos*. Mourinos is the oldest member of the Venetian family of Morino, which was in the service of Byzantium. See Pachymeres, *History*, ed. Failler and Laurent, vol. 2, bk. 6, chap. 19, p. 589, lines 5–20; Dölger, *Regesten der Kaiserurkunden des Oströmischen Reiches*, vol. 4, no. 2357.

102 Laurent, *Regestes*, no. 1595.

Athanasios I's instructions extended to a broad range of individuals, including priests, monks, men, women, and children.[103] He was particularly adamant that monks should neither eat with women nor sleep in nunneries, and vice versa. His guidance to the exarchs underscored the preservation of traditional practices and the necessity for gender separation within monastic life.[104] Athanasios was renowned for his strict views on monasticism, frequently condemning both nuns and monks for moral failings.[105]

In line with his rigorous stance, some of his successors sought to address issues like sorcery by imposing strict penalties. For instance, Kallistos I intervened in the case of Amarantina, a woman accused of sorcery, by compelling her to join the nunnery *tou Pertze*. There, she was expected to atone for her past transgressions through monastic life and repentance.[106]

The role of nunneries in the process of canonization and the construction of saintly reputations was significant. Philotheos Kokkinos provides an example from around 1347–1350, where he recounts a miracle performed by Patriarch Isidore at the nunnery *tou Pertze*. During a gathering of the entire community, Isidore cured a nun from "the illness of bloodshed" (*τῷ πάθει τῆς αἱμορροίας*), demonstrating the Patriarch's sanctity and divine favour.[107]

Similarly, Theoktistos the Stoudite, in his writings on Athanasios I, describes miracles performed by the Patriarch. In the *Life of Athanasios I*[108] and in the *translatio* of his relics,[109] he asserts that some nuns were healed by the holy patriarch. While the *Vita* does not provide specific details about the cured nuns, the *translatio* includes their names and familial connections. This inclusion of personal details was intended to enhance the credibility of the miracle accounts and strengthen the saint's reputation.

---

103 Laurent, *Regestes*, no. 1776.

104 Laurent, *Regestes*, no. 1778.

105 Athanasios I, *Correspondence*, ed. Talbot, p. 76, lines 11–12, no. 36.

106 *Patriarchal Register*, vol. 3, ed. Koder et al., pp. 32–46, no. 180 (autumn 1350?); Darrouzès, *Les regestes des Actes du patriarcat de Constantinople*, no. 2318.

107 Philotheos Kokkinos, *Vita Isidori patriarchi*, ed. Tsames, chap. 65, §2. Also, Neamonites is mentioning this disease, which is a biblical allusion. See Mitrea, *A Late Byzantine Swan Song*, 75n298.

108 Theoktistos the Stoudite, *Life of Athanasios I*, ed. Papadopoulos-Kerameus, p. 42, line 26, and p. 43, line 6.

109 Theoktistos the Stoudite, "Oratio de translatione reliquiarum sancti Athanasii Constantinopolitani," ed. Talbot, 87–90, 98; Talbot, "Cult and Pilgrimage," 271–82.

In conclusion, the relationship between female monastic communities and the official Church from the thirteenth to the fifteenth centuries was characterized by a complex interplay of support, control, and influence. The Patriarchate and local bishops generally aimed to protect and support nunneries, especially during financial and administrative difficulties. Despite this, instances of financial exploitation by some patriarchs are documented, revealing a more problematic side to their involvement. Founders, like Theodora Synadene, who were concerned about such issues sought to limit the extent of Church interference in their nunneries.

Church authorities were also responsible for overseeing the moral and spiritual conduct of nuns, enforcing adherence to canonical laws.[110] This duty often involved intervention in cases of misconduct or administrative issues within the nunneries. Additionally, nunneries played a significant role in the veneration of patriarchs, often supporting the construction of their sainthood through the documentation of miracles and divine interventions attributed to them.

Overall, while the Church sought to uphold and guide monastic communities, its involvement was multifaceted, encompassing both supportive and controlling elements. The dynamic between ecclesiastical oversight and the autonomy of female monastic institutions reflects the broader complexities of Church-monastic relations during this period.

110 Patriarch Kallistos I composed a homily for an unnamed nunnery—likely in Constantinople—after receiving accusations that the nuns were living contrary to monastic principles. See Paidas, "Secular Life's Behaviours and Debauchery Among Nuns," 343–57.

CONCLUSIONS

THE PRESENT STUDY of female monasticism in Late Byzantium explored several critical dimensions: the foundation and organization of monasteries, daily monastic life, financial structures, contributions to art and knowledge, and the relationship between female monastics and the Church.

An analysis of monastic foundations and patronage revealed intricate networks of individuals, shaped by legal, textual, and spatial frameworks. These foundations functioned not merely as religious institutions but also as instruments of power, reflecting broader societal hierarchies and imbalances. They served as expressions of political, social, and economic agency, underscoring the deeply embedded inequalities within monastic patronage networks.

An examination of monastic life elucidates the avenues of opportunity available to women who entered religious orders. While admission to a convent was occasionally a matter of personal volition, it was more frequently dictated by social or economic necessity. The age at entry, length of the novitiate, and the conditions for taking final vows varied across different communities. Nonetheless, the adoption of the religious habit afforded women access to education and the potential to attain positions of authority, which was contingent upon their qualifications. Within this institutional context, nuns were able to cultivate and exercise competencies in governance, financial oversight, and administrative leadership, thereby contesting enduring assumptions about the intellectual and practical limitations traditionally ascribed to women.

Monastic enclosure did not imply complete isolation from the outside world. Communication with family and ecclesiastical authorities remained active, facilitated in part by the physical layout of monastic spaces. Archaeological evidence from the Bebaia Elpis nunnery illustrates how architectural design reflected and reinforced female agency. Changes in the spatial organization of monastic communities reveal shifts in women's roles and their evolving authority within these institutions. By integrating textual and spatial analysis, the study underscores the multidimensional nature of female monastic foundations and their entanglement with broader political, social, and cultural structures.

These external connections are also evident in material culture—manuscripts, liturgical objects, and icons—which testify to the presence and influence of nuns. Devotion, donation, and death (the "three Ds," as termed in this study) formed the primary channels through which female monastics left their mark. Portraits of nuns appear on scrolls, books, wall paintings, mosaics, sculptures, and objects of piety. Their donations extended beyond their own communities, reaching village and urban neighbourhoods. Through such acts of patronage, nuns not only shaped the visual and devotional landscape but also played an active role in the local economy.

The financial aspects of female monasticism reveal the economic foundations that sustained these communities. Landownership was their primary asset, with properties often dispersed across distant regions. Although some communities exhibited entrepreneurial adaptability in response to gradual land losses, female involvement in economic activities was generally limited by gender-based restrictions on mobility and social interaction. To mitigate these constraints, founders typically endowed nunneries with substantial initial resources intended to ensure long-term sustainability.

Parallel patterns were observed in the lives of individual nuns. Wealthy women who entered monastic life often retained control over their personal assets, including dowries and inherited estates. Rather than directing these resources exclusively toward their convents, they frequently managed them independently, continuing to function as autonomous agents or representatives of their families.

The final chapter of this study focused on the complex social networks that connected nuns and female monasteries, particularly in the context of the ecclesiastical controversies of the late thirteenth century, the first half of the fourteenth century, and the years preceding the Fall of Constantinople. These disputes revealed a significant degree of female participation, which was mobilized through spiritual mentorship and kinship ties.

Given the complexity of this material, the analysis concentrated on the Arsenite network during the period surrounding the Union of Lyons. Utilizing Social Network Analysis, participants were categorized into two classes of nodes. The results revealed that the Arsenite movement was fragmented into smaller clusters with limited interconnectivity, suggesting a lack of cohesion that may have diminished the movement's overall effectiveness. Nevertheless, certain figures, such as Theodora Raoulaina, emerged as pivotal actors within their respective clusters.

The late Byzantine period highlights the resilience and adaptability of female monastics in response to shifting social, political, and religious conditions. Their participation in ecclesiastical debates, literary production, and cultural patronage affirms their lasting importance within Byzantine society. Furthermore, the survival of monastic communities under Ottoman rule attests to their continued relevance and influence in the post-Byzantine world. These developments are essential for understanding the enduring legacy of Byzantine female monasticism.

Appendix I

LIST OF NUNS

NOTE: Names in **bold** designate nuns not listed in the *PLP*.
An asterisk * after the name denotes uncertain dating in Late Byzantium.
This list is not intended to be exhaustive.

1. Abastagaina, ***PLP* 24**, 1264, Kephalenia, abbess of the Monastery of Megas Taxiarches
2. Adelasia, ***PLP* 292**, 1280, Fragalà Monastery, Patti/NO Sicily
3. Agathe, ***PLP* 70**, 1348, Paphos/Cyprus
4. Agathe, ***PLP* 91012**, 1344, Thessaloniki
5. Agathonike, ***PLP* 74**, 1330, Skamandros and Herakleia (Kryoneritissa Monastery)
6. Agathonike, ***PLP* 75**, 1321–1322, Philanthropos Soter Monastery, Constantinople
7. **Agnese**, Chalke Island, Rhodes, 1367 (Sigala, "Η Παναγία η Οδηγήτρια η Εννιαμερίτισσα," 333)
8. **Aikaterina Amoirisa**, 1344 (Bénou, *Codex B*, pp. 100–101, no. 47)
9. Aikaterina, ***PLP* 442**, 1343 or later
10. Aikaterina, ***PLP* 443**, 1405, Skirmalo in Paphos/Cyprus
11. Aikaterine, ***PLP* 447**, 1314, Macedonia
12. Aikaterine, ***PLP* 91098**, 1324 or earlier, Thessaloniki
13. **Alexena Kataphyge**, Hagia Triada near Psinthos, Rhodes
14. Amarantina, ***PLP* 748**, ca. 1350–1354, Constantinople
15. Anastasia, ***PLP* 856**, 1292 or before
16. Anastasia, ***PLP* 857**, second half of the fourteenth century
17. Anastasia, ***PLP* 858**, 1330, Skamandros and Herakleia (Kryoneritissa Monastery).
18. **Anastasia/Agathe**, 1302
19. **Angelina Xene**, Smyrna, 1231

20. Angelina, ***PLP* 147**, 1341, Constantinople

21. **Angelina**, sister of Xene Angelina, Smyrna, 1231

22. Anna, ***PLP* 19736**, 1360, Phalia/Cyprus

23. Anonymous, abbess in Constantinople and sister of nun Theodosia, ***PLP* 7085**, thirteenth/fourteenth century

24. **Anonymous, aunt of Sphrantzes**, end of fourteenth century, Theodora Monastery, Thessaloniki; 1387 to Lemnos; later to Kleraina Monastery in Constantinople

25. **Anonymous, daughter of Proximos**, fourteenth century, Philanthropos Soter Monastery, Constantinople

26. **Anonymous, "removed from the infidels,"** fourteenth century, Philanthropos Soter Monastery, Constantinople

27. **Anonymous, niece of Rentakes**, early thirteenth century, Smyrna area

28. **Anonymous, ex-wife of Markellos**, fifteenth century, near Hierissos

29. Anthouse, ***PLP* 996**, November 23, 1398, Phorbia Monastery, Cyprus

30. **Anysia Planitissa**, 1257, Smyrna

31. Anysia*, ***PLP* 93100**, twelfth century or later

32. Anysia, ***PLP* 1123**, 1320

33. Anysia, ***PLP* 1124**, fifteenth century or later

34. Anysia, ***PLP* 1125**, second half of thirteenth century, Vazelon Monastery, Trebizond

35. Anysia, ***PLP* 761**, April 17, 1296, Crimea

36. Anysia, ***PLP* 91256**, 1426/27, Serbia

37. Apokauchissa Irene, ***PLP* 1193**, before 1401, Kyprianou Monastery, Constantinople

38. Archotokephanina Martha, ***PLP* 1462**, fourteenth/fifteenth century, Crete

39. Asanina, Irene Komnene Palaiologina, ***PLP* 21359**, ca. 1260–after 1306, Constantinople

40. Asanina, Simonis/Sophrosyne Palaiologina, ***PLP* 1534**, ca. 1462–1464, Peloponnese

41. Aspietina, ***PLP* 1575**, 1359, Constantinople

42. Aspietissa Pheronike, ***PLP* 1579→ 91385**, 1400, Constantinople

43. Athanasia*, ***PLP* 334**, twelfth century or later
44. Athanasia, ***PLP* 333**, abbess, 1292
45. Athanasia, ***PLP* 335**, February 28, 1342, Paphos/Cyprus
46. Athanasia, ***PLP* 91070**, first half of fourteenth century, Constantinople
47. Athanasia, ***PLP* 91071**, 1355, Lemnos
48. Balda, ***PLP* 2065**, abbess, 1304, Theotokos Monastery, Messina
49. Barbara, ***PLP* 2163**, January 12, 1421, Paphos/Cyprus
50. Baropolitissa Martha, ***PLP* 91454**, 1400, Constantinople
51. Bdelena (?), ***PLP* 91482**, before 1368, Lemnos, before 1266–1283, Constantinople
52. Beloniotissa, ***PLP* 93210**, 1356/57, St. Mamas/Chalkidike
53. **Blandymerine**, fourteenth century, Serres (Bénou, *Codex B*, p. 199, no. 120, line 18)
54. **Branaina Euphrosyne**, early fourteenth century, Constantinople
55. Branaina, Eirene/Maria, Komnene Laskarina Kantakouzene Palaiologina, ***PLP* 3149**, after 1270, Constantinople
56. Briona, daughter of Koutoumalas, ***PLP* 3222**,1397, Paphos/Cyprus
57. Bryenissa, ***PLP* 3240**, before November 1360, Constantinople
58. Choumnaina, Irene Palaiologina Laskarina, ***PLP* 30936**, 1307, Philanthropos Soter Monastery, Constantinople
59. Choumnaina *kaniklina*, ***PLP* 30935**, ca. 1326–1327, Philanthropos Soter Monastery, Constantinople
60. Christodoule, ***PLP* 31001**, 1292, Chalkidike
61. **Christophile**, fourteenth century, Philanthropos Soter Monastery, Constantinople (Theoleptos of Philadelphia, *Letters*, ed. Constantinides Hero, pp. 66, line 462: no. 2)
62. Chrouse/Chrysantha, ***PLP* 31056**, 1408 (?), Paphos/Cyprus
63. **Chrysokephalina Eugenia**, 1275, Serres (Bénou, *Codex B*, p. 21, no. 1, line 1)
64. Chrysolorina Eugenia, ***PLP* 31168**, 1401, Constantinople
65. Dabalitissa Makrina, ***PLP* 5002**, d. 1426 or before, Trebizond
66. Diplobatatzina, Martha Palaiologina, ***PLP* 5516**, fourteenth century

67. Doukaina Hypomone Komnene, ***PLP* 5667**, 1289, Lykousada nunnery, Phanarion/Thessaly

68. Doukaina Theodora, ***PLP* 5664**, *basilissa* in Arta, ca. 1231–after ca. 1270, St. George (later St. Theodora) Monastery, Arta

69. Drakonto (?)[Drakontopoula] Ephrosyne, ***PLP* 5813**, 1271–1280, Crete

70. Eirenarchia, ***PLP* 5965**, 1360, Sozopolis/Thrace

71. Eleodora, ***PLP* 6007**, ca. 1350, Thessaloniki

72. Elisabet, ***PLP* 6021**, fifteenth century, Cyprus

73. Epicharis, ***PLP* 6107**, sister of Gregory Palamas, ca 1316 in Constantinople, d. ca.1326 in Berroia

74. Eudokia, ***PLP* 6233**, second half of the fourteenth century, Elateia/Asia Minor and Neapolis (Kavala?)

75. Eudosia*, ***PLP* 6246**, twelfth century or later

76. Eugenia*, ***PLP* 6176**, twelfth century or later, Macedonia

77. Eugenia, ***PLP* 6177**, end of thirteenth century (?)

78. Eugenia, ***PLP* 6178**, end of fourteenth century

79. Eugenia, ***PLP* 6179**, ca. 1270–1274, Chalkidike

80. Eugenia, ***PLP* 6180**, wife of Michael/Makarios Tornikes, great *konostavlos*, after 1320, Constantinople

81. Eugenia, ***PLP* 6181**, 1358/59, Crete

82. Eugenia, ***PLP* 6182**, fifteenth century, Crete

83. Eugenia, ***PLP* 6183**, *protosebaste*, September 1394, Constantinople

84. Eugenia, ***PLP* 91874**, before ca. 1381, Macedonia

85. Eugenia, ***PLP* 91875**, 1324 or earlier, Thessaloniki (?)

86. Eugenia, ***PLP* 93512**, ca. 1323–ca. 1340, Kroulla/Bithynia

87. Eugenia/Milica, ***PLP* 6175→ 91854**, *κνέγινα* of Serbia (1371–1405); nun since 1397/98 or earlier

88. Eulogia, ***PLP* 6275**, 1327, Thessaloniki

89. Eulogia, ***PLP* 6277**, first half of the fifteenth century

90. Euphemia, ***PLP* 6360**, *despoina* of Serbia, ca. 1364–1371

91. Euphemia, ***PLP* 6362**, 1292, Chalkidiki

92. Euphemia, ***PLP* 91911**, late thirteenth/ early fourteenth century, Skepes Monastery, Constantinople

93. Euphemia, ***PLP* 93522**, 1294, Paphos/Cyprus

94. **Euphrosyne Lagoutzikia**, 1275, Serres (Bénou, *Codex B*, p. 21, no. 1, line 1)

95. **Euphrosyne Mousarafina**, 1275, Serres (Bénou, *Codex B*, p. 21, no. 1, line 2)

96. Euphrosyne, ***PLP* 6380**, fourteenth century, Trebizond

97. Euphrosyne, ***PLP* 93524**, ca. 1323–ca. 1340, Constantinople

98. Eupraxia*, ***PLP* 6313**, twelfth century or later

99. Eupraxia, ***PLP* 6312**, *despoina* of Serbia, 1405

100. Eupraxia, ***PLP* 6314**, 1389

101. Eupraxia, ***PLP* 6315**, 1302, St. George Monastery, Hagia Triada/Crete

102. Eupraxia, ***PLP* 6316**, 1485/86, St. Nicholas Monastery, Kastoria

103. Gabala Magdalene, ***PLP* 16023**, between ca. 1323–ca. 1340, Constantinople

104. Gabraina Athanasia, ***PLP* 3321**, before July 1401, Constantinople

105. Giagoupaina, ***PLP* 4148**, around 1260 (?), Trebizond

106. Glabaina Theodosia, ***PLP* 4206**, d. after 1292, Constantinople

107. Glabaina, ***PLP* 4202**, after 1310, Constantinople

108. Glyka Euphrosyne, ***PLP* 93351**, end thirteenth century, St. John Monastery, Zoupena/Lakonia

109. Glykaina Eudokia, ***PLP* 4243**, 1325, Ainos

110. **Goudelina Anna**, *kyra* (ca. 1370–1421), Constantinople (Ganchou, "L'ultime testament," 354)

111. **Goudelina Anna/Athanasia** (ca. 1400–1457), Constantinople (Ganchou, "L'ultime testament," 354)

112. **Goudelina Raoulaina Theodora/Theodosia** (ca. 1370–1421), Constantinople (Ganchou, "L'ultime testament," 354)

113. Goudelina, Thomais/Theodoule Palaiologine, ***PLP* 91698**, fifteenth century, Constantinople

114. Helen, ***PLP* 6003**, fourteenth century (?)

115. Helen, ***PLP* 6004**, 1304, Chleion Neron/Lemnos

116. Helen, ***PLP* 6005**, since April 16, 1314, Paphos/Cyprus

117. Helenissa, ***PLP* 93495**, 1330/31

118. Hypomone *tou Mourmoura*, ***PLP* 29505**, 1339, George Kryonerites Monastery/Serres

119. Hypomone, ***PLP* 29502**, 1336, Anargyroi Monastery, Thessaloniki

120. Hypomone, ***PLP* 29503**, first half of fifteenth century (?), Karkasia Monastery, Hierapetra/Crete

121. Iagoupaina, ***PLP* 7812**, around 1260 (?), Trebizond

122. Isarina Xene, ***PLP* 8282**, *megale konostaulissa*, 1374

123. Kabakaina Kale, ***PLP* 10013**, fourteenth/fifteenth century (?), Mistras

124. Kaliaba Anysia, ***PLP* 10322**, 1291, Trebizond

125. Kalliepopoulos Margarita/Makrina, ***PLP* 10358**, 1415, Trebizond

126. Kallinika, ***PLP* 10374**, 1415, Lemnos

127. Kallinike, ***PLP* 10375**, thirteenth–fifteenth century

128. Kallinike, ***PLP* 10376**, d. December 30, 1288, Crimea

129. Kallinike, ***PLP* 10377**, 1306

130. Kallinike, ***PLP* 10378**, before 1365, Pausolype Monastery, Constantinople

131. Kallinike, ***PLP* 10379**, d. February 15, 1299, Crimea

132. Kallinike, ***PLP* 10380**, 1395–1400, Patras

133. Kallinike, ***PLP* 92268**, 1278, Polemitas, Mane/Peloponnese

134. Kallone, ***PLP* 10503**, ca. 1316–1326, Constantinople

135. Kaloeidina Hypomone, ***PLP* 10580**, 1397, Constantinople

136. **Kalognomos Euphrosyne/Helen**, after ca. 1218, thema Bagenetias, Epiros

137. Kalothetina Hypomone, ***PLP* 10588**, 1395, Thessaloniki

138. Kanabina Martha, ***PLP* 10860**, 1400, Constantinople

139. Kantakouzene Irene/Eugenia, ***PLP* 10935**, 1354–after 1363, *kyra* Martha Monastery, Constantinople

140. Kantakouzene, Eugenia Philanthropene, ***PLP* 10936**, 1391/92–1402, Bebaia Elpis Monastery, Constantinople

141. Kantakouzene, Theodora Raoulaina Palaiologina Komnene, ***PLP* 10943**, d. December 6, 1300, Andrew *in Krisei*, Constantinople

142. Kantakouzene, Thomais/Xene Komnene Doukaina Laskarina Palaiologina, ***PLP*** **10944**, around 1300, Constantinople

143. Kasiane, ***PLP*** **11330**, d. 1328 (?) or 1368(?)

144. Kasiane, ***PLP*** **93784**, thirteenth century

145. **Kataphyge Skoularopoulos**, 1482, Vazelon Monastery, Trebizond

146. Kataphyge, ***PLP*** **11460**, 1302, St. George Monastery, Hagia Triada/Crete

147. Kataphyge, ***PLP*** **11462**, 1358/59, Saviour Monastery, Blithias/Crete

148. Katenitzina/Athanasia, ***PLP*** **93798**, after April 1326, Athanasios Monastery, Constantinople

149. Katerina, ***PLP*** **11480**, 1313, Crimea

150. Katerina, ***PLP*** **11482**, 1347, Theotokos Skaphideiane Monastery, Prodromion/Crete

151. Kaukanina, Hypomone Chrysokephalina, ***PLP*** **11563**, 1400, Constantinople

152. Kleptoulia, ***PLP*** **11793**, before 1318, Krousobon/Strymon

153. Komnene Agathe, ***PLP*** **12056**, 1441/42

154. Komnene, Anna Anachoutlou, ***PLP*** **12059**, empress of Trebizond (1341–1342), d. 1342

155. Komnene, ***PLP*** **12054**, abbess, first half of the fifteenth century

156. Komnene, ***PLP*** **12055**, early fourteenth century

157. Komnene Raoulaina Strategopoulina, Anna/Antonia, ***PLP*** **26893**, foundress of Krataios monastery, late thirteenth–early fourteenth century, Constantinople

158. Komnene, Theodora Kantakouzene, ***PLP*** **12068**, empress of Trebizond 1351–1390; nun 1390–1400, Constantinople

159. Kontostephana Polyxene, ***PLP*** **13111**, fourteenth century

160. Koteanitzaina Loukiane, ***PLP*** **13325**, 1366, Trikala

161. Kypriane, ***PLP*** **13906**, end of fourteenth century, Theodora Monastery, Thessaloniki; 1387 to Lemnos; later to Kleraina Monastery in Constantinople

162. **Kyprianou *tou***, end of fourteenth century, Theodora Monastery, Thessaloniki; 1387 to Lemnos; later to Kleraina Monastery in Constantinople

163. Kyriake, ***PLP* 13953**, thirteenth century (?), Charouda in Mane/ Peloponnese

164. Kyriake, ***PLP* 93929**, thirteenth century, Kepoula in Mane/ South Peloponnese

165. Laskarina Eudokia, ***PLP* 91888**, before 1258–1309

166. **Lemniotissa Aikaterine**, 1275, Serres (Bénou, *Codex B*, p. 21, no. 1, line 2)

167. Logarina, ***PLP* 14994**, 1402, Constantinople

168. **Magdalene**, Chalke Island, Rhodes, 1367 (Sigala, "Η Παναγία η Οδηγήτρια η Εννιαμερίτισσα," 333)

169. **Magdalene *tou Kardame***, 1347, Serres (Bénou, *Codex B*, p. 150–51, no. 77)

170. Magdalene, ***PLP* 16024**, 1374/75, St. George Monastery, Longanikon/ Lakonia

171. Magdalene, ***PLP* 16025**, 1451–1461, Constantine and Helen Monastery, Nempros/Crete

172. Makaria, ***PLP* 16153**, around the middle of fifteenth century

173. Makaria, ***PLP* 16154**, before 1400

174. Makaria, ***PLP* 16155**, 1401, Kyprianou Monastery, Constantinople

175. Makrina, ***PLP* 16384**, d. 1292

176. Makrydoukaina Maria/Martha, ***PLP* 16435**, d. June 24, 1362

177. Manourina, ***PLP* 16755**, 1430 or earlier, Soter Monastery, Kotzinos/Lemnos

178. Maria/Martha, ***PLP* 16874**, mother of Basil Kourteses, 1374/75, St. George Monastery, Longanikon/Lakonia

179. Maria of Kouloudros, ***PLP* 16896**, d. December 8, 1306, Paphos/Cyprus

180. Maria, ***PLP* 16885**, ruler of Epiros and Thessaly, 1347–1359; *kyra* Martha Monastery Constantinople, 1359–1379

181. Maria, ***PLP* 16889**, thirteenth century

182. Maria/Mara Keraca, ***PLP* 16891**, empress (r. 1376–1379), Bassos monastery, Constantinople

183. **Mariamne *tou Blakou***, 1328–1329, Serres (Bénou, *Codex B*, pp. 104, 107, 109–10, nos. 50–52)

184. **Marina Sgouraina**, 1275, Serres (Bénou, *Codex B*, p. 21, no. 1, line 1)

185. Marina, ***PLP*** **16927**, fifteenth century

186. Marina, ***PLP*** **16928**, 1381, Paphos/Cyprus

187. Marina, ***PLP*** **16929**, 1359, Constantinople

188. Marina, ***PLP*** **92635**, 1348 or earlier, Monodendrion/ Thessaloniki

189. Marinia Euphrosyne, ***PLP*** **16939**, 1316, Lakedaimon

190. Martha *tou Bokolou*, ***PLP*** **16872**, d. November 4, in the fourteenth century, Paphos/Cyprus

191. Martha*, ***PLP*** **16870**, 1343 or later

192. Martha, ***PLP*** **94077**, 1332–1338, Philanthropos Soter Monastery, Constantinople

193. Martha, ***PLP*** **16866**, abbess, 1401, Kyprianos Monastery, Constantinople

194. Martha, ***PLP*** **16867**, thirteenth/ fourteenth century, Cyprus

195. Martha, ***PLP*** **16868**, d. before November 1324

196. Martha, ***PLP*** **16869**, d. March 14, 1330

197. Martha, ***PLP*** **16873**, 1400, Constantinople (?)

198. Martha, ***PLP*** **16874**, 1374/75, Lakonia

199. Martha/Maria, ***PLP*** **16871**, d. March 8, 1387

200. Maroulina, ***PLP*** **17161**, until 1361, Barangiotissa Monastery, Constantinople

201. Mastrangelaina, ***PLP*** **17242**, 1264, Kephalenia

202. Matakoudena Thekla, ***PLP*** **17258**, 1344, Mertes/Crete

203. Matrona, ***PLP*** **17399**, mid-fourteenth century, Chios

204. Mauriane Theognosia, ***PLP*** **17408**, abbess, 1400, Andrew *in Krisei*, Constantinople

205. Meizomatissa, ***PLP*** **17620**, until 1414, Constantinople

206. Melane, ***PLP*** **17637**, 1314, Thessaloniki

207. Melane, ***PLP*** **17639**, 1360–1368, Thessaloniki

208. Melane, ***PLP*** **17640**, *protohierakaria*, early fourteenth century, Constantinople

209. Melane/Martha, ***PLP*** **17638**, 1327, Thessaloniki

210. Mesopotamitissa Sophrosyne, ***PLP*** **17958**, d. February 27, 1336

211. Modene Marina/Martha, ***PLP* 19207**, 1321, Kaisaropolis/Thrace

212. Mygiarina, ***PLP* 19839**, before 1393, Trikala

213. Nikol..., ***PLP* 20385**, abbess (?), d. 1355/56

214. Nymphodora, ***PLP* 20781**, until 1445, Hierissos

215. Olympia, ***PLP* 21049**, abbess (?), thirteenth century

216. Olympias, ***PLP* 21050**, 1306

217. Palaiologina Helen/Hypomone, ***PLP* 21364**, *basilissa* of Serbia, d. November 11, 1473, Santa Maura/Leukas

218. Palaiologina Helen/Hypomone, ***PLP* 21365**, empress (1347–1397), 1392, *kyra* Martha Monastery, Constantinople

219. Palaiologina Helen/Hypomone, ***PLP* 21366**, empress (1392–1450), 1426/27–1450

220. Palaiologina Irene/Eugenia, ***PLP* 21358**, co-empress (1397–1407), d. January 1, 1440, Constantinople

221. Palaiologina Johanna (Anna)/Anastasia of Savoy, ***PLP* 21347**, empress (1328–1365/66), d. 1365/66, Thessaloniki

222. Palaiologina Maria, ***PLP* 21391**, *kralaina* of Serbia (ca. 1325–1331); nun, 1331–1355

223. Palaiologina Maria, ***PLP* 21392**, *sebaste*, ca. late thirteenth/early fourteenth century

224. Palaiologina Simonis, ***PLP* 21398**, *kralaina* of Serbia (1299–1321), after 1345, Andrew *in Krisei*, Constantinople

225. Palaiologina Tarchaneiotissa Martha/Maria, ***PLP* 21389**, before 1266–after 1267, Martha monastery

226. Palaiologina Theodora/Theodosia, ***PLP* 21379**, *tsarina* of Bulgaria, 1308–1330; 1330–1342, d. after 1342, Constantinople

227. Palaiologina, Agape Angelina Sphratzaina, ***PLP* 21341**, 1341, Hagia Maria/Chalkidike

228. Palaiologina, Anna/Anthousa Komnene Angelina Doukaina Philanthropene Maliasene, ***PLP* 21351**, 1271–1272, Nea Petra Monastery, Dryanoubaina/Thessaly

229. Komnene Raoulaina Strategopoulina, Anna/Antonia ***PLP* 26893**, early fourteenth century, Constantinople

230. Palaiologina, Eugenia Komnene, ***PLP* 21368**, *megale domestikissa*, 1321–1329, Constantinople

231. Palaiologina, Eulogia Komnene, ***PLP* 21370**, early fourteenth century, Constantinople

232. Palaiologina, Euphrosyne Komnene Doukaina Synadene, ***PLP* 21373**, first half of fourteenth century, Bebaia Elpis, Constantinople

233. Palaiologina, Irene/Eulogia Komnene, ***PLP* 21360**, 1261 (or earlier)–1284, Constantinople

234. Palaiologina, Maria/Makaria Komnene Kantakouzene, ***PLP* 21397**, empress (1427–1439), d. December 17, 1439, Constantinople

235. Palaiologina, Maria/Mariamne Komnene Branaina Laskarina Doukaina Tornikina, ***PLP* 21396**, late thirteenth/early fourteenth century

236. Palaiologina, Maria/Melane Komnene, ***PLP* 21395**, *δέσποινα τῶν Μουγουλίων* [Lady of the Mongols]; d. after 1307, *tes Panagiotisses* nunnery, Constantinople

237. Palaiologina, ***PLP* 21339**, hymnographer, d. before 1387, St. Theodora Monastery, Thessaloniki

238. Palaiologina, Rita (Maria)/Xene Doukaina, ***PLP* 21394**, co-empress (1296–1320); d. June or July 1333, Thessaloniki

239. Palaiologina, Theodora/Theodosia, ***PLP* 21379**, 1308–1330: tsarina of Bulgaria; 1330–1342: nun in Constantinople

240. Palaiologina, Theodora Doukaina Komnene, ***PLP* 21380**, empress (1259–1303), Lips nunnery, Constantinople

241. Palaiologina, Theodora/Theodoule Komnene Synadene, ***PLP* 21381**, ca. 1321–1342, Bebaia Elpis nunnery, Constantinople

242. Papagenakopoulos Anysia, ***PLP* 21729**, 1344, Vazelon Monastery, Trebizond

243. Parak/Pelagia, ***PLP* 21857**, d. March 23, 1308, Sougdaia

244. Paraskeue, ***PLP* 21885**, before 1355, Lemnos

245. Paraskeue, ***PLP* 21887**, 1401/02 (?), Theotokos tou Bryomenou (Phaneromene) monastery, Kalo Chorio/Crete

246. Pegene Euphrosyne, ***PLP* 23138**, fourteenth / fifteenth century

247. Pelagia, ***PLP* 22257**, fourteenth century, Crete

248. Pelagia, ***PLP* 22258**, 1323, Crete

249. **Penentarina Maria/Magdalene**, 1301–1304, Serres (Bénou, *Codex B*, pp. 43–45: nos. 12–13)

250. Pepagomene, ***PLP* 22340**, 1401, Constantinople
251. Perate Martha, ***PLP* 22406**, 1322–1331, Paphos/Cyprus
252. Petraliphina Euphrosyne, ***PLP* 23013**, 1329–1330, Constantinople
253. Petraliphina, ***PLP* 23011**, 1400, Constantinople
254. Phialitissa Zenobia, ***PLP* 29721**, 1401, Constantinople
255. Philanthropene Xene, ***PLP* 29746**, 1391/92–1394, Bebaia Elpis Monastery, Constantinople
256. Plato (*Πλατώ*), ***PLP* 23351**, ca. 1355–1370, Oreinos Monastery, Peloponnese
257. Platyskalitissa Anysia, ***PLP* 23350**, 1326, Thessaloniki
258. Porine Irene, ***PLP* 23565**, 1337–1344, Thessaloniki
259. Pouzoulou, Kallone he, ***PLP* 23621**, before 1401, Constantinople
260. Rabdene (*koulaïtissa*), ***PLP* 23957**, 1321, Thessaloniki
261. Ralaina, ***PLP* 24053**, 1332–1338, Philanthropos Soter, Constantinople
262. Raoulaina, Irene/Athanasia Palaiologina, ***PLP* 24142**, ca. 1289–1321, d. after 1321, Constantinople
263. Rokina, Marina te/ Marina de Rocca (?), ***PLP* 24365**, fourteenth century (?), Cyprus
264. Romani(tissa? or Romanitopoulle)... Kale, ***PLP* 24482**, 1382, Paphos/Cyprus
265. Rompaina, ***PLP* 24531**, late thirteenth/early fourteenth century, Constantinople
266. Eupraxia Sabentzina, ***PLP* 24660**, 1342 or earlier, Constantinople
267. Saberina, ***PLP* 24661**, 1264 or earlier, Kephalenia
268. Sagmataba Makaria, ***PLP* 24681**, around 1450, Trebizond
269. Sarantene Sophrosyne, ***PLP* 24882**, until 1330, Pelorygion/Strymon, Macedonia
270. Sarantene, Eleodora Tzympinissa, ***PLP* 24879**, 1348, Thessaloniki
271. Sarantene, Xene Indanina, ***PLP* 24881**, until 1330, Pelorygion/Strymon, Macedonia
272. Senacheirina Angelina, ***PLP* 25156**, 1354, *kyr David* Monastery, Philadelphia
273. Sikile, ***PLP* 25320**, 1400, Constantinople
274. Skammene Theodosia, ***PLP* 26015**, 1298, Paphos/Cyprus

275. Sophronia, ***PLP* 27347**, fifteenth century

276. Sophronia, ***PLP* 27348**, 1363/64, Eleousa Monastery, Papagiannades/Crete

277. Sophrosyne, ***PLP* 27386**, 1401/02 (?), Theotokos tou Bryomenou (Phaneromene) Monastery, Kalo Chorio/Crete

278. Soultanina, Xene Palaiologina, ***PLP* 26336**, 1344, Berroia

279. **Stamenare *tou***, before 1329, Serres (broader area) (Bénou, *Codex B*, p. 193, no. 117, line 54)

280. Stomias Makrina, ***PLP* 26839**, d. 1399, Paphos/Cyprus

281. Strategissa Eudokia*, ***PLP* 26891**, twelfth century or later

282. Synkletike, ***PLP* 27011**, 1332–1338, Constantinople

283. Syriana Martha, ***PLP* 27170**, 1365, Pausolype Monastery, Constantinople

284. Syropoulina, Zoe Melanchrene, ***PLP* 27193**, 1271–1272, Dryanoubaina/Thessaly

285. Tarchaneiotissa Eleodora, ***PLP* 27509**, 1401, Constantinople

286. Tarchaneiotissa Nostongonissa, ***PLP* 27512**, 1266–1303, Constantinople

287. Tarchaneiotissa Theodora/Theodosia, ***PLP* 27510**, *megale stratopedarchissa* (1259–1283)

288. Tarchaneiotissa, Maria Doukaina Komnene Branaina Palaiologina, ***PLP* 27511**, after 1304, Glabaina Monastery, Constantinople

289. Taronitissa Eudokia, ***PLP* 27534**, until 1275 (?), Trebizond

290. Thamar, ***PLP* 7029**, before 1355, Lemnos

291. Theodosia*, ***PLP* 7086**, twelfth century or later

292. Theodosia, ***PLP* 7085**, abbess, thirteenth/ fourteenth century, Constantinople

293. Theodote, ***PLP* 7195**, sister of Gregory Palamas, d. ca. 1339, Constantinople and Berroia

294. Theodote, ***PLP* 7196**, 1321–1322, Philanthropos Soter Monastery, Constantinople

295. **Theodoule Glykozonarou**, 1275, Serres (Bénou, *Codex B*, p. 21, no. 1, line 1)

296. Theodoule, ***PLP* 7212**, abbess, 1320/21, Theotokos Monastery, Chalkidike (?)

297. Theodoule, ***PLP* 7213**, d. 1382, Georgios *tou Koudouna* Monastery, Cyprus

298. Theodoule, ***PLP* 7214**, 1320/21, Theotokos Monastery, Chalkidike (?)

299. Theodoulia*, ***PLP* 7215**, twelfth-early fourteenth century

300. Theologitissa Makrina, ***PLP* 7519**, d. 1401, Constantinople

301. Theonymphe*, ***PLP* 7527**, twelfth century or later

302. Theopempte, ***PLP* 7530**, 1274, Elasson/Thessaly

303. Thiniatissa, ***PLP* 7738**, 1352, Constantinople

304. Thomais, ***PLP* 7758**, abbess, 1401, Pausolype Monastery, Constantinople

305. Thomais, ***PLP* 7760**, 1361–1429, Theodora Monastery, Thessaloniki; 1387 to Lemnos; later to Kleraina Monastery in Constantinople

306. Thrakesina Martha, ***PLP* 7746**, 1274–1281, Smyrna

307. Tzakalina, ***PLP* 27691**, thirteenth century, second half, St. George Monastery, called Trapeza at Skoutari

308. Tzitapina, Athanasia Tzainissa, ***PLP* 27993**, before 1304, Thessaloniki

309. Tzountzk (*Τζούντζκ*), ***PLP* 28047**, d. January 30, 1347, Sougdaia

310. Tzourakina or Tzouramina, ***PLP* 28048**, until January 1402, Constantinople

311. Tzouroulene Theodoule, ***PLP* 28059**, 1400 and earlier, Gabraina Monastery, Constantinople

312. Urre, Martha tou, ***PLP* 21195**, early fifteenth century, Cyprus

313. Xene*, ***PLP* 20847**, *hosia*, fifteenth century (?)

314. Xene, ***PLP* 20845**, fourteenth century

315. Xene, ***PLP* 20846**, 1306

316. Zagarommatina Irene/Eugenia, ***PLP* 6418**, d. 1261

317. Zena *tou Skamenou*, ***PLP* 6563**, 1349, Cyprus

318. Zenaia, ***PLP* 6565**, before July 11, 1379, Cyprus

319. Zenobia, ***PLP* 6566**, 1379/80 or earlier, Macedonia

320. **Zonaras**, nun, early thirteenth century, Smyrna area

Appendix 2

LISTS OF NUNNERIES

NOTE: The following lists present the names and locations of nunneries mentioned in late Byzantine sources, organized by century. They are not intended to be exhaustive.

Thirteenth Century

Anargyroi, Constantinople

Andrew *in Krisei,* Constantinople

Aristene, Constantinople

Athanasios, double monastery, Constantinople

Blachernitissa, Blacherna, Epiros

Carpos and Papylos (perhaps still active as a nunnery?), Constantinople

Georgiou or Trapeza, Skoutari (Üsküdar)

Gerontiou, Thessaloniki

Jacob the Persian (perhaps still active as a nunnery?), Constantinople

Kyra Martha, Constantinople

Megale Mone, Nicosia, Cyprus

Lykousada, Phanarion, Thessaly

Lips, Constantinople

Pantanassa, Athens

Pertze, Constantinople

Prodromos, Nea Petra, Demetrias, Thessaly

St. Apostoloi, Epiros, exact location unknown

Tarasiou, Constantinople

Taxiarches Monastery, Mane, Peloponnese

Theodosia nunnery, Constantinople

Theoskepastos, Trebizond

Theotokos Panagiotissa, Constantinople

Thomais nunnery, Constantinople

Skepes Monastery, Constantinople

St. Antony, Nicaea

St. George (later St. Theodora), Arta, Epiros

St. Trinity, Athens

Fourteenth Century

Akroulliou (identical to St. Anargyroi?), Thessaloniki

Anargyroi, Constantinople

Anargyroi *tes Parathyrou*, Thessaloniki

Andrew *in Krisei,* Constantinople

Anonymous monastic community where the sisters of Gregory Palamas were relocated, Berroia

Athanasios, double monastery, Constantinople

Barangiotissa Monastery, Constantinople

Bassos Monastery, Constantinople

Bebaia Elpis, Constantinople

Eleousa Monastery, Papagiannades, Crete

Elpis ton apelpismenon, Constantinople

Euouraniotissa, Constantinople

Evergetidos *tes Sebastokratorisses*, Constantinople

Fragalà, Patti/NO-Sicily

Georgios *tou Koudouna*, Cyprus

Glabaina nunnery, Constantinople

Hodegetria, Didymoteichon

Kanikleiou, Constantinople

Kantakouzenou, theme of Thessaloniki, West Chalkidiki

Kecharitomene, Constantinople

Kleraina Monastery, Constantinople

Krataios Soter, Constantinople

Kryoneritissa, Herakleia

Kryoneritissa (?), Skamandros, Asia Minor

Kyprianou Monastery, Constantinople

Kyr David, Philadelphia

Kyra Martha, Constantinople

Lips, Constantinople

Maroules, Constantinople

megales Doukaines, Constantinople

Oreinos Monastery, Peloponnese

Panachrantos, Constantinople

Pantanassa, Baionaia, Crete

Pantanassa, Constantinople, founded in the twelfth century

Pausolype, Constantinople

Pertze, Constantinople

Philanthropos Soter, Constantinople

Phorbia Monastery, Cyprus

pinkernes Theophilopoulos, Constantinople

Soter Strategopoulinas, Constantinople

St. George Monastery, Longanikon, Lakonia

St. John Damaskenos, Constantinople

St. John Monastery, Zoupena, Lakonia

St. Photidos, Serres

St. Theodora or Stephanou, Thessaloniki

tes Panagiotisses, Constantinople

Theoskepastos, Trebizond

Theotokos Monastery, Messina

Theotokos Kakabiotissa, Lemnos

Theotokos Skapheidiane, Prodromion, Crete

Trichinareai, Auxentios, Bithynia

Fifteenth Century

Anargyroi, Constantinople

Anonymous nunnery where the ex-wife of Markellos was a nun, near Hierissos

Constantine and Helen Monastery, Nempros/Crete

Euouraniotissa, Constantinople

Evergetis, Constantinople

Karkasia Monastery, Hierapetra/Crete

kathisma of Thomais, Constantinople

Kleraina Monastery, Constantinople

Kyprianou, Constantinople

Maroules, Constantinople

Pammakaristos, Constantinople

Pantanassa, Constantinople, founded in the twelfth century

Pausolype, Constantinople

Philanthropos Soter, Constantinople

Skirmalo, Paphos/Cyprus

Soter Monastery, Kotzinos, Lemnos

St. Constantin, Constantinople

St. Demetrios Perati, Crete

St. Nicholas *significato in Tauro,* Constantinople

St. Nicholas, Kastoria

St. Panteleeimon, Constantinople

St. Theodora, Thessaloniki

Povasilias, Constantinople

Theoskepastos, Trebizond

Theotokos *elpis ton apelpismenon*, at the village Dylibena, near Aigion/Peloponnese

tou Magistrou, Constantinople

BIBLIOGRAPHY

Manuscripts

Athens, Ethnike Bibliotheke tes Ellados, MS Metochion Pan. Taphou 244.
Città del Vaticano, Biblioteca Apostolica Vaticana, MS Chig. R.V. 033 (gr. 27).
——, Biblioteca Apostolica Vaticana, MS Ottob. gr. 405.
——, Biblioteca Apostolica Vaticana, MS Vat. gr. 604.
——, Biblioteca Apostolica Vaticana, MS Vat. gr. 677.
——, Biblioteca Apostolica Vaticana, MS Vat. gr. 752.
——, Biblioteca Apostolica Vaticana, MS Vat. gr. 1158.
——, Biblioteca Apostolica Vaticana, MS Vat. gr. 1787.
——, Biblioteca Apostolica Vaticana, MS Vat. gr. 1899.
Firenze, Biblioteca Medicea Laurenziana, MS Plut. VI.28.
——, Biblioteca Nazionale Centrale, Conventi Sopressi B.1.1214 (Olivieri 50).
Hagion Oros, Mone Iviron, MS 5.
——, Mone Koutloumousiou, MS 208.
——, Mone Megistes Lavras, MS B 39.
——, Mone Panteleeimonos, MS 578 (6085).
——, Mone Pantokratoros, MS 6.
——, Mone Stauroniketa, MS 56.
——, Mone Vatopediou, MS 1037.
Istanbul, Patriarchike Bibliotheke, MS Panagias 11.
London, British Library, MS Additional 22748.
Milano, Biblioteca Ambrosiana, MS F 096 sup.
Moscow, Gosudarstvennyj Istoričeskij Musej, MS Mus. Sobr. 3649.
——, Gosudarstvennyj Istoričeskij Musej, MS Sinod. gr. 343 (Vlad. 268).
München, Bayerische Staatsbibliothek, MS gr. 430.
Oxford, Bodleian Library, MS Cromwell 22.
——, Lincoln College, MS gr. 35 (Lincoln College *Typikon*).
Paris, Bibliothèque nationale de France, MS Coislin gr. 128.
——, Bibliothèque nationale de France, MS gr. 1242.
——, Bibliothèque nationale de France, MS gr. 1372.
San Lorenzo de El Escorial, Real Biblioteca, MS gr. Φ. III. 11 (230).
——, Real Biblioteca, MS gr. Ω.II.13.
Sankt-Petersburg, Rossijskaja Nacional'naja biblioteka, MS Φ. No. 906 (Gr.), gr. 243.
Sinai, Saint Catherine Monastery, MS gr. 61.
Torino, Biblioteca Nazionale Universitaria, MS B. VI. 01 (Pasini 237).

Printed Primary Sources

Actes d'Esphigménou. Edited by Jacques Lefort. Archives de l'Athos 6. Lethielleux, 1973.

Actes de Chilandar. Edited by Louis Petit and Vasilii N. Korablev. Archives de l'Athos 5. Tipografija Imperatorskoj Akademii Nauke, 1911. Reprint, 1975.

Actes de Docheiariou. Edited by Nicolas Oikonomides. Archives de l'Athos 13. Lethielleux, 1984.

Actes de Lavra. Vol. 2, *De 1204 à 1328.* Edited by André Guillou et al. Archives de l'Athos 8. Lethielleux, 1977.

Actes de Lavra. Vol. 3, *De 1329 à 1500.* Edited by André Guillou et al. Archives de l'Athos 10. Lethielleux, 1979.

Actes de Vatopédi. Vol. 1, *Des origines à 1329.* Edited by Jacques Bompaire et al. Archives de l'Athos 21. Lethielleux, 2001.

Actes de Vatopédi. Vol. 2, *Des 1330 à 1376.* Edited by Jacques Lefort et al. Archives de l'Athos 22. Lethielleux, 2006.

Actes de Xénophon. Edited by Denise Papachryssanthou. Archives de l'Athos 15. Lethielleux, 1986.

Actes de Xéropotamou. Edited by Jacques Bompaire. Archives de l'Athos 3. Lethielleux, 1964.

Actes de Zographou. Edited by Wilhelm Regel et al. Archives de l'Athos 4. Tipografija Imperatorskoj Akademii Nauke, 1907. Reprint, 1969.

Angelou, Athanasios. *Manuel Palaiologos: Dialogue with the Empress-Mother on Marriage: Introduction, Text, and Translation.* Byzantina Vindobonensia 19. Österreichische Akademie der Wissenschaften, 1991.

Angold, Michael, trans. *Germanos II, Patriarch of Constantinople (1223–1240): Select Sermons.* Translated Texts for Byzantinists 14. Liverpool University Press, 2024.

Athanasios I. *Epistulae.* Edited by Alice-Mary Maffry Talbot. In *The Correspondence of Athanasius I Patriarch of Constantinople: Letters to the Emperor Andronicus II, Members of the Imperial Family, and Officials.* Dumbarton Oaks Texts 3 and Corpus Fontium Historiae Byzantinae 7. Dumbarton Oaks, 1975.

Balsamon. *Commentary on Canon 19.* Edited by Ioannes Zepos and Panagiotes Zepos. In *Jus Graecoromanum*, vol. 1, pp. 346–48. Fexis, 1931. Reprint, Scientia, 1962.

Basil of Caesarea. *Regulae brevius tractatae.* In *Asceticon magnum sive Quaestiones*, edited by Jacques-Paul Migne. Patrologiae cursus completus: Series graeca 31, cols. 1052–1305. Migne, 1857.

——. *Regulae fusius tractatae.* In *Asceticon magnum sive Quaestiones*, edited by Jacques-Paul Migne. Patrologiae cursus completus: Series graeca 31, cols. 901–1052. Migne, 1857.

Bénou, Lisa. *Le codex B du monastère Saint-Jean-Prodrome (Serrès): A. XIIIe-XVe siècles, textes, documents.* Études sur le monde byzantin, neohellenique et balkanique 2. Association Pierre Belon, 1998.

Nikephoros Gregoras. *Antirrhetika I.* Edited by Hans-Veit Beyer. Wiener Byzantinistische Studien 12. Österreichische Akademie der Wissenschaften, 1976.

Constantine Akropolites. *Epistole.* Edited by Roberto Romano. In *Costantino Acropolita, Epistole: Saggio introduttivo, testo critico, indici.* Speculum. Contributi di Filologia Classica. D'Auria, 1991.

Constantine Meliteniotes. *Λόγοι ἀντιρρητικοὶ δύο, νῦν τὸ πρῶτον ἐκδιδόμενοι* [Two Antirrhetic Discourses, Published Now for the First Time]. In *Editio Princeps*, edited by Markos A. Orphanos. Organismos Ekdoseos Didaktikon Biblion, 1986.

Constantinides Hero, Angela. "An Unknown Letter to Matthew Kantakouzenos." In *Okeanos: Essays Presented to I. Ševčenko on His Sixtieth Birthday by His Colleagues and Students*, edited by Cyril Mango and Omeljan Pritsak, 280–88. Harvard Ukrainian Studies 7. Harvard University Press, 1984.

Constas, Nicholas, trans. "Life of Saint Theodosia." In *Byzantine Defenders of Images*, edited by Alice-Mary Talbot, 1–8. Dumbarton Oaks, 1998.

Concilium Trullanum. Edited by Giuseppe Alberigo et al. In *Conciliorum Oecumenicorum Generaliumque Decreta*, vol. 1, *The Oecumenical Councils: From Nicaea I to Nicaea II (325–787)*, edited by Giuseppe Alberigo et al., 219–93. Brepols, 2006.

Council of Carthago. Edited by Périclès-Pierre Joannou. *Discipline générale antique (iv-ix s.): Les canons des pères grecs*, vol. 2, pp. 197–436. Tipographia Italo-Orientale "S. Nilo," 1963.

Council of Chalcedon. Edited by Giuseppe Alberigo et al. In *Conciliorum oecumenicorum generaliumque decretal*, vol. 1, *The Oecumenical Councils: From Nicaea I to Nicaea II (325–787)*, edited by Giuseppe Alberigo et al., 133–51. Brepols, 2006.

Council of Constantinople (Protodeutera). Edited by Périclès-Pierre Joannou. In *Discipline générale antique (iv-ix s.): Les canons des pères grecs*, vol. 2, pp. 447–79. Tipographia Italo-Orientale "S. Nilo," 1963.

Council of Laodicea. Edited by Périclès-Pierre Joannou. *Discipline générale antique (iv-ix s.): Les canons des pères grecs*, vol. 2, pp. 130–55. Tipographia Italo-Orientale "S. Nilo," 1963.

Crostini Lappin, Barbara. "A Fourteenth-Century Homiliary for Nuns: Structure, Composition and Context of Ms. Cromwell 22." *Byzantinische Zeitschrift* 95, no. 1 (2002): 35–68.

Darrouzès, Jean. "Le mémoire de Constantin Stilbès contre les Latins." *Revue des études byzantines* 21 (1963): 50–100.

Darrouzès, Jean, and Vitalien Laurent. *Dossier grec de l'Union de Lyon (1273–1277)*. Archives de l'Orient chrétien 16. Institut français d'études byzantines, 1976.

De Gregorio Palama. Edited by Jacques-Paul Migne. Patrologiae cursus completus: Series graeca 150, cols. 875–85. Migne, 1865.

Delehaye, Hippolyte. "Vita sanctae Olympiadis et Narratio Sergiae de eiusdem Translatione." *Analecta Bollandiana* 15 (1896): 400–23.

Demetrios Chomatenos. *Ponemata*. Edited by Günter Prinzing. In *Demetrii Chomateni Ponemata diaphora*. Corpus Fontium Historiae Byzantinae 38. De Gruyter, 2002.

Demetrios Kydones. *Epistulae*. Edited by Raymond-Josef Loenertz. In *Démétrius Cydonès: Correspondance*. Studi e Testi 186 and 208. Biblioteca Apostolica Vaticana, 1960 and 1986.

Dennis, George, trans. "*Skoteine* [Boreine]*: *Testament* of Maximos for the Monastery of the Mother of God at Skoteine near Philadelphia." In *Byzantine Monastic Foundation Documents: A Complete Translation of the Surviving Founders' Typika and Testaments*, edited by John Thomas and Angela Constantinides Hero, vol. 3, pp. 1176–95. Dumbarton Oaks, 2000.

——, trans. "*Ath. Typikon*: *Typikon* of Athanasios the Athonite for the Lavra Monastery." In In *Byzantine Monastic Foundation Documents: A Complete Translation of the Surviving Founders' Typika and Testaments*, edited by John Thomas and Angela Constantinides Hero, vol. 1, pp. 205–31. Dumbarton Oaks, 2000.

Diataxis et inventarium Maximi fundatoris monasterii Boreinae. Edited by Jacques Bompaire et al. In *Actes de Vatopédi*, vol. 1, *Des origines à 1329*, edited by Jacques Bompaire et al., 142–45. Archives de l'Athos 21. Lethielleux, 2001.

Dölger, Franz. "Aus dem Wirtschaftsleben eines Frauenklosters in der byzantinischen Provinz." In *Paraspora: 30 Aufsätze zur Geschichte, Kultur und Sprache des byzantinischen Reiches*, edited by Franz Dölger and Hans Georg Beck, 350–57. Buch-Kunstverlag, 1961.

Doukas. *Historia*. Edited by Vasile Grecu. *Istoria Turco-Bizantina (1341–1462)*. Scriptores byzantini 1. Editura Academiei Republicii Populare Romine, 1958.

Ecloga. Edited by Ludwig Burgmann. *Ecloga: Das Gesetzbuch Leons III. und Konstantinos' V*. Löwenklau, 1983.

Euangelatou-Notara, Florentia. *Χορηγοί—κτήτορες—δωρητές σε σημειώματα κωδίκων: Παλαιολόγειοι χρόνοι* [Patrons—Founders—Donors in Codex Notes: Palaiologan Period]. Parousia, 2000.

Eugenios (Batopedinos). *Περιγραφή ἔμμετρος τῆς ἐν Ἄθῳ ἱερᾶς καὶ σεβασμίας Μεγίστης Λαύρας τοῦ Βατοπεδίου* [Verse Description of the Sacred and Venerable Great Lavra of Vatopedi on Athos]. Papageorgiou, 1891.

Eustathios of Thessalonike. "Adversus implacabilitatis accusationem." Edited by Theophil. Lukas Friedrich Tafel. *Eustathii metropolitae Thessalonicensis opuscula*, 98–125. Schmerber, 1832. Reprint, 1964.

Fatouros, Georgios, and Tilman Krischer, trans. *Johannes Kantakuzenos*. 2 vols. Bibliothek der griechischen Literatur 17.21. Hiersemann, 1982.

Freshfield, Edwin, trans. *A Revised Manual of Roman Law Founded Upon the Ecloga of Leo III and Constantine V of Isauria: Ecloga Privata Aucta*. Cambridge University Press, 1927.

Fusco, Roberto, ed. "L'encomio di Teoctisto Studita per Atanasio I di Costantinopoli (*BHG* 194a-b): Una orazione funebre tardo-bizantina per un patriarca a metà strada fra traditione e riforma." *Rivista di studi bizantini e neoellenici* 34 (1997): 83–153.

Ganchou, Thierry. "L'ultime testament de Géôrgios Goudélès, home d'affaires, mésazôn de Jean V et ktètôr (Constantinople, 4 mars 1421)." *Travaux et Mémoires* 16 (2010): 277–358.

Gautier, Paul. "Le *typikon* de la Théotokos Évergétis." *Revue des études byzantines* 40 (1982): 5–101.

——. "Le *typikon* de la Théotokos Kécharitôménè." *Revue des études byzantines* 43 (1985): 5–165.

Gennadios Scholarios. *Letter to Simonis*. Edited by Louis Petit et al. In *Œuvres complètes de Gennade Scholarios*, edited by Louis Petit et al., vol. 4, pp. 502–3. Maison de la bonne presse, 1935.

——. *Letter to Sophrosyne*. Edited by Louis Petit et al. In *Œuvres complètes de Gennade Scholarios*, edited by Louis Petit et al., vol. 4, pp. 234–35. Maison de la bonne presse, 1935.

——. *On the First Service of God*. Edited by Louis Petit et al. In *Œuvres complètes de Gennade Scholarios*, edited by Louis Petit et al., vol. 4, pp. 236–64. Maison de la bonne presse, 1935.

George Metochites. *Historia Dogmatica*. Edited by Guiseppe Cozza-Luzi. In *Novae Patrum Bibliothecae*, edited by Angelo Mai, vol. 8. Apud Iosephum Spithoever, 1871.

Germanos II. *Letters*. Edited by Athanasios Papadopoulos-Kerameus. In *Ἀνάλεκτα Ἱεροσολυμιτικῆς Σταχυολογίας* [Miscellaneous Writings from Collections in Jerusalem], edited by Athanasios Papadopoulos-Kerameus, vol. 1, pp. 465–66. Kirsbaum, 1891.

Giarenes, Elias. *Ο βυζαντινός λόγιος Νικόλαος Μεσαρίτης: Κείμενα και Μελετήματα* [The Byzantine Scholar Nikolaos Mesarites: Texts and Studies]. Diaulos, 2022.

Goar, Jacobus. *Euchologion sive Rituale Graecorum*. Piget, 1647. Reprint, Akademische Druck- und Verlagsanstalt, 1960.

Gouillard, Jean. "Une compilation spirituelle du XIIIe siècle: Le livre II de l'abbé Isaïe." *Echos d'Orient* 38 (1939): 72–90.

Gregoras. *Roman History*. Edited by Immanuel Bekker and Ludwig Schopen. In *Nicephori Gregorae historiae Byzantinae*. 3 vols. Corpus Scriptorum Historiae Byzantinae 19. Weber, 1829–1855.

Gregory Akindynos. *Letters*. Edited by Angela Constantinides Hero. In *Letters of Gregory Akindynos*. Corpus Fontium Historiae Byzantinae 21. Dumbarton Oaks, 1983.

Gregory of Cyprus. *Letters*. Edited by Sofia Kotzabassi. In "Scholarly Friendship in the Thirteenth Century: Patriarch Gregorios II Kyprios and Theodora Raoulaina." *Parekbolai* 1 (2011): 115–70.

——. *Letters*. Edited by Sophronios Eustratiades. In *Γρηγορίου τοῦ Κυπρίου οἰκουμενικοῦ Πατριάρχου Ἐπιστολαί καὶ Μύθοι* [Letters and Myths of the Ecumenical Patriarch Gregory of Cyprus]. Patriarchikon Typographeion, 1910.

——. *Ἐγκώμιον εἰς τὸν αὐτοκράτορα κυρὸν Μιχαὴλ Παλαιολόγον καὶ Νέον Κωνσταντῖνον* [An Encomium for the Emperor Lord Michael Palaiologos and New Constantine]. Edited by Jacques-Paul Migne. Patrologiae cursus completus: Series graeca 142, cols. 345–86. Migne, 1865.

Gregory of Nyssa. *Oratio funebris in Flacillam imperatricem*. Edited by Gunterus Heil et al. In *Gregorii Nysseni opera*, edited by Gunterus Heil et al., vol. 9.1, pp. 475–90. Brill, 1967.

Gregory Palamas. *Contra Barlaam et Acindynum*. Edited by Panagiotes K. Chrestou et al. In *Γρηγορίου τοῦ Παλαμᾶ Συγγράμματα* [Writings of Gregory Palamas], edited by Panagiotes K. Chrestou et al., vol. 4, pp. 85–100. Kyromanos, 1988.

——. *Letter to nun Xene*. Edited by Panagiotes K. Chrestou. In *Γρηγορίου τοῦ Παλαμᾶ Συγγράμματα* [Writings of Gregory Palamas], edited by Panagiotes K. Chrestou, vol. 5, pp. 193–230. Kyromanos, 1992.

——. *Letters*. Edited by Panagiotes K. Chrestou. In *Γρηγορίου τοῦ Παλαμᾶ Συγγράμματα* [Writings of Gregory Palamas], edited by Panagiotes K. Chrestou, vol. 2, pp. 315–547. Kyromanos, 1966.

——. *Orationes antirrheticae contra Acindynum*. Edited by Panagiotes K. Chrestou et al. In *Γρηγορίου τοῦ Παλαμᾶ Συγγράμματα* [Writings of Gregory Palamas], edited by Panagiotes K. Chrestou et al., vol. 3., pp. 39–506. Kyromanos, 1970.

Guilland, Rodolphe, ed. *Correspondance de Nicephore Gregoras*. Les Belles Lettres, 1927.

Guillou, André. *Les archives de Saint-Jean-Prodrome sur le Mont Menecee*. Bibliothèque Byzantine, Documents 3. Presses universitaires de France, 1955.

Guy, Jean-Claude. *Les Apophthegmes des Pères: Collection systématique, Chapitres I-IX*. Sources Chrétiennes 387. Éditions du Cerf, 1997.

Halkin, François. "Théodosie de Césarée." In *Hagiologie byzantine*, edited by François Halkin, 63–68. Société des Bollandistes, 1986.

Hausherr, Irénée. "Le Métérikon de l'abbé Isaïe." *Orientalia Christiana Periodica* 12 (1946): 286–301.

Helfer, Walter. "Das Testament des Patriarchen Isidoros." *Jahrbuch der Österreichischen Byzantinistik* 17 (1968): 76–83.

Hunger, Herbert. "Zu den restlichen Inedita des Konstantinopler Patriarchatsregisters im Cod. Vindob. Hist. Gr. 48." *Revue des études byzantines* 24 (1966): 58–68.

——. "Zwei byzantinische Urkunden der späten Palaiologenzeit aus der Österreichischen Nationalbibliothek (Suppl. gr. 143 und 144)." *Byzantinische Zeitschrift* 48 (1955): 297–308.

İnalcık, Halil. *The Survey of Istanbul 1455: The Text, English Translation, Analysis of the Text, Documents*. Türkiye İş Bankası Kültür Yayınları, 2012.

Irene Eulogia Choumnaina. *Correspondence*. Edited by Angela Constantinides Hero. In *A Woman's Quest for Spiritual Guidance: The Correspondence of Princess Irene Eulogia Choumnaina Palaiologina*. The Archbishop Iakovos Library of Ecclesiastical and Historical Sources 11. Hellenic College Press, 1986.

Joannou, Périclès-Pierre. *Discipline générale antique (iv-ix s.): Les canons des pères grecs*. 2 vols. Tipographia Italo-Orientale "S. Nilo," 1963.

John Apokaukos. *Praxis on the Blachernitissa Monastery*. Edited by Athanasios Papadopoulos-Kerameus. In "Συνοδικὰ γράμματα Ἰωάννου τοῦ Ἀποκαύκου, Μητροπολίτου Ναυπάκτου [Synodic Acts of John Apokaukos, Metropolitan of Naupaktos]." *Byzantis* 1 (1909): 3–30.

John Bekkos. *De Depositione Sua (Oratio i)*. Edited by Jacques-Paul Migne. Patrologiae cursus completus: Series graeca 141, cols. 949–69. Migne, 1865.

——. *De Depositione Sua (Oratio ii)*. Edited by Jacques-Paul Migne. Patrologiae cursus completus: Series graeca 141, cols. 969–1009. Migne, 1865.

John Chrysostom. *De sacerdotio*. Edited by Anne Marie Malingrey. In *Jean Chrysostom: Sur le sacerdoce*. Cerf, 1980.

John Eugenikos. *Letters*. Edited by Spyridon P. Lampros. In *Παλαιολόγεια καὶ Πελοποννησιακά* [Palaiologan and Peloponnesian Texts], vol. 1, pp. 154–210, 315–23. Epitrope Ekdoseos ton Kataloipon Spyridonos Lamprou, 1921.

——. *Oratio ad imperatorem Constantinum Palaeologum*. Edited by Spyridon P. Lampros. *Παλαιολόγεια καὶ Πελοποννησιακά* [Palaiologan and Peloponnesian Texts], vol. 1, pp. 123–34. Epitrope Ekdoseos ton Kataloipon Spyridonos Lamprou, 1921.

——. *Τοῦ νομοφύλακος Ἰωάννου διακόνου τοῦ Εὐγενικοῦ τῷ δεσπότῃ παραμυθητικόν* [Consolatory Address of the Nomophylax John the Deacon Eugenikos to the Despot]. Edited by Spyridon P. Lampros. In *Παλαιολόγεια καὶ Πελοποννησιακά* [Palaiologan and Peloponnesian Texts], vol. 1, pp. 56–62. Epitrope Ekdoseos ton Kataloipon Spyridonos Lamprou, 1921.

John Kantakouzenos. *History*. Edited by Ludwig Schopen. In *Ioannis Cantacuzeni eximperatoris historiarum libri iv*. Corpus Scriptorum Historiae Byzantinae 1. Weber, 1828.

Jordan, Robert, trans. "*Kecharitomene*: *Typikon* of Empress Irene Doukaina Komnene for the Convent of the Mother of God Kecharitomene in Constantinople." In *Byzantine Monastic Foundation Documents: A Complete Translation of the Surviving Founders' Typika and Testaments*, edited by John Thomas and Angela Constantinides Hero, vol. 2, pp. 649–724. Dumbarton Oaks, 2000.

Jordan, Robert H., and Rosemary Morris. *The Hypotyposis of the Monastery of the Theotokos Evergetis, Constantinople (11th–12th Centuries): Introduction, Translation and Commentary*. Ashgate, 2012.

Justinian. *Novellae*. Edited by Rudolf Schöll and Wilhelm Kroll. In *Corpus Iuris Civilis*, edited by Rudolf Schöll and Wilhelm Kroll, vol. 3. Weidmann, 1959.

Kallistos I. *Life of St. Theodosios*. Edited by Vasil N. Zlatarski. In "Žitie I žizn Prepodobnago otca našego Feodosija [The Life and Vitae of Our Venerable Father Theodosios]." *Zbornik za narodni umotvozenija nauka i kniźnina* 20 (1904): 1–41.

Konidares, Ioannes M., and Konstantinos A. Manaphes. "Ἐπιτελεύτιος βούλησις καὶ διδασκαλία τοῦ οἰκουμενικοῦ πατριάρχου Ματθαίου Α´ (1397–1410) [Final Will and Teaching of the Ecumenical Patriarch Matthew I (1397–1410)]." *Epeteris Etaireias Byzantinon Spoudon* 45 (1981–1982): 462–515.

Lampros, Spyridon."Das Testament des Neilos Damilas." *Byzantinische Zeitschrift* 4 (1895): 585–87.

——. "Ἐπιγράμματα Μάξιμου Πλανούδη [Epigrams of Maximos Planoudes]." *Neos Hellenomnemon* 13 (1916): 414–21.

——. "Νείλου Κωνσταντινουπόλεως σιγίλλιον περὶ τῆς μονῆς Λευκουσιάδος [Sigillion of Neilos, Patriarch of Constantinople, on the Monastery of Leukousias]." *Neos Hellenomnemon* 6 (1909): 174–78.

——. "Ἀνέκδοτον χρυσόβουλλον τοῦ αὐτοκράτορος Ἀνδρονίκου τοῦ Παλαιολόγου [Unedited Chrysobull of the Emperor Andronikos Palaiologos]." *Deltion tes Historikes kai Ethnologikes Etaireias tes Ellados* 1 (1883–1884): 116–19.

Laurent, Vitalien. "Le Serment anti-latin du Patriarche Joseph Ier (Juin 1273)." *Echos d'Orient* 26 (1927): 396–407.

Leo VI. *Novellae*. Edited by Spyros Troianos. In *Οι Νεαρές Λέοντος Στ´ του Σοφού* [The Novellae of Leo VI the Wise]. Herodotos, 2007.

Leone, Petrus M. A., ed. *Maximi Monachi Planudis Epistulae*. Hakkert, 1991.

Leone, Pietro Luigi M., ed. "Le epistole di Niceforo Chumno." *Epeteris Etaireias Byzantinon Spoudon* 39–40 (1972–1973): 74–95.

Loenertz, Raymond-Joseph. "Memoire d'Ogier, protonotaire, pour Marco et Marchetto nonces de Michael VIII Paléologue auprès du Pape Nicholas III. 1278 printemps-été." *Orientalia Christiana Periodica* 31 (1965): 374–408.

Magoulias, Harry, trans. *Dukas: Decline and Fall of Byzantium to the Ottoman Turks*. Wayne State University Press, 1975.

Manuel II Palaeologos. *Letters*. Edited by George T. Dennis. In *The Letters of Manuel II Palaeologus*. Corpus Fontium Historiae Byzantinae 8. Dumbarton Oaks, 1977.

Manuel Philes. *Carmina*. Edited by Emmanuel Miller. In *Manuelis Philae Carmina*, vols. 1–2. Typ. Imperiali, 1855–1857.

Martin, Jean-Marie et al. "Un acte de Baudouin II en faveur de l'abbaye Cistercienne de Sainte-Marie de Perceio (Octobre 1241)." *Revue des études byzantines* 57 (1999): 211–23.

Mercati, Giovanni. *Notizie di Procoro e Demetrio Cidone, Manuele Caleca e Teodoro Meliteniota: ed altri appunti per la storia della teologia e della letteratura bizantina del secolo XIV*. Studi e Testi 56. Biblioteca Apostolica Vaticana, 1973.

Meyer, Philipp. "Bruchstücke zweier τυπικά κτητορικά." *Byzantinische Zeitschrift* 4 (1895): 45–58.

Miklosich, Franz, and Josef Müller. *Acta et Diplomata graeca Medii Aevi sacra et profana*. Vol. 2, *Acta Patriarchatus Constantinopolitani MCCCXV–MCCCCII Tomus Posterior*. Vindobona Gerold, 1887.

——. *Acta et Diplomata graeca Medii Aevi sacra et profana*. Vol. 4, *Acta et Diplomata Monasteriorum et Ecclesiarum Orientis Tomus Primus*. Vindobona Gerold, 1891.

Millet, Gabriel, et al. *Recueil des inscriptions chrétiennes de l'Athos*. Bibliothèque des écoles françaises d'Athènes et de Rome 91. Fontemoing, 1904.

Mitrea, Mihail. *A Late Byzantine Swan Song: Maximos Neamonites and his Letters*. Master's thesis, Central European University, 2011.

Mitsiou, Ekaterini. "Regaining the True Faith: The Confession of Faith of Theodora Palaiologina." In *L'Union à l'épreuve du formulaire: Professions de foi entre Églises d'Orient et d'Occident (XIIIe-XVIIIe siècle): Proceedings of the Conference in Paris in February 2013*. Edited by Marie-Hélène Blanchet and Frédéric Gabriel, 77–96. Peeters, 2016.

Nicholas Mesarites. *Epistulae*. Edited by Annaclara Cataldi Palau. In "Nicolas Mesaritès: Deux lettres inédites (Milan, Ambrosianus F 96 sup., ff. 15v–16v)," in *Manuscripta Graeca et Orientalia: Mélanges monastiques et patristiques en l'honneur de Paul Géhin*, edited by André Binggeli et al., 187–232. Orientalia Lovaniensia Analecta 243. Peeters, 2016.

Ohme, Heinz, trans. *Das Konzil Quinisextum*. Fontes Christiani 82. Brepols, 2006.

Ouspenskij, Feodor I., and Vladimir N. Beneševič. *Τα Acta της Μονής Βαζελώνος* [The Documents of Vazelon Monastery]. Translated by Elias K. Petropoulos. Kyriakides, 2007.

Veilleux, Armand, trans. *Pachomian Koinonia: The Lifes, Rules, and Other Writings of Saint Pachomius and His Disciples*. 3 vols. Cistercian, 1980–1982.

Pachymeres. *History*. Edited by Albert Failler and Vitalien Laurent. In *Georges Pachymérès, Relations historiques*. Corpus Fontium Historiae Byzantinae 24.1–5. Les Belles Lettres, 1984–2000.

Paidas, Konstantinos. "Secular Life's Behaviours and Debauchery Among Nuns: An Unedited Homily by the Patriarch of Constantinople Kallistos I." *Zbornik Radova Vizantološkog Instituta* 52 (2015): 343–57.

Patriarchal Register. Edited by Herbert Hunger and Otto Kresten. In *Das Register des Patriarchats von Konstantinopel*, vol. 1, *Edition und Übersetzung der Urkunden aus den Jahren 1315–1331*. Corpus Fontium Historiae Byzantinae 19. Österreichische Akademie der Wissenschaften, 1981.

Patriarchal Register. Edited by Herbert Hunger et al. *Das Register des Patriarchats von Konstantinopel*, vol. 2, *Edition und Übersetzung der Urkunden aus den Jahren 1337–1350*. Corpus Fontium Historiae Byzantinae 19. Österreichische Akademie der Wissenschaften, 1995.

Patriarchal Register. Edited by Johannes Koder et al. *Das Register des Patriarchats von Konstantinopel*, vol. 3, *Edition und Übersetzung der Urkunden aus den Jahren 1350–1363*. Corpus Fontium Historiae Byzantinae 19. Österreichische Akademie der Wissenschaften, 2001.

Pavlikianov, Cyril. *The Medieval Greek and Bulgarian Documents of the Athonite Monastery of Zographou (980–1600)*. University Press "St. Kliment Ohridski," 2014.

Pertusi, Agostino, ed. *La caduta di Costantinopoli*. Vol. 1, *Le testimonianze dei contemporanei*. Fondazione Lorenzo Valla, 1976.

Pétridès, Sophron. "Chrysobulle de l'impératrice Théodora (1283)." *Echos d'Orient* 14 (1911): 25–28.

Pétridès, Sophrone. "Le *typikon* de Nil Damilas pour le monastère de femmes de Baeonia en Crète (1400)." *Isvestija Russkago Archeologičeskago Instituta v Konstantinopole* 15 (1911): 95–109.

Philotheos Kokkinos. *Logos on Gregory Palamas*. In *Φιλοθέου Κωνσταντινουπόλεως τοῦ Κοκκίνου ἁγιολογικὰ ἔργα* [Hagiographical Works of Philotheos Kokkinos, Patriarch of Constantinople], vol. 1, *Θεσσαλονικεῖς ἅγιοι* [Thessalonian Saints], edited by Demetrios Tsames, 427–591. Thessalonian Byzantine Writers 4. Kentron Byzantinon Ereunon, 1985.

——, "Vita Isidori Patriarchi." Edited by Demetrios G. Tsames. In *Φιλοθέου Κωνσταντινουπόλεως τοῦ Κοκκίνου ἁγιολογικὰ ἔργα* [Hagiographical Works of Philotheos Kokkinos, Patriarch of Constantinople], vol. 1, *Θεσσαλονικεῖς ἅγιοι* [Thessalonian Saints], edited by Demetrios Tsames, 329–423. Thessalonian Byzantine Writers 4. Kentron Byzantinon Ereunon, 1985.

Πεῖρα sive Ἐπιτομὴ νόμων [Peira or Epitome of Laws]. Edited by Ioannes Zepos and Panagiotes Zepos. In *Jus Graecoromanum*, vol. 4, pp. 11–260. Fexis, 1931. Reprint, Scientia, 1962.

Pietsch-Braounou, Efthymia. *Beseelte Bilder: Epigramme des Manuel Philes auf bildliche Darstellungen*. Österreichischern Akademie der Wissenschaften, 2011.

Previale, Luigi. "Due Monodie inedite di Matteo di Efeso (Cod. Vindob. Theol. Gr. 174 Nessel)." *Byzantinische Zeitschrift* 41 (1941): 4–39.

Pseudo-Sphrantzes. *Chronicle*. Edited by Vasile Grecu. In *Georgios Sphrantzes: Memorii 1401–1477*. Scriptores Byzantini 5. Editura Academiei Republicii Socialiste România, 1966.

Reinsch, Diether. *Die Briefe des Matthaios von Ephesos im Codex Vindobonensis Theol. Gr. 174*. Berlin: Mielke, 1974.

Rhoby, Andreas. *Byzantinische Epigramme auf Ikonen und Objekten der Kleinkunst*. Byzantinische Epigramme in inschriftlicher Überlieferung 2. Österreichische Akademie der Wissenschaften, 2010.

——. *Byzantinische Epigramme auf Stein*. Byzantinische Epigramme in inschriftlicher Überlieferung 3. Österreichische Akademie der Wissenschaft, 2014.

Riehle, Alexander, ed. *Die Briefsammlungen des Nikephoros Chumnos*. Byzantinisches Archiv 43. De Gruyter, 2023.

Rigo, Antonio. "Le lettere di Giacomo metropolita di Calcedonia alla monaca Eulogia (anni 50–60 del xiv secolo)." *Bulgaria Mediaevalis* 4–5 (2013–2014): 195–201.

Roelli, Philipp. *Marci monachi opera ascetica: Florilegium et sermones tres*. Corpus Christianorum: Series graeca 72. Brepols, 2009.

Rosenqvist, Georg Olof. *The Life of Saint Irene, Abbess of Chrysobalanton: A Critical Edition With Introduction, Notes and Indices*. Studia Byzantina Upsaliensis. Almqvist & Wiksell, 1986.

Schaff, Philip, trans. *The Seven Ecumenical Councils*. Clark, 2005.

Sinkewicz, Robert E. *Theoleptos of Philadelpheia: The Monastic Discourses*. Studies and Texts 111. Pontificial Institute of Medieval Studies, 1992.

Sphrantzes. *Memorii*. Edited by Vasile Grecu. In *Georgios Sphrantzes: Memorii 1401–1477*. Scriptores Byzantini 5. Editura Academiei Republicii Socialiste România, 1966.

Sylvestros Syropoulos. *Les "Mémoires."* Edited by Vitalien Laurent. In *Les "Mémoires" du Grand Ecclésiarque de l'Église de Constantinople Sylvestre Syropoulos sur le concile de Florence (1438–1439)*. Pont. Inst. Orientalum, 1971.

Talbot, Alice-Mary, trans. "*Philanthropos*: *Typikon* of Irene Choumnaina Palaiologina for the Convent of Christ Philanthropos in Constantinople." In *Byzantine Monastic Foundation Documents: A Complete Translation of the Surviving Founders' Typika and Testaments*, edited by John Thomas and Angela Constantinides Hero, vol. 4, pp. 1383–88. Dumbarton Oaks, 2000.

——, trans. "A Saintly Empress: Saint Theodora of Arta." In *Holy Women of Byzantium: Ten Saints' Lives in English Translation*. Edited by Alice-Mary Talbot, 323–33. Dumbarton Oaks, 1996.

——, trans. "*Anargyroi*: *Typikon* of Theodora Palaiologina for the Convent of Sts. Kosmas and Damian in Constantinople." In *Byzantine Monastic Foundation Documents: A Complete Translation of the Surviving Founders' Typika and Testaments*, edited by John Thomas and Angela Constantinides Hero, vol. 3, pp. 1287–94. Dumbarton Oaks, 2000.

——, trans. "*Bebaia Elpis*: *Typikon* of Theodora Synadene for the Convent of the Mother of God Bebaia Elpis in Constantinople." In *Byzantine Monastic Foundation Documents: A Complete Translation of the Surviving Founders' Typika and Testaments*, edited by John Thomas and Angela Constantinides Hero, vol. 4, pp. 1512–78. Dumbarton Oaks, 2000.

——, trans. "*Lips*: *Typikon* of Theodora Palaiologina for the Convent of Lips." In *Byzantine Monastic Foundation Documents: A Complete Translation of the Surviving Founders' Typika and Testaments*, edited by John Thomas and Angela Constantinides Hero, vol. 3, pp. 1254–86. Dumbarton Oaks Studies 35. Dumbarton Oaks, 2000.

——, trans. "*Neilos Damilas*: *Testament* and *Typikon* of Neilos Damilas for the Convent of the Mother of God *Pantanassa* at Baionaia on Crete." In *Byzantine Monastic Foundation Documents: A Complete Translation of the Surviving Founders' Typika and Testaments*, edited by John Thomas and Angela Constantinides Hero, vol. 4, pp. 1462–82. Dumbarton Oaks, 2000.

——, trans. "*Charsianeites*: *Testament* of Matthaios I for the Monastery of Charsianeites Dedicated to the Mother of God Nea Peribleptos." In *Byzantine Monastic Foundation Documents: A Complete Translation of the Surviving Founders' Typika and Testaments*, edited by John Thomas and Angela Constantinides Hero, vol. 4, pp. 1625–66. Dumbarton Oaks, 2000.

——, trans. "Life of St. Theodora of Thessalonike." In *Holy Women of Byzantium: Ten Saints' Lives in English Translation*. Edited by Alice-Mary Talbot, 159–63. Dumbarton Oaks, 1996.

Taxidis, Ilias. "L'éloge de saint Eudocime par Constantin Acropolite (*BHG* 606)." *Parekbolai* 3 (2013): 5–44.

Theodora Raoulaina. "Vita Theophanis et Theodori Grapti." Edited by Athanasios Papadopoulos-Kerameus. In *Ἀνάλεκτα Ἱεροσολυμιτικῆς Σταχυολογίας* [Miscellaneous Writings from Collections in Jerusalem], edited by Athanasios Papadopoulos-Kerameus, vol. 4, pp. 185–223. Kirsbaum, 1891.

Theodore Agallianos. *Contra Latinos*. Edited by Marie-Hélène Blanchet. In *Théodore Agallianos. Dialogue avec un moine contre les Latins (1442)*. Byzantina Sorbonensia 27. Publications de la Sorbonne, 2013.

——. *Sermones*. Edited by Chrestos G. Patrineles. In *Ὁ Θεόδωρος Ἀγαλλιανὸς ταυτιζόμενος πρὸς τὸν Θεοφάνην Μηδείας καὶ οἱ ἀνέκδοτοι λόγοι του* [Theodore Agallianos Identified to Theophanes of Medeia and His Unpublished Sermons], PhD diss., University of Athens, 1966.

Theodore Hyrtakenos. *Monody to Nikephoros Choumnos*. Edited by Jean François Boissonade. In *Anecdota Graeca*, edited by Jean François Boissonade, vol. 1, pp. 282–92. Regio Typographeo, 1829.

Theodore of Stoudios. *Epistulae*. Edited by Georgios Fatouros. *Theodori Studitae Epistulae*. 2 vols. Corpus Fontium Historiae Byzantinae 31. De Gruyter, 1992.

Theodore Skoutariotes. *Additamenta*. Edited by August Heisenberg and Peter Wirth. In *Georgii Acropolitae opera*, vol. 1, pp. 277–302. Teubner, 1978.

Theoktistos the Stoudite. *Life of Athanasios I*. Edited by Athanasios Papadopoulos-Kerameus. In "Zitija dvuh Vselenskih patriarhov XIV v., svv. Afanasija I i Isidora I [Lives of Two Ecumenical Patriarchs of the Fourteenth Century, Saints Athanasios I and Isidore I]." *Zapiski istoriko-filologicheskogo fakul'teta Imperatorskago S.-Peterburgskago Universiteta* 76 (1905): 1–51.

——. "Oratio de translatione reliquiarum sancti Athanasii Constantinopolitani." Edited by Alice-Mary M. Talbot. In *Faith Healing in Late Byzantium: The Posthumous Miracles of the Patriarch Athanasios I of Constantinople by Theoktistos the Stoudite*, 44–123. Holy Cross Orthodox Press, 1983.

Theoleptos of Philadelphia. *Letters*. Edited by Angela Constantinides Hero. In *The Life and Letters of Theoleptos of Philadelphia*. The Archbishop Iakovos Library of Ecclesiastical and Historical Sources 20. Hellenic College Press, 1994.

Treu, Max. *Manuelis Holoboli Orationes*. 2 vols. Programm des königlichen Victoria-Gymnasiums zu Potsdam. Brandt, 1907.

Typicon monasterii Lips. Edited by Hippolyte Delehaye. In *Deux typica byzantins de l'époque des Paléologues*, 106–36. Lamertin, 1921.

Typicon monasterii sanctorum Anargyrorum. Edited by Hippolyte Delehaye. In *Deux typica byzantins de l'époque des Paléologues*, 136–40. Lamertin, 1921.

Typicon monasterii Theotoci Bebaias Elpidos. Edited by Hippolyte Delehaye. In *Deux typica byzantins de l'époque des Paléologues*, 18–105. Lamertin, 1921, supplemented by Chrysostome Baur, "Le typikon du monastère de Notre-Dame," *Revue d'histoire ecclésiastique* 29 (1933): 635–36.

Tzannetatos, Theseus. *Πρακτικόν τῆς Λατινικῆς Ἐπισκοπῆς Κεφαλληνίας τοῦ 1264 καί ἡ Ἐπιτομή αὐτοῦ* [The Register of the Latin Bishopric of Kephalenia of 1264 and Its Summary]. Private Edition, 1965.

van Dieten, Jan-Louis, trans. *Nikephoros Gregoras: Rhomäische Geschichte*. 2 vols. Hiersemann, 1973–1979.

Ward, Benedicta, trans. *The Sayings of the Desert Fathers: The Alphabetical Collection*. Cistercian Publications, 1975. Reprint, 1984.

Secondary Works

Abu-Lughod, Janet L. *Before European Hegemony: The World System A.D. 1250–1350*. Oxford University Press 1989.

Acheimastou-Potamianou, Myrtali. "The Basilissa Anna Palaiologina of Arta and the Monastery of Vlacherna." In *Les femmes et le monachisme byzantine: Actes du symposium d'Athènes, 28–29 mars 1988 / Women and Byzantine Monasticism: Proceedings of the Athens symposium, 28–29 March 1988*, edited by Jacques Y. Perreault, Elizabeth Koubena, and Maria Toli, 43–49. Institut canadien d'archéologie à Athènes, 1991.

——. *Η Βλαχέρνα της Άρτας: τοιχογραφίες* [The Blacherna Monastery of Arta: Wall-Paintings]. Bibliotheke tes en Athenais Archaiologikes Etaireias 264. E en Athenais Etaireia, 2009.

——. "Η ζωγραφική της Άρτας στο 13° αιώνα και η μονή της Βλαχέρνας [The Painting of Arta in the Thirteenth Century and the Monastery of Blacherna]." In *The Despotate of Epirus. Proceedings of the International Symposium "The Despotate of Epirus," Arta, 27–31 May 1990*. Edited by Euangelos Chrysos, 179–203. O Skouphas, 1992.

Ahrweiler, Hélène. "La region de Philadelphie au XIVe siècle (1290–1390), dernier bastion de l'hellenisme en Asie Mineure." *Comptes rendus des séances de l'Académie des Inscriptions et Belles-Lettres* 127, no. 1 (1983): 175–97.

——. "L'histoire et la géographie de la région de Smyrne entre les deux occupations turques (1081–1317)." *Travaux et Mémoires* 1 (1965): 1–204.

Albani, Jeni. "Οι τοιχογραφίες του ναού της Αγίας Μαρίνας στον Μουρνέ της Κρήτης: Ένας άγνωστος βιογραφικός κύκλος της αγίας Μαρίνας [The Frescoes of the Church of St. Marina in Mournes, Crete: An Unknown Biographical Cycle of Saint Marina]." *Deltion tes Christianikes Archaiologikes Etaireias* 17 (1993–1994): 211–22.

Alivisatos, Hamilcar S. *Die kirchliche Gesetzgebung des Kaisers Justinian I*. Trowitzsch and Sohn, 1913. Reprint, Scientia, 1973.

Angelidi, Christina. *Pulcheria: La castità al potere, c. 399-c. 455*. Donne d'oriente e d'occidente 5. Jaca, 1998.

Archontopoulos, Theodoros, and Eleni K. Papabasileiou. "Ρόδος: Πληροφορίες για την ιστορία του τόπου μέσα από το γεγονός του θανάτου. Ταφική τοπογραφία του νησιού από τον 4ο αι. μ. Χ. έως τις αρχές του 16ου αιώνα [Rhodes: Information About the History of the Place Through the Event of Death. Burial Topography of the Island From the Fourth Century AD to the Beginning of the Sixteenth Century]." *Archaiologika Analekta ex Athenon* 39 (2006): 193–209.

Asdracha, Catherine. "A Brief Commentary to the Verses of Supplication to the Virgin, Dedicated to Her by the Despoina of Mongoulion." *Cahiers archaeologiques* 43 (1995): 183–84.

Asutay-Effenberger, Neslihan. *Die Landmauer von Konstantinopel-İstanbul: Historisch-topographische und baugeschichtliche Untersuchungen*. Millennium Studies 18. De Gruyter, 2007.

——. "Zum Datum der Umwandlung der Pammakaristoskirche in die Fethiye Camii." *Byzantion* 77 (2007): 32–41.

Athenagoras (Metropolitan). *Κατάλογος τῶν χειρογράφων τῆς ἐν Χάλκῃ Μονῆς τῆς Παναγίας*. [Catalogue of the Manuscripts at the Mother of God Monastery in Chalke]. Estia, 1933.

Bakirtzis, Charalambos. "Κουτρούβια μύρου από τη Θεσσαλονίκη [Koutroubia of Myrrh from Thessaloniki]." *Jahrbuch der Österreichischen Byzantinistik* 32, no. 3 (1982): 523–29.

Ball, Jennifer. "Decoding the Habit of the Byzantine Nun." *Journal of Modern Hellenism* 27–28 (2009–2010): 25–52.

——. "Greek Psalter." In *Pilgrimage to Sinai: Treasures From the Holy Monastery of St. Catherine*. Edited by Anastasia Drandake, 176–77. Benaki Museum, 2004.

Baltogianne, Chryssanthe. "Εικόνα της Αγίας Θεοδοσίας της Κωνσταντινουπολίτισσας στη Νάξο [Icon of Saint Theodosia of Constantinople in Naxos]." *Deltion tes Christianikes Archaiologikes Etaireias* 22 (2001): 215–28.

Bartusis, Mark C. *Land and Privilege in Byzantium: The Institution of Pronoia*. Cambridge University Press, 2013.

Beaucamp, Joëlle. "La situation juridique de la femme à Byzance." *Cahiers de civilisation médiévale* 20 (1977): 145–76.

——. *Le statut de la femme à Byzance (4e–7e siècle)*. 2 vols. De Boccard, 1990–1992.

——. "Les femmes et l'église: Droit canonique, idéologie et pratiques sociales à Byzance." In *Mother, Nun, Deaconess: Images of Women According to Eastern Canon Law*, 87–112. Kovar, 2001.

Beck, Hans Georg. *Kirche und theologische Literatur im byzantinischen Reich*. Beck, 1959.

Bees, Nikos. "Fragment d'un chrysobulle du couvent de Lycousade." *Melanges à Octave et Melpo Merlier* 3 (1957): 479–86.

Belanidiotes, Izekiel. "Ἡ ἱερὰ μονὴ Λυκουσάδος [The Holy Monastery of Lykousas]." *Theologia* 7 (1929): 162–64.

Belke, Klaus. *Bithynien und Hellespont*. Tabula Imperii Byzantini 13. Österreichische Akademie der Wissenschaften, 2020.

Belting, Hans. *Das illuminierte Buch in der spätbyzantinischen Gesellschaft*. Winter, 1970.

——. "Die Auftraggeber der spätbyzantinischen Bildhandschrift." In *Art et société à Byzance sous les Paléologues: Actes du colloque organisé par l'Association Internationale des Études Byzantines à Venise en septembre 1968*, 149–76. Bibliothèque de l'Institut hellénique d'études byzantines et post-byzantines de Venise 4. Stamperia di Venezia, 1971.

Belting, Hans, et al. *The Mosaics and Frescoes of St. Mary Pammakaristos (Fethiye Cami) at Istanbul*. Dumbarton Oaks Studies 15. Dumbarton Oaks, 1978.

Benoit-Meggenis, Rosa. *L'empereur et le moine*. MOM, 2017.

Bernicolas-Hatzopoulos, Dionysios. "The First Siege of Constantinople by the Ottomans (1393–1402) and Its Repercussions on the Civilian Population of the City." *Byzantine Studies* 10 (1983): 39–51.

Betancourt, Roland. *Byzantine Intersectionality: Sexuality, Gender and Race in the Middle Age*. Princeton University Press, 2020.

Bitha, Ioanna. "Ενδυματολογικές μαρτυρίες στις τοιχογραφίες της μεσαιωνικής Ρόδου (14ος αι.–1523). Μία πρώτη προσέγγιση [Clothing Evidence in the Frescoes of Medieval Rhodes (Fourteenth Century–1523). A first approach]." In *Ρόδος 2400 χρόνια: η πόλη της Ρόδου από την ίδρυση της μέχρι την κατάληψη από τους Τούρκους (1523)* [Rhodes 2400 Years: The City of Rhodes From its Foundation to the Occupation by the Turks (1523)], edited by Euangelia Kypraiou, 429–48. Ypourgeio Politismou, 1999–2000.

Blanchet, Marie-Hélène. *Georges-Gennadios Scholarios (vers 1400-vers 1472): Un intellectuel orthodoxe face à la disparition de l'Empire byzantine*. Archives de l'Orient Chrétien 20. Institut français d'études byzantines, 2008.

——. "L'église byzantine á la suite de l'union de Florence (1439–1445): De la contestation à la scission." *Byzantinische Forschungen* 29 (2007): 79–123.

Bolanakes, Ioannes. "Ναός Αγίας Τριάδας Ψίνθου [The Church of Holy Trinity of Psinthos]." *Archaiologikon Deltion* 50, no. B2 (1995): 825–26.

Boojamra, John Lawrence. *Church Reform in the Late Byzantine Empire: A Study for the Patriarchate of Athanasios of Constantinople*. Analekta Blatadon 35. Patriarchal Institute for Patristic Studies, 1982.

Bouras, Charalambos. "Η αρχιτεκτονική της Παναγίας του Μουχλίου στην Κωνσταντινούπολη [The Architecture of Panagia tou Mouchliou in Constantinople]." *Deltion tes Christianikes Archaiologikes Etaireias* 44 (2005): 35–50.

Bourdieu, Pierre. *Esquisse d'une théorie de la pratique, précédé de trois études d'ethnologie kabyle*. Droz, 1972.

——. *La domination masculine*. Seuil, 1998.

——. "Ökonomisches Kapital, kulturelles Kapital, soziales Kapital." In *Soziale Ungleichheiten*. Edited by Reinhard Kreckel, 183–98. Schwartz, 1983.

Brooks Hedstrom, Darlene L. "The Archaeology of Monastic Households." In *The Oxford Handbook of Christian Monasticism*, edited by Bernice M. Kaczynski, 185–203. Oxford University Press, 2020.

Brooks, Sarah. "Commemoration of the Dead: Late Byzantine Tomb Decoration (Mid-Thirteenth to Mid-Fifteenth Centuries)." PhD diss., New York University, 2002.

——. "The History and Significance of Tomb Monuments at the Chora Monastery." In *Restoring Byzantium: The Kariye Camii in Istanbul and the Byzantine Institute Restoration*, edited by Holger A. Klein, 23–31. Columbia University Press, 2004.

——. "Poetry and Female Patronage in Late Byzantine Tomb Decoration: Two Epigrams by Manuel Philes." *Dumbarton Oaks Papers* 60 (2006): 223–48.

——. "Sculpture and the Late Byzantine Tomb." In *Byzantium: Faith and Power (1267–1557): Perspectives on Late Byzantine Art and Culture*, edited by Helen C. Evans, 76–97. Yale University Press, 2006.

——. "Women's Authority in Death: The Patronage of Aristocratic Laywomen in Late Byzantium." In *Female Founders in Byzantium and Beyond*, edited by Lioba Theis, Margaret Mullett, and Michael Grünbart, 317–31. Böhlau, 2014.

Brown, Peter. *The Body and Society: Men, Women, and Sexual Renunciation in Early Christianity*. Columbia University Press, 2008.

Brubaker, Leslie, and John F. Haldon. *Byzantium in the Iconoclast Era (c. 680–850): A History*. Cambridge University Press, 2011.

——. *Byzantium in the Iconoclast Era (c. 680–850): The Sources*. Birmingham Byzantine and Ottoman Monographs 7. Ashgate, 2001.

Brundage, James A. "Juridical Space: Female Witnesses in Canon Law." *Dumbarton Oaks Papers* 52 (1998): 147–56.

Bryer, Anthony, and Judith Herrin. *Iconoclasm: Papers Given at the Ninth Spring Symposium of Byzantine Studies, University of Birmingham, March 1975*. Centre for Byzantine Studies, 1977.

Buchthal, Hugo, and Hans Belting. *Patronage in Thirteenth-Century Constantinople: An Atelier of Late Byzantine Book Illumination and Calligraphy*. Dumbarton Oaks, 1978.

Buckler, Georgina. "Women in Byzantine Law About 1100 A.D." *Byzantion* 11 (1936): 391–416.

Buckler, William H. "The Monument of a Palaiologina." In *Mélanges offerts à m. Gustave Schlumberger*, vol. 1, pp. 521–26. Geuthner 1924.

Bydén, Börje. "'Strangle Them with These Meshes of Syllogisms!': Latin Philosophy in Greek Translations of the Thirteenth Century." In *Interaction and Isolation in Late Byzantine Culture: Papers Read at a Colloquium Held at the Swedish Research Institute in Istanbul, 1–5 December, 1999*, edited by Jan Olof Rosenqvist, 133–57. Swedish Research Institute in Istanbul Transactions 13. Svenska forskningsinstitutet i Istanbul, 2004.

Bynum, Caroline Walker. *Holy Feast and Holy Fast: The Religious Significance of Food to Medieval Women*. University of California Press, 1987.

Canart, Paul. *Codices Vaticani graeci, codices 1745–1962*. Typis Polyglottis Vaticanis, 1970.

Canart, Paul, and Vittorio Peri. *Sussidi bibliografici per I manoscritti greci della Biblioteca Vaticana*. Studi e Testi 261. Bibliotheca Apostolica Vaticana, 1970.

Carr, Annemarie Weyl. "A Note on Theodore Hagiopetrites." *Scriptorium* 35 (1981): 287–90.

——. "Donors in the Frames of Icons: Living in the Borders of Byzantine Art." *Gesta* 45, no. 2 (2006): 189–98.

——. "Women and Monasticism in Byzantium: Introduction From an Art Historian." *Byzantinische Forschungen* 9 (1985): 1–15.

Caseau, Beatrice, "Objects in Churches: The Testimony of Inventories." In *Objects in Context, Objects in Use Material Spatiality in Late Antiquity*, edited by Luke Lavan, Ellen Swift, and Toon Putzeys, 549–79. Late Antique Archaeology 5. Brill, 2008.

Catafygiotou-Topping, Eva. "Women Hymnographers in Byzantium." *Diptycha Etaireias Byzantinon kai Metabyzantinon Meleton* 3 (1982–1983): 98–111.

Cavallo, Gugliemo. *Η ανάγνωση στο Βυζάντιο* [Reading in Byzantium]. Translated by Smaragda Tsochantaridou and Paolo Odorico. Agra, 2008.

de Certeau, Michel. *L'Invention du Quotidien*. vol. 1. Union générale d'éditions, 1980.

Charalampous, Dionysios. *Γυναικείος ορθόδοξος μοναχισμός κατά τα Πατερικά Κείμενα* [Female Orthodox Monasticism According to the Patristic Texts]. Pantokratoros, 2008.

Chassoura, Olympia. *Les peintures murales byzantines des églises de Longanikos-Laconie*. Kardamitsa, 2002.

Cheynet, Jean-Claude. "Le bullaire monastique à Byzance." In *Lire les Archives de l'Athos*, edited by Olivier Delouis and Kostis Smyrlis, 243–85. Travaux et Mémoires 23, no. 2. ACHCByz, 2019.

Chitwood, Zachary. "The Testament of the Nun Maria (Kale): Commemorative Dining, Memoria and Servitude in Byzantium at the Time of the First Crusade." *Endowment Studies* 7 (2023): 97–126.

Christophorake, Ioanna. "Χορηγικές μαρτυρίες στους ναούς της μεσαιωνικής Ρόδου (1204–1522) [Testimonies of Patronage in the Churches of Medieval Rhodes (1204–1522)." In *Ρόδος 2400 χρόνια: η πόλη της Ρόδου από την ίδρυση της μέχρι την κατάληψη από τους Τούρκους (1523)* [Rhodes 2400 Years: The City of Rhodes From its Foundation to the Occupation by the Turks (1523)], edited by Euangelia Kypraiou, 449–64. Ypourgeio Politismou, 1999–2000.

Chrysos, Euangelos. "Η Ανατολή συναντά τη Δύση: Προβλήματα επικοινωνίας και πρωτοκαθεδρίας στη Σύνοδο της Φλωρεντίας [East Meets West: Problems of Communication and Primacy at the Council of Florence]." In *Κλητόριον είς μνήμην Νίκου Οίκονομίδη* [A Banquet in Memory of Nikos Oikonomides], edited by Phlorentia Evangelatou-Notara and Triantaphyllista Maniate-Kokkine, 49–62. Banias, 2005.

Chrysostomides, Elias. "Το corpus των επιστολών του Γεωργίου-Γρηγορίου Κυπρίου [The Letter Corpus of George-Gregory of Cyprus]." PhD diss., Thessaloniki, 2015.

Ćirić, Jasmina. "Brickwork and Façade: Envisioning the Apse of the Church of Saint John the Baptist at the Lips Monastery." In *Πάντα ῥεῖ. Change in Thirteenth-Century Byzantine Architecture, Art, and Material Culture*, edited by Jenny P. Albani and Ioanna Christoforaki, 77–102. Brepols, 2022.

Congourdeau, Marie-Hélène. "Nicolas Cabasilas et Matthieu Cantacuzène." In *Pour une poétique de Byzance. Hommage à Vassilis Katsaros*, edited by Stephanos Efthymiadis et al., 85–98. De Boccard, 2015.

Connor, Carolyn L. "Female Saints in the Church Decoration of the Troodos Mountains in Cyprus." In *Medieval Cyprus: Studies in Art, Architecture and History in Memory of Doula Mouriki*, edited by Nancy Patterson Ševčenko and Christopher Frederick Moss, 211–28. Princeton University Press, 1999.

——. *Women of Byzantium*. Yale University Press, 2004.

Constantinides, Costas N. "Byzantine Scholars and the Union of Lyons (1274)." In *The Making of Byzantine History: Studies Dedicated to Donald M. Nicol*, edited by Roderick Beaton and Charlotte Roueché, 86–93. Variorum Reprints, 1993.

——. *Higher Education in Byzantium in the Thirteenth and Early Fourteenth Centuries (1204-ca. 1310)*. Cyprus Research Centre, 1982.

Constantinides Hero, Angela. "Theoleptos of Philadelphia (ca. 1250–1322): From Solitary to Activist." In *Twilight of Byzantium: Aspects of Cultural and Religious History in the Late Byzantine Empire. Papers From the Colloquium Held at Princeton University 8–9 May 1989*, edited by Slobodan Ćurčić and Doula Mouriki, 27–38. Princeton University, 1991.

Constantinou, Stavroula. *Female Corporeal Performances: Reading the Body in Byzantine Passions and Lives of Holy Women*. Uppsala University Library, 2005.

——. "Holy Actors and Actresses: Fools and Cross-Dressers as the Protagonists of Saints' Lives." In *The Ashgate Research Companion to Byzantine Hagiography*, edited by Stephanos Efthymiadis, vol. 2, pp. 343–62. Ashgate, 2014.

Cormack, Robin. "Icon of the Triumph of Orthodoxy." In *Byzantium: Treasures of Byzantine Art and Culture from British Collections*, edited by David Buckton, 129–30. British Museum, 1994.

Cotsonis, John. "Onomastics, Gender, Office and Images on Byzantine Lead Seals: A Means of Investigating Personal Piety." *Byzantine and Modern Greek Studies* 32 (2008): 1–37.

Coxe, Henry Octavius. *Catalogus codicum mss. qui in collegiis aulisque Oxoniensibus hodie adservantur*. e Typographeo academico, 1852.

Crossley, Nick, et al. *Social Network Analysis for Ego-Nets*. SAGE, 2015.

Crostini, Barbara, and Glenn Peers. *A Book of Psalms from Eleventh-Century Constantinople: On the Complex of Texts and Images in Vat. gr. 752*. Studi e Testi Series 504. Biblioteca Apostolica Vaticana, 2016.

Crow, James G., et al. *The Water Supply of Byzantine Constantinople*. Society for the Promotion of Roman Studies, 2008.

Cunningham, Mary B. "Messages in Context: The Reading of Sermons in Byzantine Churches and Monasteries." In *Images of the Byzantine World. Visions, Messages and Meanings: Studies presented to Leslie Brubaker*, edited by Angeliki Lymberopoulou, 83–98. Farnham, 2011.

Cupane, Carolina. "Magie und Zauberei im späten Byzanz im Lichte des Patriarchatsregisters von Konstantinopel." *Historicum* 96 (2008): 49–53.

Cupane, Carolina, and Ewald Kislinger. "Bemerkungen zur Abtreibung in Byzanz." *Jahrbuch der Österreichischen Byzantinistik* 35 (1985): 21–49.

Curtis, Daniel R. *Coping with Crisis: The Resilience and Vulnerability of Pre-Industrial Settlements*. Ashgate, 2014.

Cutler, Antony. *The Aristocratic Psalters in Byzantium*. Bibliothèque des Cahiers archéologiques 13. Picard, 1984.

Cutler, Antony, and Paul Magdalino. "Some Precisions on the Lincoln College *Typikon*." *Cahiers archeologiques* 27 (1978): 179–98.

Čvetković, Branislav. "The Investiture Relief of Arta, Epiros." *Zbornik Radova Vizantološkog Instituta* 33 (1994): 103–12.

Dalby, Andrew. *Tastes of Byzantium: The Cuisine of a Legendary Empire*. Tauris, 2010.

Darrouzès, Jean. *Les regestes des Actes du patriarcat de Constantinople*. Vol. 1, *Les actes des patriarches: Fasc. 5/6/7. Les regestes de 1310 à 1376/1377 à 1410/1410 à 1453*. Le patriarcat byzantin, série 1. Socii Assumptionistae Chalcedonenses, 1991.

——. *Le registre synodal du Patriarcat byzantin au XIVe siècle: Étude paléographique et diplomatique*. Archives de l'Orient Chrétien 12. Institut français d'études byzantines, 1971.

——. *Recherches sur les ΟΦΦΙΚΙΑ de l'église byzantine*. Archives de l'Orient Chrétien 11. Institut français d'études byzantines, 1970.

Davies, Eversley. "From Womb to the Tomb: The Byzantine Life Course AD 518–1204." PhD diss., University of Birmingham, 2013.

De Andrés, Gregorio. *Catálogo de los códices griegos de la Real Biblioteca de El Escorial*. Vol. 3. El Escorial, 1967.

De Meester, Placide. *De monachico statu iuxta disciplinam Byzantinam*. Sacra Congregazione per la Chiesa Orientale, Codificazione Canonica Orientale, Fonti; ser. 2, fasc. 10. Typis Polyglottis Vaticanis, 1942.

——. "Les typiques de fondation (τυπικά κτητορικά)." *Studi bizantini e neoellenici* 6 (1940): 489–508.

De Montfaucon, Bernard. *Bibliotheca Coisliniana olim Segueriana sive Manuscriptorum omnium Graecorum*. Ludovicum Guérin et Carolum Robustel, 1715.

De'Cavalieri, Pio Franchi. *Codices graeci Chisiani et Borgiani*. Typis Polyglottis Vaticanis, 1927.

Demacopoulos, George E. "The Popular Reception of the Council of Florence in Constantinople, 1439–1453." *St. Vladimir's Theological Quarterly* 43 (1999): 37–53.

Demangel, Robert, and Ernest Mamboury. *Le quartier des Manganes et la première région de Constantinople*. Recherches Françaises en Turquie. De Boccard, 1939.

Demus, Otto. "Studien zur byzantinischen Buchmalerei des 13. Jahrhunderts." *Jahrbuch der Österreichischen Byzantinischen Gesellschaft* 9 (1960): 77–89.

Devreesse, Robert. *Catalogue des manuscrits grecs*. Vol. 2, *Le fonds Coislin*. Imprimerie Nationale, 1945.

——. *Codices Vaticani graeci*. Vol. 3, *Codices 604–866*. Typis Polyglottis Vaticanis, 1950.

Dölger, Franz. *Regesten der Kaiserurkunden des Oströmischen Reiches von 565–1453*. Vol. 4, *Regesten von 1282–1341*. Beck, 1960.

——. *Regesten der Kaiserurkunden des oströmischen Reiches von 565–1453*. Vol. 5, *Regesten von 1341–1453*. Beck, 1965.

Dölger, Franz, and Peter Wirth. *Regesten der Kaiserurkunden des Oströmischen Reiches*. Vol. 3. Beck, 1977.

Dosse, François. *Michel de Certeau: Le marcheur blesse*. Découverte, 2002.

Drandakes, Nikolaos B. "Ο σπηλαιώδης ναός του Άι-Γιαννάκη στη Ζούπενα [The Cave Church of Ai-Giannakes in Zoupena]." *Deltion tes Christianikes Archaiologikes Etaireias* 13 (1985–1986): 79–92.

——. "Ὁ Ἁϊ-Γιαννάκης τοῦ Μυστρά [The Church of Ai-Giannakes in Mystras]." *Deltion tes Christianikes Archaiologikes Etaireias* (1987–1988): 61–82.

——. "Τὸ Παλιομονάστηρο τῶν Ἁγίων Σαράντα στή Λακεδαίμονα καὶ τὸ ἀσκηταριό του [The Old Monastery of St. Saranta in Lakedaimon and Its Hermitage." *Deltion tes Christianikes Archaiologikes Etaireias* 16 (1991–1992): 115–38.

——. "Ἔρευναι εἰς τὴν Μάνην [Research in Mane]." *Praktika Archaiologikes Etaireias* (1974): 110–38.

——. "Ὁ Ταξιάρχης τῆς Χαροῦδας καὶ ἡ κτητορικὴ ἐπιγραφή του [The Taxiarches Church of Charouda and its Founding Inscription]." *Lakonikai Spoudai* 1 (1972): 287–88.

Effenberger, Arne. "Die Klöster der beiden Kyra Martha und die Kirche des Bebaia Elpis Klosters in Konstantinopel." *Millennium* 3 (2006): 255–93.

——. "Ein byzantinisches Emailkreuz mit Besitzerinschrift." *Deltion tes Christianikes Archaiologikes Etaireias* 31 (1983): 115–24.

——. "Theodosia von Konstantinopel: Kult und Kultort: Ergänzende Überlegungen zu ihrem phagiographischen Dossier.'" *Jahrbuch der Österreichischen Byzantinistik* 61 (2011): 121–34.

——. "Zu den Eltern der Maria Dukaina Komnene Branaina Tarchaneiotissa." *Jahrbuch der Österreichischen Byzantinistik* 57 (2007): 169–82.

——. "Zu den Gräbern in der Pammakaristoskirche." *Byzantion* 77 (2007): 170–96.

——. "Zur Restaurierungstatigkeit des Michael Dukas Glabas Tarchaneiotes im Pammakaristoskloster und zur Erbauungszeit des Parekklesion." *Zograf* 31 (2006–7): 79–94.

Efthymiadis, Stephanos, and Andreas Mazarakis. "Questions de chronologie sur Ramon Muntaner (Ch. 234) et Georges Pachymérès (XIII, 27–38): La prise de Phocée et de Thasos en 1307." *Nea Rhome* 5 (2008): 303–22.

Ehrhard, Albert. *Überlieferung und Bestand der hagiographischen und homiletischen Literatur der griechischen Kirche, Texte und Untersuchungen*. 3 vols. Hinrichs, 1937–1952.

Elden, Stuart. *Understanding Henri Lefebvre: Theory and the Possible*. Continuum, 2004.

Elm, Susanna K. *"Virgins of God": The Making of Asceticism in Late Antiquity*. Oxford University Press, 1994.

Erler, Ingolf. "Das Buch als soziales Symbol: Die Umwandlung von objektiviertem kulturellem Kapital in symbolisches Kapital." Master's thesis, Universität Wien, 2005.

Erler, Mary C., and Maryanne Kowaleski. *Gendering the Master Narrative: Women and Power in the Middle Ages*. Cornell University Press, 2003.

Euangelatou-Notara, Florentia. "ΑΔΕΛΦΑΤΟΝ. ΨΥΧΙΚΟΝ: Evidence from Notes on Manuscripts." *Byzantion* 75 (2005): 164–70.

Eustratiades, Sophronios. "Ὁ πατριάρχης Ἀρσένιος ὁ Αὐτωρειανός (1255–1260 καὶ 1261–1267) [The Patriarch Arsenios Autoreianos (1255–1260 and 1261–1267)]." *Hellenika* 1 (1928): 78–94.

Evans, Helen C. *Byzantium: Faith and Power (1261–1557)*. Metropolitan Museum of Art, 2004.

Evert-Kappesowa, Halina. "La société byzantine et l'Union de Lyon." *Byzantinoslavica* 10 (1949): 28–41.

——. "Une page de l'histoire des relations byzantino-latines." *Byzantinoslavica* 16 (1955): 297–317.

——. "Une page de l'histoire des relations byzantino-latines: Le clergé byzantin et l'Union de Lyon (1274–1282)." *Byzantinoslavica* 13 (1952–1953): 68–92.

——. "Une page de l'Histoire des relations byzantino-latines: 2. La fin de l'Union de Lyon." *Byzantinoslavica* 17 (1956): 1–18.

Failler, Albert. "Pachymeriana Novissima." *Revue des études byzantines* 55 (1997): 221–46.

Fassoulakis, Stergios. *The Byzantine Family of Raoul-Ral(l)es.* Fassoulakis, 1973.

Feissel, Dennis, and Anne Philippidis-Braat. "Inventaires en vue d'un recueil des inscriptions historiques de Byzance. 3: Inscriptions du Péloponnèse (à l'exception de Mistra)." *Travaux et Memoires* 9 (1985): 267–395.

Felloni, Giuseppe. *Amministrazione ed etica nella Casa di San Giorgio (1407–1805): Lo statuto del 1568.* Bibliotheca dell'"Archivio storico italiano" 36. Olschki, 2014.

Feron, Ernestus, and Fabianus Battaglini. *Codices manuscripti graeci Ottoboniani Bibliothecae Vaticanae.* ex Typographeo Vaticano, 1893.

Finlay, Victoria. *The Brilliant History of Color in Art.* Getty, 2014.

Firatli, Nezih. *La sculpture byzantine figurée au Musée Archéologique d'Istanbul.* Librairie d'Amérique et d'Orient, 1990.

Fonkič, Boris L'vovič. "Zametki o grečeskich rukopisjach Sovietskich chranilišč [Notes on Greek Manuscripts From Soviet Archives]." *Vizantijskij Vremmenik* 36 (1974): 134–38.

Foskolou, Vasiliki. "Blessing For Sale? On the Production and Distribution of Pilgrim Mementoes in Byzantium." *Byzantinische Zeitschrift* 105, no. 1 (2012): 53–84.

Foss, Clive. *Nicaea: A Byzantine Capital and Its Praises.* Hellenic College Press, 1996.

——. *Survey of Medieval Castles of Anatolia.* Vol. 2. *Nicomedia.* British Institute of Archaeology at Ankara 21. British Institute of Archaeology at Ankara, 1996.

Frazee, Charles A. "Late Roman and Byzantine Legislation on the Monastic Life from the Fourth to the Eighth Centuries." *Church history* 51 (1982): 263–79.

Fryde, Edmund. *The Early Palaeologan Renaissance (1261-c. 1360).* The Medieval Mediterranean 27. Brill, 2000.

Fugger, Verena, and Rudolf Stefec. "Das illuminierte *Typikon* des Eugenios-Klosters in Trapezunt." *Jahrbuch der Österreichischen Byzantinistik* 64 (2014): 41–66.

Gabra, Gawdat, and Tim Vivian. *Coptic Monasteries: Egypt's Monastic Art and Architecture.* American University in Cairo, 2002.

Galatariotou, Catia. "Byzantine Women's Monastic Communities: The Evidence of the ΤΥΠΙΚΑ." *Jahrbuch der Österreichischen Byzantinistik* 38 (1988): 263–90.

Galavaris, Giorgos. "Two Icons of St. Theodosia at Sinai." *Deltion tes Christianikes Archaiologikes Etaireias* 17 (1993–1994): 313–16.

Gamillscheg, Ernst, et al. *Repertorium der griechischen Kopisten 800–1600.* Vol. 3. *Rom mit Vatikan.* Österreichische Akademie der Wissenschaften, 1997.

Ganchou, Thierry. "Héléna Notara Gateliousaina d'Ainos et le Sankt Peterburg Bibl. Publ. gr. 243." *Revue des études byzantines* 56 (1998): 141–68.

Gansell, Amy Rebecca. "Amulet Portraying the Woman with the Issue of Blood." In *Byzantine Women and Their World*, edited by Ioli Kalavrezou and Angeliki Laiou, 283–84. Harvard University Art Museums, 2003.

——. "Prayer for Pregnancy." In *Byzantine Women and Their World*, edited by Ioli Kalavrezou and Angeliki Laiou, no. 174, 292–93. Harvard University Art Museums, 2003.

Garland, Lynda. *Byzantine Empresses: Women and Power in Byzantium, AD 527–1204.* Routledge, 1999.

Gastgeber, Christian. "Das *Typikon* Lincoln College gr. 35 und das Patriarchat von Konstantinopel." *Scripta* 7 (2014): 95–110.

Gaul, Niels. "Writing 'with Joyful and Leaping Soul': Sacralization, Scribal Hands, and Ceremonial in the Lincoln College *Typikon*." *Dumbarton Oaks Papers* 69 (2015): 243–71.

Geanakoplos, Deno John. *Emperor Michael Palaeologos and the West 1258–1282: A Study in Byzantine-Latin Relations*. Harvard University Press, 1959.

Geelhaar, Tim, and John Thomas. *Stiftung und Staat im Mittelalter: Eine byzantinisch-lateineuropaische Quellenanthologie in komparatistischer Perspektive*. Stiftungsgeschichten 6. De Gruyter, 2011.

Georgopoulou-Verra, Myrto. "Βυζαντινά μονύδρια και ασκηταριά στην περιοχή του όρους Σκόλλις στην Αχαΐα [Byzantine Monasteries and Hermitages in the Area of Mount Skollis in Achaia]." In *Monasticism in the Peloponnese 4th–15th c.*, edited by Voula Konti, 113–29. Ethniko Idryma Ereunon, 2004.

Gerola, Giuseppe. *Monumenti veneti nell'isola di Creta*. 4 vols. Officine dell'Istituto d'Arti Grafiche, 1932.

Gerstel, Sharon E. J. *Rural Lives and Landscapes in Late Byzantium: Art, Archaeology and Ethnography*. Cambridge University Press, 2015.

Gerstel, Sharon E. J., and Alice-Mary Talbot. "Nuns in the Byzantine Countryside." *Deltion tes Christianikes Archaiologikes Etaireias* 27 (2006): 481–90.

Gerstel, Sharon E. J., and Sophia Kalopissi-Verti. "Female Church Founders: The Agency of the Village Widow in Late Byzantium." In *Female Founders in Byzantium and Beyond*, edited by Lioba Theis, Margaret Mullett, and Michael Grünbart, 195–211. Böhlau, 2014.

Giannopoulos, Nikolaos I. "Αἱ παρὰ τὴν Δημητριάδα βυζαντιναὶ μοναὶ [The Byzantine Monasteries by Demetrias]." *Epeteris Etaireias Byzantinon Spoudon* 1 (1924): 210–40.

Giard, Luce. *Michel de Certeau*. Centre Georges Pompidou, 1987.

Gilchrist, Robert. *Gender and Material Culture: The Archaeology of Religious Women*. Routledge, 2008.

Gill, Joseph. *Byzantium and the Papacy, 1198–1400*. Rutgers University Press, 1979.

——. *The Council of Florence*. Cambridge University Press, 1959. Reprint, 1961.

Gioffreda, Anna. "Giovanni Ciparissiota e il Contra Nilum Cabasilam: L'autore e il suo testo." *Medioevo Greco* 17 (2017): 87–106.

Gkoutziokostas, Andreas. "Observations on the Dating of the *Typikon* of the Lips Monastery." *Jahrbuch der Österreichischen Byzantinistik* 59 (2009): 79–85.

Gones, Demetrios P. *Τὸ συγγραφικὸν ἔργον τοῦ οἰκουμενικοῦ πατριάρχου Καλλίστου Α´* [The Writings of the Ecumenical Patriarch Callistus I]. University of Athens, 1980.

Gounarides, Paris. *Τὸ κίνημα τῶν Ἀρσενιατῶν (1261–1310): Ἰδεολογικές διαμάχες τὴν ἐποχή τῶν πρώτων Παλαιολόγων* [The Arseniate Movement (1261–1310): Ideological Disputes During the Era of the Early Palaiologoi]. Domos, 1999.

——. "Ιωάννης Βέκκος εχθρός Ρωμαίων [Ioannes Bekkos enemy of the Romans]." In *The Balkans and the Eastern Mediterranean, 12th–17th Centuries. Proceedings of the International Symposium in Memory of D. A. Zakythinos*, edited by Katerina Nikolaou and Linos Maurommates, 29–40. Ethniko Idryma Ereunon, 1998.

——. "Πολιτικές διαστάσεις της συνόδου Φεράρας-Φλωρεντίας [Political Dimensions of the Ferrara-Florence Synod]." *Thesaurismata* 31 (2001): 107–29.

Grabar, André. *L'art byzantin*. Editions d'art et d'histoire, 1938.

——. *Sculptures byzantines du Moyen Âge*. Picard et Maisonneuve, 1976.

Granstrem, Evgenija E. "Каталог греческих рукописей ленинградских хранилищ [Catalogue of Greek Manuscripts in Leningrad Archives]." *Vizantijskij Vremmenik* 31 (1971): 132–44.

Gregoropoulos, Ioannes. *Θεολήπτου Φιλαδελφείας τοῦ Ὁμολογητοῦ (1250–1322): βίος καὶ ἔργα* [Theoleptos of Philadelpheia the Confessor (1250–1322): Life and Works]. Tertios, 1996.

Grünbart, Michael. "Female Founders—Das Konzept: Zu Stiftungshandlungen in der byzantinischen Welt." In *Female Founders in Byzantium and Beyond*, edited by Lioba Theis, Margaret Mullett, and Michael Grünbart, 317–31. Böhlau, 2014.

——. *Formen der Anrede im byzantinischen Brief vom 6. bis zum 12. Jahrhundert*. Wiener byzantinistische Studien 25. Österreichische Akademie der Wissenschaften, 2005.

——. "Paideia Connects: The Interaction Between Teachers and Pupils in Twelfth-Century Byzantium." In *Networks of Learning: Perspectives on Scholars in Byzantine East and Latin West, c. 1000–1200*, edited by Sita Steckel et al., 18–31. Byzantinistische Studien und Texte 6. LIT, 2014.

Haldon, John Frederick. "Limnos, Monastic Holdings and the Byzantine State: ca. 1261–1453." In *Continuity and Change in Late Byzantine and Early Ottoman Society: Papers Given at a Symposium at Dumbarton Oaks in May 1982*, edited by Anthony Bryer and Heath Lowry, 161–215. Dumbarton Oaks, 1986.

Hamburger, Jeffrey F. *Nuns as Artists: The Visual Culture of a Medieval Convent*. University of California Press, 1997.

Hamburger, Jeffrey F., and Robert Suckale. "Between This World and the Next: The Art of Religious Women in the Middle Ages." In *Crown and Veil. Female Monasticism from the Fifth to the Fifteenth Centuries*, edited by Jeffrey F. Hamburger and Susan Marti. Translated by Dietlinde Hamburger, 76–108. Columbia University Press, 2008.

Hand, Joni M. *Women, Manuscripts and Identity in Northern Europe, 1350–1559*. Ashgate, 2013.

Hannick, Christian, and Gudrun Schmalzbauer. "Die Synadenoi." *Jahrbuch der Österreichischen Byzantinistik* 25 (1976): 125–61.

Harlfinger, Dieter. "Einige Aspekte der handschriftlichen Überlieferung des Physikkommentars des Simplikios." In *Simplicius, sa vie, son oeuvre, sa survie: Actes du Colloque international de Paris (28 sept.–1 oct. 1985)*, edited by Ilsetraut Hadot, vol. 1, 267–86. Peripatoi 15. De Gruyter, 1987.

Harmless, William, S.J. *Desert Christians: An Introduction to the Literature of Early Monasticism*. Oxford: Oxford University Press, 2004.

Harpham, Geoffrey Galt. *The Ascetic Imperative in Culture and Criticism*. University of Chicago Press, 1987.

Harris, Jonathan P. "The Goudelis Family in Italy After the Fall of Constantinople." *Byzantine and Modern Greek Studies* 33, no. 20 (2009): 168–79.

Hatlie, Peter. *The Monks and Monasteries of Constantinople, ca. 350–850*. Cambridge University Press, 2007.

Hatzaki, Myrto. *Beauty and the Male Body in Byzantium: Perceptions and Representations in Art and Text*. Palgrave Macmillan, 2009.

Hausherr, Irénée. "Note sur l'inventeur de la méthode hésychaste." *Orient Chretienne* 20 (1930): 179–82.

Hennessy, Cecily. "The Lincoln College *Typikon*: Influences of Church and Family in an Illuminated Foundation Document for a Palaiologan Convent in Constantinople." In *Under the Influence: The Concept of Influence and the Study of Illuminated Manuscripts*, edited by Alixe Bovey and John Lowden, 97–109. Publications of the Research Centre for Illuminated Manuscripts 1. Brepols, 2007.

Herman, Emil. "Das bischöfliche Abgabenwesen im Patriarchat von Konstantinopel vom XI. bis zur Mitte des XIX. Jahrhunderts." *Orientalia Christiana Periodica* 5 (1939): 434–513.

——. "Ricerche sulle istituzioni monastiche byzantine: Typika ktetorika, caristicari e monastery liberi." *Orientalia Christiana Periodica* 6 (1940): 293–375.

Herrin, Judith. "'Femina Byzantina': The Council in Troullo on Women." *Dumbarton Oaks Papers* 46 (1992): 97–105.

——. *Unrivalled Influence: Women and Empire in Byzantium*. Princeton University Press, 2013.

——. *Women in Purple: Rulers of Medieval Byzantium*. Phoenix, 2002.

Hiestand, Rudolf. "Die erste Ehe Isaaks II. Angelos und seine Kinder." *Jahrbuch der Österreichischen Byzantinistik* 47 (1997): 199–208.

Hill, Barbara. *Imperial Women in Byzantium 1025–1204*. Longman, 1999.

Hillier, Bill, and Julienne Hanson. *The Social Logic of Space*. Cambridge University Press, 1984.

Hilsdale, Cecily J. *Byzantine Art and Diplomacy in an Age of Decline*. Cambridge University Press, 2014.

Hutter, Irmgard. *Corpus der byzantinischen Miniaturenhandschriften*. Vol. 5. Oxford College Libraries. Hiersemann, 1997.

——. "Die Geschichte des Lincoln College *Typikons*." *Jahrbuch der Österreichischen Byzantinistik* 45 (1995): 79–114.

Ivanov, Sergey A. *Holy Fools in Byzantium and Beyond*. Translated by Simon Franklin. Oxford University Press, 2006.

——. *In Search of Constantinople: A Guidebook Through Byzantine Istanbul and Its Surroundings*. Translated by Sara Buzadzhi and Deborah Hoffman. Kitap Yayınevi, 2021.

Jacoby, David. "The Urban Evolution of Latin Constantinople (1204–1261)." In *Byzantine Constantinople. Monuments, Topography and Everyday Life*, edited by Nevra Nečipoglu, 277–97. Brill, 2001.

James, Liz. *Empresses and Power in Early Byzantium*. Leicester University Press, 2001.

Janin, Raymond. *Constantinople byzantine: Développement urbain et repertoire topographique*. Archives de l'Orient Chrétien 4A. Institut français d'études byzantines, 1964.

——. *La géographie ecclésiastique de l'Empire byzantine*. Vol. 1, *Le siège de Constantinople et le Patriarcat œcuménique*, fasc. 3. *Les églises et les monastères*. Institut français d'études byzantines, 1969.

——. "Le monachisme byzantine au Moyen Âge: Commende et typika (Xe-XIV siècles)." *Revue des études byzantines* 22 (1964): 5–44.

——. *Les églises et les monastères des grands centres Byzantins: Bithynie, Hellespont, Latros, Galèsios, Trébizonde, Athènes, Thessalonique*. Institut français d'études byzantines, 1975.

——. "Les monastères du Christ Philanthrope à Constantinople." *Études Byzantines* 4 (1946): 135–62.

Jeffreys, Elizabeth. "The *Sebastokratorissa* Irene as Patron." In *Female Founders in Byzantium and Beyond*, edited by Lioba Theis, Margaret Mullett, and Michael Grünbart, 177–94. Böhlau, 2014.

Johnstone, Pauline. *The Byzantine Tradition in Church Embroidery*. Tiranti, 1967.

Kadushin, Charles. *Understanding Social Networks: Theories, Concepts, and Findings*. Oxford University Press, 2012.

Kafescioğlou, Çiğdem. *Constantinopolis/Istanbul: Cultural Encounter, Imperial Vision, and the Construction of the Ottoman Capital*. The Pennsylvania State University Press, 2009.

Kalopissi-Verti, Sophia. *Dedicatory Inscriptions and Donor Portraits in Thirteenth-Century Churches of Greece*. Österreichische Akademie der Wissenschaften, 1992.

———. "Δωρεές γυναικών στην υστεροβυζαντινή περίοδο [Women's Donations in the Late Byzantine Period]." In *Γυναίκα στο Βυζάντιο: Λατρεία και τέχνη: Ειδικό θέμα του 26ου συμποσίου Βυζαντινής και μεταβυζαντινής Αρχαιολογίας και τέχνης, Αθήνα 12–14 Μαΐου 2006* [Woman in Byzantium: Worship and Art: Special Theme of the 26th Symposium on Byzantine and Post-Byzantine Archaeology and Art, Athens 12–14 May 2006], edited by Maria Panagiotide-Kesisoglou, 243–56. Politistiko Idryma Omilou Peiraios, 2012.

Kambourova, Tania. "Le don de l'Église—une affaire couple?" In *Female Founders in Byzantium and Beyond*, edited by Lioba Theis, Margaret Mullett, and Michael Grünbart, 213–29. Böhlau, 2014.

Karamaouna, Nota, et al. "Female Donors in Thirteenth Century: Wall-Paintings in Cappadocia." In *Female Founders in Byzantium and Beyond*, edited by Lioba Theis, Margaret Mullett, and Michael Grünbart, 231–42. Böhlau, 2014.

Katsafados, Panayotis Stam. "Νέα στοιχεία για τις αφιερωτικές επιγραφές (13ος αιώνας) του ναού των Αγίων Θεοδώρων Ανω Πούλας, Μέσα Μάνης [New Evidence on the Dedicatory Inscriptions (13th century) in the Church of Hagioi Theodoroi, Ano Poula, Inner Mane]." *Deltion tes Christianikes Archaiologikes Etaireias* 36 (2016): 275–88.

Kazhdan, Alexander. "The Italian and Late Byzantine City." *Dumbarton Oaks Papers* 49 (1995): 1–32.

Kazhdan, Alexander, and Alice-Mary Talbot. "Stauropegion." In *Oxford Dictionary of Byzantium*, edited by Alexander Kazhdan, vol. 3, pp. 1946–1947.

———. "Women and Iconoclasm." *Byzantinische Zeitschrift* 84/85 (1991/92): 391–408.

Kianka, Frances. "The Letters of Demetrios Kydones to Empress Helena Kantakouzene Palaiologina." *Dumbarton Oaks Papers* 46 (1992): 155–64.

Kidonopulos, Vassilios. *Bauten in Konstantinopel 1204–1328: Verfall und Zerstörung, Restaurierung, Umbau und Neubau von Profan- und Sakralbauten*. Mainzer Veröffentlichungen zur Byzantinistik 1. Harrassowitz, 1994.

———. "The Urban Physiognomy of Constantinople from the Latin Conquest Through the Palaiologan Era." In *Byzantium, Faith, and Power (1261–1557): Perspectives on Late Byzantine Art*, edited by Sarah T. Brooks, 98–117. Yale University Press, 2007.

Kiilerich, Bente. "Attire and Personal Appearance in Byzantium." In *Byzantine Culture: Papers From the Conference "Byzantine Days of Istanbul" Held on the Occasion of Istanbul being European Cultural Capital 2010, Istanbul May 21–23, 2010*, edited by Dean Sakel, 439–51, 479–511 (illustrations). Türk Tarih Kurumu, 2014.

Kiousopoulou, Antonia. *Βασιλεύς ή οικονόμος: Πολιτική εξουσία και ιδεολογία πριν την Άλωση* [Emperor or Manager: Political Power and Ideology Before the Fall]. Polis, 2007.

——. "Ἡ κοινωνικὴ διάσταση τῆς σύγκρουσης ἀνάμεσα στοὺς ἑνωτικούς καὶ τοὺς ἀνθενωτικούς τὸν 15° αἰώνα [The Social Dimension of the Conflict Between the Unionists and Anti-Unionists in the 15th Century]." *Mnemon* 23 (2001): 25–36.

Kitchin, George William. *Catalogus codicum mss. qui in Bibliotheca Aedis Christi apud Oxonienses adversantur*. Clarendon, 1867.

Koder, Johannes, and Friedrich Hild. *Hellas und Thessalien*. Tabula Imperii Byzantini 1. Österreichische Akademie der Wissenschaften, 1976.

Kohler, Timothy A. "Complex Systems and Archaeology." In *Archaeological Theory Today*, edited by Ian Hodder, 93–123, 2nd edn. Polity, 2012.

Kolbaba, Tia M. *The Byzantine Lists: Errors of the Latins*. Illinois Medieval Studies. University of Illinois Press, 2000.

——. "Byzantine Perceptions of Latin Religious 'Errors': Themes and Changes from 850 to 1350." In *The Crusades from the Perspective of Byzantium and the Muslim World*, edited by Angeliki E. Laiou and Roy Parviz Mottahedeh, 117–43. Dumbarton Oaks, 2001.

——. *Inventing Latin Heretics: Byzantines and the Filioque in the Ninth Century*. Western Michigan University, 2008.

——. "The Orthodoxy of the Latins in the Twelfth Century." In *Byzantine Orthodoxies: Papers from the Thirty-Sixth Spring Symposium of Byzantine Studies, University of Durham, 23–25 March 2002*. Edited by Andrew Louth and Augustine Casiday, 199–214. Society for the Promotion of Byzantine Studies 12. Ashgate, 2006.

Kondyli, Fontini. "Tracing Monastic Economic Interests and Their Impact on the Rural Landscape of Late Byzantine Lemnos." *Dumbarton Oaks Papers* 64 (2010): 129–50.

Konidares, Ioannes. *Το δίκαιον της μοναστηριακής περιουσίας: Από του 9ου μέχρι και του 12ου αιώνος* [The Law of Monastic Property: From the Ninth to the Twelfth Century]. Sakkoulas, 1979.

——. *Νομικὴ θεώρηση τῶν μοναστηριακῶν τυπικῶν* [Legal View of Monastic Typika]. Sakkoulas, 1984.

——. "Η θέση της χήρας στη βυζαντινή κοινωνία [Widow's Position in the Byzantine Society]." *Byzantina* 16 (1991): 35–42.

Koubena, Elizabeth. "A Survey of Aristocratic Women Founders of Monasteries in Constantinople Between the Eleventh and the Fifteenth Centuries." In *Les femmes et le monachisme byzantine: Actes du symposium d'Athènes, 28–29 mars 1988/ Women and Byzantine Monasticism: Proceedings of the Athens Symposium, 28–29 March 1988*, edited by Jacques Y. Perreault, Elizabeth Koubena, and Maria Toli, 25–32. Institut canadien d'archéologie à Athènes, 1991.

Kountoura-Galake, Eleonora. "Ιωάννης Σταυράκιος: ένας λόγιος στη Θεσσαλονίκη της πρώιμης Παλαιολόγειας εποχής [John Stavrakios: A Scholar in Thessaloniki of the Early Palaeologan Era]." *Symmeikta* 16 (2003–2004): 379–94.

Kountoura-Galaki, Eleonora, and Ekaterini Mitsiou. *Women and Monasticism in the Medieval Eastern Mediterranean: Decoding a Cultural Map*. Ethniko Idryma Ereunon, 2019.

Kouroupou, Matoula, and Jean-François Vannier. "Commémoraisons des Comnènes dans le *typikon* liturgique du monastère du Christ Philanthrope (MS. Panaghia Kamariotissa 29)." *Revue des études byzantines* 63 (2005): 41–69.

Kouroupou, Matoula, and Paul Géhin. *Catalogue des manuscrits conservés dans la Bibliothèque du Patriarcat Oecuménique: Les manuscrits du monastère de la Panaghia de Chalki*. Brepols, 2008.

Kraus, Christof Rudolf. *Kleriker im späten Byzanz: Anagnosten, Hypodiakone, Diakone und Priester 1261–1453*. Mainzer Veröffentlichungen zur Byzantinistik 9. Harrassowitz, 2007.

Krausmüller, Dirk. "From Individual Almsgiving to Communal Charity: The Impact of the Middle Byzantine Monastic Reform Movement on the Life of Monks." *Jahrbuch der Österreichischen Byzantinistik* 66 (2016): 111–26.

Kresten, Otto, and Martin Schaller. "Diplomatische, chonologische und textkritische Beobachtungen zu Urkunden des Chartulars B des Ioannes Prodromos-Klosters bei Serrhai." In *Sylloge Diplomatico-Palaeographica*, vol. 1. *Studien zur byzantinischen Diplomatik und Palaographie*, edited by Christian Gastgeber and Otto Kresten, 179–232. Österreichische Akademie der Wissenschaften, 2010.

Kubina, Krystina. *Die enkomiastische Dichtung des Manuel Philes: Form und Funktion des literarischen Lobes in der frühen Palaiologenzeit*. Byzantinisches Archiv 38. De Gruyter, 2020.

Kugeas, Sokrates. "Zur Geschichte der Münchener Thukydideshandschrift." *Byzantinische Zeitschrift* 16 (1907): 588–609.

Külzer, Andreas. *Ostthrakien (Eurōpē)*. Tabula Imperii Byzantini 12. Österreichische Akademie der Wissenschaften, 2008.

Lähnemann, Henrike, and Schlotheuber, Eva. *Unerhörte Frauen: Die Netzwerke der Nonnen im Mittelalter*. Propyläen, 2023.

Laiou, Angeliki. "The Agrarian Economy: Thirteenth–Fifteenth Centuries." In *The Economic History of Byzantium: From the Seventh through the Fifteenth Century*, edited by Angeliki E. Laiou, vol. 2, pp. 311–75. Dumbarton Oaks Studies 39. Dumbarton Oaks, 2002.

——. "Economic Activities of Vatopedi in the Fourteenth Century." In *Ιερά Μονή Βατοπεδίου. Ιστορία και Τέχνη* [Holy Monastery of Vatopedi. History and Art], edited by Paris Gounarides, 55–72. Athonika Symmeikta 7. Ethniko Idryma Ereunon, 1999.

——. "Family Structure and the Transmission of Property." In *A Social History of Byzantium*, edited by John Haldon, 51–75. Wiley-Blackwell, 2009.

——. *Gender, Society and Economic Life in Byzantium*. Variorum Reprints, 1992.

——. *Mariage, amour et parenté à Byzance aux XIe-XIIIe siècles*. De Boccard, 1992.

——. "Sex, Consent and Coercion in Byzantium." In *Consent and Coercion to Sex and Marriage in Ancient and Medieval Societies*, edited by Angeliki E. Laiou, 109–221. Dumbarton Oaks, 1993.

——. "The Role of Women in Byzantine Society." *Jahrbuch der Österreichischen Byzantinistik* 31, no. 1 (1981): 233–60.

Lampakes, Stylianos. *Γεώργιος Παχυμέρης: πρωτέκδικος και δικαιοφύλαξ: Εισαγωγικό δοκίμιο* [George Pachymeres: Protekdikos and Dikaiophylax: An Introductory Essay]. Monographs 5. Ethniko Idryma Ereunon, 2004.

Lampropoulos, Kosmas. *Ιωάννης Απόκαυκος: Συμβολή στην έρευνα του βίου και του συγγραφικού έργου του* [John Apokaukos: Contribution to the Research of his Life and Writings]. Historical Monographies 6. Basilopoulos, 1988.

Lampros, Spyridon. *Catalogue of the Greek Manuscripts on Mount Athos*. Vol. 1. Cambridge University Press, 1895.

——. "Ἑλληνίδες βιβλιογράφοι καὶ κυρίαι κωδίκων κατὰ τοὺς μέσους αἰῶνας καὶ ἐπί τουρκοκρατίας [Greek Women Scribes and Manuscript Owners in the Middle Ages and During the Turkokratia]." *Epistemonike Epeteris tou Ethnikou Panepistemiou* (1902–1903): 229–64.

Laurent, Vitalien. "Kyra Martha: Essai de topographie et de prosopographie byzantine." *Echos d'Orient* 38 (1939): 296–320.

——. "La direction spirituelle à Byzance." *Revue des études byzantines* 8 (1950): 64–84.

——. "Le métropolite de Thessalonique Gabriel (1397–1416/19) et le couvent de la Νέα Μονή." *Hellenika* 13 (1954): 241–55.

——. "Les grandes crises religieuses à Byzance: La fin du schisme arsénite." *Bulletin de la Section Historique de l'Académie Roumaine* 26, no. 2 (1945): 225–313.

——. *Les regestes des Actes du patriarcat de Constantinople.* Vol. 1, *Les actes des patriarches*, fasc. 4, *Les regestes des 1208 à 1309.* Le patriarcat byzantin, série 1. Institut français d'études byzantines, 1971.

——. "Une fondation monastique de Nicéphore Choumnos." *Revue des études byzantines* 12 (1954): 32–44.

——. "Une princesse byzantine au cloître: Irène-Eulogie Choumnos Paléologine, fondatrice du couvent de femmes τοῦ Φιλανθρώπου Σωτῆρος." *Echos d' Orient* 29 (1930): 29–60.

Lefebvre, Henri. *La production de l'espace.* Anthropos, 1974.

Leonte, Florin "A Late Byzantine Patroness: Helena Kantakouzene Palaiologina." In *Female Founders in Byzantium and Beyond*, edited by Lioba Theis, Margaret Mullett, and Michael Grünbart, 345–54. Böhlau, 2014.

Leontiades, Ioannes G. *Die Tarchaneiotai: Eine prosopographisch-sigillographische Studie.* Kentro Byzantinon Ereunon, 1998.

Likhačeva, Vera D. *Византийская миниатюра: памятники византийской миниатюры ИХ–ХВ веков в собраниях советского союза* [Byzantine Illuminations: Monuments of Byzantine Illuminations of the Ninth to the Fiftheenth Centuries in the Collections of the Soviet Union]. Iskusstvo, 1977.

——. "Роль бытовых реалий и пейзажа в миниатюрах рукописи Государственной публичной библиотеки гр. № 243 [The Role of the Author's Recitations and Paintings in the Illuminated Manuscript of the State Public Library, No. 243]." *Vizantijskij Vremmenik* 27 (1967): 229–42.

Loberdou-Tsigarida, Katia. "Βυζαντινή μικροτεχνία [Byzantine Miniature Objects]." In *The Holy and Great Monastery of Vatopaidi: Tradition—History—Art*, edited by Ioakeim Papangelos and Panagiotis Grabbalos, vol. 2, pp. 458–99. Athonite Center of Orthodox Culture, 1998.

Loukaki, Marina. "Monastères de femmes à Byzance du XIIe siècle jusqu' à 1453." In *Les femmes et le monachisme byzantine: Actes du symposium d'Athènes, 28–29 mars 1988 / Women and Byzantine Monasticism: Proceedings of the Athens Symposium, 28–29 March 1988*, edited by Jacques Y. Perreault, Elizabeth Koubena, and Maria Toli, 33–42. Institut canadien d'archéologie à Athènes, 1991.

Loverdou-Tsigarida, Katia. "Cross of the Empress Helena Palaiologina, Dionysiou Monastery." In *Treasures of Mount Athos: Catalogue of the Exhibition "Treasures of Mount Athos,"* edited by Athanasios A. Karakatsanis, 346–47. Holy Community of Mt. Athos, 1997.

Lubinsky, Crystal Lynn. *Removing Masculine Layers to Reveal a Holy Womanhood: The Female Transvestite Monks of Late Antique Eastern Christianity.* Brepols, 2013.

Luckhardt, Courtney. *The Charisma of Distant Places: Travel and Religion in the Early Middle Ages.* Routledge, 2020.

Macrides, Ruth. "Dowry and Inheritance in the Late Period: Some Cases from the Patriarchal Register." In *Eherecht und Familiengut in Antike und Mittelalter*, edited by Dieter Simon, 89–98. Schriften des Historischen Kollegs Kolloquien 22. Oldenbourg, 1992.

——. "The Transmission of Property in the Patriarchal Register." In *La transmission du patrimoine: Byzance et l'aire mediterraneenne*. Travaux et Mémoires du Centre de Recherche d'Histoire et Civilisation de Byzance, Monographies 11. De Boccard, 1998.

Macridy, Theodore. "The Monastery of Lips and the Burials of the Palaeologi." *Dumbarton Oaks Papers* 18 (1964): 253–77.

Magdalino, Paul. "Adelphaton." In *Oxford Dictionary of Byzantium*, edited by Alexander Kazhdan, vol. 1, p. 19. Oxford University Press, 1991.

——. "Some Additions and Corrections to the List of Byzantine Churches and Monasteries in Thessalonica." *Revue des études byzantines* 35 (1977): 277–85.

Maguire, Henry. *The Icons of Their Bodies: Saints and Their Images in Byzantium*. Princeton University Press, 2000.

Majeska, George P. *Russian Travelers to Constantinople in the Fourteenth and Fifteenth Centuries*. Dumbarton Oaks Studies 19. Dumbarton Oaks, 1984.

Mango, Cyril, and Ernest J. W. Hawkins, "Additional Notes." *Dumbarton Oaks Papers* 18 (1964): 299–315.

Maniate-Kokkine, Triantaphyllitsa. "Γυναίκα καὶ "ἀνδρικὰ" οἰκονομικὰ προνόμια [Women and "Male" Economic Privileges]." In *Κλητόριον εἰς μνήμην Νίκου Οἰκονομίδη* [A Banquet in Memory of Nikos Oikonomides], edited by Phlorentia Evangelatou-Notara and Triantaphyllista Maniate-Kokkine, 403–70. Banias, 2005.

Maniatis, George C. "Organization, Market Structure, and Modus Operandi of the Private Silk Industry in Tenth-Century Byzantium." *Byzantinische Zeitschrift* 53 (1999): 263–332.

Manolova, Divna. "Discourses of Science and Philosophy in the Letters of Nikephoros Gregoras." PhD Diss., Budapest, 2014.

Margarou, Elene L. *Τίτλοι και επαγγελματικά ονόματα γυναικών στο Βυζάντιο: Συμβολή στη μελέτη για τη θέση της γυναίκας στη Βυζαντινή κοινωνία*. [Titles and Professional Names of Women in Byzantium: Contribution to the Study of the Position of Women in Byzantine Society]. Kentro Byzantinon Ereunon, 2000.

Marinis, Vasileios. "The Monastery tou Libos: Architecture, Sculpture, and Liturgical Planning in Middle and Late Byzantine Constantinople." PhD diss., University of Illinois at Urbana-Champaign, 2005.

——. "Sacred Dimensions: Church Building and Ecclesiastical Practice." In *The Cambridge Companion to Constantinople*, edited by Sarah Bassett, 180–99. Cambridge Companions to the Ancient World. Cambridge University Press, 2022.

——. "Tombs and Burials in the Monastery tou Libos in Constantinople." *Dumbarton Oaks Papers* 63 (2009):147–66.

Marsengill, Katherine. *Portraits and Icons: Between Reality and Spirituality in Byzantine Art*. Studies in Byzantine History and Civilization 5. Brepols, 2013.

Martínez Manzano, Teresa. "Prontuario para una abadesa: El Escur. Φ III 11 e Irene Cumno (con una propuesta de la escritura inédita de Mateo Blastares)." *Byzantinische Zeitschrift* 114 (2021): 269–324.

Matschke, Klaus Peter, and Franz Tinnefeld. *Die Gesellschaft im späten Byzanz: Gruppen, Strukturen und Lebensformen*. Böhlau, 2001.

Maxwell, Kathleen. "Another Lectionary of the 'Atelier' of the Palaiologina, Vat. Gr. 352." *Dumbarton Oaks Papers* 37 (1983): 47–54

Melichar, Petra. *Empresses of Late Byzantium: Foreign Brides, Mediators and Pious Women*. Lang, 2019.

——. "Imperial Women as Emissaries, Intermediaries, and Conciliators in the Palaiologan Era." *Jahrbuch der Österreichischen Byzantinistik* 67 (2017): 103–12.

Melicharová, Petra. "Crown, Veil and Halo: Confronting Ideals of Royal Female Sanctity in the West and in the Byzantine East in Late Middle Ages (13th–14th century)." *Byzantion* 77 (2007): 315–44.

Melvani, Nicholas. "The Duplication of the Double Monastery of Christ Philanthropos in Constantinople." *Revue des études byzantines* 74 (2016): 361–84.

——. "The Last Century of the Chora Monastery: A New Look at the Tomb Monuments." *Byzantinische Zeitschrift* 114 (2021): 1219–39.

——. *Late Byzantine Sculpture*. Studies in the Visual Cultures of the Middle Ages 6. Turnhout: Brepols, 2013.

——. "The Monument of a Palaiologina and the Monastery of Kyra Martha in Constantinople." *Arkeoloji ve Sanat Dergisi* 155 (2017): 161–74.

Meyendorff, John. *Byzantine Hesychasm: Historical, Theological and Social Problems*. Variorum Reprints, 1974.

——. *Introduction à l'étude de Grégoire Palamas*. Seuil, 1959.

Mitsiou, Ekaterini. "Aspekte der Wirtschafts- und Sozialgeschichte des späten Byzanz in den Akten des Patriarchatsregisters." *Historicum* 96 (2008): 32–42.

——. "Byzantine Monastic Space: Selection, Modification and Configuration Patterns." In *Community and Seclusion: Defining the Religious Life in the South Asian Traditions, in Buddhism, in Eastern and Western Christianity*, edited by Mirko M. Breitenstein and Gert Melville, 175–98. Vita Regularis 79. LIT, 2021.

——. "Byzanz. Monastischer Raum und Raumordnung." In *Geist und Gestalt: Monastische Raumkonzepte als Ausdrucksformen religiöser Leitideen*, edited by Gert Melville and Jörg Sonntag, 197–218. Vita Regularis 69. LIT, 2016.

——. "Das Doppelkloster des Patriarchen Athanasios I. in Konstantinopel: Historisch-prosopographische und wirtschaftliche Beobachtungen." *Jahrbuch der Österreichischen Byzantinistik* 58 (2008): 87–106.

——. "Das Leben der Kirche von Konstantinopel im Spiegel des Patriarchatsregisters: Zwischen Ideal und Devianz—Mönche, Kleriker, Laien, Konvertiten, Häretiker und Zauberer." *Ostkirchliche Studien* 58 (2009) 208–25.

——. "Die Dominikaner als Experten in der Romania (13.–14. Jahrhundert)." In *Praktiken und Räume des Wissens. Expertenkulturen in Geschichte und Gegenwart*, edited by Marian Füssel et al., 43–53. Göttingen 2019.

——. "Die Netzwerke einer kulturellen Begegnung: Byzantinische und lateinische Klöster in Konstantinopel im 13. und 14. Jh." In *Abrahams Erbe: Konkurrenz, Konflikt und Koexistenz der Religionen im europäischen Mittelalter*, edited by Klaus Oschema, Ludger Lieb, and Johannes Heil, 359–72. Das Mittelalter: Beihefte 2. De Gruyter, 2015

——. "'Ευλογίες': Ταπεινά προσκυνηματικά αναμνηστικά ανεκτίμητης αξίας ['Eulogiai': Humble but Priceless Pilgrimage Memorabilia]." In *Byzantium Without Glamour: Humble Objects and Their Usage in Everyday Life of the Byzantines*, edited in Anastasia Yiangaki and Angeliki Panopoulou, 195–229. Ethniko Idryma Ereunon, 2018.

——. "Female Monastic Communities in Byzantium and the Role of Silence." In *De monialibus in byzantino orbe: Essays on Byzantine Women Monasticism*, edited by Barbara Crostini Lappin and Rosa Maria Parrinello. *Rivista di storia del cristianesimo* 15, no. 1 (2018): 57–70.

——. "Female Monastic Space and Patronage in Late Byzantine Constantinople." In *Women and Monasticism in the Medieval Eastern Mediterranean: Decoding a Cultural Map*, edited by Eleonora Kountoura Galaki and Ekaterini Mitsiou, 365–81. Ethniko Idryma Ereunon, 2019.

——. "Historisch-Geographisches aus dem Patriarchatsregister: Angaben zu den konstantinopolitanischen Klöstern." In *Junge Römer—Neue Griechen*, edited by Mihailo Popović and Johannes Preiser-Kapeller, 141–65. Phoibos, 2008.

——. "Mobile Criminals: Crime and Punishment in Thirteenth-Century Byzantine Epirus." In *Microstructures and Mobility in Byzantium*, edited by Claudia Rapp and Jannis Stouraitis, 117–35. Moving Byzantium Series. Vandenhoeck & Ruprecht, 2024.

——. "The Monastery of Kecharitomene and the Contribution of the Assumptionists to the Study of Female Monasticism in Byzantium." In *L'apport des Assomptionnistes français aux études byzantines: Une approche critique. Actes du colloque de Bucarest, 25–27 septembre 2014*, edited by Marie-Hélène Blanchet and Ionut A. Tudorie, 327–44. Archives de l'Orient Chrétien 21. Institut français d'études byzantines, 2017.

——. "The Monastery of Sosandra: A Contribution to Its History, Dedication and Localisation." *Bulgaria Mediaevalis* 2 (2011): 665–83.

——. "Networks of Nicaea: 13th Century Socio-Economic Ties, Structures and Prosopography." In *Liquid and Multiple: Individuals and Identities in the Thirteenth-Century Aegean*, edited by Guillaume Saint-Guillan and Dionysios Stathakopoulos, 91–104. ACHCByz, 2012.

Mitsiou, Ekaterini, and Johannes Preiser-Kapeller. "Church and Religion." In *Brill's New Pauly Supplements II—Volume 10: History and Culture of Byzantium*, edited by John N. Dillon, translated by Duncan A. Smart, 251–79. Brill, 2020.

——. "Moving Hands: Types and Scales of Labour Mobility in the Late Medieval Eastern Mediterranean (1200–1500 CE)." In *Micro-Spatial Histories of Global Labour*, edited by Anne Gerritsen and Christian De Vito, 29–67. Palgrave Mcmillan, 2017.

Morris, Rosemary. *Monks and Laymen in Byzantium, 843–1118*. Cambridge University Press, 1995.

Morrisson, Cécile, and Jean-Claude Cheynet. "Prices and Wages in the Byzantine World." In *The Economic History of Byzantium: From the Seventh through the Fifteenth Century*, edited by Angeliki E. Laiou, vol. 2, pp. 815–78. Dumbarton Oaks Studies 39. Dumbarton Oaks, 2002.

Mouriki, Doula. "Portraits of St. Theodosia in Five Sinai Icons." In *Θυμίαμα στη μνήμη της Λασκαρίνας Μπούρα* [Incense in the Memory of Laskarina Boura], 213–19. Benaki Museum, 1994.

Moutsopoulos, Nikolaos K. *Οι βυζαντινές εκκλησίες της Άρτας* [The Byzantine Churches of Arta]. Parateretes, 2002.

Müller-Wiener, Wolfgang. *Bildlexikon zur Topographie Istanbuls: Byzantion-Konstantinupolis-Istanbul bis zum Beginn des 17. Jahrhunderts*. Wasmuth, 1977.

Mullett, Margaret E. "Aristocracy and Patronage in the Literary Circles of Comnenian Constantinople." In *The Byzantine Aristocracy: IX to XIII Centuries*, edited by Michael Angold, 173–201. British Archaeological Reports, International Series 221. British Archaeological Reports, 1984.

——. "Founders, Refounders, Second Founders, Patrons." In *Founders and Refounders of Byzantine Monasteries*, edited by Margaret Mullett, 1–27. Belfast Byzantine Enterprises, 2007.

Nelson, Robert S. *Theodore Hagiopetrites: A Late Byzantine Scribe and Illuminator*. Österreichische Akademie der Wissenschaften, 1991.

Nelson, Robert S., and John Lowden. "The Palaeologina Group: Additional Manuscripts and New Questions." *Dumbarton Oaks Papers* 45 (1991): 59–68.

Newman, Mark E. J., Albert-Laszlo Barabási, and Duncan J. Watts. *The Structure and Dynamics of Networks*. Princeton University Press, 2006.

Neyzi, Elif. "Monasticism in Late Byzantine Constantinople (1261–1453): Urban, Social, and Institutional History." PhD diss., University of Edinburgh, 2024.

Nicol, Donald M. *The Byzantine Family of Kantakouzenos ca. 1100–1460: A Genealogical and Prosopographical Study*. Dumbarton Oaks, 1968.

——. *The Byzantine Lady: Ten Portraits 1250–1500*. Cambridge University Press, 1994.

——. "The Byzantine Reaction to the Second Council of Lyons, 1274." In *Studies in Church History*, edited by Geoffrey John Cuming and Derek Baker, 113–46. Cambridge University Press, 1971.

——. "The Greeks and the Union of the Churches: The Preliminaries to the Second Council of Lyons, 1261–1274." In *Medieval Studies Presented to Aubrey Gwynn, S.J.*, edited by John A. Watt, John B. Morrall, and Francis Xavier Martin, 454–80. The Three Candles, 1961.

——. *The Last Centuries of Byzantium: 1261–1453*. Hart-Davies, 1972.

Nikolaou, Katerina. *Η γυναίκα στη μέση βυζαντινή εποχή: Κοινωνικά πρότυπα και καθημερινός βίος στα αγιολογικά κείμενα* [The Woman in the Middle Byzantine Period: Social Models and Everyday Life in the Hagiographical Texts]. Ethniko Idryma Ereunon, 2005.

Nousia, Fevronia. "Theodora Raoulaina's Autograph Codex Vat. gr. 1899 and Aelius Aristides." In *Byzantine Commentaries on Ancient Greek Texts, 12th–15th Centuries*, edited by Baukje van den Berg et al., 339–359. Cambridge University Press, 2022.

Nystazopoulou-Pelekidou, Maria G. *Βυζαντινή διπλωματική: Τα έγγραφα των δημοσίων λειτουργών* [Byzantine Diplomatics: The Documents of the Civil Servants]. Banias, 2014.

——. "Τὰ πλοῖα τῆς Μονῆς Πάτμου (11ος–13ος αἰώνας)." In *Ι. Μονή Αγ. Ιωάννου του Θεολόγου: 900 χρόνια ιστορικής μαρτυρίας (1088–1988)* [Holy Monastery of St. John the Theologian: 900 Years of Historical Testimony (1088–1988)], edited by Athanasios D. Komines, 93–114. Etaireia Byzantinon kai Metabyzantinon Meleton, 1989.

Oikonomides, Nicolas. "The Holy Icon as an Asset." *Dumbarton Oaks Papers* 45 (1991): 35–44.

——. *Hommes d'affaires grecs et latins à Constantinople (XIIIe-XVe siècles)*. Institut d'Etudes Médiévales, 1979.

——. "The Monastery of Patmos and Its Economic Functions (11th–12th Centuries)." In *Social and Economic Life in Byzantium*, edited by Nicolas Oikonomides, 1–17. Variorum Reprints, 2004.

——. "Theodora δέσποινα τῶν Βουλγάρων in a Prostagma of Michael IX (September 1318)." *Byzantine Studies/Études Byzantines* 5 (1978): 201–11.

Oltean, Daniel. *Devenir moine à Byzance: coutumes sociales, règles monastiques et rituels liturgiques*. Orientalia Lovaniensia 291. Peeters, 2020.

Orlandos, Anastasios. "Ὁ τάφος τῆς Ἁγίας Θεοδώρας [The Grave of St. Theodora]" *Archeion Byzantinon Mnemeion Ellados* 2 (1936): 105–15.

——. *Μοναστηριακὴ Ἀρχιτεκτονική* [Monastic Architecture]. Hestia, 1958.

Ostrogorsky, Georg. "Das Chrysobull des Despoten Johannes Orsini für das Kloster von Lykusada." *Zbornik Radova Vizantološkog Instituta* 11 (1968): 205–13.

——. *Pour l'histoire de la féodalité byzantine*. Translated by Henri Grégoire and Paul Lemerle. Corpus Bruxellense Historiae Byzantinae: Subsidia 1. L'Institut de philologie et d'histoire orientales et slaves, 1954.

Ousterhout, Robert. "Water and Healing in Constantinople: Reading the Architectural Remains." In *Life Is Short, Art Long: The Art of Healing in Byzantium: New Perspectives*, edited by Tanman Gülru, and Brigitte Pitarakis, 6577. İstanbul Research Institute, 2018.

Pahlitzsch, Johannes. "Zum Loskauf von griechischen Gefangenen und Sklaven in spätbyzantinischer Zeit. Formen und Akteure." *In Gefangenenloskauf im Mittelmeerraum: Ein interreligiöser Vergleich. Akten der Tagung vom 19. bis 21. September 2013 an der Universität Paderborn*, edited by Heike Grieser and Nicole Priesching, 123–42. Olms, 2015.

Papachryssanthou, Dionysia. *Ο αθωνικός μοναχισμός: αρχές και οργάνωση* [Athonite Monasticism: Principles and Organization]. Morphotiko Hidryma Ethnikes Trapezes, 1992.

Papadopoulos-Kerameus, Athanasios. "Ἡ ἐν τῷ νησίῳ Σωζοπόλεως βασιλικὴ μονὴ Ἰωάννου τοῦ Προδρόμου καὶ ἡ τύχη τῆς βιβλιοθήκης αὐτῆς [The Royal Monastery of John the Baptist on the Island of Sozopolis and the Fate of its Library]." *Vizantijskij Vremmenik* 7 (1900): 661–95.

Papadopoulou, Barbara. N. *Η Βυζαντινή Άρτα και τα μνημεία της* [Byzantine Arta and Its Monuments]. Tameio Archaiologikon Poron, 2002.

Papadopulos, Averkios Th. *Versuch einer Genealogie der Palaiologen 1259–1453*. Pilger-Druckerei, 1938.

Papagianne, Eleutheria. "Οι κληρικοί των βυζαντινών γυναικείων μονών και το άβατο [The Clergy of the Byzantine Nunneries and the Abaton." *Byzantiaka* 6 (1986): 75–94.

——. "Η αγορά των ακινήτων στην Κωνσταντινούπολη σύμφωνα με τις αποφάσεις του πατριάρχη Ματθαίου Α΄ [The Real Estate Market in Constantinople According to the Decisions of Patriarch Matthew I]." In *Money and Markets in the Palaiologoi Era*, edited by Nikolaos G. Moschonas, 145–55. Ethniko Idryma Ereunon, 2003.

Papamastorakes, Titos. "Επιτύμβιες παραστάσεις κατά τη μέση και ύστερη βυζαντινή περίοδο [Funerary Representations in the Middle and Late Byzantine period]." *Deltion tes Christianikes Archaiologikes Etaireias* 19 (1996–1997): 285–304.

Papazotos, Thanases. *Η Βέροια και οι ναοί της, 11ος–18ος αιώνας* [Berroia and Its Churches, 11th–18th Century]. Tameio Archaiologikon Poron, 1994.

Parani, Maria. "'The Joy of the Most Holy Mother of God the Hodegetria the One in Constantinople': Revisiting the Famous Representation at the Blacherna Monastery, Arta." In *Viewing Greece: Cultural and Political Agency in the Medieval and Early Modern Mediterranean*, edited by Sharon Gerstel, 113–45. Brepols, 2016.

——. "Negotiating Gender Identity Through the Visual Arts." In *The Routledge Handbook on Gender and Sexuality in Byzantium*, edited by Mati Meyer and Charis Messis, 419–42. Routledge, 2024.

Parpulov, Georgi. "Lincoln College MS, Gr. 35: New Description." *Medieval Manuscripts in Oxford Libraries*. Accessed August 31, 2024, https://medieval.bodleian.ox.ac.uk/catalog/manuscript_16083.

——. "Ornament and Status: Three Early Palaeologan Illuminated Manuscripts." *Estudios bizatinos* 11 (2023): 101–16.

——. *Toward a History of Byzantine Psalters ca. 850–1350 AD*. Plovdiv, 2014.

Patedakes, Manoles S. "Οι διαθήκες των πατριαρχών της πρώιμης Παλαιολόγειας περιόδου (1255–1309) [The Wills of the Patriarchs of the Early Palaiologan Period (1255–1309)]." *Thesaurismata* 37 (2007): 65–86.

Patlagean, Évelyne. *Ο ελληνικός Μεσαίωνας: Βυζάντιο, 9ος–15ος αιώνας* [The Greek Middle Ages: Byzantium, 9th–15th Century]. Traslated by Despoina Lampada. Patakes, 2014.

——. "L'histoire de la femme déguisée en moine et l'évolution de la sainteté féminine à Byzance." *Studi medievali* 17, no. 2 (1976): 597–623.

——. "Transactions immobilières à Thessalonique vers 1260–vers 1430." In *Money and Markets in the Palaiologoi Era*. Edited by Nikolaos G. Moschonas, 133–44. Ethniko Idryma Ereunon, 2003.

Patrich, Yosef. *Sabas, Leader of Palestinian Monasticism: A Comparative Study in Eastern Monasticism, Fourth to Seventh Centuries*. Dumbarton Oaks, 1995.

Pazaras, Theochares. *Ανάγλυφες σαρκοφάγοι και επιτάφιες πλάκες της μέσης και ύστερης βυζαντινής περιόδου στην Ελλάδα* [Relief Sarcophaguses and Tombstones of the Middle and Late Byzantine Period in Greece]. Tameio Archaiologikon Poron, 1988.

Peers, Glenn. *Sacred Shock: Framing Visual Experience in Byzantium*. Pennsylvania State University Press, 2004.

Pérez Martín, Inmaculada. *El patriarca Gregorio de Chipre (ca. 1240–1290) y la transmision de los textos clasicos en Bizancio*. Consejo Superior de Investigaciones Científicas, 1996.

——. "Irene Cumno y el 'taller de la Paleologuina.'" *Scrittura e Civilta* 9 (1995): 223–34.

——. "L'Escorial Ω-II-13 (gr. 530) et sa copiste Anna." *Revue des études byzantines* 83 (forthcoming, 2025).

——. "Le conflit de l'Union des Églises (1274) et son reflet dans l'enseignement supérieur de Constantinople." *Byzantinoslavica* 56 (1995): 411–22.

Petanovič, Luka. *Elena: L'ultima emperatrice bizantina*. Donne d'Oriente e d'Occidente 18. Jaca, 2006.

Petit, Louis. "La profession de foi de l'imperatrice Théodora." *Echos d'Orient* 18 (1916/1919): 286–87.

Piault, Colette. *Familles et biens en Grece et a Chypre*. Harmattan, 1985.

Pitouli, Sofia. *A Vlach Nun and Her Thirteenth-Century Monastery*. Master's thesis, University of California, 2021.

Politis, Linos, "Eine Schreiberschule im Kloster τῶν Ὁδηγῶν." *Byzantinische Zeitschrift* 51 (1958): 261–87.

Popović, Svetlana. "The 'Trapeza' in Cenobitic Monasteries: Architectural and Spiritual Contexts." *Dumbarton Oaks Papers* 52 (1998): 281–303.

Pratsch, Thomas. *Theodoros Studites (759–826): Zwischen Dogma und Pragma*. Lang, 1998.

Prazniak, Roxann. *Sudden Appearances: The Mongol Turn in Commerce, Belief, and Art*. University of Hawaii Press, 2019.

Preiser-Kapeller, Johannes. *Der Episkopat im späten Byzanz: Ein Verzeichnis der Metropoliten und Bischöfe des Patriarchats von Konstantinopel in der Zeit von 1204 bis 1453*. Müller, 2008.

——. "Heptaskalon und weitere Anlegestellen am Goldenen Horn." In *Die byzantinischen Häfen Konstantinopels*, edited by Falko Daim, 99–108. Byzanz zwischen Orient und Okzident 4. Römisch-Germanischen Zentralmuseums, 2016.

——. "Mapping Networks of Women in the Late Medieval Eastern Mediterranean: Concepts, Tools and Selected Results." In *Women and Monasticism in the Medieval Eastern Mediterranean: Decoding a Cultural Map*, edited by Eleonora Kountoura Galaki and Ekaterini Mitsiou, 349–63. Ethniko Idryma Ereunon, 2019.

Psilakes, Nikos. *Μοναστήρια και ερημητήρια της Κρήτης* [Monasteries and Hermitages of Crete]. 2 vols. Archiepiskope Kretes, 1992–1993.

Puech, Vincent. "The Byzantine Aristocracy and the Union of the Churches (1274–1283): A Prosopographical Approach." In *Liquid and Multiple: Individuals and Identities in the Thirteenth-Century Aegean*, edited by Guillaume Saint-Guillan and Dionysios Stathakopoulos, 45–54. ACHCByz, 2012.

——. "La refondation religieuse de Constantinople par Michel VIII Paléologue (1261–1282): un acte politique." In *Religion et société urbaine au Moyen-Âge: Études offertes à Jean-Louis Biget par ses anciens élèves*, edited by Patrick Boucheron and Jacques Chiffoleau, 351–62. Publications de la Sorbonne, 2000.

——. "L'aristocratie et le pouvoir à Byzance au XIIIe siècle (1204–1310)." 2 vols. PhD diss., Université de Versailles-Saint-Quentin-en-Yvelines, 2000.

Radle, Gabriel. "The Veiling of Women in Byzantium: Liturgy, Hair, and Identity in a Medieval Rite of Passage." *Speculum* 94 (2019): 1070–1115.

Rapp, Claudia. "Figures of Female Sanctity: Byzantine Edifying Manuscripts and Their Audience." *Dumbarton Oaks Papers* 50 (1996): 313–44.

Rawlings, Craig, et al. *Network Analysis: Integrating Social Network Theory, Method, and Application with R*. Structural Analysis in the Social Sciences 52. Cambridge University Press, 2023.

Reuter, Timothy. "Nobles and Others: The Social and Cultural Expression of Power Relations in the Middle Ages." In *Nobles and Nobility in Medieval Europe: Concepts, Origins, Transformations*, edited by Anne J. Duggan, 85–98. Boydell Press, 2000.

Rhoby, Andreas. "Poetry on Commission in Late Byzantium (13th–15th Century)." In *A Companion to Byzantine Poetry*, edited by Wolfram Hörandner et al., 264–304. Companions to the Byzantine World 4. Brill, 2019.

Riehle, Alexander. "Authorship and Gender (and) Identity: Women's Writing in the Middle Byzantine Period." In *The Author in Middle Byzantine Literature: Modes, Functions, and Identities*, edited by Aglaia Pizzone, 245–62. Gruyter, 2014.

——. "Epistolography, Social Exchange and Intellectual Discourse (1261–1453)." In *A Companion to the Intellectual Life of the Palaeologan Period*, edited by Sofia Kotzabassi, 211–51. Brill, 2023.

——. "Funktionen der byzantinischen Epistolographie: Studien zu den Briefen und Briefsammlungen des Nikephoros Chumnos (ca. 1260–1327)." PhD diss., Ludwig-Maximilians-Universität, 2011.

——. "*Καί σε προστάτιν ἐν αὐτοῖς τῆς αὐτῶν ἐπιγράψομεν σωτηρίας*: Theodora Raulaina als Stifterin und Patronin." In *Female Founders in Byzantium and Beyond*, edited by Lioba Theis, Margaret Mullett, and Michael Grünbart, 299–315. Böhlau, 2014.

Rigo, Antonio. "Il metropolita di Pentapolis Natanaele a Costantinopoli (fine del XIV secolo)." In *Γαληνοτάτη: Τιμή στη Χρύσα Μαλτέζου* [Serenissima: Honour to Chrysa Maltezou], edited by Gogo K. Varzeliote and Kostas G. Tsiknakes, 697–707. Benaki Museum, 2013.

——. "L'assemblea generale athonita del 1344 su un gruppo di monaci bogomili." *Cristianesimo nella storia* 5 (1984): 475–506.

——. "La direction spirituelle des moniales à Byzance (XIIIe-XVe siècles). In *Women and Monasticism in the Medieval Eastern Mediterranean: Decoding a Cultural Map*, edited by Eleonora Kountoura Galaki and Ekaterini Mitsiou, 283–300 and plate 1 at 385. Ethniko Idryma Ereunon, 2019.

——. *Mistici bizantini*. Einaudi, 2008.

——. "Nota sulla dottrina ascetico-spirituale di Teolepto Metropolita di Filadefia (1250/51–1322)." *Rivista di Studi Byzantini e Neoellenici* 24 (1987): 165–200.

——. "Principes et canons pour le choix des livres et la lecture dans la littérature spirituelle byzantine." *Bulgaria Mediaevalis* 3 (2012): 171–85.

Ringrose, Kathryn M. "The Byzantine Body." In *The Oxford Handbook of Women and Gender in Medieval Europe*, edited by Judith M. Bennett and Ruth Mazo Karras, 362–78. Oxford University Press, 2013.

Rizzo Nervo, Francesca. "Teodora Raoulena: Tra agiografia e politica." In *Syndesmos: Studi in onore di Rosario Anastasi*, edited by Antonio Carile et al., 147–62. Università di Catania, 1991.

Roberg, Burkhard. *Das Zweite Konzil von Lyon (1274)*. Schöningh, 1990.

——. *Die Union zwischen der griechischen und der lateinischen Kirche auf dem II. Konzil von Lyon (1274)*. Röhrscheid, 1964.

Rydén, Lennart. "The Holy Fool." In *The Byzantine Saint*, edited by Sergei Hackel, 106–13. Fellowship of St. Alban and St. Sergius, 1981.

Ryder, Edmund C. "The Despoina of the Mongols and Her Patronage at the Church of the Theotokos ton Mougoulion." *Journal of Modern Hellenism* 27 (2009–2010): 71–102.

Saint-Guillain, Guillaume. "Propriétés et bienfaiteurs de l'abbaye constantinopolitaine de Sainte-Marie du Perchay." *Thesaurismata* 41/42 (2011–2012): 9–40.

——. "Sainte-Marie du Perchay, abbaye cistercienne à Constantinople." In *Puer Apuliae: Mélanges offerts à J.-M. Martin*, edited by Enrico Cuozzo et al., 593–603. ACHCByz, 2008.

Salaville, Sévérien. "Un directeur spirituel à Byzance au début du XIVe siècle: Théolepte de Philadelphie." In *Mélanges Joseph de Ghellinck: Moyen Âge, époques moderne et contemporaine 1951*, edited by Joseph de Ghellinck, 877–78. Duculot, 1951.

Samara, Demetra. *Θεόδωρος Μουζάλων: η ζωή και το συγγραφικό έργο ενός λογίου του 13ου αιώνα* [Theodore Mouzalon: The Life and Writings of a 13th-Century Scholar]. Kentro Byzantinon Ereunon, 2018.

Samori, Francesca. "A Self-Portrait of an Unyielding Unionist: The *Historia Dogmatica* of George Metochites and the Fight for Church Unity." *Parekbolai* 12 (2022): 67–103.

Saradi-Mendelovici, Helen. "A Contribution to the Study of the Byzantine Notarial Formulas: The Infirmitas Sexus of Women and the Sc. Velleianum." *Byzantinische Zeitschrift* 83 (1990): 72–90.

Savramis, Demosthenes. *Zur Soziologie des byzantinischen Mönchtums*. Brill, 1962.

Schaeffer, Hartmut. *Die Gül Camii in Istanbul: Ein Beitrag zur mittelbyzantinischen Kirchenarchitektur Konstantinopels.* Wasmuth, 1973.

Schilbach, Erich. *Byzantinische Metrologie.* Beck, 1970.

Schmalzbauer, Gudrun. "Die Tornikioi in der Palaiologenzeit." *Jahrbuch der Österreichischen Byzantinistik* 19 (1968): 131–32.

Schreiner, Peter. "Die topographische Notiz über Konstantinopel in der Pariser Suda-Handschrift: Eine Neuinterpretation." In *AETOS: Studies in Honour of Cyril Mango,* edited by Ihor Sevcenko and Irmgard Hutter, 273–83. Teubner, 1998.

——. "Kopistinnen in Byzanz: Mit einer Anmerkung zur Schreiberin Eugenia im Par. Lat. 7560." *Rivista di Studi Bizantini e Neoellenici* N. S. 36 (1999): 35–45.

Schwingel, Markus. *Pierre Bourdieu zur Einführung.* Junius, 2011.

Seibt, Werner. "The Sons of Senek'erim Yovhannēs, the Last King of Vaspurakan." *Revue des études arméniennes* 37 (2016–2017): 119–33.

Shahar, Shulamith. *The Fourth Estate: A History of Women in the Middle Ages.* Rev. ed. Routledge, 2003

Shaw, Teresa M. *The Burden of the Flesh: Fasting and Sexuality in Early Christianity.* Fortress, 1998.

Shawcross, Teresa. "In the Name of the True Emperor: Politics of Resistance After the Palaiologan Usurpation." *Byzantinoslavica* 66 (2008): 203–27.

Shawcross, Teresa, et al. *Reading in the Byzantine Empire and Beyond.* Cambridge University Press, 2018.

Sherry, Lee Frances. "The Poem of Maria Komnene Palaiologina to the Virgin and Mother of God, the Chorine." *Cahiers archaeologiques* 43 (1995): 181–82.

Shields, Rob. *Lefebvre, Love and Struggle: Spatial Dialectics.* Routledge, 1999.

Shukurov, Rustam. *The Byzantine Turks, 1204–1461.* Brill, 2016.

Sigala, Maria Z. "Η Παναγία η Οδηγήτρια η Εννιαμερίτισσα στη Χάλκη της Δωδεκανήσου (1367) [The Virgin Mary Hodegetria the Nine-Days-Old in Chalki of Dodecanese (1367)]." *Archaiologikon Deltion* 55 (2000): 329–81.

Silvas, Anna M. *The Asketikon of St. Basil the Great.* Oxford University Press, 2005.

——. *Macrina the Younger: Philosopher of God.* Brepols, 2008.

Simon, Dieter. "Vertragliche Weitergabe des Familienvermögens in Byzanz." In *Hommes et richesses dans l'Empire byzantin*, edited by Vassiliki Kravari et al., vol. 2, 183–96. Lethielleux, 1991.

Smyrlis, Kostis. *La fortune des grands monastères byzantins: Fin du X*[e]*-milieu du XIV*[e] *siècle.* Centre de Recherche d'Histoire et Civilisation de Byzance, Monographies 21. ACHCByz, 2006.

——. "The Management of Monastic Estates: The Evidence of the Typika." *Dumbarton Oaks Papers* 56 (2002): 245–61.

——. "The State, The Land, and Private Property: Confiscating Monastic and Church Properties in the Palaiologan Period." In *Church and Society in Late Byzantium,* edited by Dimitar G. Angelov, 58–87. Medieval Institute Publications, 2009.

——. "Τα μοναστήρια στο Ύστερο Βυζάντιο: Οικονομικός ρόλος και σχέσεις με το κράτος (13ος–15ος αιώνας)." In *Μοναστήρια, οικονομία και πολιτική: Από τους μεσαιωνικούς στους νεώτερους χρόνους* [Monasteries, Economy, and Politics from Medieval to Modern Times], edited by Elias Kolobos, 53–68. Panepistemiakes Ekdoseis Kretes, 2012.

Sode, Claudia. *Jerusalem—Konstantinopel—Rom: Die Viten des Michael Synkellos und der Brüder Theodoros und Theophanes Graptoi.* Altertumswissenschaftliches Kolloquium 4. Steiner, 2001.

Soule, Warren Becket. "The Stauropegial Monastery." *Orientalia Christiana Periodica* 66 (2000): 147–67.

Soustal, Peter. *Makedonien, südlicher Teil.* Tabula Imperii Byzantini 11. Österreichische Akademie der Wissenschaften, 2022.

——. *Thrakien (Thrake, Rodope und Haimmimontos).* Tabula Imperii Byzantini 6. Österreichische Akademie der Wissenschaften, 1991

Spatharakis, Iohannes. *The Portrait in Byzantine Illuminated Manuscripts.* Brill, 1976.

Spatharakis, Ioannis. *Dated Byzantine Wall Paintings of Crete.* Alexandros, 2001.

Spearing, Elizabeth. *Medieval Writings on Female Spirituality.* Penguin, 2002.

Stathakopoulos, Dionysios. "I Seek Not My Own: Is There a Female Mode of Charity and Patronage?" In *Female Founders in Byzantium and Beyond,* edited by Lioba Theis, Margaret Mullett, and Michael Grünbart, 383–97. Böhlau, 2014.

Stauridou-Zaphraka, Alkmene. "Το Κοντοσκάλιο και το Επτάσκαλο: Συμβολή στη Μελέτη των λιμανιών της Κωνσταντινούπολης κατά την Ύστερη περίοδο [Kontoskalion and Eptaskalo: A Contribution to the Study of the Ports of Constantinople in the Late Period]." *Byzantina* 13 (1985): 1303–28.

——. "Η Μονή Μωσελέ και η Μονή των Ανθεμίου [The Monastery Mosele and the Monastery of Anthemios]." *Byzantina* 12 (1983): 66–92.

Stefec, Rudolf. "Beiträge zur Urkundentätigkeit epirotischer Herrscher in den Jahren 1205–1318." *Nea Rhome* 11 (2014): 249–370.

——. "Zur Schnittdekoration kretischer Handschriften." In *Miscellanea Bibliothecae Apostolicae Vaticanae* 19 (2012): 501–33.

Stickler, Günter. *Manuel Philes und seine Psalmenmetaphrase.* VWGÖ, 1992.

Stolfi, Anna. "La biografia di Irene-Eulogia Cumnena Paleologhina (1291–1355): Un riesame." *Cristianesimo nella storia* 20 (1999): 1–40.

Stolte, Bernhard H. "Law for Founders." In *Founders and Refounders of Byzantine Monasteries,* edited by Margaret Mullett, 121–39. Belfast Byzantine Enterprises, 2007.

Studer-Karlen, Manuela. "Mise en scene multiple et lecture simultanée: La 'création' d'une sainte." In *Parerga: Pour Victor I. Stoichita,* 79–94. Droz, 2022.

——. "Walking Through the Narthex: The Rite in the Chora." In *Biography of a Landmark. The Chora Monastery and Kariye Camii in Constantinople/Istanbul from Late Antiquity to the 21st Century,* edited by Manuela Studer-Karlen, 31–73. Mediterranean Art Histories Series 7. Brill, 2023.

Sykoutres, Ioannis. "Περὶ τὸ σχίσμα τῶν Ἀρσενιατῶν [On the Arsenite Schism]." *Hellenika* 2 (1929): 267–332; *Hellenika* 3 (1930): 15–44; and *Hellenika* 5 (1932): 107–26.

Szell, Michael, et al. "Trade, Conflict and Sentiments: Multirelational Organization of Large-Scale Social Networks." *PNAS* 107, no. 31 (2010): 13636–641.

Talbot, Alice-Mary. "A Comparison of the Monastic Experience of Byzantine Men and Women." *Greek Orthodox Theological Review* 30 (1985): 1–20.

——. "Affirmative Action in the 13th Century: An Act of John Apokaukos Concerning the Blachernitissa Monastery in Arta." In *Philellen: In Honour of Robert Browning,* edited by Costas N. Constantinides et al., 399–409. Instituto ellenice di studi bizantini e postbizantini di Venezia, 1996.

——. "Bluestocking Nuns: Intellectual Life in the Convents of Late Byzantium." In *Okeanos: Essays presented to Ihor Sevcenko on his Sixtieth Birthday by his Colleagues and Students,* edited by Cyril Mango and Omeljan Pritsak, 604–18. Harvard Ukranian Studies 7. Harvard Ukrainian Research Institute, 1983.

——. "Building Activity in Constantinople Under Andronikos II: The Role of Women Patrons in the Construction and Restoration of Monasteries." In *Byzantine Constantinople: Monuments, Topography and Everyday Life*, edited by Nevra Necipoğlu, 329–43. Brill, 2001.

——. "The Conversion of Byzantine Monasteries from Male to Female and Vice-Versa." In Πολυπλευρος Νους*: Miscellanea für Peter Schreiner zu seinem 60. Geburtstag mit einem Geleitwort von Herbert Hunger*, edited by Cordula Scholz and Georgios Makris, 360–64. Byzantinisches Archiv 19. Saur, 2000.

——. "Cult and Pilgrimage: The Translation of Relics in the Palaiologan Period." In *Pilgrimage of Life: Studies in Honour of Professor René Gothóni*, edited by Riku Hämäläinen, 271–82. Maahenki, 2010.

——. "Empress Theodora Palaiologina, Wife of Michael VIII." *Dumbarton Oaks Papers* 46 (1992): 295–303.

——. "Epigrams in Context: Metrical Inscriptions on Art and Architecture of the Palaiologan Era." *Dumbarton Oaks Papers* 53 (1999): 75–90.

——. "Epigrams of Manuel Philes on the Theotokos tes Peges and Its Art." *Dumbarton Oaks Papers* 48 (1994): 135–65.

——. "Female Patronage in the Palaiologan Era: Icons, Minor Arts and Manuscripts." In *Female Founders in Byzantium and Beyond*, edited by Lioba Theis, Margaret Mullett, and Michael Grünbart, 259–74. Böhlau, 2014.

——. "Founders Choices: Monastery Site Selection in Byzantium." In *Founders and Refounders of Byzantine Monsteries*, edited by Margaret Mullett, 43–62. Belfast Byzantine Enterprises, 2007.

——. "Holy Springs and Pools in Constantinople." In *Istanbul and Water*, edited by Paul Magdalino and Nina Ergin, 161–74. Peeters, 2015.

——. "Kyra Martha Nunnery." In *Oxford Dictionary of Byzantium*, edited by Alexander Kazhdan, vol. 2, p. 1163. Oxford University Press, 1991.

——. "Literati and the Revival of Hagiography in the Early Palaiologan Period (1261–1328)." In *Κυπριακή Αγιολογία. Πρακτικά Α΄ ΔιεΘνούς Συνεδρίου* [Cypriot Hagiography. Acts of the First International Symposium], edited by Theodoros Giagkou and Chrysostomos Nasses, 435–46. Politistike Akademia "Hagios Epiphanios," 2012.

——. "Mealtime in Monasteries: The Culture of the Byzantine Refectory." In *Eat, Drink, and Be Merry (Luke 12:19): Food and Wine in Byzantium. Papers of the 37th Annual Spring Symposium of Byzantine Studies, in Honour of Professor A. A. M. Bryer*, edited by Leslie Brubaker and Kallirroe Linardou, 109–23. Society for the Promotion of Byzantine Studies Publications 13. Ashgate, 2007.

——. "Old Age in Byzantium." *Byzantinische Zeitschrift* 77 (1984): 267–78.

——. "Old Wine in New Bottles: The Rewriting of Saints' Lives in the Palaeologan Period." In *The Twilight of Byzantium: Aspects of Cultural and Religious History in the Late Byzantine Empire*, edited by Slobodan Ćurčić and Doula Mouriki, 15–26. Princeton University Press, 2019.

——. "Personal Poverty in Byzantine Monasticism: Ideals and Reality." *Travaux et Mémoires* 16 (2010): 829–41.

——. "The Restoration of Constantinople Under Michael VIII." *Dumbarton Oaks Papers* 47 (1993): 243–61.

——. *Studies in Byzantine Monasticism*. Routledge, 2024

——. *Varieties of Monastic Experience in Byzantium, 800–1453*. University of Notre Dame Press, 2019.

——. "Women's Space in Byzantine Monasteries." *Dumbarton Oaks Papers* 52 (1998): 113–27.

Talbot, Alice-Mary, and Stamatina McGrath. "Monastic Onomastics." In *Monastères, images, pouvoirs et société à Byzance*, edited by Michel Kaplan, 89–120. Éditions de la Sorbonne, 2015.

Taxides, Elias. *Μάξιμος Πλανούδης: Συμβολή στη μελέτη του corpus των επιστολών του* [Maximos Planoudes: Contribution to the Study of the Corpus of His Letters]. Byzantine Texts and Studies 58. Kentro Byzantinon Ereunon, 2012.

Taxidis, Ilias. "Public and Private Libraries in Byzantium." In *A Companion to the Intellectual Life of the Palaeologan Period*, edited by Sofia Kotzabassi, 458–490. Brill, 2023.

Teleles, Ioannes. *Μετεωρολογικά φαινόμενα και κλίμα* [Meteorological Phenomena and Climate]. Ponemata 5. Academy of Athens, 2004.

Teteriatnikov, Natalia. "The Place of the Nun Melania (the Lady of the Mongols) in the Deesis Program of the Inner Narthex of Chora, Constantinople." *Cahiers archeologiques* 43 (1995): 163–80.

Theotekne (Hagiostephanitissa). *Ἡ θέση τῆς μοναχῆς στὴν Ὀρθόδοξη Ἐκκλησία* [The Position of the Nun in the Orthodox Church]. Hiera Mone Hagiou Stephanou, 2003.

Thiermeyer, Andreas-Abraham. "Das Meterikon: Das frühe Christentum und die Frauen." *Bollettino della Badia Greca di Grottaferrata* 2 (2005): 303–5.

Thomas, John Philip. *Private Religious Foundations in the Byzantine Empire*. Dumbarton Oaks Studies 24. Dumbarton Oaks, 1987.

Tinnefeld, Franz. "Das Schisma zwischen Anhängern und Gegnern des Patriarchen Arsenios in der orthodoxen Kirche von Byzanz (1265–1310)." *Byzantinische Zeitschrift* 105 (2012): 143–65.

——. *Die Briefe des Demetrios Kydones: Themen und literarische Form*. Mainzer Veröffentlichungen zur Byzantinistik 11. Harrassowitz, 2010.

Toumpouri, Marina. "Changes and Innovation: Reassessing Thirteenth Century Byzantine Manuscript Illumination." In *Πάντα ῥεῖ: Change in Thirteenth-Century Byzantine Architecture, Art, and Material Culture*. Edited by Jenny P. Albani and Ioanna Christoforaki, 171–206. Brepols, 2022.

Treu, Max. "Manuel Holobolos." *Byzantinische Zeitschrift* 5 (1896): 538–59.

Troianos, Spyros N. *Οι πηγές του Βυζαντινού δικαίου* [The Sources of Byzantine Law]. 3rd ed. Sakkoulas, 2011.

Trone, Robert H. "A Constantinopolitan Double Monastery of the Fourteenth Century: The Philanthropic Saviour." *Byzantine Studies/Études Byzantines* 10 (1983): 81–87.

Tsamakda, Vasiliki. *A Companion to Byzantine Illustrated Manuscripts*. Brill, 2017.

Tsigaridas, Euthymios N., and Katia Loberdou-Tsigarida. *Ιερά Μεγίστη Μονή Βατοπαιδίου: Βυζαντινές εικόνες και επενδύσεις* [Great Monastery of Vatopedi: Byzantine Icons and Inlays]. Hiera Megiste Mone Batopaidiou, 2006.

Tsougarakis, Nickiphoros I. *The Latin Religious Orders in Medieval Greece, 1204–1500*. Medieval Church Studies 18. Brepols, 2012.

Turyn, Alexander. *Codices graeci Vaticani saeculis XIII et XIV scripti annorumque notis instructi*. Biblioteca Apostolica Vaticana, 1964.

Underwood, Paul A. *Kariye Djami*. Vol. 1, *Historical Introduction and Description of the Mosaics and Frescoes*. Pantheon, 1966.

——. "Notes on the Work of the Byzantine Institute in Istanbul: 1954." *Dumbarton Oaks Papers* 9–10 (1955–1956): 291–300.

Uspenskij, Porfiri. *Vostok christianskij: Istorija Afona* [The Christian East: A History of Athos]. 3 vols. Fronckevič, 1877.

van Dieten, Jan-Louis. "Der Streit in Byzanz und die Rezeption der Unio Florentina." *Ostkirchliche Studien* 39 (1990): 160–80.

van Millingen, Alexander. *Byzantine Churches in Constantinople: Their History and Architecture*. Macmillan, 1912

Verpeaux, Jean. "Les *oikeioi*: Notes d'histoire institutionnelle et sociale." *Revue des études byzantines* 23 (1965): 89–99.

——. *Nicéphore Choumnos: Homme d'état et humaniste byzantin (ca.1250/55–1327)*. Picard et Cie, 1959.

Vickers, Michael. "The Hippodrome at Thessaloniki." *Journal of Roman Studies* 62 (1972): 25–32.

Vladimir (Archimandrit). *Sistematičeskoe opisanie rukopisei Moskovskoj Sinodalnoj biblioteki* [Systematic Description of the Manuscripts of the Moscow Synodal Library]. Sinodalnaja tipografija, 1894.

Vogel, Marie, and Victor Gardthausen. *Die griechischen Schreiber des Mittelalters und der Renaissance*. Harrassowitz, 1909.

Volk, Otto. "Die byzantinischen Klosterbibliotheken von Konstantinopel, Thessalonike und Kleinasien." PhD diss., Ludwig-Maximilians-Universität, 1954.

Volk, Robert. *Gesundheitswesen und Wohltätigkeit im Spiegel der byzantinischen Klostertypika*. Miscellanea Byzantina Monacensia 28. Institut für Byzantinistik und neugriechische Philologie der Universität, 1983.

Waring, Judith Sarah. "Byzantine Monastic Libraries in the Eleventh and Twelfth Centuries." PhD diss., Queen's University of Belfast, 1999.

Wasserman, Stanley and Katherine Faust. *Social Network Analysis: Methods and Applications*. Cambridge University Press, 1999.

Weißbrod, Ursula. *"Hier liegt der Knecht Gottes": Gräber in byzantinischen Kirchen und ihr Dekor (11. bis 15. Jahrhundert) unter besonderer Berücksichtigung der Höhlenkirchen Kappadokiens*. Harrassowitz, 2003.

Werner, Ernst. "Spätbogomilisch-adamitische Spekulationen und Praktiken in religions-historischer Sicht." *Byzantine Studies* 1 (1974): 40–53.

White, Despina. "Property Rights of Women: The Changes in the Justinian Legislation Regarding the Dowry and the Parapherna." *Jahrbuch der Österreichischen Byzantinistik* 32 (1982): 539–48.

Wilson, Nigel G. "The Libraries of the Byzantine World." *Greek, Roman and Byzantine Studies* 8 (1967): 53–80.

Woodfin, Warren Theriot. *The Embodied Icon: Liturgical Vestments and Sacramental Power in Byzantium*. Oxford University Press, 2012.

Wybrew, Hugh. *The Orthodox Liturgy: The Development of the Eucharistic Liturgy in the Byzantine Rite*. SPCK, 1989. Reprint, 2013.

Xexakes, Nikolaos. "Ἰωάννης Βέκκος καὶ αἱ θεολογικαὶ ἀντιλήψεις αὐτοῦ [John Bekkos and His Theological Views]." PhD diss., University of Athens, 1981.

Yota, Élisabeth. "L'image du donateur dans les manuscrits illustrés byzantins." In *Donations et donateurs dans le monde byzantine: Actes du colloque international de l'Université de Fribourg 13–15 mars 2008*. Edited by Jean-Michel Spieser and Élisabeth Yota, 265–92. Réalités Byzantines 14. Desclée de Brouwer, 2012.

Zarras, Nektarios. *Ideology and Patronage in Byzantium: Dedicatory Inscriptions and Patron Images from Middle-Byzantine Macedonia and Thrace*. Byzantios: Studies in Byzantine History and Civilization 21. Brepols, 2023.

Zeses, Theodoros. *Γεννάδιος Β΄ Σχολάριος: Βίος, συγγράμματα, διδασκαλία* [Gennadios II Scholarios: Life, Writings, Teaching.] Analekta Blatadon 30. Patriarchikon Idryma Paterikon Meleton, 1980. Reprint, 1988.

Zhishman, Joseph von. *Das Stifterrecht (Τὸ κτητορικὸν δίκαιον) in der morgenländischen Kirche*. Hölder, 1888.

Zorzi, Niccolo. "Una copista, due copisti, nessuna copista? Teodora Raulena e i due codici attribuiti alla sua mano." *Medioevo greco: Rivista di storia e filologia bizantina* 19 (2019): 259–82.

Websites

"Coins and Seals Collection, Dumbarton Oaks." Accessed March 11, 2025, https://www.doaks.org/resources/seals.

"Euchologia-Project." Austrian Academy of Sciences, Institute for Medieval Research, Department of Byzantine Research (PI: Prof. Claudia Rapp). Accessed March 11, 2025, https://www.oeaw.ac.at/en/imafo/research/byzantine-research/communities-and-landscapes/euchologia-project.

"*ORA-LITE." Accessed March 11, 2025, https://www.cmu.edu/casos-center/research/tools/ora-lite.html.

Prosopographie der mittelbyzantinischen Zeit Online, s.v. "Theodoros Studites, no. 7574." Accessed March 11, 2025, https://www.degruyter.com/database/PMBZ/entry/PMBZ18819/html.

Thesaurus Linguae Graecae. Accessed March 11, 2025, https://stephanus.tlg.uci.edu/.

INDEX OF PLACES

This index includes place names appearing at least twice in the book. The recurrent location of Constantinople was excluded, but locations within the capital are listed under the city's name.

INDEX OF PERSONS

This index does not include all names mentioned in this book, but only a selection of the most important persons. PLP numbers are not provided for nuns; for these, consult the list of nuns in Appendix 1.